POEMS

OF

PAUL HAMILTON HAYNE

Paul Hamilton Hayne

POEMS

OF

PAUL HAMILTON HAYNE

𝔆omplete 𝔈dition

WITH NUMEROUS ILLUSTRATIONS

AMS PRESS
NEW YORK

Reprinted from the edition of 1882, Boston
First AMS EDITION published 1970
Manufactured in the United States of America

Library of Congress Catalogue Card Number: 74-101918
SBN: 404-03167-6

AMS PRESS, INC.
NEW YORK, N. Y. 10003

TO

COLONEL JOHN G. JAMES,

PRESIDENT OF THE STATE AGRICULTURAL AND MECHANICAL COLLEGE OF TEXAS,

𝔗𝔥𝔢𝔰𝔢 𝔙𝔢𝔯𝔰𝔢𝔰,

IN WHICH HE HAS TAKEN SO UNSELFISH AN INTEREST,

ARE

AFFECTIONATELY DEDICATED.

BIOGRAPHICAL SKETCH.

IT had little to do with Byron's success as a poet that he was born in the purple of the English aristocracy; or with the quality of Shelley's genius that he was the son of a Sir Timothy, who prided himself on a descent from a long line of British squires; or that Algernon Swinburne's father was a baronet. And yet if our poets have gentle blood in their veins, other things being equal, we prefer that they should have it.

Good birth, as a general thing, argues good breeding, refinement, education, fixed social position, and a wide margin of generous leisures; all of which have much to do with the outcome of a poet's life.

We do not believe that Tennyson would ever have written as he has, if it had been his fortune to labor for his daily bread. Even had the genius all been there, the wide leisures would have been wanting, and he would have produced his poems, not as Goethe, at his "unhasting ease," — absolutely free from all exigence, — but under the pressure of a goad, which would have destroyed all their beautiful spontaneity.

It is therefore to the advantage of our poet, PAUL HAMILTON HAYNE, that he had ancestors. It may sound somewhat unrepublican perhaps, to hear him wish, as he does in one of his keen sonnets, that these same ancestors had been content to stay in their four-hundred-year-old Shropshire Manor-House, enjoying the positive good England gave them, rather than go sailing over seas in quest of what might be of questionable benefit; but we can forgive him, in view of his antecedents on this side the water, of which he may be proud as well. His English progenitors settled, early in colonial days, in Charleston, South Carolina, and from the first were of importance in the civil affairs of the young State. They furnished noble patriots, who shed their blood in Revolutionary days, for the liberties of their adopted country. The name of the renowned statesman and orator, Robert G. Hayne, who was the poet's uncle, has become the possession of the country. While in the Senate of the United States, he was not afraid to match his strength with Webster's, and he was governor of South Carolina when to be governor of the Palmetto State was an honor worth the winning.

The subject of this sketch is the only child of Lieutenant Hayne, a naval officer, who died at sea when his son was an infant; his mother, recently deceased, was a South Carolina lady, of good English and Scotch descent. He was born in Charleston, January 1st, 1830, and educated at Charleston College, from which he was graduated. Inheriting the prestige of a noble name, high position, and a sufficient amount of wealth, the world was before the youth, and he was free to choose his path. From earliest boyhood his fondness for literature, particularly poetry, was pronounced, and there was everything around him to foster this love. The Charleston of thirty-five years ago was a very different place from the Charleston of to-day. The old Huguenot element, with its aristocratic names and associations, was strong, and the large admixture of good English blood helped to make its people just a little exclusive. Boston herself did not gather the mantle of her self-importance in a more queenly manner about her than did this city by the sea. There was a decided literary element, too, among its higher classes. Legarè's wit and scholarship brightened its social circle; Calhoun's deep shadow loomed over it from his plantation at Fort Hill; Gilmore Simms's genial culture broadened its sympathies. The latter was the Mæcænas to a band of brilliant youths who used to meet for literary suppers at his beautiful home; and here it was that the love for old Elizabethan lore, and the study of the classics of the English tongue, which has always characterized Mr. Hayne, found one of its best stimulants.

No sooner had he graduated than he threw himself actively into literary life. He became connected with the journalism of the city, and when the enthusiastic group of young scholars established a Literary Monthly Magazine (*Russell's*) Mr. Hayne was appointed its editor.

His first volume of Poems was published by the old house of Ticknor & Co., Boston, in 1855, when he was some twenty-five years old, his second in 1857, and his third in 1860. These all met with such success as encouraged him to adopt fully a literary life as his vocation.

In the meantime he had married Miss Mary Middleton Michel, of Charleston, the daughter of an eminent French physician, who received a gold medal from Napoleon the Third, for services under the first Napoleon at the battle of Leipsic. Of the poet's wife it is but the scantest justice to say that she has been the inspiration, the stay, the joy of his life. No poet ever was more blessed in a wife, and she it is, who, by her self-renunciation, her exquisite sympathy, her positive, material help, her bright hopefulness, has made endurable the losses and trials that have crowded Mr. Hayne's life. Those who know how to read between the lines can see everywhere the influence of this irradiating and stimulating presence.

Then came the disasters of the civil war. Mr. Hayne, whose health, delicate from his childhood, would not allow him to take field service, became an aid on Governor Pickens's staff. During the bombardment of his native city, his beautiful home was burned to the ground, and his large, handsome library utterly lost. Even the few valuables, such as the old family silver, which he succeeded in securing and removing to a bank in Columbia for safe-keeping, were swept away in the famous "march to the sea;" and there was nothing left for the homeless and ruined man but exile among the "Pine Barrens" of Georgia. There he established himself, in utter seclusion, in a veritable cottage (or rather *shanty*, dignified at first as "Hayne's Roost"), behind whose screens of vines, among the peaches, melons, and strawberries of his own raising, he has fought the fight of life with uncomplaining bravery, and persisted in being happy.

Here, then, at "Copse Hill," nested amid his greenery and his pines, our poet has lived for fifteen years,—content with little of this world's gear, happy in his chosen work, writing as his frail health would permit, and in manly independence. In 1872, the Lippincotts published his *Legends and Lyrics*, and in 1873 his edition of his friend Henry Timrod's Poems appeared, accompanied by one of the most pathetic biographical memorials of which literature gives an example. In 1875, *The Mountain of the Lovers* was published. A Life of Gilmore Simms (still in MS.) was also written, with Memorial Sketches of Governor Hayne and Mr. Legarè,—so that these years of seclusion have been well filled up with literary labor; and during the past five years the names of not many writers have appeared more frequently, perhaps, in the pages of our current literature, than that of the recluse of "Copse Hill." Here he has interpreted Nature, we think, with as clear an insight as the poet of Rydal Mount. He has made the melancholy moanings of his Georgia pines sob through his verses. He has given voices to the *Midnight Thunder;* to the *Windless Rain*; to the *Muscadines of the Southern Forests;* to their *Woodland Phases;* to the *Aspects of the Pines*, as has not been heretofore done.

It were superfluous to enter upon any criticism of his poems, nor is this the place for it. They are left with the reader, who, if he cannot, of himself, find therein the aromatic freshness of the woods, — the swaying incense of the cathedral-like aisles of pines, — the sough of dying summer winds, — the glint of lonely pools, and the brooding notes of leaf-hidden mocking-birds, — would not be able to discern them, however carefully the critic might point them out.

MARGARET J. PRESTON.

CONTENTS.

YOUTHFUL POEMS.

SONNETS.

DRAMATIC SKETCHES.

POEMS OF THE WAR.

LEGENDS AND LYRICS.

LATER POEMS.

HUMOROUS POEMS.

POEMS FOR CHILDREN.

LIST OF ILLUSTRATIONS.

HOME OF PAUL HAMILTON HAYNE,
"Copse Hill," Ga.

YOUTHFUL POEMS.

1850–1860.

THE WILL AND THE WING.

To have the will to soar, but not the
    wings,
Eyes fixed forever on a starry height,
Whence stately shapes of grand imagin-
    ings
Flash down the splendors of imperial
    light;

And yet to lack the charm that makes
    them ours,
The obedient vassals of that conquering
    spell,
Whose omnipresent and ethereal powers,
Encircle Heaven, nor fear to enter Hell;

This is the doom of Tantalus — the
    thirst
For beauty's balmy fount to quench the
    fires
Of the wild passion that our souls have
    nurst
In hopeless promptings — unfulfilled de-
    sires.

Yet would I rather in the outward state
Of Song's immortal temple lay me
    down,
A beggar basking by that radiant gate
Than bend beneath the haughtiest em-
    pire's crown!

For sometimes, through the bars, my
    ravished eyes
Have caught brief glimpses of a life
    divine,
And seen afar, mysterious rapture rise
Beyond the veil that guards the inmost
    shrine.

"THE LAUGHING HOURS BEFORE HER FEET."

THE laughing Hours before her feet,
Are scattering spring-time roses,
And the voices in her soul are sweet
As music's mellowed closes;
All hopes and passions, heavenly
    born,
In her, have met together,
And Joy diffuses round her morn
A mist of golden weather.

As o'er her cheek of delicate dyes,
The blooms of childhood hover,
So do the tranced and sinless eyes,
All childhood's heart discover;
Full of a dreamy happiness,
With rainbow fancies laden,
Whose arch of promise grows to bless
Her spirit's beauteous Adenne.

She is a being born to raise
Those undefiled emotions,
That whisper of our sunniest days,
And most sincere devotions;
In her, we see renewed and bright,
That phase of earthly story,
Which glimmers in the morning light,
Of God's exceeding glory.

Why, in a life of mortal cares,
Appear these heavenly faces,
Why, on the verge of darkened years,
These clear, celestial graces?
'Tis but to cheer the soul that faints
With pure and blest evangels,
To prove, if Heaven is rich with saints,
That Earth may have her angels.

Enough! 'tis not for me to pray
That on her life's sweet river,
The calmness of a virgin day
May rest, and rest forever;
I know a guardian Genius stands
Beside those waters lowly,
And labors with ethereal hands
To keep them pure and holy.

EVE OF THE BRIDAL.

YES! it has come; the strange, o'ermas-
tering hour,
When buoyant hopes, and tender, trem-
ulous fears
Sway the full heart with a divided power,
The flush of sunshine, and the touch of
tears!

Oh! for a spell to charm away thy
care,
As I *could* charm, were I but near thee
now
To chide coy flickerings of that half de-
spair
Of virginal shame upon thy downcast
brow;

A fitful gloom 'mid blushes of bright joy,
Like those transparent clouds in summer
days,
That cast their transient shadows of alloy
Across the noontide's else too dazzling
blaze;

Yet, from the fair hills of this foreign
shore,
I waft thee benedictions on the wind,
Hopes that a peaceful bliss forevermore
May rule the gracious empire of thy mind.

And blessing thus, the dreary distance
dies,
And in a clearer than Agrippa's glass,
The enamored fancy, — what pale vis-
ions rise,
Brightening to shape and beauty ere they
pass?

A room where sunset's glory deep,
though dim,
Girds thy rich chamber with luxurious
grace,
Rounds the fair outline of each delicate
limb,
And crowns with chastened ray thine elo-
quent face,

In shimmering folds thy raiments soft
and rare,
Swell with the passionate heavings of thy
breast,
O'er whose young loveliness, the en-
tranced air,
Languidly breathing, seeks voluptuous
rest.

Thy hand —(in two brief hours no longer
thine) —
Gleams near a gossamer curtain, stirred
with sighs,
And the full, star-like tears begin to
shine
In the blue heaven of thy bewildering
eyes.

Tears for the girlhood, almost past
away,
Its innocent life, its wealth of tender
lore,
Tears for the womanhood, whose opening
day,
May not reveal the untried scene before.

Not bitter tears! for him thou lov'st is
true,
And all thy being quivers into flame,
A swift delicious flame that thrills thee
through,
Whene'er thy memory lingers on his
name.

Ev'n now I see thee turn thy timid head,
Luxuriant-locked, towards a dim retreat,
Where twilight shadows veil thy bridal
bed,
And golden gloom and tender silence
meet.

MY FATHER.

My father! in the vague, mysterious
    past,
My boyish thoughts have wandered
    o'er and o'er,
To thy lone grave upon a distant shore,
The wanderer of the waters, still at last.

Never in childhood have I blithely
    sprung
To catch my father's voice, or climb
    his knee;
He was a constant pilgrim of the sea,
And died upon it when his boy was
    young.

He perished not in conflict nor in
    flame,
No laurel garland rests upon his
    tomb;
Yet in stern duty's path he met his
    doom;
A life heroic, though unwed to fame!

First in vague depths of fancy, scarce-
    defined,
Love limned his wavering likeness on
    my soul,
Till through slow growths it waxed a
    perfect whole
Of clear conceptions, brightening heart
    and mind.

His careless bearing and his manly
    face,
His cordial eye; his firm-knit, stalwart
    form,
Fitted to breast the fight, the wreck,
    the storm;
The sailor's frankness and the soldier's
    grace.

In dreams, in dreams we've mingled, and
    a swell
Of feeling mightier for the eyes'
    eclipse,
The music of a blest Apocalypse,
Thrilled through my spirit with its mys-
    tic spell:

Ah, then! ofttimes a sadder scene will
    rise,
A gallant vessel through the mist-
    bound day,
Lifting her spectral spars above the bay,
Gloomily swayed against gray glimmer-
    ing skies.

O'er the dim billows thundering, peals a
    boom
Of the deep gun that bursteth as a
    knell,
When the brave tender to the brave
    farewell —
And strong arms bear a comrade to the
    tomb.

. . . . .

The opened sod: a sorrowing band be-
    side —
One rattling roll of musketry, and
    then,
A man no more among his fellow-men,
Darkness his chamber, and the earth his
    bride,

My father sleeps in peace; perchance
    more blest
Than some he left to mourn him, and
    to know
The bitter blight of an enduring woe,
Longing (how oft!) with him to be at
    rest.

———◆———

SONG.

Fly, swiftly fly
    Through yon fair sky,
    O purple-pinioned Hours!
And bring once more the balmy night,
When from her lattice, silvery bright,
Love's beacon-star — her taper — shines
Between those dark manorial pines,
    Above the myrtle-bowers.

Fly, breezes, fly,
    And waft my sigh
    With love's warm fondness fraught,
'Twill stir my lady's languid mood,
Where, in her verdurous solitude,

She sits and thinks, a moonlight grace
Cast o'er her beauteous brow and face,
Touched by a passionate thought!

Glide, rivulet, glide
    With whispering tide,
Through coverts low and deep,
To woo her with the airy call,
The music faint, the far-off fall,
Of fairy streams in fairy climes,
Or pleasant lapse of fairy rhymes,
    Soft as her breath in sleep.

Fly, swiftly fly
    Through yon calm sky,
O gentle-hearted dove!
And pausing on her favorite tree,
Murmur your plaint so tenderly,
That, born of that sweet tone, a charm
Her very heart of hearts may warm
    With rosy bliss of love.

Fly, swiftly fly
    Through yon fair sky,
O purple-pinioned Hours!
And bring once more the balmy night,
When from her lattice, silvery bright,
Love's beacon-star — her taper — shines
Between those dark manorial pines
    Above the myrtle-bowers!

----◆----

SONG.

Ho! fetch me the winecup! fill up to the
    brim!
For my heart has grown cold, and my
    vision is dim,
And I fain would bring back for a mo-
    ment the glow,
The swift passion that age has long
    chilled with its snow;
Ho! fetch me the winecup! the red
    liquor gleams,
With a promise to waken youth's rapture
    of dreams,
And I'll drain the bright draught for that
    promise divine,
Though Death, Death the spectre, should
    hand me the wine.

'Tis not life that I live, for the blood-
    currents glide
Through my wan shrunken veins in so
    sluggish a tide,
That my heart droops and withers; what!
    life call you this ?
O! rather, consumed by one keen thrill
    of bliss,
Would I die with youth's glory revivified
    round me,
The deep eyes that blessed, and the white
    arms that bound me;
O! rather than brood in this dusk of de-
    sire,
Sink down, like yon marvellous sunset,
    all fire,
The soul clad with wings, and the brain
    steeped in light;
Then come, potent wizard! I call on thy
    might,
Breathe a magical mist o'er the ravage of
    Time,
Roll back the sad years to the flush of my
    prime,
And I'll drain thy bright draught for
    that vision divine,
Though Death, Death the Spectre, should
    hand me the wine!

----◆----

BY THE GRAVE.

[Extract from an unfinished narrative poem.]

This is the place — I pray thee, friend,
Leave me alone with that dread grief,
Whose raven wings o'erarch the grave,
Closed on a life how sad and brief!

Already the young violets bloom
On the light sod that shrouds her
    form,
And Summer's awful sunshine strikes
Incongruous on the spirit's storm.

She died, and did not know that I,
Whose heart is breaking in this gloom,
Had shrined her love, as pilgrims shrine
A blossom from some saintly tomb.

And, ah! indeed, it *was* a tomb,
The tomb of Hope, so ghastly-gray,
Whence sprung that flower of love that
 grew
Serenely on the Hope's decay.

A pallid flower that bloomed alone,
With no warm light to keep it fair,
But nurtured by the tears that fell,
Even from the clouds of our despair.

She perished, and her patient soul
Passed to God's rest, nor did she know

I kept the faith we could not plight
In honor, or in peace below.

But, Love! at last, all, all is clear.
You see the flame of that fierce fate,
Which blazed between my life, and
 yours,
And left them both — how desolate!

And well you comprehend that now
My heart is breaking where I stand,
But 'mid the ruin, shrines its faith,
A relic from love's Holy Land.

"Come! come! and seek us here,
In these cool deeps."

SONG OF THE NAIADS.

GAY is our crystal floor,
 Beneath the wave,
With strange gems flaming o'er
 The Genii gave;
Sweet is the purple light
That haunts our happy sight,
And low and sweet the lulling strains
 that sigh
While the tides pause, and the faint
 zephyrs die.

Come! come! and seek us here,
 In these cool deeps,
Where all is calmly fair,
 And sorrow sleeps:
Thy burning brow shall rest,
Couched on a tender breast,
And, charmed to bliss, thy soul shall
 catch the gleams
Of mystic glories in Elysian dreams.

Come! ere the earth grows drear,
 The tempests rave,
And the fast-failing year
 Is nigh its grave:
Thy summer, too, is past,
Wouldst thou have peace at last?
O! here she dwells serenely in still caves,
And waits to woo thee underneath the
 waves.

—◇—

LETHE.

A DUMB, dark region through whose
 desolate heart
Creeps a dull river with a stagnant
 flood;
Its skies are sombre-hued, and dreary
 clouds,
No wind hath ever stirred, hang low and
 dim

Above the barren woodlands; all things
  droop
In slumber; the little willow stoops to
  kiss
The waves, but not a ripple murmurs
  back
Its salutation, and wan starlike flowers
Yield a white radiance to the failing
  sense,
And odors pregnant with the charms of
  rest,
And glamour of Oblivion; all things
  droop
In slumber; for whate'er hath passed the
  bounds
Of this miraculous kingdom, bird or
  beast,
Men lured from action, or soul-sick of
  life,
Weary and heartsore, maids in love's
  despair,
Or mothers stricken by their first-born's
  crime —
All sink without a struggle to deep
  peace.
Prone in the gleam the river casts abroad,
A gleam more pallid than the light of
  Hades,
Lie those who sought this region ages
  since;
Their upturned brows are smooth, and
  tranced with calm.

And on their shadowy lips a waning
  smile
Fitfully glimmers; round them rest the
  forms
Of savage beasts; the lion all unnerved,
Drowsy and passionless, his huge limbs
  relaxed,
And curved to lines of languor: the fierce
  pard
Tamed to a breathless quiet, whilst afar,
Gloom the gaunt shapes of mighty brutes
  of eld,
The world's primeval tenants; all things
  droop
In slumber; even the sluggish river's
  flow

Sounds like the dying surges of the sea
To ears far inland, or the feeblest sigh
Of winds that faint on lofty mountain-
  tops.
This is the realm — " Oblivion " — this
  the stream
Which mortals have called — " Lethe!"

THE REALM OF REST.

IN the realm that Nature boundeth
Are there balmy shores of peace,
Where no passion-torrent soundeth,
And no storm-wind seeks release ?
Rest they 'mid the waters golden,
Of some strange untravelled sea,
Where low, halcyon airs have stolen,
Lingering round them slumbrously ?

Shores begirt with purple hazes,
Mellowed by gray twilight's beams,
Whose weird curtains shroud the mazes,
Wandering through a realm of dreams;
Shores, where Silence wooes Devotion,
Action faints, and echo dies,
And each peace-entranced emotion
Feeds on quiet mysteries.

If there be, O guardian Master,
Genius of my life and fate,
Bear me from the world's disaster,
Through that kingdom's shadowy gate;
Let me lie beneath its willows,
On the fragrant, flowering strand,
Lulled to rest by breezeless billows,
Thrilled with airs of Elfin-land.

Slumber, flushed with faintest dreamings;
Deep that knows no answering deep,
Unprofaned by phantom-seemings,
— Mockeries of Protéan sleep; —
Noiseless, timeless, *half* forgetting,
May that sleep Elysian be,
While serener tides are setting,
Inward, from the roseate sea.

Hark! to mine a voice is calling,
Sweet as tropic winds at night,
Gently dying, faintly falling
From some marvellous mystic height,

Troubled Thought's unhallowed riot
By its wandering glamour kissed,
Feels a charm of sacred quiet
Fold it, like enchanted mist.

"There's a realm, thy footsteps nearing,"
[Thus the voice to mine replies,]
" Where the heavy heart despairing,
Breathes no more its life in sighs;
'Tis a realm, imperial, stately,
Refuge of dethronèd Years,
Calm as midnight, towering greatly,
Through a moonlit veil of tears.

" Though an empire, freedom reigneth,
Kingly brow, and subject knee,
Each with what to each pertaineth,
Slumbering in equality;
'Tis a sleep, divorced from dreamings,
Deep that knows no answering deep,
Unprofaned by phantom-seemings —
Noiseless, wondrous, timeless sleep.

" On its shores are weeping willows,
Action faints, and Echo dies,
And the languid dirge of billows,
Lulls with opiate symphonies;
But beside that murmurous ocean
All whc rest, repose in sooth,
And no more the stilled emotion
Stirs to joy, or wakens ruth.

" Thou *shalt* gain these blest dominions,
Thou *shalt* find this peaceful ground,
Shaded by Oblivion's pinions,
Startled by no mortal sound;
Noiseless, timeless, ALL forgetting,
Shall thy sleep Elysian be,
While eternal tides are setting
Inward from that mystic sea."

———◆———

THE ISLAND IN THE SOUTH.

THE ship went down at noonday in a
    calm,
When not a zephyr broke the crystal sea.
We two escaped alone: we reached an
    isle
Whereon the water settled languidly

In a long swell of music; luminous skies
O'erarched the place, and lazy, broad
    lagoons
Swept inland, with the boughs of plan-
    tain trees
Trailing cool shadows through the dense
    repose;
All round about us floated gentle airs,
And odors that crept upward to the
    sense
Like delicate pressures of voluptuous
    thought.
I, with a long bound, leapt upon the
    shore
Shouting, but she, pavilioned in dark
    locks,
Sobbed out thanksgiving; 'twixt the
    world and us,
Distance that seemed Eternity outrolled
Its terrible barriers; on the waste a Fate
Stood up, and stretching its blank hands
    abroad
Muttered of desolation. Did we weep,
And groaning cast our foreheads in the
    dust ?
So it *had* been, but in each other's eyes
Smiled a new world, dearer than that
    which rose
Beneath the lost stars of the faded West.
That very morn the white-stoled priest of
    God
Had blessed us with the church's choicest
    prayers,
And these did gird us like a sapphire
    wall
When the floods threatened, and the
    ghastly doom
Moaned itself impotent; free we were to
    love
To the full scope of passion; a few suns,
And in the deep recesses of the woods
We built ourselves a cabin; the dim spot
Was fortressed by the tropic's giant
    growths,
Luxuriant Titans of a hundred years;
And the vines, laced and interlaced be-
    tween,
Drooped with a flowery largess many-
    hued.

It was a place of Faëry; songs of birds
That glimmered in and out among the
    leaves,
Like magical dreams embodied, wooed
    the winds
To gentlest motion of benignant wings;
And the sun veiled his radiance, and the
    stars
Peered through the shadowy stillness
    with a light
So spiritual, the forest seemed to wane
In tremulous lines waved down the sil-
    very aisles.
There lived, there loved we, as none else
    have lived
And loved, I think, since the primeval
    blight
Rained down its discords, and death
    clinched the curse.
No shallow mockeries of a worn-out age,
Effete and helpless, bound young passion
    round
With the cold fetters of detested forms:
Civilization was not there to set
Its specious seal of custom on our hearts,
Prisoning the bolder virtues; we might
    dare
To act, speak, think, as the true nature
    moved,
Untutored and majestic; our souls grew
To the stature of the spirit, that looks
    down
From the unpolluted regnancy of heavens
That hold no curses; the glad universe
Showered rare benedictions on our path;
Matter was merged in poesy: the winds
From the serene Pacific, the quick gales
From mountainous ridges in the upper-
    most air,
The eternal chorus of far seas serene,
The harmony of forests, the small voice
That trembles from the happy rivulet's
    breast,   [phy,
All touched us with that sweet philoso-
Which, if we woo the visible world
    aright,
Blesses experience with new gates of
    sense
Where through we gain Elysium.

So the years
Were winged and odorous with a thou-
    sand joys,
Of which the poor slave to the hollow
    law
We term society, hath had no dream;
Our love was comprehensive, full, divine,
Rounding the perfect orbit wherein life
Should gravitate to God, even as the
    spheres
Roll to the central fire; love mastered
    life
As maelstroms suck still waters, love
    the one
Electric current through act, reason, will,
Throbbing like inspiration ; no vain
    touch
Of weak, fantastic passion, no thin glow
Of morbid longing, fluttering feebly up
From shallow brains, stirred to a dubious
    flame,
And tortured with false throes of senti-
    ment —
(That bastard whimperer to the deity,
    Love —
As a changeling to the Titans) — no red
    heat
Of base desire, fusing the delicate
    thought
To chaos; but a steadfast, genial sun,
A luminous glory, gentle as intense,
Making our fate a heaven of warmth,
    light, rest,
Whose very clouds were halos, and whose
    storms
Were tempered into music. Thus time
    stole
On muffled wings through the still air of
    bliss,
Gathering our ripened hopes, and sowing
    seeds
Of joy to come. My innocent bud had
    flowered
To beauty — oh! such beauty as these
    lips,
Touched though they were with fire,
    might not profane
With shackles of mean utterance. Oh,
    God! God!

"We reached an isle
Whereon the waters settled languidly."

Why didst thou take her from me ? why
transform
The passionate presence in my shielding
arms
To this poor phantom of a broken brain,
Mocking my woe with shadows ? On a
night
When the still sea was calmest, the bright
stars
Most bright, and a warm breathing on
the wind
Spoke of perpetual summer, a strange
voice
I scarce could hear, said: " It is evening
time,"
And a wan hand my eyes were blind to
note
Beckoned her far away.
The awful grief
Closed round me like an ocean. I was
mad,
And raved my memory from me. When
again
The world dawned, as a dreary landscape
dawns
Grotesquely through the sluggish mists
of March,
I walked once more in a great capital's
streets,
A savage 'midst the civilized, a man —
Shattered and wrecked, I grant you, —
still a man
Amongst the puppets that usurp the
name
And act the fraud so basely, that the
Fiend
Wearies to death the echoes of his hell
In laughter at them. I *am* with you still,
Emasculate denizens of the stifling mart,
Where heaven's free winds are throttled
in the fumes
Of furnaces, and the insulted sun
Glooms through the crowding vapors at
midday,
Like a God, re-collecting to himself
His immortality; where nerveless limbs
Bear nerveless bodies to their separate
dens
Of torture, and lean, wide-eyed revellers

Foster the hungering worm that never
dies,
And fan the lurid fire unquenchable;
Where stealthy avarice lurks in wait to
sack
The widow's house ; and license of low
minds,
Loaded with prurient knowledge, and
no hearts
(Self-worship having killed them), make
the world
A Pandemonium.   I *am* with you still;
But the hours creep on to a more fortu-
nate time;
A vessel swells her broad sails in the bay,
And the breeze bloweth seaward; I will
seek
My island in the southern waves again;
A thousand memories urge me, tones
that slept
Waken to invitation; I can feel
The Hesperian beauty of that realm of
peace
Flushing my brain and fancy; but
through all
The ruddy vision glides a tender shade,
And pauses with mute meaning by a
grave.

—◆—

ODE.

Delivered on the First Anniversary of the Car-
olina Art Association, Feb. 10, 1856.

THERE are two worlds wherein our souls
may dwell,
With discord, or ethereal music fraught,
One the loud mart wherein men buy and
sell
(Too oft the haunt of grovelling moods
of Hell),
The other, that immaculate realm of
thought,
In whose bright calm the master-work-
men wrought,
Where genius lives on light,
And faith is lost in sight,
Where crystal tides of perfect harmony
swell

Up to the heavens that never held a
    cloud,
And round great altars reverent hosts
    are bowed,
Altars upreared to love that cannot
    die,
To beauty that forever keeps its youth,
To kingly grandeur, and to virginal
    truth,
    To all things wise and pure,
Whereof our God hath said, "Endure!
    endure!
    Ye are but parts of me,
The *hath been*, and the evermore *to be*,
Of my supremest Immortality!"

We falter in the darkness and the dearth
Which sordid passions and untamed de-
    sires
Create about us; universal earth
Groans with the burden of our sensual
    woes;
The heart heaven gave for homage is
    consumed
By the wild rages of unhallowed fires;
The blush of that fine glory which
    illumed
The earlier ages, hath gone out in gloom;
There is no joy within us, no repose,
One creed our beacon, and one god our
    hold,
    The creed, the god, of gold;
The heavenward wingèd Instinct that
    aspires,
Like a lost seraph with dishevelled
    plume,
Pants humbled in the "slough of deep
    Despond;"
The present binds us, there is no Beyond,
No glorious Future to the soul content
With the poor husks and garbage of this
    world;
And are indeed the wings of worship
    furled
Forevermore ? Is no evangel blent,
No sweet evangel, with the hiss and
    hum
Of the century's wheels of progress ?
    Science delves

Down to the earth's hot vitals, and ex-
    plores
Realms arctic and antarctic, the strange
    shores
Of remote seas, or with raised vision
    stands,
All undismayed, amidst the starry lands:
Man too, material man, our baser
    selves,
She hath unmasked even to the source of
    being;
    Almost she seems a god,
    Deep-searching and far-seeing;
And yet how oft like some wild funeral
    wail
Which goes before the burial of our
    hopes,
Emerging from the starry-blazoned copes
Of highest firmaments, or darkest vale
Of the nether earth, or from the burdened
    air
Of chambers where this mortal frame lies
    bare,
Probed to the core, her saddening ac-
    cents come;
"What! call'st thou man a seraph ? nay,
    a clod,
The veriest clod when his frail breath is
    spent,
Man shows to us who know him ;
    what is he ?
A speck! the merest dew-globe 'midst
    the sea
    Of life's infinity;"
Or, "we have probed, dissected all we
    can,
But never yet, in any mortal man,
Found we the spirit ! thing of time and
    clay,
Eat, drink, enjoy thy transient insect-
    day!"
Thus Science; but while still her mock-
    ing voice
Rings with a cold sharp clearness in our
    ears,
Her beauteous sister, on whose brow the
    years
Have left no cankering vestige of de-
    cay,

Eternal Art, she of the fathomless eyes
Brimming with light, half worship, half
surprise,
In whose right hand a branch of fadeless
palms,
Plucked from the depths of golden shad-
owed calms,
Points upward to the skies,
She answers in a minor, sweet and
strange
The while, all graces in her aspect meet,
And Doubt and Fear shrink shuddering
at her feet,
"I bring a nobler message! Soul, re-
joice!
Rise with me from thy troublous toils of
sense,
Thy bootless struggles, born of impo-
tence,
Rise to a subtler view, a broader range
Of thought and aim;
Mine is a sway ideal,
But still the works I prompt, alone, are
real;
Mine is a realm from immemorial time
Begirt by deeds and purposes sublime,
Whose consecration is faith's quenchless
flame,
Whose voices are the songs of poet-
sages,
Whose strong foundations resting on the
ages,
The throes and crash of empires have
not shaken,
Nor any futile force of human rages.

"Come! let us enter in!
Behold, the portal gates stand open
wide!
Only, from off thy spirit shake the dust
Of any thought of sin,
Or sordid pride,
For sacred is the kingdom of my trust,
By mind, and strength, and beauty sanc-
tified."

She spake! and o'er the threshold of a
sphere,
A marvellous sphere, they passed;

From the deep bosom of the purpling
air
A lambent glory broke along the
vast
Horizon line, whence clouds, like incense,
rolled
Athwart a firmamental arc of gold
And sapphire; clouds not vapor-born,
But clasping each the radiant seeds of
morn,
Which suddenly, clear zenith heights at-
tained,
Burst into light, unfolding like a flower,
From out whose quivering heart a mystic
shower
Of splendor rained:
A spell was hers to conquer time and
space,
For from the desert grandeur of that
place
A hundred temples rise,
The marble poems of the bards of old,
Whereon 'twere well to look with rever-
ent eyes,
Because they body noblest aspirations,
Ethereal hopes, and winged imagina-
tions,
Whether to fabled Jove their walls were
raised,
Or on their inner altar offerings blazed
To wise Athèna, or, in Christian Rome
Beneath St. Peter's mighty circling
dome,
A second Heaven, the golden censers
swing,
The clear-toned choirs those hymns of
rapture sing,
Which, on harmonious waves of gratula-
tion,
The outburst of the sense of deep salva-
tion,
Uplift the spirit where the Incarnate
Word
Amid the praise no ear of man hath
heard,
The peace no mind of man can compre-
hend,
Awaits to welcome Time's worn wander-
ers home!

"But look again!" Art's eager Genius
    cried:
    "Thou hast not seen the end,
Scarce the beginning!" As she spake, a
    tide
Of all the mighty masters, loved, adored,
From out the shining distant spaces
    poured,
All those who fashioned, through an
    inward dower,
The concrete forms of beauty and of
    power;
Whether from white Pentelic quarries
    brought,
The voiceless stone uprose, a breathing
    thought,
Or, from the mystic rays of rainbows
    drawn,
And colors of the sunset and the dawn,
The painter's pencil his ideal fine,
    Had clothed in hues divine;
    Or, skilled in living words
Melodious as the natural voice of birds
(But each a sentient thing, a meaning
    grand,
It is not given to all to understand),
The poet from the shade of breezy
    woods,
    From barren seaside solitudes,
And from the pregnant quiet of his soul
Outbreathed the numbers that forever
    roll
Perennial, as the fountains of the sea,
And deep almost as deep eternity!

Near and yet nearer the bright concourse
    came,
    Their faces all aflame,
As when of yore the quick creative thrill
Did smite them into utterance, and the
    throng,
Awed by the fiery burden of the song,
    Grew reverent pale and still;
O! solemn and sublime Apocalypse
That wresteth, from the dreary death-
    eclipse,
The sacred presence of these marvellous
    men!
Yonder the visible Homer moves again,

Moves as he moved below,
Save that his smitten vision
Rekindled at the fount of fire Elysian,
Burns with a subtler, grander, deeper
    glow;
And yonder Æschylus, with "thunder-
    ous brow,"
Scarred by the lightning of his own crea-
    tions,
Wrapped in a cloud of sombre medita-
    tions,
Hath seized the tragic muse, as if to
    her
He scorned to bend an humble worship-
    per,
    But would extort her gifts;
    Then Shakespeare mild,
Blessed with the innocent credence of a
    child,
With a child's thoughts and fancies un-
    defiled,
    And yet a Magian strong
To whom the springs of terrible fears
    belong,
Of majesty, and beauty, and delight,
To the weird charm of whose infallible
    sight,
    The heart's emotions,
Though turbid as the tides of darkest
    oceans,
Shone clear as water of the woodland
    brooks—
He passed with wisdom thronèd in his
    looks
Attempered by the genial heats of
    wit;
While close beside him, his grand coun-
    tenance lit
By thoughts like those which wrought
    his Judgment Day,
    Grave Michel Angelo
    His massive forehead lifts,
In a strange Titan fashion, unto Heaven;
Next Raphael comes, with calm and star-
    like mien,
Fresh from the beatific ecstasy,
His face how beautiful, and how serene!
Since God for him the awful veil had
    riven

That shrouds Divinity,
And rolled before his wondering mind
 and eye
Visions that we should gaze on but — to
 die!

They passed, and thousands more passed
 by with them;
Again Art's Genius spake: " Lo! these
 are they
Who, through stern tribulations,
Have raised to right and truth the sub-
 ject nations;
 Lo! these are they,
Who, were the whole bright concourse
 swept away,
Their fame's last barrier, built the surge
 to stem
Of chaos and oblivion, whelmed be-
 neath
The pitiless torrent of eternal death,
Would yet bequeath to races unbegot
The precepts of a faith which faileth
 not;
Pointing, from troublous toils of time
 and sense,
From bootless struggles born of impo-
 tence,
 To that fair realm of thought,
In whose bright calm these master-
 workmen wrought,
Where crystal tides of perfect music
 swell
Up to the heavens that never held a
 cloud,
And round great altars worshipping
 hosts are bowed—
Altars upreared to love that cannot
 die,
To beauty that forever keeps its youth,
To kingly grandeur, and to virginal
 truth,
 To all things wise and pure,
Whereof our God hath said: ' Endure!
 endure!
 Ye are but parts of me,
The HATH BEEN, and the evermore TO
 BE,
Of my supremest Immortality!' "

QUEEN GALENA, OR THE SULTANA BETRAYED.

HOLD! let the heartless perjurer go!
Speak not! strike not! he is *my* foe,
From me, me only, comes the blow —
I will repay him woe for woe;
Look in my eyes! my eyes are dry,
I breathe no plaint, I heave no sigh,
But — will avenge me ere I die.

Think you that I shall basely rest,
And know the bosom mine hath prest,
Is couched upon a colder breast?
Think you that I shall yield the West,
The Orient soul *my* nature nurst,
Till the black seed of treachery burst
And blossomed to this deed accurst?

My rival! O! her glance is meek,
Her faltering presence wan, and weak
As the faint flush that tints her cheek.
'Tis not on *her* that I would wreak
My vengeance — sooner would I wring
Life from an insect-birth of spring
Than palter with so poor a thing.

But he — I tell you if he flew,
As it was once his wont to do,
Repentant — pleading — quick to woo,
With all his wild heart flaming through
The glance of passion — it were sweet,
Yea, more! 'twere righteous, just, and
 meet,
To slay him kneeling at my feet!

He *shall not* wed her; by Heaven's light
He shall not; o'er my lurid sight·
Throbs a thick fire; the ancient might
Of a stern race is stirred to-night;
My sovereign claim annul — disown!
I will repay him groan for groan,
Or — stab him at the altar-stone!

———◆———

THE POET'S TRUST IN HIS SORROW.

O GOD! how sad a doom is mine,
 To human seeming:
Thou hast called on me to resign
So much — much! —*all* — but the divine
 Delights of dreaming.

I set my dreams to music wild,
  A wealth of measures;
My lays, thank Heaven! are undefiled,
I sport with Fancy as a child
  With golden leisures.

And long as fate, not wholly stern,
  But this shall grant me,
Still with perennial faith to turn
Where Song's unsullied altars burn
Nought, nought shall daunt me!

What though my worldly state be low
  Beyond redressing;
I own an inner flame whose glow
Makes radiant all the outward show;
  My last great blessing!

———◆———

THE BROOK.

But yesterday this brook was bright,
And tranquil as the clear moonlight,
That wooes the palms on Orient shores,
But now, a hoarse, dark stream, it pours
Impetuous o'er its bed of rock,
And almost with a thunder-shock
Boils into eddies, fierce and fleet,
That dash the white foam round our
  feet,
A raging whirl of waters, rent
As if with angry discontent!

A tempest in the night swept by,
Born of a murk and fiery sky,
And while the solid woodlands shook,
It wreaked its fury on the brook.
The evil genius of the blast
Within its quiet bosom passed,
And therefore this transfigured tide,
Which used as lovingly to glide
As thought through spirits sanctified,
Rolls now a whirl of waters, rent
As if with angry discontent.

I knew, of late, a creature, bright
And gentle as the clear moonlight,
The tenderest and the kindest heart
That ever played Love's selfless part,

Across whose unperturbèd life,
A sudden passion swept, in strife,
With wild, unhallowed forces rife.
It stirred her nature's inmost deep,
That nevermore shall rest or sleep,
Remorse, its rugged bed of rock,
O'er which for aye, with thunder-shock,
The tides of feeling, fierce and fleet,
Are dashed to foam or icy sleet,
A raging whirl of waters, rent
By something worse than discontent!

———◆———

NATURE THE CONSOLER.

Gladly I hail these solitudes, and
  breathe
The inspiring breath of the fresh wood-
  land air,
Most gladly to the past alone bequeath
  Doubt, grief, and care;
I feel a new-born freedom of the mind,
Nursed at the breast of Nature, with the
  dew
Of glorious dawns; I hear the mountain
  wind,
Clear as if elfin trumpets loudly blew,
Peal through the dells, and scale the
  lonely height,
Rousing the echoes to a quick delight,
Bending the forest monarchs to its
  will,
'Till all their pond'rous branches shake
  and thrill
In the wide-wakening tumult; far above
The heavens stretch calm and blessing;
  far below
The mellowing fields are touched with
  evening's glow,
And many a pleasant sight and sound I
  love
Would gently woo me from all thoughts
  of woe:
Sunlighted meadows, music in the
  grove,
From happy bird-throats, and the fairy
  rills
That lapse in silvery murmurs through
  the hills;

"Gladly I hail these solitudes, and breathe
The inspiring breath of the fresh woodland air."

Great circles of rich foliage, rainbow-
    crowned
By autumn's liberal largess, whilst
    around
Grave sheep lie musing on the pastoral
    ground,
    Or sending a mild bleat
    To other flocks afar,
The fleecy comrades they are wont to
    meet
Homeward returning 'neath the vesper
    star!

Oh, genial peace of Nature! divine calm
That fallest on the spirit, like the rain
Of Eden, bearing melody and balm
To soothe the troubled heart and heal its
    pain,
Thy influence lifts me to a realm of joy,
A moonlight happiness, intense but
    mild,
Unvisited by shadow of alloy,
And flushed with tender dreams and fan-
    cies undefiled.

The universe of God is still, not dumb,
For many voices in sweet undertone
    To reverent listeners come;
And many thoughts, with truth's own
    honey laden,
Into the watcher's wakeful brain have
    flown,
    Charming the inner ear
With harmonies so low, and yet so clear,
So undefined, yet pregnant with a feeling,
An inspiration of sublime revealing,
That they whose being the strong spell
    shall hold,
    Do look on earthly things
Through atmospheres of rich imaginings,
    And find, in all they see,
    A meaning manifold;
The forces of divine vitality
Break through the sensual gloom
    About them furled,
All instinct with the radiant grace and
    bloom
Caught from the glories of a lovelier
    world.

A lovelier world! in the thronged space
    on high,
Dwells there indeed a fairer star than
    ours,
Circled by sunsets of more gorgeous dye,
And gifted with an ampler wealth of
    flowers?
Can heavenly bounty lavish richer stores
Of color, fragrance, beauty, and delight
    On mortal or immortal sight,
In any sphere that rolls around the sun?
See what a splendor from the dying day
Through the grand forest pours!
Now, lighting up its veteran-crests with
    glory,
Now, slanting down the shadows dim and
    hoary,
Till, in the long-drawn gloom of leafy
    glades,
At the far close of their impervious
    shades,
The purple splendor softly melts away!

Now, overarched by dewy canopies,
And awed by dimness that is hardly
    gloom,   [lips,
We stand amidst the silence with hushed
Watching the dubious glimmer of the
    skies
Paled by the foliage to a half-eclipse,
    And struggling for full room,
With intermittent gleams, that quickly
    die
In throbs and tremors, waning suddenly
To the mere ghosts of flame, to appari-
    tions
Impalpable as star-beams in deep seas,
Lost in the dark below the surface-
    ruffling breeze.
        [tions,
Latest of all these marvellous transi-
And crowning all with their ineffable
    grace,
The eyes of the night's empress, witch-
    ing sweet,
Scatter the shadows in each secret
    place,
So that, where'er her beamy glances
    fleet,

Shot through and through, as if with
    arrowy might,
The dusky gloaming falls before her
    shafts of light.

THE SOUL-CONFLICT.

DEFEATED! but never disheartened!
    Repulsed! but unconquered in will,
Upon dreary discomfitures building
    Her virtue's strong battlements still,
The soul, through the siege of tempta-
    tions,
    Yields not unto fraud, nor to might,
Unquelled by the rush of the passions,
    Serene 'mid the tumults of fight.

She sees a grand prize in the distance,
    She hears a glad sound of acclaims,
The crown wrought of blooms amaran-
    thine,
    The music far sweeter than Fame's.
And so, 'gainst the rush of the passions
    She lifts the broad buckler of right,
And so, through the glooms of tempta-
    tion,
    She walks in a splendor of light.

THE PRESENTIMENT.

OVER her face, so tender and meek,
    The light of a prophecy lies,
That has silvered the red of the rose on
    her cheek,
    And chastened the thought in her eyes!

Beautiful eyes, with an inward glance,
    To the spirit's mystical deep;
Lost in the languid gleam of a trance,
    More solemn and saintly than sleep.

And, forever and ever, she seems to hear
    The voice of a spirit implore,
" Come! enter the life that is noble and
    clear;
    Come! grow to my heart once more."

And, forever and ever, she mutely turns
    From a mortal lover's sighs;

And fainter the red of the rose-flush
    burns,
    And deeper the thought in her eyes.

The seeds are warm of the churchyard
    flowers,
    That will blossom above her rest,
And a bird that shall sing by the old
    church towers,
    Is already fledged in its nest!

And so, when a blander summer shall
    smile,
    On some night of soft July,
We will lend to the dust her beauty
    awhile,
    In the hush of a moonless sky.

And later still, shall the churchyard
    flowers,
    Gleam nigh with a white increase;
And a bird outpour, by the old church
    towers,
    A plaintive poem of peace.

THE TWO SUMMERS.

THERE is a golden season in our year,
Between October's hale and lusty cheer,
And the hoar frost of winter's empire
    drear;

Which, like a fairy flood of mystic tides,
Whereon divine tranquillity abides,
The kingdom of the sovereign months
    divides;

The wailing autumn winds their requiems
    cease,
Ere winter's sturdier storms have gained
    release,
And heaven and earth alike are bright
    with peace.

O soul! thou hast thy golden season
    too!
A blissful interlude of birds and dew,
Of balmy gales, and skies of deepest blue!

That second summer, when thy work is
    done,
The harvest hoarded, and the mellow sun
Gleams on the fruitful fields thy toil has
    won;

Which, also, like a fair mysterious tide,
Whereon calm thoughts like ships at
    anchor ride,
Doth the broad empire of thy years di-
    vide.

This passed, what more of life's brief
    path remains,
Winds through unlighted vales, and dis-
    mal plains,
The haunt of chilling blight, or fevered
    pains.

Pray, then, ye happy few, along whose
    way   [ray,
Life's Indian summer pours its purpling
That ye may die ere dawns the evil day.

Sink on that season's kind and genial
    breast,
While peace and sunshine rule the cloud-
    less west,
The elect of God, whom life and death
    have blessed!

———◆———

LINES.

"Though dowered with instincts keen and
        high."
                        "I weep
My youth, and its brave hopes, all dead and
        gone,
In tears which burn." — PARACELSUS.

THOUGH dowered with instincts keen and
    high,
    With burning thoughts that wooed the
        light,
The scornful world hath passed him by,
    And left him lonelier than the night.

Yes! cold and hopeless, one by one
    The stars of faith have quenched their
        flame,
And like a waning polar sun,
    Declines the latest hope of fame.

He longed to sing one noble song,
    To thrill, with passion's living breath,
The fools whose scorn had worked him
        wrong,
    And baffle fate, and conquer death.

Dear God! dost thou endow with powers,
    Whose aspirations mock the bars
Of time and sense, whose vision towers
    Irradiate 'mid thy sovereign stars,

Only to furnish some faint gleams
    Of loftier beauty, quick withdrawn,
Leaving a frenzied hell of dreams,
    And wailings for the vanished dawn?

The oracles of fancy mute,
    Ambition's priests dethroned and fled,
He wanders with a tuneless lute,
    Through dreary regions of the dead.

But from that place of bale uploom
    The phantoms of unburied years,
The haunting care, the grief, the gloom,
    The treacherous hopes, the pale-eyed
        fears

That stormed his spirit's brave design,
    That clogged its wings, betrayed its
        trust,
Defaced its creed, and dashed the wine
    In song's bright chalice, to the dust.

Ah, Heaven! could he retrace his life
    From out this realm of doubt and
        dearth,
He would not court thought's eagle
        strife,
    But clasp the calm that clings to earth.

Above, the threatening thunders wait
    For dauntless souls that dare aspire,
But lowly lives are safe from hate,
    And peace is wed to meek desire.

Yet, birds that breast the turbulent air
    Are worthier than the things that
        creep,
And nobler is a high despair
    Than weak content, or sluggish sleep.

SONG.

O! YOUR eyes are deep and tender,
    O! your charmèd voice is low,
But I've found your beauty's splendor
    All a mockery and a show;
Slighted heart and broken promise
    Follow wheresoe'er you go.

All your words are fair and golden,
    All your actions false and wrong,
Not the noblest soul's beholden
    To your weak affections long;
Only true in — lover's fancy,
    Only constant in — his song.

ON A PORTRAIT.

A widower muses over the likeness of his dead
wife.

THE face, the beautiful face,
    In its living flush and glow,
The perfect face in its peerless grace
    That I worshipped long ago;
That I worshipped when youth was
        strong and bold,
    That I worship now,
Though the pulse of youth grows faint
        and low,
    And the ashes of hope are cold.

The face, the beautiful face,
    Ever haunting my heart and brain,
Bringing ofttimes a dream of heaven,
    Ofttimes the pang of a pain
Which darteth down like a lightning
        flash
    To the dreadful deeps,
Where the gems of a shipwrecked life
        are cast,
    And its dead cold promise sleeps.

Sweet face! shall I meet thee again,
    In the passionless land of palms,
By the verge of Heaven's enchanted
        streams
    In the hush of its perfect calms;
Or, forever and ever, and evermore,
    While the years depart,
    While the ages roll,

Walk the glooms of a ghostly shore,
    Made wild by a phantom-haunted
        brain,
    And a cloud-encircled soul;
By a haunted brain and a cheerless
        heart,
    While the years and the ages roll?

No answer comes to my cry,
    Though out of the depths I call:
Not the faintest gleam of a hopeful
        beam
    Shines over the shroud and pall.
My soul is clothed with sackcloth and
        dust,
    And I look from my widowed hearth
    With a vacant eye on the tumult
        and stir
    Of this weary, dreary earth;
For my soul is dead and its hopes are
        dust,
And the joy of passion, the strength of
        trust,
    These passed from the world with
        her.

THE SHADOW.

THE pathway of his mournful life hath
        wound
Beneath a shadow; just beyond it play
The genial breezes, and the cool brooks
        stray
Into melodious gushings of sweet sound,
Whilst ample floods of mellow sunshine
        fall
Like a mute rain of rapture over all.

Oft hath he deemed the spell of darkness
        lost,
And shouted to the dayspring; a full
        glow   [woe,
Hath rushed to clasp him; but the subtle
Unvanquished ever, with the might of
        frost,
Regains its sad realm, and with voice
        malign
Saith to the dawning joy: "This life is
        mine!"

Still smiles the brave soul, undivorced
    from hope!
And, with unwavering eye and warrior
    mien,
Walks in the shadow, dauntless and
    serene,
To test, through hostile years, the ut-
    most scope
Of man's endurance — constant to essay
All heights of patience free to feet of
    clay.

Still smiles the brave soul, undivorced
    from hope!
But now, methinks, the pale hope gath-
    ers strength;
Glad winds invade the silence; streams,
    at length,
Flash through the desert; 'neath the
    sapphire cope
Of deepening heavens he hails a happier
    day,
And the spent shadow mutely wanes
    away.

THE WINTER WINDS MAY WILDLY RAVE.

THE winter winds may wildly rave,
    How wildly o'er thy place of rest!
But, love! thou hast a holier grave,
    Deep in a faithful human breast.

There, the embalmer, Memory, bends,
    Watching, with softly-breathed sighs,
The mystic light her genius lends
    To fadeless cheeks and tender eyes.

There in a fathomless calm, serene,
    Thy beauty keeps its saintly trace,
The radiance of an angel mien,
    The rapture of a heavenly grace.

And there, O gentlest love! remain
    (No stormy passion round thee raves),
Till, soul to soul, we meet again,
    Beyond this ghostly realm of graves.

UNDER SENTENCE.

PLACE — *Scotland.*   TIME — *Thirteenth Century.*

OFF! off! No treacherous priest for me!
What's Heaven? what's Hell? Eternity!
It hath no meaning to *mine* ear,
Unless —— Stay, father! Canst thou
    swear
By holy Rood, that I shall meet
Him there, whose crime made murder
    sweet?
Him whose black soul I've hurled be-
    fore?
He's gone! How cold my dungeon
    floor!
And the rack wrenches still! This hand,
Which stiffened to a fire-hot band
Of steel, crushing his base breath out,
They've foully mangled! See that gout
Of blood there — there, too! What
    care I?
It did its work well: let it lie!

I'd give ten mortal lives, I trow,
As full of sweets as mine of woe,
To feel that quivering throat once more;
To view the blue-tinged, strangling gore
Spout from his lips! To watch the dim
Film o'er those cruel eyeballs swim,
And the black anguish of his stare,
Dashed blind with horror! Lords! be-
    ware
Much trifling! We are dogs, ye ken,
Who yet may rise, and smite like men.

What's this? Ah, yes! the flower I took
From *her!* I think her dying look
Baptized it, for it keeps so fair.
I wonder if they decked her hair
With other flowers like this, ere yet
They lowered her beauty to the wet,
Dark mould? If maiden dust to flowers
(Some say so) turns, not all the bowers
This spring shall warm will equal those
To blossom from her pure repose!

My nuptial night! God's blood! what
    right
Had *I* to nuptials? To the bright

Keen joy that burns on wedded lips ?
My life-star could not break the eclipse
Wherein 'twas born! So that dark doom
Which hounds me to a shameful tomb,
Ordained that the fiend's trick they
    used
Should trap me! Faith, love, peace
    abused,
I woke to find my heart bereft
Of its *one* treasure! What was left ?
What, but that mandate Vengeance,
    hissed
With hot tongue thro' a seething mist
Of passion; the fierce mandate, "Kill ? "
Aye! but *she*, too, lay blanched and
    still.

Blanched on the couch I dreamed would
    be
My wedding couch! Oh, infamy!
His outrage smote her to the heart;
It crashed the gates of life apart,
Where through her shuddering soul took
    flight!
But ere the death-dew dimmed her sight,
She gave me, as I said, this flower,
And — one long smile! To my last hour
I've shrined her smile! If, if some-
    where
There *be* a heaven, benign and fair,
Its saints, I feel, must smile so there!

Dread God! couldst thou have marked
    my wrong,
Yet sheathed thy lightning ? I was
    strong
And lusty as the hillside roe;
Could wield the brand and bend the
    bow
So deftly, that his lordship deigned
To show me favor! Was it feigned ?
I know not! His *last* kindness took
A strange shape truly; for it shook
My hopes to atoms! Yet *he* fell
Prone with them! Shall we meet in
    hell ?

I ask again. Ha! if we do
And there's a single nerve, or thew,

Or muscle left to naked soul,
I'll strangle him once more; enroll
My ruthless arms round breast and
    throat,
And wring from out his gorge that note
Of palsied fear! I'll do 't, tho' all
The devils should pull me back, and
    call
Fresh torments on my anguished head:
Doubtless they'll take *his* part instead.

Of *mine*, being devils, and he the worst;
A prince amongst their tribes accurst
By this time; for a month has sped,
Beshrew me, since he joined the dead,
The damned dead! Full time I trow,
For all the bounds of hell to know
That Satan's rivalled! Hark without!
The gathering tramp, the approaching
    shout
Of thousands! Well, their scaffold's
    high;
Fair chance for all to see me die!

———◆———

THE VILLAGE BEAUTY.

THE glowing tints of a tropic eve,
Burn on her radiant cheek,
And we know that her voice is rich and
    low,
Though we never have heard her speak;
So full are those gracious eyes of light,
That the blissful flood runs o'er,
And wherever her tranquil pathway
    tends
A glory flits on before!

O! very grand are the city belles,
Of a brilliant and stately mien,
As they walk the steps of the languid
    dance,
And flirt in the pauses between;
But beneath the boughs of the hoary
    oak,
When the minstrel fountains play,
I think that the artless village girl
Is sweeter by far than they.

O! very grand are the city belles,
But their hearts are worn away
By the keen-edged world, and their lives
    have lost
The beauty and mirth of May;
They move where the sun and the starry
    dews
Reign not; they are haughty and bold,
And they do not shrink from the cursed
    mart,
Where faith is the slave of gold.

But the starry dews and the genial sun
Have gladdened *her* guileless youth;
And her brow is bright with the flush of
    hope,
Her soul with the seal of truth;
Her steps are beautiful on the hills
As the steps of an Orient morn,
And Ruth was never more fair to see
In the midst of the autumn corn.

AFTER DEATH.

THE passionate sobs of the dear friends
    that came
To look their last upon my living frame,
And catch the fainting accents of my
    breath,
That fluttered in the atmosphere of
    death,
Were hushed to silence, and the uncer-
    tain light,
That flickered o'er the arras to my sight,
Grew paler and more tremulous, as life
Sunk 'neath the power of that unequal
    strife,

Which pits humanity against the spell
Of one all flesh hath found invincible!

I could not see my foe: but the whole
    space
Was redolent of pestilence, and grace
Of all things beautiful, and grand and
    free,
Seemed lost in darkness evermore to
    me:
I struggled with the invisible arm that
    wound
So sternly round me, but could give no
    sound
To the great agony that whelmed my
    soul
In surges wilder than the eternal roll
Of a world's waters, thundering round
    the Pole.

Downward, still downward, the relent-
    less hand
Pressed on my being, and the iron wand
Of his malign enchantment struck my
    heart
With a dull force that made the life-blood
    start
Forever from its courses; then a sense
Of coming rest, more dreamless and in-
    tense
Than ever wrapped mortality in still
And throbless freedom from all thoughts
    of ill,
Stole o'er the vanquished form and glim-
    mering sight,
Till silence ruled, with nothingness and
    night!

SONNETS.

SONNETS.

OCTOBER.

THE passionate summer's dead! the sky's
⟨aglow
With roseate flushes of matured desire,
The winds at eve are musical and low,
As sweeping chords of a lamenting
lyre,
Far up among the pillared clouds of fire,
Whose pomp of strange procession up-
ward rolls,
With gorgeous blazonry of pictured
scrolls,
To celebrate the summer's past renown;
Ah, me! how regally the heavens look
down,
O'ershadowing beautiful autumnal woods
And harvest fields with hoarded in-
crease brown,
And deep-toned majesty of golden floods,
That raise their solemn dirges to the
sky,
To swell the purple pomp that floateth by.

LIFE AND DEATH.

I. — LIFE.

SUFFERING! and yet majestical in pain;
Mysterious! yet, like spring-showers in
the sun,
Veiling the light with their melodious
rain,
Life is a warp of gloom and glory spun;
Its darkling phases are as clouds that
mourn
Beneath the loftier splendors of an arch
Where deathless orbs in golden daylight
burn,

And God's great pulses beat their music
march.
The heaven we worship dimly girt with
tears,
The spirit-heaven, what is it but a life,
Lifting its soul beyond our mortal years
That oft begin, and ever end with strife:
Strife we must pass to win a happier
height,
Nature but travails to reveal us — light.

II. — DEATH.

THEN whence, O Death! thy dreariness?
We know
That every flower the breeze's flattering
breath
Wooes to a blush, and love-like mur-
muring low,
Dies but to multiply its bloom in death:
The rill's glad, prattling infancy, that
fills
The woodlands with its song of innocent
glee,
Is passing through the heart of shadowy
hills,
To swell the eternal manhood of the
sea:
And the great stars, Creation's minstrel-
fires
Are rolling toward the central source
of light,
Where all their separate glory but ex-
pires
To merge into one world's unbroken
might;
There is no death but change, soul
claspeth soul,
And all are portion of the immortal
whole.

SHELLEY.

BECAUSE they thought his doctrines
    were not just,
Mankind assumed for him the chasten-
    ing rod,
And tyrants reared in pride, and strong
    in lust,
Wounded the noblest of the sons of
    God;
The heart's most cherished benefactions
    riven,
Basely they strove to humble and
    malign
A soul whose charities were wide as
    heaven,
Whose *deeds*, if not his *doctrines*, were
    divine;
And in the name of Him, whose sun-
    shine warms
The evil as the righteous, deemed it
    good
To wreak their bigotry's relentless
    storms
On one whose nature was not under-
    stood.
Ah, well! God's ways are wondrous; it
    may be
His seal hath not been set to man's
    decree.

POETS OF THE OLDEN TIME.

THE brave old poets sing of nobler
    themes
Than those weak griefs which harass
    craven souls;
The torrent of their lusty music rolls
Not through dark valleys of distempered
    dreams,
But ·murmurous pastures lit by sunny
    streams;
Or, rushing from some mountain height
    of thought,
Swells to strange meaning that our
    minds have sought
Vainly to gather from the doubtful
    gleams

Of our more gross perceptions. Oh,
    their strains
Nerve and ennoble manhood! no shrill
    cry,
Set to a treble, tells of querulous woe;
Yet numbers deep-voiced as the mighty
    main's
Merge in the ringdove's plaining, or the
    sigh
Of lovers whispering where sweet rivu-
    lets flow.

"NOW, WHILE THE REAR-GUARD."

Now, while the rear-guard of the flying
    year,
Rugged December on the season's verge
Marshals his pale days to the mournful
    dirge
Of muffled winds in far-off forests drear,
Good friend! turn with me to our in-door
    cheer;
Draw nigh; the huge flames roar upon
    the hearth,
And this sly sparkler is of subtlest birth,
And a rich vintage, poet souls hold
    dear;
Mark how the sweet rogue wooes us!
    Sit thee down,
And we will quaff, and quaff, and drink
    our fill,
Topping the spirits with a Bacchanal
    crown,
Till the funereal blast shall wail no more,
But silver-throated clarions seem to
    thrill,
And shouts of triumph peal along the
    shore.

"PENT IN THIS COMMON SPHERE."

PENT in this common sphere of sensual
    shows,
I pine for beauty; beauty of fresh mien,
And gentle utterance, and the charm
    serene,
Wherewith the hue of mystic dream-land
    glows;

I pine for lulling music, the repose
Of low-voiced waters, in some realm be-
tween
The perfect Adenne, and this clouded
scene
Of love's sad loss, and passion's mourn-
ful throes;
A pleasant country, girt with twilight
calm,

In whose fair heaven a moon of shadowy
round
Wades through a fading fall of sunset
rain;   [balm,
Where drooping lotos-flowers, distilling
Gleam by the drowsy streamlets sleep
hath crown'd,
While Care forgets to sigh, and Peace
hath balsamed Pain.

"BETWEEN THE SUNKEN SUN AND THE NEW MOON."

BETWEEN the sunken sun and the new
moon,
I stood in fields through which a rivulet
ran
With scarce perceptible motion, not a
span
Of its smooth surface trembling to the
tune
Of sunset breezes: "O delicious boon,"
I cried, "of quiet! wise is Nature's
plan,
Who, in her realm, as in the soul of
man,

Alternates storm with calm; and the loud
noon
With dewy evening's soft and sacred
lull:
Happy the heart that keeps *its* twilight
hour,
And, in the depths of heavenly peace
reclined,
Loves to commune with thoughts of
tender power;
Thoughts that ascend, like angels beau-
tiful,
A shining Jacob's ladder of the mind."

ANCIENT MYTHS.

YE pleasant myths of Eld, why have ye
    fled ?
The earth has fallen from her blissful
    prime
Of summer years, the dews of that sweet
    time
Are withered on its garlands sere and
    dead.
No longer in the blue fields overhead
We list the rustling of immortal wings,
Or hail at eve the kindly visitings
Of gentle Genii to fair fortunes wed :
The seas have lost their Nereids, the sad
    streams
Their gold-haired habitants, the moun-
    tains lone
Those happy Oreads, and the blithesome
    tone
Of Pan's soft pipe melts only in our
    dreams ;
Fitfully fall the old faith's broken gleams
On our dull hearts, cold as sepulchral
    stone.

O GOD! WHAT GLORIOUS SEASONS BLESS THY WORLD !

O GOD! what glorious seasons bless thy
    world !
See! the tranced winds are nestling on
    the deep,
The guardian heavens unclouded vigil
    keep
O'er the mute earth; the beach birds'
    wings are furled
Ghost-like and gray, where the dim bil-
    lows curled
Lazily up the sea-strand, sink in
    sleep,
Save when the random fish with light-
    ning leap
Flashes above them, the far sky's im-
    pearled
Inland, with lines of silvery smoke that
    gleam
Upward from quiet homesteads, thin
    and slow :

The sunset girds me like a gorgeous
    dream
Pregnant with splendors, by whose mar-
    vellous spell,
Senses and soul are flushed to one deep
    glow,
The golden mood of thoughts ineffable!

"ALONG THE PATH THY BLEEDING FEET."

ALONG the path thy bleeding feet have
    trod,
O Christian Mother! do the martyr-years,
Crownèd with suffering through the mist
    of tears |God;
Uplift their brows, thorn-circled, unto
Most bitterly our Father's chastening rod
Hath ruled within thy term of mortal
    days,
Yet in thy soul spring up the tones of
    praise,
Freely as flowers from out a burial-sod :
Nor hath a tireless faith essayed in vain
To win from sorrow that diviner rest,
Which, like a sunset, purpling through
    the rain
Of dying storms, maketh the darkness
    blest ;
Grief is transfigured, and dethronèd
    Fears,
Pale in the glory beckoning from the
    West.

" TOO OFT THE POET IN ELABORATE VERSE."

Too oft the poet in elaborate verse,
Flushed with quaint images and gorgeous
    tropes,
Casteth a doubtful light, which is not
    hope's,
On the dark spot where Death hath
    sealed his curse
In monumental silence. Nature starts
Indignant from the sacrilege of words
That ring so hollow, and forlornly girds
Her great woe round her; there's no
    trick of Art's,

But shows most ghastly by a new-made
     tomb.
I see no balm in Gilead; he is lost,
The beautiful soul that loved thee, thy
     life's bloom,
Is withered by the sudden blighting
     frost;
O Grief ! how mighty ; Creeds ! how
     vain ye are:
Earth presses closely, — Heaven is cold
     and far.

—◇—

MOUNTAIN SONNETS.

[Written on one of the Blue Ridge range of
Mountains.]

HERE let me pause by the lone eagle's
     nest,
And breathe the golden sunlight and
     sweet air,
Which gird and gladden all this region
     fair
With a perpetual benison of rest;
Like a grand purpose that some god hath
     blest,
The immemorial mountain seems to rise,
Yearning to overtop diviner skies,
Though monarch of the pomps of East
     and West;
And pondering here, the genius of the
     height
Quickens my soul as if an angel spake,
And I can feel old chains of custom
     break,   [light;
And old ambitions start to win the
A calm resolve born with them, in whose
     might
I thank thee, Heaven ! that noble
     thoughts awake.

Here, friend! upon this lofty ledge sit
     down,
And view the beauteous prospect spread
     below,
Around, above us; in the noonday glow
How calm the landscape rests! yon dis-
     tant town,
Enwreathed with clouds of foliage like a
     crown

Of rustic honor; the soft, silvery flow
Of the clear stream beyond it, and the
     show
Of endless wooded heights, circling the
     brown
Autumnal fields, alive with billowy
     grain;
Say! hast thou ever gazed on aught more
     fair
In Europe, or the Orient ? What do-
     main
(From India to the sunny slopes of
     Spain)
Hath beauty, wed to grandeur 'n the air,
Blessed with an ampler charm a more
     benignant reign ?

The rainbows of the heaven are not more
     rare,
More various and more beautiful to view,
Than these rich forest rainbows, dipped
     in dew
Of morn and evening, glimmering every-
     where
From wooded dell to dark-blue moun-
     tain mere;
O Autumn! wondrous painter! every
     hue
Of thy immortal pencil is steeped
     through
With essence of divinity; how bare
Beside thy coloring the poor shows of
     Art,
Though Art were thrice inspired; in
     dreams alone
(The loftiest dreams wherein the soul
     takes part)
Of jasper pavements, and the sapphire
     throne
Of Heaven, hath such unearthly bright-
     ness shone
To flush and thrill the visionary heart!

—◆—

COMPOSED IN AUTUMN.

WITH these dead leaves stripped from a
     withered tree,
And slowly fluttering round us, gentle
     friend,

Some faithless soul a sad presage might
    blend;
To me they bring a happier augury;
Lives that shall bloom in genial sun-
    shine free,
Nursed by the spell Love's dews and
    breezes send,
And when a kindly Fate shall speak the
    end,
Down dropping in Time's autumn si-
    lently;
All hopes fulfilled, all passions duly
    blessed,
Life's cup of gladness drained, except
    the lees,
No more to fear or long for, but the
    rest
Which crowns existence with its dream-
    less ease;
Thus when our days are ripe, oh! let us
    fall
Into that perfect Peace which waits for
    all!

GREAT POETS AND SMALL.

Shall I not falter on melodious wing,
In that my notes are weak and may not
    rise
To those world-wide entrancing harmo-
    nies,
Which the great poets to the ages sing?
Shall my thought's humble heaven no
    longer ring
With pleasant lays, because the empyreal
    height
Stretches beyond it, lifting to the light
The anointed pinion of song's radiant
    king?   [flight
Ah! a false thought! the thrush her fitful
Ventures in vernal dawns; a happy note
Trills from the russet linnet's gentle
    throat,
Though far above the eagle soars in
    might,
And the glad skylark — an ethereal
    mote —
Sings in high realms that mock our
    straining sight.

MY STUDY.

This is my world! within these narrow
    walls,
I own a princely service; the hot care
And tumult of our frenzied life are
    here
But as a ghost, and echo; what befalls
In the far mart to me is less than
    naught;
I walk the fields of quiet Arcadies,
And wander by the brink of hoary
    seas,
Calmed to the tendance of untroubled
    thought:
Or if a livelier humor should enhance
The slow-timed pulse, 'tis not for present
    strife,
The sordid zeal with which our age is
    rife,
Its mammon conflicts crowned by fraud
    or chance,
But gleamings of the lost, heroic life,
Flashed through the gorgeous vistas of
    romance.

TO ——.

Belovèd! in this holy hush of night,
I know that thou art looking to the
    South,
Fair face and cordial brow bathed in the
    light
Of tender Heavens, and o'er thy deli-
    cate mouth
A dewy gladness from thy dark eyes
    shed;
O eloquent eyes! that on the evening
    spread
The glory of a radiant world of dreams
(The inner moonlight of the soul that
    dims
This moonlight of the sense), and o'er
    thy head,
Thrown back, as listening to a voice of
    hymns,
Perchance in thine own spirit, violet
    gleams

"This is my world! within these narrow walls,
I own a princely service."

From modest flowers that deck the
    window-bars,
While the winds sigh, and sing the far-
    off streams,
And a faint bliss seems dropping from
    the stars.
O! pour thine inmost soul upon the air
And trust to heaven the secrets that
    recline
In the sweet nunnery of thy virgin
    breast;
Speak to the winds that wander every-
    where, —
And sure must wander hither — the
    divine
Contentment, and the infinite, deep
    rest
That sway thy passionate being, and lift
    high
To the calm realm of Love's eternity,
The passive ocean of thy charmèd
    thought;
And tell the aerial element to bear
The burden of thy whispered heart to
    me,
By fairy alchemy of distance wrought
To something sacred as a saintly prayer,
A spell to set my nobler nature free.

TO W. H. H.

How like a mighty picture, tint by tint,
This marvellous world is opening to thy
    view!
Wonders of earth and heaven; shapes
    bright and new,
Strength, radiance, beauty, and all things
    that hint
Most of the primal glory, and the print
Of angel footsteps; from the globe of
    dew
Tiny, but luminous, to the encircling
    blue,
Unbounded, thou drink'st knowledge
    without stint;
Like a pure blossom nursed by genial
    winds,
Thy innocent life, expanding day by day,

Upsprings, spontaneous, to the perfect
    flower;
Lost Eden-splendors round thy path-
    way play,
While o'er it rise and burn the starry
    signs
Which herald hope and joy to souls of
    power.

I pray the angel in whose hands the sum
Of mortal fates in mystic darkness lies,
That to the soul which fills these deep-
    ening eyes,
Sun-crowned and clear, the spirit of
    Song may come;
That strong-winged fancies, with melo-
    dious hum
Of plumèd vans, may touch to sweet sur-
    prise
His poet nature, born to glow and rise,
And thrill to worship though the world
    be dumb;
That love, and will, and genius, all may
    blend
To make his soul a guiding star of time,
True to the purest thought, the noblest
    end,
Full of all richness, gentle, wise, com-
    plete,
In whose still heights and most ethereal
    clime,
Beauty, and faith, and plastic passion
    meet.

LINES.

YE cannot add by any pile ye raise,
One jot or tittle to the statesman's
    fame;
That the world knows; to the far future
    days
Belongs his glory, and its radiant flame
Will burn, when ye are dead, decayed,
    forgot;
Therefore, your opposition matters not;
The thin-masked jealousies of present
    time,
Unburied in his grave, survive to keep

Rampant the hate he deemed his highest
  praise,
And the rude clash of discord o'er his
  sleep;
But for his great, wise acts, his faith
  sublime,
All that the soul of genius sanctifies,
These mount where viler passions cannot
  climb,
These live where palsied malice faints
  and dies.

Still must the common voice denounce
  the deed,
The common heart swell with an out-
  raged pride,
That the poor purchase of that paltry
  meed
His country owed him should be thus
  denied;
Shame on the Senate! shame on every
  hand
Which did not falter when recording
  there,
The basest act achieved for many a year,
To fire the scorn of the whole Southern
  land;
Nor the South only, for our foes will cry
Out on your petty pasteboard chivalry!
The people who refuse to crown the
  great
And good with honor, do themselves
  eclipse,
And doubly shameless is the recreant
  State,
Whose condemnation comes from her
  own lips.

"AN IDLE POET DREAMING."

An idle poet, dreaming in the sun,
One given to much unhallowed va-
  grancy
Of thought and step; who, when he
  comes to die,

In the broad world can point to nothing
  done;
No chartered corporations, no streets
  paved
With very princely stone-work, no vast
  file
Of warehouses, no slowly-hoarded pile
Of priceless treasure, no proud sceptre
  waved
O'er potent realms of stock, no magic
  art
Lavished on curious gins, or works of
  steam;
Only a few wild songs that melt the
  heart,
Only the glow of some unearthly dream,
Embodied and immortal; what are these?
Sneers the sage world; chaff, smoke,
  vain phantasies!

Yet stock depreciates, even banks decay,
Merchant and architect are lowly laid
In purple palls, and the shrewd lords of
  trade
Lament, for they were wiser in their
  day
Than the clear sons of light; but prithee,
  how
Doth stand the matter, when the years
  have fled;
What means yon concourse thronging
  where the dead
Old singer sleeps; say! do they seek him
  now?
Now that his dust is scattered on the
  breath
Of every wind that blows; what meaneth
  this?
It means, thou sapient citizen, that
  death
Heralds the bard's true life, as with a
  kiss,
Wakens two immortalities; then bow
To the world's scorn, O poet, with calm
  brow.

DRAMATIC SKETCHES.

DRAMATIC SKETCHES.

ANTONIO MELIDORI.

[AMONG the heroes of the modern Greek revolution, none, perhaps, were so distinguished for acts of individual daring, and a spirit of romantic and chivalrous adventure, as Captain Antonio Melidori, a native of Candia. He waged against the Turks a partisan conflict, which was often eminently successful. His own deeds of strength, and reckless hardihood, made him terrible to the foe, who were persuaded finally to look upon him as one whose life was " charmed."

It did not prove so, however, as he fell a victim to the rage and jealousy of some of his own company. Having been invited by the malcontents to a feast, Rousso (the chief of the conspirators, whom Antonio appears to have rivalled successfully both in love and war), whilst in the very act of embracing the patriot, plunged a dagger into his bosom.

There is a tradition that Antonio loved a beautiful maiden, Philota, whom in the stirring and anxious scenes of the revolution he was ultimately led to neglect, if not to forsake. A writer in " Chambers' Journal " has from this episode in the private career of the Greek partisan taken the material for a touching and graphic narrative, which has been closely, often literally followed in the composition of the ensuing " sketch."]

SCENE I.

[A place not far from the summit of Mount Psiloriti, in the Isle of Candia. Philota discovered with a basket of grapes upon her head; she looks eagerly upward. Time, a little before sunset.]

PHILOTA.

WHY comes he not ? Here on this emer-
ald sward,
Close to the cool shade of these ancient
rocks,
We have met, and fondly lingered in the
sunset,
Eve after eve, since first he said, " I love
thee!"
Never, Antonio, hast thou been ere now
A loiterer! wherefore should my heart
beat fast,
And my breath thicken, and the dew of
fear
Stand chill upon my forehead ? Is't an
omen ?

[At this moment Antonio is seen bounding
quickly down the mountain ; he reaches Philota
and embraces her.]

ANTONIO.

Thou hast waited long, Philota, hast thou
not ?

PHILOTA.

'Tis true, Antonio! but thou know'st an
hour,
Nay, a bare minute, drags the weariest
length
When thou art from me!

ANTONIO.

Thanks, dearest, and, forgive me,
I did but dream upon the hill-top yonder
And, dreaming thus, forgot thee.

PHILOTA.

Forgot me!

ANTONIO.

Nay, nay, I mean not that! thy face, thy
smiles,
Thy deep devotion, in my heart of hearts,
I keep them shrined forever, but my
thoughts
Turned truant; who can hold his
thoughts, Philota,
In a leash always ? prithee reascend

The mountain with me, I would show
   the place
Which tempted my weak thoughts to
   wander thus.

[*They reach the most elevated portion of the
mountain, whence a wide circuit of land and
sea becomes visible.*]

PHILOTA.

How beautiful! how glorious! see, my
   love,
There's not a cloud, or shadow of cloud
   in heaven;
Even here, the winds breathe faintly,
   and afar
O'er the broad circuit of the watery
   calm,
Peace broods upon the ocean, rules the
   air,
And up the sunset's dazzling pathway
   walks
Like a saint entering Paradise.
            'Twere sweet,
How sweet, Antonio, amid scenes like
   these,
To live and love forever!

ANTONIO [*absently*].
            Dost thou think so?
Ay!—well—perhaps——

PHILOTA.
            He heeds me not, his eye
Is cold and stern; what troubles thee,
   Antonio?

ANTONIO.
Trouble! I am not troubled.

PHILOTA.
            But thou art,
I know thou art; would'st thou deceive
   Philota?

ANTONIO.
Now by the saints, not so; dismiss the
   fear
Which, like a tremulous shadow, breaks
   the calm
Of those soft eyes! [*after a pause*]
            The matter, in brief, is this:
Tracking our mountain paths at early
   dawn,
Rousso—thou knowest him—hailed me
   from the rocks,

With words that sounded like the battle
   trumpets;
"It comes!" he cried; "the war-cloud
   rolls this way;
We too shall hear its thunders"——

PHILOTA.
            Ay! and feel
Its bolts perchance,—there's lightning
   in such clouds!

ANTONIO.
What if there be! who would not brave
   them all,—
All, for a cause like ours? Believe me,
   Love,
We stand upon the brink of troublous
   times:
All shall be changed here: men,—brave
   Grecian men,—
The blood of heroes in them,—cannot
   pause,
Storing the honey, harvesting the olive,
Or humbly following the tame herds-
   man's trade,
Whilst Freedom calls to conflict.
            Look, Philota!
Dost mark yon lurid flash across the bay?
Our soldiers test their cannon! hark,
   below,
The drums of Affendouli—how they
   ring!
Already thousands of bold mountaineers
Have formed beneath his banners; dost
   thou hear me?

PHILOTA.
And wouldst thou wish to join them?
   Ah! I see,
I see it all!—a trouble on thy brow,
Borne upward from the restless gloom
   within,
Hath clouded o'er thy peace. I,—a
   frail girl,
And gifted only with the wealth of love,
How can I satisfy the burning need
Of a strong man's ambition?. Yes, tis so,
'Tis even so!—love is the woman's
   heaven,
Her hope, her god, her life-blood! yet
   to man,
What is it but a pastime?

ANTONIO.
Speak not thus

Oh, speak not thus, Philota! I have
loved
Thee, only thee, — so help me, Virgin
Mother!
But comrades from whose lips a taunt is
bitter,
Have dared to hint ——

PHILOTA.
What!

ANTONIO.
That I chose to stay,

Delving, like some base slave, our bar-
ren soil,
When not a Sphakiote that can carry
arms
Has failed to seize them. Liars! pesti-
lent liars,
I would have proved the falsehood were
it not ——

PHILOTA.
For me — Philota! — well! I love thee
dearly,
Deeply, — God knows, — but I would
have this love
To crown thee as a garland, — not as a
chain
To bind and fetter — thou art free, An-
tonio! —

ANTONIO.
But hast thou thought of all which fol-
lows this?
Thou shalt be left alone, no bridal feast
Can cheer the olive harvest!

PHILOTA.
I have thought,

And am determined; — thou art free,
Antonio!

ANTONIO.
Oh, thanks, thanks, thanks! — lift up
thy hopes, Philota,
Up to the height of mine! our cause is
just,
And a just Fate shall guard it; where-
soe'er
Free thought finds utterance, and the
patriot-soul

Thrills at the deeds of heroes, — we may
look
For a "God speed!" The prayers of
noble men,
The tears of women, — the whole world's
applause
Do wait upon us!
Methinks I see the end,
A free, grand Commonwealth of Gre-
cian States,
Built upon chartered rights, — each
sealed with blood!

PHILOTA.
Enough! enough! Antonio, thou shalt
go!
Greece is thy mistress, now.

SCENE II.

[The cottage of Philota, at the foot of Mount
Psiloriti. Philota discovered at the window,
looking out upon the night, which is bleak
and stormy.]

PHILOTA.
Hark! how those lusty trumpeters, the
winds,
Urge on the black battalions of the
clouds;
And see! the swollen rivulets rushing
down
The sides of Psiloriti! Yesterday,
'Neath the clear calm of the serenest
morn
Earth ever stole from Paradise, they
swept,
Bright curves of laughing silver in the
sunshine;
But now, an overmastering rush of
floods,
They thunder to the heavens, that an-
swer back
From the wild depths of gloom, — an
awful tempest!

[*Enter* ANTONIO *hastily.*]

ANTONIO.
Where is the priest, Philota? where is
Andreas?
Was he not here to-night?

PHILOTA.
Ay! but left some half hour since!

ANTONIO.
                    What say you?
Oh, the poor father! — then 'twas him I
    saw
Pent 'twixt the mountain torrents; he is
    lost!
The good old man! — and yet, not so,
    not so!
Give me yon oaken staff, — and, hold; a
    flask
Of the best vintage; I'll be back anon,
And the dear father with me: —

[*Exit Antonio. Philota kneels before an image
of the Virgin, and prays for the safety of her
lover. After the lapse of some minutes, enter
Rousso stealthily, wrapped in a cloak, which
partly conceals his features.*]

ROUSSO [*aside*].
Faith! a pretty picture!
Now, were I what fools call poetical,
I'd worship her, whilst she adores the
    saint, —
A lovelier saint herself, and nearer truly
To the just standard of divinity
Than yonder painted image; there's the
    curve,
The old Greek curve, in the voluptuous
    swell
Of those full lips; the passion in her eyes
Is shadowed off to melancholy meaning,
Only to waken to meridian life,
When a like passion touches it to flame.

PHILOTA [*praying*].
Oh, merciful Mother! save him, — save
    Antonio!

ROUSSO [*aside*].
Oh, potent Devil! claim him, — claim
    Antonio!
What! shall this malapert boy dispute
    my love?

[*Philota, rising, discovers Rousso, towards
whom (mistaking him for Antonio), she rushes,
as if about to cast herself into his arms, but
discovering her error, she shrinks back.*]

PHILOTA.
                    You here!
ROUSSO [*advancing*].
I crave protection, shelter, — may I stay?
PHILOTA.
At a safe distance, Sir!

ROUSSO.
            Why, what means this?
I looked for kindlier welcome!

PHILOTA.
            Wherefore, Rousso?
What thou hast asked, I grant, — pro-
    tection, shelter;
Durst thou claim more than these?

ROUSSO.
I' faith thy temper is most strange and
    wayward!
Because, some months agone, not quite
    myself,
I ventured at the harvest of the olive,
Upon one innocent liberty ——

PHILOTA.
                    No liberty,
With me, at least, bold man! is rated
    thus!

ROUSSO.
I do repeat, that I was not myself;
Blame the hot wine of Cyprus; spare
    your slave! [*Kneeling.*]

PHILOTA.
A slave, indeed! —
            ROUSSO.   [Iota;
But one who stoops to conquer, fair Phi-
If I have knelt, 'tis only that I may
Rise thus, and clasp thee! Hold, no
    foolish cries,
No weak, vain strugglings! Think'st
    thou that the storm
Pealing adown the mountain's rugged
    steeps
Can bear these feeble wailings to thy
    friends?
Come, come, Philota! — if thou could'st
    believe it,
I am the very worthiest of thy vassals;
List for an instant, while I paint the
    beauty
Of a far Eden waiting for the light,
The sundawn of thine eyes: —
                    Amid the waves
Of the Ægean, bosomed in the calm
Of ever-during summer, sleeps an isle
Whereon the ocean ripples into music;
Through whose luxuriant wilderness of
    blooms,

The soft winds sigh their breath away in
    dreams,
Where — (the deuce take me! I forget
    my part) —
Where — where — where — i' sooth, a
    place
To live, to love, to die in, and revisit
From the sad vale of shadows, with a
    touch
Of mortal fondness, overmastering death:
Wilt thou go thither with me? Nay,
    thou must!

[*As Rousso attempts to carry Philota from
the apartment, she recovers, and, by a sudden
effort, releases herself from his arms.*]

ROUSSO.

Pardon, Philota! 'tis my eager love
Which thus hath urged me on; thou
    tremblest! what?
I would not make thee fear me.

PHILOTA.
            Fear! fear!
If my cheek pales, it is not cowardice
That plays the tyrant to the exiled
    blood;
If my frame trembles, there are other
    moods
Than that thou speak'st of, to unstring
    its firmness;
Thy presence brings no terrors; dost thou
    talk
Of fear to a Greek woman?

ROUSSO.
No! no! not fear, but love!

PHILOTA.
        Man, man! I pray thee
Blaspheme not thus! what canst thou
    know of love?
'Tis true thou speak'st it boldly; from
    thy lips
The word falls with a rounded fullness
    off,
And yet, believe me, thou hast used a
    phrase,
(A sacred phrase, and wretchedly pro-
    faned),
Which, were thy years thrice lengthened
    out beyond

The general limit of our mortal lives,
And thou be made to pass through all
    extremes
Of multiform experience, it could never
Enter thy sordid soul to comprehend!

ROUSSO.
Bravely delivered! by my soul, I think
We both make good declaimers! Where
    did'st learn
That pretty speech, Philota?

PHILOTA.
          Wilt thou leave me?

ROUSSO.
Pshaw! thou art less than courteous.
    Leave thee? no!
I will not leave thee! Hark ye, my proud
    damsel,
I am not one with whom 'tis safe to
    trifle,
Thou knowest, or shalt know this; so,
    mark my words,
Long have I wooed thee fairly, would
    have won thee,
Yea, and endowed thee with both wealth
    and station;
Twice hast thou heard my proffer, twice
    with loathing
Spurned it, and me; I shall not woo thee
    thrice
With honeyed words; no, 'tis the strong
    arm now.
I am prepared for all; come on!

[*He seizes Philota a second time, but enter on
the instant Antonio, with the Monk Andreas
leaning upon him.*]

PHILOTA [*faintly*].
          Saved! saved!

ANTONIO.
Ha, Rousso, I have heard it whispered
    oft
Amongst thy watchful brethren in this
    isle,
That underneath that smooth and flatter-
    ing front
There lurked a mine of blackest villany!
Faith! I denied it once; what shall I
    say
When next the public voice decries you,
    sir?

ROUSSO.

A jest! I do assure you but a jest!
This cloak, which in your self-devoted
flight
To rescue the dear father, Andreas
(How glad I am to see his saintship
safe),
You dropped some furlongs from the
mountain's base,
I cast, in sportive fashion, on my person,
And deeming that Philota would rejoice
To hear that thou had'st so far braved
the force
O' th' treacherous elements, I called
upon her;
She did me the vast honor to confound
Your humble servant with Antonio,
And 'ere I was aware, sprang to my
arms,
With such a blinded ecstasy of rapture,
That I had wellnigh sunk into the earth,
From the mere stress of native modesty!
A jest, a jest, and nothing but a jest.

ANTONIO.

Such jesting may be dangerous, — be-
ware!

SCENE III.

[A year is supposed to have elapsed. The
town of Sphakia after nightfall. Enter con-
fusedly a band of Sphakiote soldiers, with
Rousso amongst them. The streets are crowded
with women, many of whom are heard lament-
ing the death of Antonio Melidori.]

ROUSSO [*in a disguised voice*].

Why will ye clamor thus, ye foolish
jades ?
Your handsome favorite, your renowned
commander,
Is no more dead than I am!

A WOMAN.

Say'st thou so ?
Where then is Melidori ?

ROUSSO [*still disguising his voice*].

Would'st thou learn ?
Women of Sphakia, your immaculate
captain,
He for whose welfare, upon bended
knees,

Ye nightly pray to heaven, whose name
your infants
Lisp in their very slumbers, hath be-
trayed us!
Hold! hear me out! I am no dubious
witness;
Thrice, whilst the battle raged along our
front,
I saw the traitor creeping like a dog
Between the Turkish outposts!

[*Antonio appears in the rear, with a child in
his arms.*]

ANTONIO.

It is false!
Here is your leader, Sphakiotes; what
base slanderer
Dares to pronounce me traitor ? I but
paused
To save this weeping innocent, whose
mother
Fell by some coward's sword!

ROUSSO.

Ha, Sphakiotes, see,
The noble Melidori waxes tender,
Soft as a woman! he must love the
Moslem,
Who fosters thus their offspring! by the
saints
A lusty brat! He'll thrive, good friends,
believe me,
And grow betimes, to cut our infants'
throats!

ANTONIO.

Let him who speaks stand forth; I would
confront
My bold accuser. What! he clings to
the dark!
Fit place for lies and liars!
Friends, I scorn
To parley with this viper; there's a way,
One only way, to deal with reptiles,
crush them,
Thus, thus, and thus,
When they have crawled too near us;

[*Stamping violently upon the earth.*]

Till then, why let the ugly beasts hiss
on,
And spit their harmless venom.

BIRTHPLACE OF PAUL HAMILTON HAYNE.
Charleston, S.C.

[*Turning to the women.*]

Mothers, wives,
Maidens of Sphakia, are there none
amongst ye
Ready to take this poor unfortunate?
Just for my sake, fair countrywomen,
list,
List to the blessèd word: — "The merci-
ful
Shall obtain mercy!"

ROUSSO.

Heed him not, I say,
But seize the infidel whelp, and let him
rock
On a steel bayonet! What! have we re-
pelled
The invading foe, exterminated wholly
His forces and his empire, that we dare
Cherish his cubs among us? — and for
what?
" Just for his sake, fair countrywomen,
— his,
And mercy's!" Who showed mercy to
our children,
When the Turk ravaged Scio? The
young devil, —
Hear how he shrieks! ho! send him
down to hell!
Down to his father! he's a grateful
spirit,
And thankful for small favors!

[*The crowd begin to murmur, and move threat-
eningly towards* ANTONIO.]

ANTONIO.

Shame upon you!
Though the poor boy were fifty times a
Moslem,
I'll rear him as my own; he shall not
perish;
Perchance, who knows, when I have died
for you,
For you, and Grecian liberty, this babe,
Reared as a Greek, may yet avenge my
death,
As none of you, false brethren, dare
avenge it!
Once more I say, — Mothers, wives,
maids of Sphakia,

Is there not one amongst ye to whose
tendance
I may commit this trembling casta-
way?

PHILOTA [*veiled*].

Give me the child, — I'll nurture him
with love,
And gentlest usage.

ANTONIO [*starting*].

Heavens! what voice is that?
You here, Philota? I had hoped you
dwelt
Safely within the close heart of the
mountains!

PHILOTA.

The mountains are not safe.

ANTONIO.

Why then did'st thou
Keep such strict silence? Answer me,
Philota,
How hast thou lived. This peasant's
dress ——

PHILOTA.

Is fittest
For me, Antonio, — by my handiwork,
And daily labor, I now earn my bread, —
For was it meet an unknown peasant
girl
Should claim, as her betrothed, great
Melidori,
Captain of Sphakia?

ANTONIO.

O, thou generous heart!
But stay, — the rabble must not. catch
our words;
Take thou the babe, — under the city-
walls
I'll meet thee in the gloaming,

SCENE IV.

[A place under the city walls, — time, an hour
after sunset.]

ANTONIO, [*embracing* PHILOTA con-
strainedly].
How kind thou art!

PHILOTA.

I but obeyed your mandate!

ANTONIO.

Nay, why so cold ? my troth is thine,
    Philota, —
Dost thou remember ?

PHILOTA.

            Would'st thou have me do so ?
Methought that dream was over, — by
    thy wish.

ANTONIO.

By heaven! I never said so!

PHILOTA.

            Yet thy heart,
Thy heart, Antonio, spake the keen de-
    sire,
Although thy lips kept silence; — I have
    learned
To read thy spirit like an open book,
And cannot be deceived; — all's changed
    with us;
Never again, as in the time that's past,
Shall we, hand linked in hand, explore
    the vales,
Or walk the shining hill-tops; thou hast
    risen
Far, far above my level; a great man,
Among the greatest, — thou wert mad
    t' espouse
A humble girl like me; I ask it not;
My love but burdens thy aspiring hopes,
So, I beseech thee, dwell no more upon
    it:
Antonio, for thy welfare I would give
My soul's life; shall I then refuse to
    yield
A personal joy, that thou may'st win
    and wed
The immortal virgin — Glory ? Dream
    it not!
Oh! dream it not!

ANTONIO.

        Now, gracious God, forgive me!
It were presumption, should I kiss thy
    feet,
Thou pure, unselfish woman! yet thy
    words
Are true, too true, and I dare not gain-
    say them.
One thing believe, Philota, I am
    wretched,

Yes, far more so than thou art:

[*After a pause.*]
                    — Did'st thou know
The terrible life I lead in this dread war-
    fare,
Through what an atmosphere of blood
    and carnage
It is my doom to move, as through the
    air
Of some plague-stricken city, thick with
    curses;
Did'st know the numberless dangers,
    that like demons
(Many unseen, — and therefore doubly
    fearful),
Which hover 'round the soldier, hour by
    hour
O'ershadowing life with the black gloom
    of death;
Did'st know the coarse companions, the
    rude manners
Of vile extortioners, bent alone on prey,
And personal profit, and the thousand
    evils
Gendered of strife, and strife's unhal-
    lowed passions,
O, thou would'st shrink from following
    such base courses,
Even as an angel from the brink of hell!

PHILOTA.

Thou wrong'st my love, and hast de-
    ceived thyself;
Where'er thou art, to me that place is
    heaven;
Antonio, God alone, God and my soul
Know what I might, and would have
    been to thee!
I would have shared thy fortunes, joined
    my fate
For weal or woe, for honor or disgrace,
For life or death to thine; have tracked
    thy steps,
(If need it were,) through seas of blood
    and carnage,
Strengthened thy weakness, buoyed thy
    sinking hopes,
Nor, at the worst, have shed one wo-
    man's tear

To shake thy manhood. Had heaven
    blessed thy cause,
I would have striven to make my spirit
    worthy
To mount with thee; so, when the orbèd
    glory
Shone like the fire of sunrise round thy
    brow,
No man dare say that with that lustre
    mingled
One blush of shame for Melidori's wife!
This might have been, and this shall
    never be. | *Wildly.* |
I' th' name of mercy, by thy mother's
    soul,
And the dear past, I pray thee leave me
    now,
While still thou lov'st me (dost thou
    not ?) a little.
        ANTONIO.
And thou — and thou, Philota ? ——
        PHILOTA.
            I shall dwell
In peace; [*aside*] ay! broken hearts are
    peaceful!
        ANTONIO.
            But where ? ——
        PHILOTA.
What matter where, so that I live in
    peace ?
Grieve not, Antonio.   In my humble
    station
One thought shall bring content; — "he
    was not false,"
No mortal maiden stole Antonio's heart!
        ANTONIO.
            Blessèd words!
'Tis true I love but thee!
        PHILOTA.
            Then do not sorrow.
Love, I forgive thee; thou hast wronged
    me not.
And for the child — ah, I shall dream it
    thine;
Tend it as thine, and when the years
    have ripened
That infant soul, 'tis mine to lead to
    virtue,
I'll teach the boy how noble was the act

Whereby Antonio saved him; I'll be
    happy,
Oh, trust me, Love! so very, very
    happy!
        ANTONIO.
Then be it so, Philota.   I would bless
    thee,
But am not worthy; still, thou shalt be
    blessed.
        PHILOTA.
And thou, too, if the Virgin hear my
    prayers;
And now that we are friends, *but* friends,
    though firm ones,
Beseech thee, list my tidings.   There's
    a foe,
A deadly, treacherous foe in thine own
    camp,
And one who vows thy ruin; it is Rousso;
Thou knowest how first his envious, bit-
    ter temper
Was stung to hatred; since that time,
    thy will
Hath often clashed with his; besides,
    thy fame
In these fierce wars hath far o'ertopped
    his credit;
So he has sworn thy death; the voice
    was his,
That goaded on thy soldiers to rebellion;
And, as I threaded my uncertain path-
    way,
A short hour since, through the dark
    streets of Sphakia,
I heard thy name in whispers; two dim
    forms
(Men, as I knew by their hoarse tones,)
    conferred
With hurried, stealthy gestures, and one
    sentence
Startled me like a knell: — "His tomb
    is open,"
A deep voice said; "Antonio's tomb is
    open!"
Oh, then, beware.   As lowly as thou
    deem'st me,
I'll watch above thy safety; the soft dove
May warn the eagle of the midnight
    spoiler!

ANTONIO.

And thy own life and safety ——

PHILOTA.

I am here
To spend them both for thee. But hark!
thy name
Is shouted by thy comrades in the valley.
The hour has come that parts us. Fare
thee well!

[*She gives him her hand.*]

ANTONIO.

'Twas not our wont to part in this cold
fashion;
Come, one more kiss, Philota! let me feel
We were indeed betrothed; one last, last
kiss!   [*They embrace and part.*]

SCENE V.

[An apartment in the house of Affendouli,
the Governor-General of Candia. Enter An-
tonio, and Affendouli, conversing.]

AFFENDOULI.

These private bickerings are the fruitful
cause
Of all disgrace and failure; let us end
them!

ANTONIO.

Most willingly! I have no feud with
any,
Saving one quarrel, forced upon me,
chief!

AFFENDOULI.

True, true! but even now a courier waits,
Charged with a special message of good
will,
From Rousso, and his brother, Anag-
nosti;
They say, " We plead for peace! all per-
sonal hate
Henceforth be quelled between us; we
would join
Our troop to Melidori's, and our banners
Wave side by side with his." Accept
their proffer!

ANTONIO.

I will!

AFFENDOULI.

To show thou art sincere, fail not to test
Their hospitality.

ANTONIO.

As how?

AFFENDOULI.

They give
A solemn feast of unity and friendship,
To which thou art invited. Go, I charge
thee.

ANTONIO.

Trust me, I shall be there, what day's
appointed
Whereon to hold this festival of love?

AFFENDOULI.

This very day; thou knowest the camp
of Rousso?

ANTONIO.

Ay! I'll be there anon!

[*Exit Antonio. Enter, after a brief interval,
Philota, with a hurried and anxious mien.*]

PHILOTA.

Oh, pardon, pardon!
Most gracious Governor! but I come to
seek
Ant—— Ant——, that is, the Captain
Melidori,
With tidings of grave import.

AFFENDOULI.

Ha!
Thou luckless messenger! he has de-
parted.
Gone——

PHILOTA [*wildly*].

Where, where?

AFFENDOULI.

To feast with Rousso.

PHILOTA [*rushing out*].

Then is he lost! O merciful God, pro-
tect us!

SCENE VI.

[An open space in a wood, — tables arranged
for a banquet, — Rousso, Anagnosti, Antonio
Melidori, and their followers, discovered feast-
ing.]

ANAGNOSTI.

A soldier's life forever! freè to pass
In feast or fray! how glorious this wild
banquet
Compared to those dull, formal feasts of
old,

Held at the olive harvest! Speak, Antonio,
Give us thy thought upon it: what! art
    silent?

ROUSSO.

Urge him no more; perchance Antonio
    pines
For the sweet quiet of that mountain
    life,
Which thou hast called so dull; its days
    of dream,
Its nights of warm voluptuous dalliance!

ANTONIO.

No, no, by heaven! those times are dead
    to me;
They had their pleasures, but not one to
    match
The keen delights of glory, the true
    honor
Which follows patriot service.

ROUSSO.
          Gallant words,
Brave, and high-sounding; but for me
    and mine,
We do not fight for shadows!

ANTONIO [*coldly*].
          I'm at fault,
Not clearly comprehending, sir, your
    meaning.

ROUSSO.

Oh! thou dost well to speak of glory,
    honors,
We know what rich rewards await thee,
    chief,
When the war's ended; spoils, and wealth
    and beauty.
But yestermorn, I saw thy winsome
    lady,
The bride to be, old Affendouli's daughter.
Nay, shrink not, man, she is a lovely
    maid,
Fair as her father's generous; what an
    eye!
Half arch, half languishing; and what a
    breast!
That heaves as 'twould burst outward to
    the day,

And strike men mad with its white
    panting passion!
No lovelier woman lives, unless, unless—
It be that poor young thing who doted
    on thee,
Before the war, — what was her name?
    Philota?

ANTONIO.

Thy thoughts run on fair damsels; let
    us talk
Like soldiers, not like brain-sick boys in
    love.

ROUSSO.

With all my heart; only, one pledge to
    thee,
And Affendouli's daughter!

ANTONIO.
          I have borne
This jesting with the patience of a saint,
But now 'tis stretched to license. Prithee,
    cease!

ROUSSO.

God, how he winces! if Philota —

ANTONIO.
          Villain!
Utter that sacred name again——

ROUSSO [*rising suddenly and drawing
    his dagger*].
          Oh, ho!
Wilt fight, wilt fight! I'm ready for thee;
    come.

ANTONIO [*aside*].

(He shall not trap me thus.) Thou art
    my host;
'Twere shame, yea, bitter shame, this
    brawl should end
In blows and bloodshed! when the time
    befits,
          [*To* ROUSSO].

Doubt not that I shall call thee to account
For this day's work; meanwhile I leave
    a board
Where clownish insult poisons all your
    cups!

[*As he is about to depart, Anagnosti approaches,
    with an air of conciliation.*]

ANAGNOSTI.

Well spoken, noble captain, thou wert
wronged;
But Rousso is so hasty! He repents;
Let not this solemn feast of unity
Break up in discord.

ROUSSO.

No, no, no, Antonio!
I do repent! Prithee embrace me, friend,
In sign of reconcilement.

[*Rousso approaches Melidori with an unsteady
step; while in the act of embracing, he stabs
him in the side. Philota rushes upon the scene,
with a cry of agony, and throws herself beside
Antonio, whose head she supports.*]

PHILOTA.

Too late! O God, too late! He faints,
he dies!
Why stare ye thus upon us, cruel men?
Wine, wine, another cup, how slow ye
move!
My scarf is drenched with blood, — ye
pitiless fools!
Will not a creature loan me wherewithal
To bind his wretched wound up? There,
'tis stanched,
And he revives! Antonio, speak to me,
I am Philota!

ANTONIO [*his mind wandering*].

Where hast thou been, my love, this
weary time?
Am I not true? I charge thee, heed
them not!
The girl is nothing to me; Rousso's
tongue,
His sharp false tongue first joined our
names together;
She loves another, and I love but thee;
Draw nearer, let me whisper. I have
dreamed,
Oh, such a dream! the valleys flowed
with blood,
And ruin compassed all our island round,
And every town was sacked, and, hark
ye, nearer!
I saw a mother murdered by a knave,
A coward knave, because she would not
yield
Her body to him; but I saved her child,

And here he is, a pretty, pretty boy!
Take him, Philota. Ah, my heart, my
heart!
It pains me sorely; 'twas a terrible
dream,
But now, thank Heaven, 'tis over! Thou
art pale;
What makes thee pale? Bear up, my
dearest love!
This morn we shall be wedded, and I
think
We will not part again. I had a foe,
His name is Rousso; but we are so
happy,
Let us forgive all foes; invite him thither,

PHILOTA [*weeping*].

He breaks my heart —

ANTONIO.

How keen the wind is!
Keen, keen, and chill; it was not wont
to blow
So coldly at this season: I am sick,
Yea, sick of very joy; but joy kills not;
My lids are heavy; I would sleep,
Philota.
Wake me at early dawn; I told my
mother,
That I would bring thee home, to-mor-
row morn.

[*He dies.*]

ALLAN HERBERT.

SCENE I.

[The hall of a country house in Westmore-
land, surrounded with portraits of the M. . . .
family. Allan Herbert, and Jocelyn, an old
domestic, are seen standing before the likeness
of a lady, young, and wonderfully fair.]

HERBERT.

The canvas speaks!

JOCELYN.

Ay, sir, 'tis very like;
Was she not beautiful?

HERBERT.

Was; yes, and is;
She had not lost one bloom when late I
saw her.

"The canvas speaks."

JOCELYN.

Sir, she is dead!

HERBERT.

Ay, so they say, old man;
And yet I see her nightly, — in my
  dreams;
I tell you that her cheek is round and
  fair
As summer's fulness, that her eyes are
  lustrous,
And she, a perfect presence clasped in
  light!
Thus will she look, on resurrection
  morning.

JOCELYN [aside].

Alas, poor gentleman! how many loved
  her,
And loved her vainly! Pardon, sir, your
  name ?

HERBERT.

My name is Allan Herbert.

JOCELYN.

Herbert, Herbert!
Where have I heard that dainty name
  before ? (musing)
Oh, now I have it; my young mistress,
  sir,
She who is dead, was wont to read a
  book
A delicate gold-edged volume, that I'm
  sure
Bore some such name within it; she
  would sit
Beneath yon grape vine trellis toward the
  south
(This window, sir, commands it), and
  for hours,
Nay, days, bend o'er her favorite pages;
  once
She left the book behind her, and I saw
Its leaves were touched with tears.

HERBERT.

Where is it now ?
That book your mistress loved ? Let
  me behold it!

JOCELYN.

In sooth, sir, I have never seen it since,

Or, if I have [hesitating], it lies beyond
  our reach.

HERBERT.

What meanest thou ?

JOCELYN.

I mean that while she lay
Decked for her burial, whilst I stood be-
  side her,
Looking my last upon her tranquil fea-
  tures,
The robe of death was fluttered by the
  wind,
A low sad wailing wind, that swept aside
The drapery for a moment, and I marked
The glimmer of the gold-edged pages
  placed
Right on her bosom! Master, you are
  pale,
You tremble; I have rudely touched the
  spring
Of some deep-seated sorrow!

HERBERT.

Yes, old man;
A sorrow most unlike to common griefs,
That pass like clouds or shadows; mine
  is mingled
With the dark hues of treachery and re-
  morse;
A rayless, blank eclipse, through which
  I wander,
Accursed and hopeless; sometimes in a
  vision
Comes the sweet face of her I foully
  wronged,
And stabs me with a smile!

JOCELYN.

Did'st wrong her, Sir ?
Did'st wrong my lady ?

HERBERT.

Lead me to the grave;
I know 'tis near at hand.

JOCELYN.

The grave! what grave ?
Moreover, — if you wronged her ———

HERBERT.

If I wronged her!
Why dost thou taunt me with it ? thou
    on earth
With Mercy still beside thee, — I — in
    Hell ?

JOCELYN.

Madman!

HERBERT.

I am not mad, my friend, but only
    wretched;
Once more, I pray thee, show me where
    she sleeps.

JOCELYN.

I must obey him; this way, — follow me.

SCENE II.

[A forest. — Deep in the shade a single
monument appears, covered with wild-flowers
and roses.]

HERBERT [*alone*].

'Tis fit she should be buried in this place
So fragrant and so peaceful; O, my love!
Thou hast grown dull of hearing! I may
    call
'Till the lone echoes shiver with thy
    name,
Thou wilt not heed me; dust, dust, dust
    indeed!
And thou — more glorious than the
    morning star;
More tender than the love-light of the
    eve!
They tell me thou shalt rise again,
    Christ's bride,
Not mine, most beautiful, yet changed;
Perchance I shall not know thee, or per-
    chance,
The human love which made thine eyes
    like heaven —
My heaven of hope and worship — shall
    be lost
In some diviner splendor ! all is
    hushed,
No smallest whisper trembles gently up
From the deep grave to soothe me; 'tis
    in vain

I agonize in thought.   Eternal Nature!
She whom I once called " mother,"
    wears an aspect
Callous and pitiless.   I fain would solve
This terrible mystery that weighs down
    my soul
With nightmare fancies.   Let me die in
    peace,
O God! and if I may not see her more
Through all the long eternities, nor hear
Her voice of tender pardon, let me rest
Next to some stream of Lethe, and re-
    pose
In everlasting slumbers!———

[*Enter* JOCELYN.]

JOCELYN.

Come, let us hence! the darkness creeps
    upon us;
See, Sir! there's not a spark of sunset
    left
In all the waning West.

HERBERT.

Well, what of that!
I live in darkness, — the light burns my
    spirit,
It mocks and tortures me! Begone, I
    say,
And leave me to the dismal shade thou
    fearest!

JOCELYN.

Good Sir, be counselled — stay not in
    the wood;
Thine eye is troubled, and thy visage
    weary; —
'Tis a rash venture!

HERBERT.

Sooth to say, I thank thee;
Thou could'st not serve long in the house-
    hold blessed
By her most merciful presence, and not
    catch
Some tenderness of temper; — take my
    thanks!
Yet will I stay in this same dreary wood,
And watch until the night is overpast.

JOCELYN.

Thou'lt find it lonely.

HERBERT.
Oh, I have my thoughts,
A stirring company, that never slumber.

JOCELYN.
Why, worse and worse! I've heard, such
restless thoughts
Engender a sore sickness ———

HERBERT.
Of the mind;
Yet is my case already desperate,
Past healing, and past comfort. Go thy
way.
Thou kind old man, thou canst not
shake my purpose,
But when the last star wanes before the
dawn,
Come back; my night will then be over-
past,
And my watch ended; till that hour,
farewell!

———————◆———————

FROM THE CONSPIRATOR,

AN UNPUBLISHED TRAGEDY.

SCENE.

[A garden ; Arnold De Malpas and Catharine
discovered walking slowly towards a summer-
house in the distance].

CATHARINE.
Art thou prepared to risk all this, De
Malpas ?

DE MALPAS.
Ay! this, and more, if I but thought —
                    [*Hesitating*].

CATHARINE.
          What, Arnold ?

DE MALPAS.
If I but thought that when the strife was
over,
The feeble prince hurled down, the
throne secured,
She, for whose love I braved the people's
hate,
Malice of rulers, and the headsman's
axe,
Would deign to share with me that
perilous height.

CATHARINE.
She! Oh, thou hast a lady-love!

DE MALPAS.
Cruel! Wouldst thou put by my passion
thus,
With a feigned jest ? Catharine, I stake
my all,
Manhood's strong hopes and purpose,
the heart's wealth,
And the mind's store of hard-bought
lore, my peace
Of conscience, and my soul's immortal
life,
To lift thee to the summit of thy wish;
(Oh! I have proved thee, and I know
thy thoughts),
And yet, thou feignest ignorance!

CATHARINE.
          Dear De Malpas,
Forgive me! let us both throw by the
mask!
I hate the queen; even in our girlish
days,
She was my rival; her mild-mannered
arts
Stole suitors from me; the old priest, our
teacher,
Though I eclipsed her ever in the school,
And shamed her dullness with keen-
witted words
And quicker apprehension, shone on her
With sunny aspect, sleeked her golden
hair,
Fondled and soothed and petted, whilst
for me,
The apter scholar, he reserved harsh
looks,
And harsher tones; (well, the old fool is
dead!
In after time, some friend of holy church,
Some zealous friend, proved that his
saintship taught
Schism and heresy, and so—he perished)!
But for this queen, this Eleanor! our
souls
Nursed yearly a more fixed hostility;
We sat together at the knightly jousts,
And watched the conflict with high
beating hearts,

Flushed cheeks, and fluttering pulses;
    she from fear,
I with the mounting heat of martial
    blood,
Thrilled with the music of the battle's
    roar,
The ring of mighty lances on steel helms,
Clangor of shields, and neighing of wild
    steeds:
One morn my knight was victor; as he
    placed
The crown of gems and laurel on my
    brow,
Methought that I was born to be a queen,
Not the brief ruler of a festal throng,
But 'stablished kingdoms, and a host of
    men
Bound to my sway forever!

DE MALPAS.
                    A true thought!
O, noble Catharine! thy aspiring spirit
Fires my purpose, and gives wings to
    action;
Thy rival hath sped past thee in the
    race,
But she shall fall midway; the blinded
    monarch
Walks on the brink of an abysmal deep,
And soon shall topple over; then, a vic-
    tor,
(Not from the conflict with half-blunted
    spears,
In friendly tournament), but the tumult
    fierce
Of revolution, and the crash of states,
Shall set a weightier crown about thy
    brows,
And hail thee ruler, — not of festal
    throngs,
But 'stablished kingdoms, and a host of
    men
Bound to thy sway forever!

.   .   .   .

DE MALPAS.

Speak, Bolton! what say these, my faith-
    ful friends,
Touching my present life ?

BOLTON.
                    Why, Master Arnold,
I' sooth they're much divided; some as-
    sert,
That thou art moonstruck; that some
    morbid fancy,
Whether of love or pride, hath seized
    upon thee;
Others, that thou hast simply lost thy
    trust
In man and in thyself; and others still,
That thou hast sunk to base, inglorious
    ease,
Urging the languid currents of the blood
With fiery spurs of sense; a few there
    are,
Few, but most faithful, who at dead of
    night
In secret conclave, with low-whispered
    words
And pallid faces glancing back aghast,
Speak of a monstrous wrong, which
    thou ——

DE MALPAS.
    [*Starting up, and seizing Bolton.*]
Unhappy wretch! therein thou speak'st
    thy doom!
That prying, curious spirit is thy fate.
                [*Stabs him suddenly.*]
Did I not warn thee of it ?

BOLTON.
                    Oh! I die!
Yet my soul swells and lightens; all the
    future
Flashes before me like a revelation.
Arnold De Malpas! thou shalt gain thine
    end!
The aged king shall fall, the throne be
    thine!
But, as thou goest to claim it, as thy
    foot
Presses the royal dais (mark my words)!
A bolt shall fall from heaven, sudden,
    swift,
Even as thy blow on me, thou'lt writhe
    i' the dust,
Down-trodden by the hostile heel of
    thousands,

Whilst she, for whom thou'st turned
    conspirator,
Smiling, shall gaze from out her palace
    doors,
And wave her broidered scarf, and join
    the music
Of her low witching laughter to the
    sneers
Of courtly parasites; "De Malpas bore
His honors bravely, did he not, my
    lords ?
Now, by our lady, 'tis a grievous fall!"
" Yet pride, thou know'st, sweet Catha-
    rine,"—
              " Ay, ay, ay!
" Prithee, Francisco, wilt thou dance to-
    night ?"

        DE MALPAS.

What, fool! wilt prate forever ? Hence,
    I say,
And entertain the devil with thy dream-
    ings!
          [*Stabs him again.*]

   .   .   .   .   .

        DE MALPAS.

Thou hast been to court, Bernaldi, hast
    thou not ?

        BERNALDI.

Ay! all the forenoon!

        DE MALPAS.

        Didst thou see the lady,
Catharine of Savoy, whose miraculous
    beauty
Hath set all Spain aflame ?

        BERNALDI.

        I did, my cousin,
But, I am bold to speak it, liked her not;
Her beauty is the beauty of the serpent,
Masking a poisonous spirit; there's no
    depth
Of womanly nature in her gleaming
    eyes,
Falsest when most they flatter; men have
    said
She owns the Borgia's blood; I know not
    that,
But, by St. Mark! she owns their temper,
    cousin!

EXPERIENCE IN POVERTY.

A. How bitterly you speak!
B.   I have good warrant.
A. Well, for my part, I hold your creed
    is false,
Uncharitable, monstrous! I have seen
The world, sir; studied men and man-
    ners in it;
And though no doubt some selfishness
    and craft
May evermore be found by those who
    seek them,
Peering too closely underneath the
    mask
Of multiform conventions, yet, by heaven,
The world's a fair, good, reasonable
    world
To all who follow reason! Your high
    fancies,
Whose goal is vague impossibility,
Of course must miss their mark! We
    live not, sir,
In Eden, or the golden age.
B.   Right! right!
You talk as is most natural in one
To whom all life hath been a gay parade,
A frolic pastime!— to whom subtle for-
    tune
Hath never turned her dark and lowering
    front,
But round whose footsteps sowed with
    golden showers
Obsequious knaves and sweet-tongued
    servitors
Have fawned and lied and flattered, till
    your days
Borne bravely onward over perfumed
    tides
Passed like a steady bark 'twixt shores of
    flowers,
You know the world! its men and modes
    forsooth!
Wait, sir, until your purse grows lean as
    mine,
And fate within the compass of one evil
(A gaunt and loathsome poverty), in-
    cludes
All ills that flesh is heir to! disrespect

From insolent curs that now you'd
    hardly stoop
To soil your lordly boot with! studied
    coldness
Of ancient friends whose easy faith de-
    clines
With your decreasing wine-butts! covert
    sneers,
Or open insult from the gaudy throng
Of parasites, who breathe alone in sun-
    shine!
Grief without balm, and pain that knows
    not pity;
Dark days, and maddening midnights,
    and the pang
Of outraged feeling, and the soul's de-
    spair:
Ay! wait, I say, until from depths like
    these,
The lonely thunder growling overhead,
And misery like a cataract raging round
Your path of ruin, wild and desperate
    eyes
Are lifted to the summits of past hope,
Receding ever with their shows of joy,
Less real than the mirage, or the domes
Which sunset builds on clouds of phan-
    tasy!
Wait till the fiend that's born of famished
    hours
Shall grasp your hand in bony fellow-
    ship,
And lead you through the mist of ghastly
    dreams,
Helpless and tottering, to the brink of
    death!
Ha! ha! you shrink! the picture does
    not please
Your dainty fancy! Well, soft optimist,
Confess there's somewhat you have still
    to learn
Of this same fair, good, reasonable world!

THE TRUE PHILOSOPHY.

I'D have you use a wise philosophy,
In this, as in all matters, whereupon
Judgment may freely act; truth ever lies

Between extremes; avoid the spend-
    thrift's folly
As you'd avoid the road of utter ruin;
For wealth, or at the least, fair compe-
    tence,
Is honor, comfort, hope, and self-respect;
All, in a word, that makes our human
    life
Endurable, if not happy: scorn the cant
Of sentimental Dives, wrapped in pur-
    ple,
Who over jewelled wine-cups and rich
    fare,
Affects to flout his gold, and prattles
    loosely
Of sweet content that's found in poverty:
As for the miser, he's a madman simply,
One who the means of all enjoyment
    holds,
Yet never dares enjoy: no, no, Anselmo,
Use with a prudent, but still liberal hand
That store the gods have given you; thus,
    my friend,
'Twixt the Charybdis of a churlish mean-
    ness,
And the swift Scylla of improvident
    waste,
You'll steer your bark o'er smooth, in-
    nocuous seas,
And reach at last a peaceful anchorage.

LOVE'S CAPRICES.

COME, sweetheart, hear me! I have
    loved thee well,
God knoweth. Through all these years
    my holiest thoughts,
Like those pure doves nurtured in an-
    tique temples,
Have fluttered ever round thine image
    fair,
And found in thee their shrine. No
    tenderest hope
Of mine, which hath not warmed its
    radiant wings
Within that heaven, thy presence, and
    drank strength
And sunshine from it.

How hast thou responded?
Sometimes thine eyes, like Eden gates
    unclosed,
Would pour such beams of sacred pas-
    sion down,

That all my soul was flooded with its joy,
And I, methought, breathed as immor-
    tals breathe,
A deathless light and ether. Then,
    when most

"Come, sweetheart, hear me!"

I dreamed me happy, a strange change
    would come,
Sudden as strange; some wind of cold
    caprice,
Blowing, I knew not whence, an icy cloud
Upbore, and o'er the splendor of thy
    brow,

Of late so frankly beautiful, there hung
Ominous shadows, crossed by gleams of
    scorn;
Trifles as slight as eider-down have power
To move or sting thee, and a swarm of
    humors,
Gendered of morbid fancy, buzz and hiss

About some vacant chambers of thy
    mind,
By idle thoughts left open, making
    harsh,
Rude discord, where, if healthful will
    had sway,
Angels, perchance, might lift celestial
    voices!

Love, love, thou wrong'st thyself, and
    that sweet nature,
Sweet at the core, for all such small de-
    spites,
Wherewith kind heaven endowed thee;
    yet, beware!
Caprice, though frail its shafts, a poi-
    soned barb
Hath bound on each; their points are
    sharp to wound,
And the wounds rankle! Giants great
    as Love
Have perished merely of an insect's
    venom,
And who through all God's universe can
    touch
Love's pulseless heart to warmth and
    life again?

CREEDS.

FRIEND, 'mid the complex and unnum-
    bered creeds
Which meet and jostle on this mortal
    scene,
And sometimes fight _à l'outrance_, I
    perceive
Some precious seed of truth ennobling all:
Encased, it may be, like the mummy's
    wheat,
Locked in dead forms, yet waiting but a
    breath
Of honest air, an inch of wholesome soil,
To bloom and flourish heavenward;
    therefore, friend,
Walk hand in hand with clear-eyed
    Charity,
And Faith sublime, though simple, like
    a child's,

Who feels through densest midnight,
    next his own,
The loving throb of a kind father's
    heart.

THE UNIVERSALITY OF GRIEF.

I GRANT you that our fate is terrible,
Bitter as gall. What then? Will lam-
    entation,
Childish complaint, everlasting wailings,
Grief, groans, despair, help to amend
    our doom?
Glance o'er the world — the world is full
    of pain
Akin to ours. If some dark spirit
    touched
Our vision to miraculous clearness,
    sights
Would meet our eyes, at which the cold-
    est heart
Might weep blood-tears; there's not a
    moment passes
Which doth not bear its load of agonies
Out to the dim Eternity beyond;
The primal curse of earth, with heavier
    weight,
Descends on special victims; yet, bethink
    you,
All sorrow hath its bounds, o'er which
    there stands
That friend of misery, gentle-hearted
    Death.
Balms of oblivion holds he, and the
    realm
Wherein he rules hath murmurous caves
    of sleep.

THE PENITENT.

THOU see'st yon woman with the grave
    pelisse
Lined with dark sables? Is she not de-
    vout?
Her soul is in the service, and her eyes
Are dim with weeping, — weeping for
    the follies

Of a misguided youth; thus saith the
    world,
But I, who know her ladyship, know
    this:
She weeps that youth itself, and the lost
    triumphs
Which followed in its train; the scores
    of lovers
Dead now, or married off; the rout, the
    joust,
The sweet flirtations, merry carnivals,
And — (oh! supremest memory of all!) —
The banded serenaders 'neath the lattice,
Lifting the voice of passion in the night:
And one among the minstrels loved her
    well,
But him she laughed to scorn, his heart
    was riven;
She trampled on the purest pearl of love,
And cast it to the dogs; well, God is
    just!
She scorned his sacred gift, and so must
    walk,
Henceforth a lonely woman on the
    earth!

DRAMATIC FRAGMENT.

WE might have been! ah, yes! we might
    have been
Among the laurelled noblemen of
    thought,
Who lift their species with them as they
    climb
To deathless empire in the realm of
    gods;
But some dark power — we will not call
    it Fate —
We dare not call it Providence — hath
    seized
The helm of our strange destinies, and
    steered
Right onward to the breakers. All is
    lost!
Hope's siren song of promise faints in
    sighs,
And joy — (but she ne'er charmed us,
    save in days

Of dim-remembered childhood);— let it
    pass!
Our lot's the lot of millions; for on life
A blight is preying, and a mystic wrong
Hath set our heartstrings to the tune of
    grief!

REWARD OF FICKLENESS.

ALTON.

YOU see that man with the quick eyes
    and brow,
Too ponderous almost for his slender
    frame,
His dark locks tinged with gray; you'd
    hardly think it,
But he's a moral dandy, *dilettante*
(As your Italians say), whose fickle taste
Leads him, like some fastidious bee, from
    flower
To flower of social pastime! A fair girl,
Pretty and piquante, fills his heart to-
    day;
On airy wings of sentiment he hovers
Lovingly round her, feeds the beauteous
    creature
On honeyed nothings in a tone so sweet,
They seem the genuine fruit of a strong
    soul
Nurtured by passion, and true adoration;
Then on the morrow when he meets once
    more
"That Cynthia of the minute," a cold
    crust
Of iciest form and etiquette o'erspreads
His words, look, bearing; the whole man
    is changed —
As if a Tropic landscape, bright with
    sunlight,
Had grown to frozen hardness in an
    hour: —
A demon, fickle, trifling, and capricious
O'errules his spirit always! with men
    likewise,
It is his pride to play the same vile
    game!
Why, sir, your patience would be taxed
    to count

His dupes within the year! he'll take a
youth,
Bright-minded, trusting, whom per-
chance he meets
In casual fashion on the public square,
Caress, solicit, flatter him — at length
Bear the poor fool, elate and jubilant,
To banquet at his own well-ordered
board,
Ply him with curious questions, draw
him out
To make display of all his raciest wit,
And when, like a squeezed orange, all
his sap's
Exhausted, — faith! Sir Dainty down
the wind
Whistles his victim with a cool assur-
ance,
Which is the calm sublime of impu-
dence!
In fine, the man's a worn-out Epicurean,
A ceaseless hunter after new sensations,
To whom the world's a storehouse
crammed with hearts
And minds for his amusement! as for
hearts,
He'll toss 'em up, as jugglers toss their
balls,
Proud of his sleight of hand, his impish
cunning,
His matchless turns of quick dexterity!
And if the baubles break, he's sore
amazed
That aught should be so brittle! yet
thanks God
The earth is full of these same delicate
toys;
And so he hurls the shattered plaything
by,
To re-assume his honest, juggling tricks,
And charm his weary leisure-time with
lies;
A silken, soft, fair-spoken, dangerous
knave.

MARCUS.

Some day he'll find his match!

ALTON.

Ay! you may swear to that;
Some woman versed in every social art,

Some rare, majestic creature, whose rich
beauty
Will set his amorous senses in a blaze;
Slowly around him she will draw the
net
Of fascinations, multiform and strange;
Enchant his fancy with her regal wit,
His taste with every charm of female
guile,
Inflame him with voluptuous blandish-
ments,
By turns, sooth, flatter, madden, vow
she loves
At one delicious moment, then the next
As warmly swear she loathes him! by a
spell
Invisible, but potent as the sun,
She'll lead him, fawning, quivering to
her feet,
And at the last, O! consummation just!
When on the very brink of blest frui-
tion,
He hovers, arms outstretched, and soul
aglow,
She'll freeze to sudden marble, wave him
off
With such calm haughtiness of queenly
scorn,
Imperious, crushing, fatal, that, by heav-
en,
I should not wonder if the terrible sting
Of disappointment and deceived desires,
Of baffled passion, wounded self-conceit,
And hope so swiftly murdered by de-
spair,
Struck to the core of being, and this
man
Falser than hell to others, perished
wholly,
By his own pestilent trickery done to
death!

———◆———

A CHARACTER.

A.　HE is a man whose complex char-
acter
Few can decipher rightly; but for me
I have found the key at last!

B. What make you of it?

A. As mournful and as blurred a page, perchance,
As ever pained the seeker after truth:
Listen! this man, when like a factory slave
I toiled for some bald pittance in the city,
Came to me (unsolicited, remember),
With words of cheer, and honeyed courtesies;
His tone was soft as dulcet airs of May;
His heart the very fount of sympathy!
"What," said he, "shall you grind your genius here,
Down to the last faint edge; waste your rich thoughts"
(Mark you the subtle flattery of this language),
"Upon a thankless, ignorant, brutal fool,
Who plays the patron with the grace of Bottom,
His ass's head from out your flowering fancies
Grinning in dull and idiot self-applauses;
By every gentle muse this shall not be!"
Straightway, with hand caressing as a woman's,
He led me from hard desk and stifling air,
Forth to his bowery home amid the hills,
There fed me, sir, on kindness, day by day,
Until this starved and tortured spirit grew
Healthy and hale again! No wish had I,
He did not hasten blithely to forestall!
He called me "brother," drew from shy reserves
Of knowledge, feeling, poesy, full stores
Of all my wealth — by heart or brain amassed —
Ha! by Apollo! what rare times were those
We spent in 'rapt communion with the bards
Each worshipped, and what jovial laughter shook

The flying night-winds, when our graver books
Were cast aside, and he an artful mimic,
A famed *raconteur*, many a humorous scene
Enacted with such raciness of wit
Despair itself had checked its tears — to smile;
In brief, by every wile a man could use
To knit his fellow's heart-strings to his own,
He made me love him! other friends were gone
Forlornly mouldering in far churchyard shades
And therefore — undivided, ardent, sure,
Affection centred all its warmths on him!

And now, when wholly his, I would have dared
For him all danger (you will scarce believe it),
But suddenly, as sometimes on calm seas,
The watcher from some lonely headland views
A gallant bark sink swiftly in the deep,
Dissolving like a vision — thus his friendship,
Its glittering flags of promise flaunting still
The tranquil sunlight, sunk before mine eyes
And left me gazing like a man distraught
Across the mocking solitude!

B. What more?

A. What more? Why, truly, sir, the tale is done.
'Twas a sharp close, I grant you, to a dream
Which rose so fairly; yet there's comfort in 't!

B. Comfort!

A. Ay, ay! rare comfort in the thought
That tho' my years should reach the utmost verge
Of mortal life, I shall not dream again!

But pshaw! push on the bottle, 'tis the
  last
Of a full bin that constant friend of
  mine,
That loyal, noble, pure Samaritan,
Gave me, with vows of everduring love,
Three months ago at Christmas! Stay,
  a toast:
"Fair health, long life, immortal honor
  crown
The man who's constant only to — him-
  self!"

MORALS OF DESPERATION.

THE man who's wholly ruined, sir, fears
  nothing;
How can he when all's lost to him al-
  ready?
There is a desperate gayety which comes
To buoy one up in such a strait as this;
Under whose spell, it is a sort of witch-
  craft,
Men lose all sense of wrong, or rather
  take
Wrong for their right, rejoicing even in
  crime.
Faith, now, I'd hardly answer for my-
  self,
If in some garden solitude, like this, sir,
At the hour of midnight (hark! the deep
  church tower
Is tolling twelve), haply I chanced to
  meet
A pompous millionaire, a man who stag-
  gers
Under his golden burden, like a ship
Reeling 'neath too much canvass; I
  should ease
My laboring comrade, thus and thus, of
  all
His glittering superfluities; this ring
Is a brave diamond, and will serve me
  bravely;
And ha! by Pluto! what a massive chain
Meanders like a miniature Pactolus
Across your worship's vest; my lord, no
  wonder

You grow asthmatic with a weight like
  that
Pressed on your gasping lungs; I'll free
  you from it;
And blessed saints! but here's a fair-knit
  purse,
And fairly filled, too! Shame it were in
  sooth
To keep this gift of your sweet para-
  mour,
Therefore, behold me! I pour out this
  coin;
O Jesu! what rich music! but the purse
Duly return you! haste, your worship,
  haste,
Or else these itching palms will find fresh
  work
About your silken doublet, and bright
  hose,
Or those trussed points you needs must
  clasp with jewels;
Ay, haste, and take you comfort in the
  text
Which the wise Messer Salvatore Duomo
Dins in our ears each sacred Sabbath
  morning,
That "blessed, three times blessed, are
  the poor!"

THE CONDEMNED.

As in those lands of mighty mountain
  heights,
The streams, by sudden tempests over-
  charged,
Sweep down the slopes, bearing swift
  ruin with them,
So I and all my fortunes were engulf'd
In sudden, swift, complete destruction;
The morning found me happy, rich,
  contented,
But ere the sunset that black ruin
  came,
And stared me in the face.

                    Sir, I had reach'd
A stage of middle life, when chains of
  habit

Cannot be broken, save by giant
   wrenches,
When to be rudely hurled from life-long
   grooves
Of thought and progress, leaves the
   staunchest mind

Broken, amazed, despondent. What
   had I,
A scholar, recluse, dreamer, thou may'st
   say,
In common with the work-day world of
   men ?

"Almighty Nature, the first law of God,
   Perforce I followed."

Yet, goaded on by fierce necessity,
I sought work in the crowded haunts of
   cities,
Thinking to draw on knowledge as a
   bank,
Exhaustless, opulent, whereby all needs,
Not born of random, loose extrava-
   gance,

Would be assuredly answered.   Ah!
   poor fool:
Too soon experience clove the shining
   mist
Of hopeful fantasy, and like a wind,
Sullen at first and slow, but raised ere
   long
To tempest-madness, rent the veil away

O'er which a steel-blue melancholy
   heaven
Glared on me, like a mocking eye in
   death:
Then came by turn mistrust, despon-
   dence, dread,
And last, despair, with frenzy; the brute
   instincts,
That sleep like tigers, jungled, in the
   blood,
With hale or pampered bodies, at the
   sting
Of loathsome famine, woke, and raged
   and tore,
Till Conscience, whose fair seat is in the
   soul,
Till Reason, whose deep life is in the
   brain,
Lay silent, murdered. A mere animal
   thing —
Hyena, tiger, wolf — whate'er thou
   wilt —
I seized my prey and rent it. What to
   me
The complex figments of your juggling
   laws ?
Nature with countless clamorous tongues
   cried out,
" Thou hungerest, diest; snatch thy food
   from fate,
Though 'twixt thee and the life-sustain-
   ing bread
A hundred sleek, smooth, sneering ty-
   rants stand
Laughing to scorn thine untold agonies!"
Almighty Nature, the first law of God,
Perforce I followed; the false codes of
   man
Perforce I broke. And so, for this, for
   this,
Man's law that fain would run a tilt at
   God,
Its puny weapon shivering like a reed,
'Gainst the great bosses of Jehovah's
   buckler,
Appoints me death. Well, well, I fear
   not death,
Trusting that death, perchance, is but a
   night

Shorn of all morrow, a long, dreamless
   slumber,
O'er which the ages, hoar and solemn
   nurses,
Chant their majestic lullabies, that hold
Spells of oblivion; either thus, or I,
Whose life-sun rose in shadow, sets in
   blood,
Shall find a nobler being in some star
Beyond the silvery Pleiads.

       Friend, thy hand;
Alone of all earth's creatures do I love
   thee:
Thee, and the little soft-eyed, pensive
   child,
Thy fairy daughter. Strange! but when
   I drink
Light from the founts of her large, seri-
   ous eyes,
I seem to near a trembling, spiritual
   joy,
To thrill upon the utmost verge and
   brink
Of mystic revelations. Prithee, there-
   fore,
Bring the fair child once more; I yearn
   to carry
The dream of her sweet, pitiful, angel's
   face,
To cheer the realm of shadows. Will
   she come ?

ANTIPATHIES.

LOVE is no product of the obedient will,
It hath its root in those deep sympa-
   thies,
Mere ties of blood are powerless to con-
   trol;
I love thee not because around thy heart
An Arctic nature hath built up the ice
Of thawless winter: vain it is to strive
Against the law of just antipathies:
The Tropic sunlight burns not at the
   Poles,
Nor blooms the lustrous foliage of the
   East

Among the rocky, storm-bound Hebrides;
To all my gods thou art antipodal,
Therefore, again, good sir! I love thee
   not.

————◆————

MISCONSTRUCTION.

How man misjudges man! the outward
   seeming,
Gesture, or glance, or utterance that may
   iar

Against some petty, pampered, poor con-
   ceit,
Unworthy, undefined, is straightway
   made
To prove a vast obliquity of soul,
And shallow disputants, with ponderous
   show
Of judgment that provokes the wise to
   scorn,
Exhort the virtuous by the foul abuse
Which damns them to the level of their
   speech.

POEMS OF THE WAR.

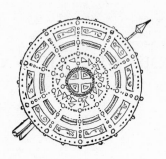

POEMS OF THE WAR.

1861–1865.

These poems are republished with no ill-feeling, nor with the desire to revive old issues; but only as a record and a sacred duty: —

"Fidelis ad urnam!"

MY MOTHER-LAND.

"Animis Opibusque Parati."

MY Mother-land! thou wert the first to
    fling
Thy virgin flag of freedom to the breeze,
The first to front along thy neighboring
    seas,
The imperious foeman's power;
But long before that hour,
While yet, in false and vain imagining,
Thy sister nations would not own their
    foe,
And turned to jest thy warnings, though
    the low,
Portentous mutterings, that precede the
    throe
Of earthquakes, burdened all the omin-
    ous air;
While yet they paused in scorn,
Of fatal madness born,
Thou, oh, my mother! like a priestess
    bless'd
With wondrous vision of the things to
    come,
Thou couldst not calmly rest
Secure and dumb —
But from thy borders, with the sounds of
    drum
And trumpet rose the warrior-call,—
(A voice to thrill, to startle, to appall!)—
*"Prepare! the time grows ripe to meet
    our doom!"*

Thy careless sisters frowned, or mocking
    said:
"We see no threatening tempest over-
    head,
Only a few pale clouds, the west wind's
    breath
Will sweep away, or melt in watery
    death."

*" Prepare! the time grows ripe to meet
    our doom!"*
Alas! it was not till the thunder-boom
Of shell and cannon shocked the vernal
    day,
Which shone o'er Charleston Bay,*
That startled, roused, the last scale fallen
    away
From blinded eyes, our South, erect and
    proud,
Fronted the issue, and, though lulled too
    long,
Felt her great spirit nerved, her patriot
    valor strong.

.   .   .   .   .

Death! What of death? —
Can he who once drew honorable breath
    In liberty's pure sphere,
    Foster a sensual fear,
When death and slavery meet him face
    to face,

---

* Fort Sumter, March, 1861.

Saying: " Choose thou between us; here,
the grace
Which follows patriot martyrdom, and
there,
Black degradation, haunted by despair."

The very thought brings blushes to the
cheek!
I hear all 'round about me murmurs
run,
Hot murmurs, but soon merging into
one
Soul-stirring utterance — hark! the peo-
ple speak:

" Our course is righteous, and our aims
are just!
Behold, we seek
Not merely to preserve for noble wives
The virtuous pride of unpolluted lives,
To shield our daughters from the servile
hand,
And leave our sons their heirloom of
command,
In generous perpetuity of trust;
Not only to defend those ancient laws,
Which Saxon sturdiness and Norman
fire
Welded forevermore with freedom's
cause,
And handed scathless down from sire to
sire —
Nor yet our grand religion, and our
Christ,
Unsoiled by secular hates, or sordid
harms,
(Though these had sure sufficed
To urge the feeblest Sybarite to arms) —
But more than all, because embracing
all,
Ensuring all, self-government, the
boon
Our patriot statesmen strove to win and
keep,
From prescient Pinckney and the wise
Calhoun
To him, that gallant knight,
The youngest champion in the Senate
hall,

Who, led and guarded by a luminous
fate,
His armor, Courage, and his war-horse,
Right,
Dared through the lists of eloquence to
sweep
Against the proud Bois Guilbert of de-
bate!*

" There's not a tone from out the teem-
ing past,
Uplifted once in such a cause as ours,
Which does not smite our souls
In long reverberating thunder-rolls,
From the far mountain-steeps of ancient
story,
Above the shouting, furious Persian
mass,
Millions arrayed in pomp of Orient
powers,
Rings the wild war-cry of Leonidas
Pent in his rugged fortress of the rock;
And o'er the murmurous seas,
Compact of hero-faith and patriot bliss
(For conquest crowns the Athenian's
hope at last),
Come the clear accents of Miltiades,
Mingled with cheers that drown the
battle-shock
Beside the wave-washed strand of Sala-
mis.

" Where'er on earth the self-devoted
heart
Hath been by worthy deeds exalted thus,
We look for proud exemplars; yet for
us
It is enough to know
Our fathers left us freemen; let us show
The will to hold our lofty heritage,
The patient strength to act our father's
part.

" Yea! though our children's blood
Rain 'round us in a crimson-swelling
flood,

---

* *Vide* the Senatorial debate on "Foote's
Resolution," in 1832.

Why pause or falter? — that red tide
    shall bear
The ark that holds our shrinèd liberty,
Nearer, and yet more near
Some height of promise o'er the ensan-
    guined sea.

" At last, the conflict done,
The fadeless meed of final victory won,
Behold! emerging from the rifted dark
Athwart a shining summit high in
    heaven,
    That delegated Ark!
No more to be by vengeful tempests
    driven,
But poised upon the sacred mount,
    whereat
The congregated nations gladly gaze,
Struck by the quiet splendor of the
    rays
That circle freedom's blood-bought Ara-
    rat!"

Thus spake the people's wisdom; unto
    me
Its voice hath come, a passionate augury!
Methinks the very aspect of the world
Changed to the mystic music of its
    hope.
For, lo! about the deepening heavenly
    cope
The stormy cloudland banners all are
    furled,
    And softly borne above
Are brooding pinions of invisible love,
    Distilling balm of rest and tender
        thought
    From fairy realms, by fairy witchery
        wrought:
O'er the hushed ocean steal ethereal
    gleams
Divine as light that haunts an angel's
    dreams;
And universal nature, wheresoever
My vision strays — o'er sky, and sea, and
    river —
    Sleeps, like a happy child,
    In slumber undefiled,
A premonition of sublimer days,

When war and warlike lays
At length shall cease,
Before a grand Apocalypse of Peace,
Vouchsafed in mercy to all human
    kind —
A prelude and a prophecy combined!

——◆——

ODE.

[In honor of the bravery and sacrifices of the
    soldiers of the South.]

WITH bayonets slanted in the glittering
    light,
    With solemn roll of drums,
With star-lit banners rustling wings of
    might,
    The knightly concourse comes!
The flower and fruit of all the tropic
    lands,
The unsheathed brightness of their stain-
    less brands
    Blazing in courtly hands,
One glorious soul within those thousand
    eyes,
One aim, one hope, one impulse from
    the skies,
    While silent, awed and dumb,
A nation waits the end in dread sur-
    mise,
    They come! they come!

The summer flaunts her vivid leaves
    above
    The unwonted scene,
The summer heavens embrace with
    smiles of love
    The hill-slopes green;
Far in the uppermost realms of silent
    air
Peace sits enthroned and happy, but on
    earth
The cymbals clash, and the shrill trum-
    pets blare,
And Death, like some grim mower on
    the plain,
    Topped by the ripened grain,
Whets his keen scythe, and shakes it
    fearfully!

Our serried lines march sternly to the
    front,
Where decked as if they rose to celebrate
    A joyous festal morn,
In glistening pomp and splendid bla-
    zonry,
    Slow moving as in scorn
Of those weak bands that guard the pass
    below,
Come gorgeous, flushed and proud, the
    cohorts of the foe!

They wheel! deploy, are stationed, down
    the cleft
    Of the long gorge their signal thun-
        ders run!
A sullen answer echoes from our left
    And the great fight's begun!
O! who shall picture the immortal
    fray?
Our Southern host that day
Breasted the onset of the invading sea
With wills of adamant; but stern-
    weighted strength,
Like waves by some infernal alchemy
Hardened, transformed to solid metal,
    burning
At white heat as they struck, and aye
    returning
Hotter and more resistless than before
(All flecked atop with foam of human
    gore),
Pierced here and there our crumbling
    ranks at length,
    Which as a mountain shore,
Rock-ribbed and iron founded, still had
    stood,
    And outward hurled
In bloody sprayings, that tremendous
    flood
Which, with wild charge and furious
    brunt on brunt,
Had dashed against us like a fiery world!

Unceasing still poured on the fateful
    tide,
And plumèd victory ever seemed to ride
On the red billows of the northland war!
    Our glory and pride

Had fallen,—fallen in the terrible
    van,—
Like wine the life-streams ran;
"Back! back!" cried one (it was the
    voice of Bee,
Lifted in wrath and bitter agony),
"We're driven backward!" unto whom
    there came
An answer, like the rush of steady flame,
'Twixt ribs of iron, "We will give them
    yet
    The bayonet!
The sharp edge of the Southern bayo-
    net!"
At which the other's face flushed up,
    and caught
Light like a warrior-angel's, and he
    sprang
To the front rank, while swift as pas-
    sionate thought
Leaped forth his sword, and this high
    summons rang:
    "See! see! where fixed and grand,
Like a stone wall the braves of Jackson
    stand!
Forward!" and on he rushed with
    quivering breath,
    On to his Spartan death!

Unceasing still poured down the fateful
    tide,
And plumèd victory ever seemed to ride
O'er the red billows of the northland
    war!
    When faint and far,
Far on our left there rose a sound that
    thrilled
All souls, and even the battle's thunder-
    ous pulse
(Or so we deemed) for briefest space
    was stilled;
A sound, low hissing as a meteor-star,
But gathering depth of volume, till it
    burst
    In one great flamelike cheer,
That seemed to rend and lift the cloud
    accurst,
    The poisonous-clinging cloud
    That wrapped us in its shroud,

While wounded men leaped on their feet
  to hear,
And dying men upraised their eyes to
  see
How on the conflict's lowering canopy,
Dawned the first rainbow hues of vic-
  tory!

Have you watched the condor leap
From his proud Andean rock,
And with hurtling pinions sweep
On the valley-pasturing flock?
Have you watched an eygre vast
On the rude September blast
Roll adown with curvèd crest
O'er the low sands of the West?
O! thus and thus they came
(Four thousand men and more),
Hearts, faces, — all aflame,
And the grandeur of their wrath
Whirled the tyrant from their path
As the frightened rack is driven
By the unleashed winds in heaven;
Then, maddened, tossed about
In a reckless, hopeless rout,
The Northern army fled
O'er their dying and their dead,
And the Southern steel flashed out,
And their vengeful points were red
With the hot heart's tide that flowed
Where they sabred as they rode!
And the news sped on apace
(Where the Rulers, in their place,
Sat jubilant, one and all),
Till a shadow seemed to fall
Round their joyance like a pall,
And the inmost senate-hall
Pealed an echo of disgrace!
At the set of July's sun
They stood quivering and undone,
For the eagle standards waned and the
  Southern "stars" had won!

Thus loomed serene and large
Upon that desperate contest's lurid
  marge
Our orb of destiny; millions of hearts
  Throb with bold exultation,
Till there starts

From mountain fastness, and from wav-
  ing plain,
From wooded swamp and mist-encircled
  main,
  From hamlet, city, field,
  And the rich midland weald,
The spirit of the antique hero time!
O! 'twas a sight sublime
To watch the upheaval of the popular
  soul,
The stormy gathering, — the majestic roll
Upward of its wild forces, by the awe
Of Right and Justice steadied into law!
Faith lent our cause its heavenly conse-
  cration!
  Hope its omnipotent might!
And Fame stood ready, with her flowers
  of light,
To crown alike the living and the dead,
While in the broadening firmament o'er-
  head
We seemed to read the fiat of our fate,
  "Ye are baptized, — a Nation!
Amongst the freest, free, — amongst the
  mightiest, great!"
An ominous hush! and then the scat-
  tered clouds
  In the dark northern heaven
(Clouds of a deadlier strife),
  Urged by the poison wind
  Of rage and rapine, sullenly com-
  bined,
Charged with the bolts of ruin! what
  were shrouds,
Crimsoned with gore? the widowed
  spirit riven?
The desecration of God's gift of life,
To that one thought (three fiery strands
  uniting,
  Hot from a Hadéan loom),
"Conquest!" "Revenge!" Suprema-
  cy?" The blighting
Of untold promises, the grief, the gloom,
The desolate madness and the anguish
  blind,
  All spreading on and on
From murdered sire to subjugated son,
Were less than nothing to the arrogant
  pride

Which treaties, compacts, honor, laws
　　defied,
And aimed above the wrecks of temple
　　and tower
To rear the symbols of its merciless
　　power!

　　Four deadly years we fought,
Ringed by a girdle of unfaltering fire,
That coiled and hissed in lessening cir-
　　cles nigher.
　　Blood dyed the Southern wave;
From ocean border to calm inland river,
There was no pause, no peace, no respite
　　ever.
　　Blood of our bravest brave
Drenched in a scarlet rain the western
　　lea,
Swelled the hoarse waters of the Tennes-
　　see,
Incarnadined the gulfs, the lakes, the
　　rills,
　　And from a hundred hills
Steamed in a mist of slaughter to the
　　skies,
Shutting all hope of heaven from mortal
　　eyes.
The Beaufort blooms were withered on
　　the stem;
　　The fair gulf city in a single night
　　Lost her imperial diadem;
And wheresoe'er men's troubled vision
　　sought,
They viewed MIGHT towering o'er the
　　humbled crest of RIGHT!

　　But for a time, but for a time, O
　　　　God!
The innate forces of our knightly blood
Rallied, and by the mount, the fen, the
　　flood,
　　Upraised the tottering standards of
　　　　our race.
O grand Virginia! though thy glittering
　　glaive
Lies sullied, shattered in a ruthless
　　grave,
How it flashed once! They dug their
　　trenches deep

(The implacable foe), they ranged their
　　lines of wrath;
But watchful ever on the imminent
　　path
Thy steel-clad genius stood;
North, South, East, West, — they strove
　　to pierce thy shield;
　　Thou would'st not yield!
Until, — unconquered, yea, unconquered
　　still,
Nature's weakened forces answered not
　　thy will,
And gored with wound on wound,
Thy fainting limbs and forehead sought
　　the ground;
And with thee the young nation fell, a
　　pall
Solemn and rayless, covering one and
　　all!
God's ways are marvellous; here we
　　stand to-day
Discrowned, and shorn, in wildest dis-
　　array,
The mock of earth! yet never shone the
　　sun
On sterner deeds, or nobler victories
　　won.
Not in the field alone; ah, come with
　　me
To the dim bivouac by the winter's sea;
Mark the fair sons of courtly mothers
　　crouch
O'er flickering fires; but gallant still, and
　　gay
As on some bright parade; or mark the
　　couch
In reeking hospitals, whereon is laid
The latest scion of a line perchance,
Whose veins were royal; close your
　　blurred romance,
Blurred by the dropping of a maudlin
　　tear,
And watch the manhood here;
That firm but delicate countenance,
Distorted sometimes by an awful pang,
Born in meek patience; when the trum-
　　pets rang
"To horse!" but yester-morn, that ar-
　　dent boy

Sprung to his charger, thrilled with hope
 and joy
To the very finger-tips, and now he lies,
The shadows deepening in those falcon
 eyes,
 But calm and undismayed,
As if the death that chills him, brow and
 breast,
Were some fond bride who whispered,
 " Let us rest! "

Enough! 'tis over! the last gleam of hope
Hath melted from our mournful horo-
 scope,
 Of all, of all bereft,
 Only to us are left
Our buried heroes and their matchless
 deeds;
These cannot pass; they hold the vital
 seeds
Which in some far, untracked, un-
 visioned hour
May burst to vivid bud and glorious
 flower.
 Meanwhile, upon the nation's bro-
 ken heart
Her martyrs sleep. O! dearer far to her,
Than if each son, a wreathèd conqueror,
 Rode in triumphant state
 The loftiest crest of fate;
O! dearer far, because outcast and low,
She yearns above them in her awful woe.
One spring its tender blooms
Hath lavished richly by those hallowed
 tombs;
One summer its imperial largess spread
Along our heroes' bed;
One autumn wailing with funereal blast,
The withered leaves and pallid dust
 amassed
All round about them, till bleak winter
 now
Hangs hoar-frost on the grasses, and the
 bough
. In dreary woodlands seems to thrill and
 start,
Thrill to the anguish of the wind that
 raves
Across those lonely desolated graves!

CHARLESTON.

CALMLY beside her tropic strand,
 An empress, brave and loyal,
I see the watchful city stand,
 With aspect sternly royal;
She knows her mortal foe draws near,
 Armored by subtlest science,
Yet deep, majestical, and clear,
 Rings out her grand defiance.
Oh, glorious is thy noble face,
 Lit up by proud emotion,
And unsurpassed thy stately grace,
 Our warrior Queen of Ocean!

First from thy lips the summons came,
 Which roused our South to action,
And, with the quenchless force of
 flame,
 Consumed the demon, Faction;
First, like a rush of sovereign wind,
 That rends dull waves asunder,
Thy prescient warning struck the blind,
 And woke the deaf with thunder;
They saw, with swiftly kindling eyes,
 The shameful doom before them,
And heard, borne wild from Northern
 skies,
 The death-gale hurtling o'er them:

Wilt thou, whose virgin banner rose,
 A morning star of splendor,
Quail when the war-tornado blows,
 And crouch in base surrender ?
Wilt thou, upon whose loving breast
 Our noblest chiefs are sleeping,
Yield thy dead patriots' place of rest
 To scornful alien keeping ?
No! while a life-pulse throbs for fame,
 Thy sons will gather round thee,
Welcome the shot, the steel, the flame,
 If honor's hand hath crowned thee.

Then fold about thy beauteous form
 The imperial robe thou wearest,
And front with regal port the storm
 Thy foe would dream thou fearest;
If strength, and will, and courage fail
 To cope with ruthless numbers,

And thou must bend, despairing, pale,
  Where thy last hero slumbers,
Lift the red torch, and light the fire
  Amid those corpses gory,
And on thy self-made funeral pyre,
  Pass from the world to glory.

STUART.

A CUP of your potent "mountain dew,"
  By the camp-fire's ruddy light;
Let us drink to a spirit as leal and true
  As ever drew blade in fight,
And dashed on the foeman's lines of
    steel,
  For God and his people's right.

By heaven! it seems that his very name
  Embodies a thought of fire;
It strikes on the ear with a sense of flame,
  And the life-blood boundeth higher,
While the pulses leap and the brain ex-
    pands,
  In the glow of a grand desire.

Hark! in the day-dawn's misty gray,
  Our bugles are ringing loud,
And hot for the joy of a coming fray,
  Our souls wax fierce and proud,
As we list for the word that shall launch
    us forth,
  Like bolts from the mountain-cloud.

We list for the word, and it comes at
    length,
  In a strain so mighty and clear,
That we rise to the sound with an added
    strength,
  And our hearts are glad to hear,
And a stir, like the breath of the boding
    storm
  Thrills through us, from van to rear.

Then, with the rush of the whirlwind
    freed,
  We rush, by a secret way,
And merry on sabre, and helmet, and
    steed,

Do the autumn sunbeams play,
And the devil must sharpen his keenest
    wits,
  To rescue "his own" to-day.

Ho, ye who dwell in the fertile vales
  Of the pleasant land of Penn,
Who feast on the fat of her fruitful
    dales,
  How little ye dream or ken
That the southern Murat has bared his
    brand,
  That the Stuart rides again.

"Close up, close up! we have travelled
    long,
  But a jovial night's in store,
A night of wassail, and wit, and song,
  In yon cosy town before.
Quick, sergeant! spur to the front in
    haste,
  And knock at the mayor's door."

Behold, he comes with a ghost-like
    grace,
  And his knee-joints out of tune;
And the cold, cold sweat runs down his
    face,
  I' the light of the autumn moon,
While his husky voice, like an ancient
    crone's,
  Dies in a hollow croon.

He cannot speak; but his buxom dame,
  With her trembling daughters nigh,
Shrieks out, "Oh, honor their virgin
    fame,
  Pass the poor maidens by."
(Whereon, with a grievous heave and
    sob,
  She paused in her speech — to cry.)

"Rise up! we leave to the churlish brood
  Our vengeance hath sought ere now,
The fame which springs from the ruth-
    less mood
  That crimsons a woman's brow;
For sons are we of a kindly race,
  And bound by a knightly vow.

"Rise up! we war with the strong alone;
  For where was the caitiff found,
To sport with an outraged woman's
    moan,
  Where the southern trumpets sound?

 . . . . .

"Enough! while I speak of the past, my
    lad,

There's coming — (hush! lean thee
    near!) —
There's coming a raid that shall drive
    them mad,
  And cover their land with fear;
And you and I, by the blessing of
    God,
  Ay, you and I shall be there."

"They arose with the sun, and caught life
from his light."

BEYOND THE POTOMAC.

THEY slept on the field which their valor
    had won,
But arose with the first early blush of
    the sun,
For they knew that a great deed re-
    mained to be done,
  When they passed o'er the river.

They arose with the sun, and caught life
    from his light,
Those giants of courage, those Anaks in
    fight,
And they laughed out aloud in the joy
    of their might,
  Marching swift for the river.

On, on! like the rushing of storms
  through the hills;
On, on! with a tramp that is firm as
  their wills;
And the one heart of thousands grows
  buoyant, and thrills,
    At the thought of the river.

Oh, the sheen of their swords! the fierce
  gleam of their eyes!
It seemed as on earth a new sunlight
  would rise,
And, king-like, flash up to the sun in
  the skies,
    O'er their path to the river.

But their banners, shot-scarred, and all
  darkened with gore,
On a strong wind of morning streamed
  wildly before,
Like wings of death-angels swept fast to
  the shore,
    The green shore of the river.

As they march, from the hillside, the
  hamlet, the stream,
Gaunt throngs whom the foemen had
  manacled, teem,
Like men just aroused from some ter-
  rible dream,
    To cross sternly the river.

They behold the broad banners, blood-
  darkened, yet fair,
And a moment dissolves the last spell
  of despair,
While a peal, as of victory, swells on the
  air,
    Rolling out to the river.

And that cry, with a thousand strange
  echoings, spread,
Till the ashes of heroes were thrilled in
  their bed,
And the deep voice of passion surged up
  from the dead,
    "*Ay, press on to the river!*"

On, on! like the rushing of storms
  through the hills,
On, on! with a tramp that is firm as
  their wills;
And the one heart of thousands grows
  buoyant and thrills,
    As they pause by the river.

Then the wan face of Maryland, hag-
  gard and worn,
At this sight lost the touch of its aspect
  forlorn,
And she turned on the foemen, full-
  statured in scorn,
    Pointing stern to the river.

And Potomac flowed calmly, scarce
  heaving her breast,
With her low-lying billows all bright in
  the west,
For a charm as from God lulled the
  waters to rest
    Of the fair rolling river.

Passed! passed! the glad thousands
  march safe through the tide;
Hark, foeman, and hear the deep knell
  of your pride,
Ringing weird-like and wild, pealing up
  from the side
    Of the calm-flowing river.

'Neath a blow swift and mighty the ty-
  rant may fall;
Vain, vain! to his gods swells a desolate
  call;
Hath his grave not been hollowed, and
  woven his pall,
    Since they passed o'er the river?

------◆------

BEAUREGARD'S APPEAL.

YEA! since the need is bitter,
  Take down those sacred bells,
Whose music speaks of hallowed joys,
  And passionate farewells!

But ere ye fall dismantled,
  Ring out, deep bells! once more:
And pour on the waves of the passing
      wind
  The symphonies of yore.

Let the latest born be welcomed
  By pealings glad and long,
Let the latest dead in the churchyard
      bed
  Be laid with solemn song.

And the bells above them throbbing,
  Should sound in mournful tone,
As if, in grief for a human death,
  They prophesied their own.

Who says 'tis a desecration
  To strip the temple towers,
And invest the metal of peaceful notes
  With death-compelling powers?

A truce to cant and folly!
  Our people's ALL at stake,
Shall we heed the cry of the shallow
      fool,
  Or pause for the bigot's sake?

Then crush the struggling sorrow!
  Feed high your furnace fires,
And mould into deep-mouthed guns of
      bronze,
  The bells from a hundred spires.

Methinks no common vengeance,
  No transient war eclipse,
Will follow the awful thunder-burst
  From their adamantine lips.

A cause like ours is holy,
  And it useth holy things;
While over the storm of a righteous
      strife,
  May shine the angel's wings.

Where'er our duty leads us,
  The grace of God is there,
And the lurid shrine of war may hold
  The Eucharist of prayer.

THE SUBSTITUTE.

[THE crime of McNeil, perpetrated in one of
our Western States, has now met with the rep-
robation of Christendom.   But at the time
the following verses — cast, as the reader will
perceive, in a partly dramatic mould — were
composed, *ten* Confederates had been hastily
executed by order of a Federal commander, on
a charge afterwards proven to be false ; and
one of the unfortunate victims (a mere youth)
voluntarily sacrificed his life to rescue his
friend, a man advanced in years and with a
large family.
  In the poem this latter individual is repre-
sented as unaware of the youth's resolve until
it has been executed.
  Between the first and second parts of the
piece, about *twenty-four hours* are supposed to
have elapsed.]

PART I.

[PLACE — *A Federal Prison — A Confederate
    chained, and a Visitor, his Friend.*]

"How say'st thou? die to-morrow?
        Oh! my friend!
    The bitter, bitter doom!
What hast thou done to tempt this
        ghastly end —
    This death of shame and gloom?"

"What done? Do tyrants wait for
        guilty deeds,
    To find or prove a crime —
They, who have cherished hatred's fiery
        seeds:
    Hot for the harvest-time?

"A sneer! a smile! vague trifles light as
        air —
    Some foolish, false surmise —
Lead to the harrowing drama of despair
    Wherein — the victim dies!

"And I shall perish! Comrade, heed
        me not!
    For thus my tears must start —
Not for the misery of my blasted lot,
    But hers who holds my heart!

"And theirs, the flowers that wreathe
        my humble hearth
    With roseate blush and bloom.

To-morrow eve, they stand alone on
      earth,
  Beside their father's tomb!

"There's Blanche, my serious beauty,
      lithe and tall,
  With pensive eyes and brow —
There's Kate, the tenderest darling of
      them all,
  Whose kisses thrill me now!

"There's little Rose, the sunshine of our
      days —
  A tricky, gladsome sprite —
How vividly come back her winsome
      ways,
  Her laughters, and delight!

"And my brave boy — my Arthur! Did
      his arm
  Second his will and brain,
I should not groan beneath this iron
      charm,
  Clasping my chains in vain!

"Oh, Christ! and hath it come to this?
      Will none
  Ward off the ghastly end?
And yet methinks I heard the voice of
      one
  Who called the old man — Friend!

"May all the curses caught from deepest
      hell
  Light on the blood-stained knave
Who laughs to hear the patriot's funeral
      knell,
  Blaspheming o'er his grave!

"Away!   Such dreams are madness!
      My pale lips
  Had best besiege Heaven's ear,
But in the turmoil of my mind's eclipse,
  No thought, no wish is clear.

"Dear friend, forgive me!   Sorrow,
      frenzy, ire —
  My bosom's raging guests —
By turn have whelmed me in their floods
      of fire,
  Fierce passions, swift unrests.

"And now, farewell!   The sentry's
      warning hand,
  Taps at my prison bars.
We part, but not forever!   There's a
      land,
  Comrade, beyond the stars!"

"Yea!" said the youth, and o'er his
      kindling face
  A saint-like glory came,
As if some prescient Angel, breathing
      grace,
  Had touched it into flame.

PART II.

[PLACE — *The same Prison.* PERSONS — *Confederate Prisoner, together with McNeil and the Jailer.*]

The hours sink slow to sunset!   Sud-
      denly
  Rose a deep, gathering hum;
And o'er the measured stride of soldiery
  Rolled out the muffled drum!

The prisoner started! crushed a stifling
      sigh,
  Then rose erect and proud!
Scorn's lightning quivering in his stormy
      eye,
  'Neath the brow's thunder-cloud!

And girding round his limbs and stal-
      wart breast
  Each iron chain and ring,
He stood sublime, imperial, self-pos-
      sessed —
  And haughty as a king!

The "dead march" wails without the
      prison gate
  Up the calm evening sky;
And ruffian jestings, born of ruffian hate,
  Make loud, unmeet reply!

The hired bravoes, whose pitiless features
      pale
  In front of armed men,
But whose *magnanimous* courage will
      not quail
  Where none can strike again!

"The flowers that wreathe my humble hearth
With roseate blush and bloom."

The "dead march" wails without the
    prison wall,
Up the calm evening sky:
And timed to the dread dirge's rise and
    fall,
Move the fierce murderers by!

They passed; and wondering at his doom
    deferred,
The captive's lofty fire
Sank in his heart, by torturing memories
    stirred
Of husband, and of sire!

But hark! the clash of bolt and opening
    door!
The tramp of hostile heel!
When lo! upon the darkening prison
    floor,
Glared the false hound — McNeil.

And next him, like a bandog scenting
    blood,
Roused from his drunken ease,
The grimy, low-browed jailer glowering
    stood,
Clanking his iron keys.

"Quick! jailer! strike yon rebel's fetters
    off,
And let the old fool see
What ransom [with a low and bitter
    scoff],
What ransom sets him free."

As the night traveller in a land of foes
The warning instinct feels,
That through the treacherous dimness
    and repose
A shrouded horror steals.

So, at these veilèd words, the captive's
    soul
Shook with a solemn dread,
And ghostly voices, prophesying dole,
Moaned faintly overhead.

His limbs are freed! his swarthy, scowl-
    ing guide
Leads through the silent town,

Where from dim casements, black with
    wrathful pride,
Stern eyes gleam darkly down.

They halted where the woodland
    showered around
Dank leaflets on the sod,
And all the air seemed vocal with the
    sound
Of wild appeals to God.

Heaped, as if common carrion, in the
    gloom,
Nine mangled corpses lay —
All speechless now — but with what
    tongues of doom
Reserved for judgment day.

And near them, but apart, one youthful
    form
Pressed a fair upland slope,
O'er whose white brow a sunbeam flicker-
    ing warm,
Played like a heavenly hope.

There, with the same grand look which
    yester-night
That face at parting wore,
The self-made martyr in the sunset light
Slept on his couch of gore.

The sunset waned; the wakening forest
    waved,
Struck by the north wind's moan,
While he, whose life this matchless death
    has saved
Knelt by the corse — alone.

———◆———

BATTLE OF CHARLESTON HARBOR,
    April 7, 1863.

Two hours, or more, beyond the prime
    of a blithe April day,
The Northmen's mailed "Invincibles"
    steamed up fair Charleston Bay;
They came in sullen file, and slow, low-
    breasted on the wave,
Black as a midnigh front of storm, and
    silent as the grave.

A thousand warrior-hearts beat high as
these dread monsters drew
More closely to the game of death across
the breezeless blue,
And twice ten thousand hearts of those
who watch the scene afar,
Thrill in the awful hush that bides the
battle's broadening star.

Each gunner, moveless by his gun, with
rigid aspect stands,
The reedy linstocks firmly grasped in
bold, untrembling hands,
So moveless in their marble calm, their
stern, heroic guise,
They look like forms of statued stone
with burning human eyes!

Our banners on the outmost walls, with
stately rustling fold,
Flash back from arch and parapet the
sunlight's ruddy gold —
They mount to the deep roll of drums,
and widely echoing cheers,
And then, once more, dark, breathless,
hushed, wait the grim cannon-
eers.

Onward, in sullen file, and slow, low-
glooming on the wave,
Near, nearer still, the haughty fleet glides
silent as the grave,
When shivering the portentous calm o'er
startled flood and shore,
Broke from the sacred Island Fort the
thunder wrath of yore!*

The storm has burst! and while we speak,
more furious, wilder, higher,
Dart from the circling batteries a hundred
tongues of fire;
The waves gleam red, the lurid vault of
heaven seems rent above —
Fight on, oh, knightly gentlemen! for
faith, and home, and love!

---

* Fort Moultrie.

There's not, in all that line of flame, one
soul that would not rise,
To seize the victor's wreath of blood,
though death must give the
prize;
There's not, in all this anxious crowd
that throngs the ancient town,
A maid who does not yearn for power to
strike one foeman down!

The conflict deepens! ship by ship the
proud Armada sweeps,
Where fierce from Sumter's raging breast
the volleyed lightning leaps,
And ship by ship, raked, overborne, 'ere
burned the sunset light,
Crawls in the gloom of baffled hate be-
yond the field of fight!

CHARLESTON AT THE CLOSE OF 1863.

WHAT! still does the mother of treason
uprear
Her crest 'gainst the furies that darken
her sea,
Unquelled by mistrust, and unblanched
by a fear,
Unbowed her proud head, and un-
bending her knee,
Calm, steadfast and free!

Ay! launch your red lightnings! blas-
pheme in your wrath!
Shock earth, wave, and heaven with
the blasts of your ire;
But she seizes your death-bolts yet hot
from their path,
And hurls back your lightnings and
mocks at the fire
Of your fruitless desire!

Ringed round by her brave, a fierce cir-
clet of flame
Flashes up from the sword-points that
cover her breast;
She is guarded by love, and enhaloed by
fame,

And never, we swear, shall your foot-
steps be pressed,
  Where her dead heroes rest.

Her voice shook the tyrant, sublime from
  her tongue
Fell the accents of warning! a prophet-
  ess grand —
On her soil the first life notes of liberty
  rung,
And the first stalwart blow of her
  gauntleted hand
  Broke the sleep of her land.

What more ? she hath grasped in her
  iron-bound will
The fate that would trample her honors
  to earth;
The light in those deep eyes is luminous
  still
  With the warmth of her valor, the
    glow of her worth,
  Which illumine the earth.

And beside her a knight the great Bayard
  had loved,
  "Without fear or reproach," lifts her
    banner on high;
He stands in the vanguard majestic, un-
  moved,
  And a thousand firm souls when that
    chieftain is nigh,
    Vow "'tis easy to die!"

Their words have gone forth on the fet-
  terless air,
  The world's breath is hushed at the
    conflict! Before
Gleams the bright form of Freedom, with
  wreaths in her hair —
  And what though the chaplet be crim-
    soned with gore —
    We shall prize her the more!

And while Freedom lures on with her
  passionate eyes
  To the height of her promise, the
    voices of yore

From the storied profound of past ages
  arise,
  And the pomps of their magical music
    outpour
    O'er the war-beaten shore!

Then gird your brave empress, O heroes!
  with flame
  Flashed up from the sword-points that
    cover her breast!
She is guarded by Love and enhaloed by
  Fame,
  And never, stern foe! shall your foot-
    steps be pressed
    Where her dead martyrs rest!

———◆———

SCENE IN A COUNTRY HOSPITAL.

HERE, lonely, wounded and apart,
  From out my casement's glimmering
    round,
I watch the wayward bluebirds dart
  Across yon flowery ground;
How sweet the prospect! and how fair
The balmy peace of earth and air.

But, lowering over fields afar,
  A red cloud breaks with sulphurous
    breath,
And well I know what gory star,
  Is regnant in his house of death;
Yet faint the conflict's gathering roll,
To the fierce tempest in my soul.

I, who the foremost ranks had led,
  To strike for cherished home and land,
Groan idly on this torturing bed,
  With broken frame and palsied hand,
So nerveless, 'tis a task to scare,
The insects fluttering round my hair.

O God! for one brief hour again,
  Of that grim joy my spirit knew,
When foemen's life-blood poured like
    rain,
  And sabres flashed and trumpets blew:
One hour to smite, or smitten die
On the wild breast of victory!

It may not be; my pulses beat
    Too feebly, and my heart is chill.
Death, like a thief with stealthy feet
    Draws nigh to work his ruthless will;
Hope, Honor, Glory, pass me by,
But *he* stands near with mocking eye!

Ay, smooth the couch! — pour out the
    draught,
    That, hapily, for a season's space,
Hath power to charm his fatal shaft,
    And warn the death-damps off my face,
A blest reprieve! — a wondrous boon,
Thank Heaven! this — all — ends with
    me soon.

———◆———

VICKSBURG. — A BALLAD.

For sixty days and upwards,
    A storm of shell and shot
Rained round us in a flaming shower,
    But still we faltered not.
"If the noble city perish,"
    Our grand young leader said,
"Let the only walls the foe shall scale
    "Be ramparts of the dead!"

For sixty days and upwards,
    The eye of heaven waxed dim;
And e'en throughout God's holy morn,
    O'er Christian prayer and hymn,
Arose a hissing tumult,
    As if the fiends in air
Strove to engulf the voice of faith
    In the shrieks of their despair.

There was wailing in the houses,
    There was trembling on the marts,
While the tempest raged and thundered,
    'Mid the silent thrill of hearts;
But the Lord, our shield, was with us,
    And ere a month had sped,
Our very women walked the streets
    With scarce one throb of dread.

And the little children gambolled,
    Their faces purely raised,
Just for a wondering moment,
    As the huge bombs whirled and blazed,

Then turned with silvery laughter
    To the sports which children love,
Thrice-mailed in the sweet, instinctive
    thought
    That the good God watched above.

Yet the hailing bolts fell faster,
    From scores of flame-clad ships,
And about us, denser, darker,
    Grew the conflict's wild eclipse,
Till a solid cloud closed o'er us,
    Like a type of doom and ire,
Whence shot a thousand quivering
    tongues
    Of forked and vengeful fire.

But the unseen hands of angels
    Those death-shafts warned aside,
And the dove of heavenly mercy
    Ruled o'er the battle tide;
In the houses ceased the wailing,
    And through the war-scarred marts
The people strode, with step of hope,
    To the music in their hearts.

———◆———

THE LITTLE WHITE GLOVE.

The early springtime faintly flushed the
    earth,
And in the woods, and by their favorite
    stream
The fair, wild roses blossomed modestly,
Above the wave that wooed them: there
    at eve,
Philip had brought the woman that he
    loved,
And told his love, and bared his burning
    heart.
She, Constance, — the shy sunbeams
    trembling oft,
Through dewy leaves upon her golden
    hair, —
Made him no answer, tapped her pretty
    foot,
And seemed to muse: "To-morrow I
    depart,"
Said Philip, sadly, "for wild fields of
    war;

Shall I go girt with love's invisible
mail,
Stronger than mortal armor, or, all
stripped
Of love and hope, march reckless unto
death?"

A soft mist filled her eyes, and over-
flowed
In sudden rain of passion, as she
stretched
Her delicate hand to his, and plighted
troth,

"And by their favorite stream,
The fair, wild roses blossomed modestly
Above the wave that wooed them."

With lips more rosy than the sun-bathed
flowers;
And Philip pressed the dear hand fer-
vently,
Wherefrom in happy mood, he gently
drew
A small white glove, and ere she guessed
his will,
Clipped lightly from her head one golden
curl,
And bound the glove, and placed it next
his heart.

"Now I am safe," cried Philip; "this
pure charm
Is proof against all hazard or mischance.
Here, yea, unto this self-same spot I vow
To bring it stainless back; and you shall
wear

This little glove upon our marriage
eve."
And Constance heard him, smiling
through her tears.
Another springtime faintly flushed the
earth,
And in the woods, and by their favorite
stream,
The fair, wild roses blossomed modestly
Above the wave that wooed them: there
at eve
Came a pale woman with wild, wander-
ing eyes,
And tangled, golden ringlets, and weak
steps
Tottering towards the streamlet's rip-
pling marge,
She seemed phantasmal, shadowy, like
the forms

By moonlight conjured up from a place
    of graves;
There, crouching o'er the stream, she
    laved and laved
Some object in it, with a strained regard.
And muttered fragments of distempered
    words,
Whereof were these: "He vowed to
    bring it back,
The love-charm that I gave him — my
    white glove —
Stainless and whole. He has not kept
    his oath!
Oh, Philip, Philip! have you cast me off,
Off, like this worthless thing you send
    me home,
Tattered and mildewed? Look you!
    what a rent,
Right through the palm! It cannot be
    my glove;
And look again; what horrid stain is
    here?
My glove; you placed it next your heart,
    and swore
To keep it safe, and on this self-same
    spot,
Return it to me on our marriage eve;
And now — and now — I *know* 'tis not
    my glove, —
Yet Philip, sweet! it was a cruel jest,
You surely did not mean to fright me
    thus?
For hark you! as I laved the loathsome
    thing,
To see what stain defiled it —(do not
    smile,
I feel that I am foolish, foolish, Phil-
    ip) —
But, God of Heaven! I dreamed that
    stain was *blood!* "

STONEWALL JACKSON.

THE fashions and the forms of men
    decay,
The seasons perish, the calm sunsets die,
Ne'er with the *same* bright pomp of
    cloud or ray

To flush the golden pathways of the sky;
All things are lost in dread eternity, —
States, empires, creeds, the lay
Of master poets, even the shapes of
    love,
Bear ever with them an invisible shade,
Whose name is Death; we cannot breathe
    nor move,
But that we touch the darkness, till dis-
    mayed,
We feel the imperious shadow freeze our
    hearts,
And mortal hope grows pale and flutter-
    ing life departs.
All things are lost in dread eternity,
Save that majestic virtue which is given
Once, twice, perchance beneath our
    earthly heaven,
To some great soul in ages: O! the lie,
The base, incarnate lie we call the world,
Shakes at his coming, as the forest
    shakes,
When mountain storms, with bannered
    clouds unfurled,
Rush down and rend it; sleek conven-
    tion drops
Its glittering mass, and hoary, cob-
    webbed rules
Of petty charlatans or insolent fools
Shrink to annihilation, — Truth awakes,
A morning splendor in her fearless
    eyes,
    Touching the delicate stops
Of some rare lute which breathes of
    promise fair,
    Or pouring on the covenanted air
A trumpet blast which startles, but
    makes strong,
    While ancient Wrong,
Driven like a beast from his deep-cav-
    erned lair,
    Grows gaunt, and inly quakes,
Knowing that retribution draws so near!

    Whether with blade or pen
    Toil these immortal men,
Theirs is the light supreme, which genius
    wed
    To a clear spiritual dower.

Hath ever o'er the aroused nations shed
  Joy, faith, and power;
Whether from wrestling with the god-
  like thought,
They launch a noiseless blessing on
  mankind,
Or through wild streams of terrible car-
  nage brought,
  No longer crushed and blind,
  Trampled, dishevelled, gored,
They proudly lift, where kindling soul
  and eye
May feast upon her beauty as she stands
(Girt by the strength of her invincible
  bands),
And freed through keen redemption of
  the sword,
Thy worn, but radiant form, victorious
  Liberty!

We bow before this grandeur of the
  spirit;
  We worship, and adore
God's image burning through it ever-
  more;
And thus, in awed humility to-night,*
As those who at some vast cathedral
  door
Pause with hushed faces, purified de-
  sires,
  We contemplate his merit,
Who lifted failure to the heights of fame,
And by the side of fainting, dying right,
Stood, as Sir Galahad pure, Sir Lance-
  lot brave,
  The quick, indignant fires
Flushing his pale brow from the passion-
  ate mind
No strength could quell, no sophistry
  could bind,
Until that moment, big with mystic doom
  (Whose issue sent
  O'er the long wastes of half a conti-
    nent
Electric shudders through the deepening
  gloom),

* This Ode was originally written to be deliv-
ered before a Southern patriotic association.

When in his knightly glory "Stonewall"
  fell,
And all our hearts sank with him; for we
  knew
Our staff, our bulwark broken, the fine
  clew
To freedom snapped, his hands had
  held alone,
Through all the storms of battle over-
  blown, —
Lost, buried, mouldering in our hero's
  grave.

O soul! so simple, yet sublime!
  With faith as large, and mild
As that of some benignant, trustful
  child,
Who mounts to heaven on bright, ethe-
  real stairs
Of tender-worded prayers, —
Yet strong as if a Titan's force were
  there
To rise, to act, to suffer, and to dare, —
  O soul! that on our time
Wrought, in the calm magnificence of
  power
To ends *so* noble, that an antique light
Of grace and virtue streamed along thy
  way,
  Until the direst hour
Of carnage caught from that immaculate
  ray
  A consecration, and a sanctity!
Thou art not dead, thou nevermore canst
  die,
  But wide and far,
Where'er on Christian realms the morn-
  ing star
Flames round the spires that tower
  towards the sky, —
  Thy name, a household word,
In cottage homes, by palace walls, is
  heard,
Breathed with low murmurs, reveren-
  tially!

Even as I raise this faltering song to
  one,
Who now beyond the empires of the sun,

Looks down perchance upon our mourn-
  ful sphere,
With the deep pity of seraphic eyes,
Fancy unveils the future, and I see
Millions on millions, as year follows year,
Gather around our warrior's place of rest
In the green shadows of Virginian hills;
Not with the glow of martial blazonry,
  With trump and muffled drum,
  Those pilgrim millions come,
But with bowed heads, and measured
  footsteps slow,
As those who near the presence of a
  shrine,
  And feel an air divine,
All round about them blandly, sweetly
  blow,
While like dream-music the faint fall of
  rills,
  Lapsing from steep to steep,
  The wood-dove 'plaining in her covert
  deep,
And the long whisperings of the ghostly
  pine
(Like ocean-breathings borne from tides
  of sleep),
With every varied melody expressed
In Nature's score of solemn harmonies,
Blends with a feeling in the reverent
  breast
Which cannot find a voice in mortal
  speech,
So deep, so deep it lies beyond the reach
Of stammering words, — the pilgrims
  only know
That slumbering, O! so calmly there,
  below
The dewy grass, the melancholy trees,
  Moulders the dust of him,
By whose crystalline fame, earth's scar-
  let pomps grow dim,
  The crownèd heir
  Of two majestic immortalities,
That which is earthly, and yet scarce of
  earth,
  Whose fruitful seeds
Were his own grand, self-sacrificing
  deeds,
  And that whose awful birth

Flowered into instant perfectness sub-
  lime,
  When done with toil and time,
He shook from off the raiments of his
  soul,
The weary conflict's desecrating dust,
For stern *reveillés*, heard the angels
  sing,
For battle turmoils found eternal calm,
Laid down his sinless sword to clasp the
  palm,
And where vast heavenly organ-notes
  outroll
Melodious thunders, 'mid the rush of
  wing,
And flash of plume celestial, paused in
  peace,
A rapture of ineffable release
To know the long fruition of the just!

———◆———

SONNETS.

I.

ON THE CHIVALRY OF THE PRESENT
TIME.

AH! foolish souls and false! who loudly
  cried
"True chivalry no longer breathes in
  time."
Look round us now; how wondrous, how
  sublime
The heroic lives we witness; far and
  wide,
Stern vows by sterner deeds are justified;
Self abnegation, calmness, courage,
  power,
Sway with a rule august, our stormy
  hour,
Wherein the loftiest hearts have wrought
  and died —
Wrought grandly, and died smiling.
  Thus, oh God,
From tears, and blood, and anguish, thou
  hast brought
The ennobling act, the faith-sustaining
  thought —
'Till in the marvellous present, one may
  see

A mighty stage, by knight and patriots
trod,
Who had not shunned earth's haughtiest
chivalry.

II.

ELLIOTT IN FORT SUMTER.

AND high amongst these chiefs of iron
grain,
Large-statured natures, souls of Spartan
mien,
Superbly brave, inflexibly serene,
Man of the stalwart hope, the sleepless
brain,
Well dost thou guard our fortress by the
main!
And what, though inch by inch old
Sumter falls,
There's not a stone that forms those
sacred walls,
But holds a tongue, which shall not
speak in vain!
A tongue that tells of such heroic mood,
Such nerved endurance, such immaculate
will,
That after times shall hearken and grow
still,
With breathless admiration, and on thee
(Whose stern resolve our glorious cause
made good).
Confer an antique immortality!

———◇———

OUR MARTYRS.

I AM sitting alone and weary,
  By the hearth of my darkened room,
And the low wind's *miserere*,
  Makes sadder the midnight gloom.
"There's a nameless terror nigh me —
  There's a phantom spell on the air,
And methinks, that the dead glide by me,
  And the breath of the grave's in my
    hair!"

'Tis a vision of ghastly faces,
  All pallid and worn with pain,
Where the splendor of manful graces
  Shines dim thro' a scarlet rain: —

In a wild and weird procession
  They sweep by my startled eyes,
And stern with their Fate's fruition,
  Seem melting in blood-red skies.

Have they come from the shores super-
    nal;
  Have they passed from the spirit's
    goal,
'Neath the veil of the life eternal
  To dawn on my shrinking soul?
Have they turned from the choiring
    angels,
  Aghast at the woe and dearth,
That war with his dark evangels
  Hath wrought in the loved of earth?

Vain dream! amid far-off mountains
  They lie where the dew mists weep,
And the murmur of mournful fountains
  Breathes over their painless sleep;
On the breast of the lonely meadows
  Safe, safe, from the despot's will,
They rest in the starlit shadows,
  And their brows are white and still,

Alas! for our heroes perished!
  Cut down at their golden prime,
With the luminous hopes they cherished,
  On the height of their faith sublime!
For them is the voice of wailing
  And the sweet blush-rose departs.
From the cheeks of the maidens paling
  O'er the wreck of their broken hearts.

And alas! for the vanished glory
  Of a thousand household spells!
And alas! for the tearful story
  Of the spirit's fond farewells!
By the flood, on the field, in the forest,
  Our bravest have yielded breath,
Yet the shafts that have smitten the
    sorest,
  Were launched by a viewless death.

Oh, Thou! that hast charms of healing,
  Descend on a widowed land,
And bind o'er the wounds of feeling,
  The balms of thy mystic hand;

Till the lives that lament and languish,
Renewed by a touch divine,
From the depths of their mortal anguish,
May rise to the calm of Thine.

FORGOTTEN.

FORGOTTEN! Can it be a few swift
rounds
Of Time's great chariot wheels have
crushed to naught
The memory of those fearful sights and
sounds,
With speechless misery fraught —
Wherethro' we hope to gain the Hespe-
rian height,
Where Freedom smiles in light?

Forgotten! scarce have two dim autumns
veiled
With merciful mist those dreary burial
sods,
Whose coldness (when the high-strung
pulses failed,
Of men who strove like gods)
Wrapped in a sanguine fold of senseless
dust
Dead hearts and perished trust!

Forgotten! While in far-off woodland
dell,
By lonely mountain tarn and murmur-
ing stream,
Bereavèd hearts with sorrowful passion
swell —
Their lives one ghastly dream
Of hope outwearied and betrayed desire,
And anguish crowned with fire!

Forgotten! while our manhood cursed
with chains,
And pilloried high for all the world to
view,
Writhes in its fierce, intolerable pains,

Decked with dull wreaths of rue,
And shedding blood for tears, hands
waled with scars,
Lifts to the dumb, cold stars!

Forgotten! Can the dancer's jocund feet
Flash o'er a charnel-vault, and maid-
ens fair
Bend the white lustre of their eyelids
sweet,
Love-weighed, so nigh despair,
Its ice-cold breath must freeze their
blushing brows,
And hush love's tremulous vows?

Forgotten! Nay: but all the songs we
sing
Hold under-burdens, wailing chords of
woe;
Our lightest laughters sound with hollow
ring,
Our bright wit's freest flow,
Quavers to sudden silence of affright,
Touched by an untold blight!

Forgotten! No! we cannot all forget,
Or, when we do, farewell to Honor's
face,
To Hope's sweet tendance, Valor's un-
paid debt,
And every noblest Grace,
Which, nursed in Love, might still be-
nignly bloom
Above a nation's tomb!

Forgotten! Tho' a thousand years should
pass,
Methinks our air will throb with mem-
ory's thrills,
A conscious grief weigh down the falter-
ing grass,
A pathos shroud the hills,
Waves roll lamenting, autumn sunsets
yearn
For the old time's return!

LEGENDS AND LYRICS.

LEGENDS AND LYRICS.

1865–1872.

DAPHLES.

AN ARGIVE STORY.

ONCE on the throne of Argos sat a maid,
Daphles the fair; serene and unafraid
She ruled her realm, for the rough folk were brought
To worship one they deemed divinely wrought
In beauty and mild graciousness of heart:
Nobles and courtiers, too, espoused her part,
So that the sweet young face all thronged to see,
Glanced from her throne-room's silken canopy
(Broidered with leaves, and many a snow-white dove),
Rosily conscious of her people's love.
Only the chief of a far frontier clan,
A haughty, bold, ambitious nobleman,
By law her vassal, but self-sworn to be
From subject-tithe and tribute boldly free,
And scorning most this weak girl-sovereign's reign,
Now from the mountain fastness to the plain
Summoned his savage legions to the fight, —
Wherein he hoped to wrench the imperial might
From Daphles, and confirm his claim thereto.
But Doracles, the insurgent chief, could know

Naught of the secret charm, the subtle stress
Of beauty wed to warm unselfishness,
Which, in her hour of trial, wrapped the Queen
Safely apart in golden air serene
Of deep devotion, and fond faith of those
The steadfast hearts betwixt her and her foes.
The oldest courtier, schooled in state-craft guile,
Some loyal fire at her entrancing smile
Felt strangely kindled in his outworn soul;
Far more the warrior youths her soft control
Moulded to noble deeds, till all the land,
Aroused at Love's and Honor's joint command,
Bristled with steel and rang with sounds of war.

Still rashly trusting in his fortunate star,
This arrogant thrall who fain would grasp a crown,
Backed by half-barbarous hordes, marched swiftly down
'Twixt the hill ramparts and the Western Sea.
First, blazing homesteads greet him, whence did flee
The frightened hinds through fires themselves had lit
'Mid the ripe grain, lest foes should reap of it;
Or here and there, some groups of aged folk,

Women and men bent down beneath the
yoke
Of cruel years and babbling idiot speech.
" Methinks," cried Doracles, " our arms
will reach
The realm's unshielded heart; for lo! the
breath,
The mere hot fume of rapine and of
death
Which flames before our legions like a
blight
Withers this people's valor and their
might."

The fifes played shriller; the wild
trumpet's blast
Smote the great host and thrilled them
as it passed;
While clashing shields, and spears which
caught the morn,
And splendid banners in strong hands
upborne,
And plumèd helms, and steeds of match-
less race,
And in the van that clear, keen eagle
face
Of Doracles, firm set on shoulders tall,
Squared like a rock, and towering o'er
them all,
With all the pomp and swell of martial
strife,
Woke the burnt plains and bleak de-
files to life.
So phalanx after phalanx glittering filed
Firm to the front: their haughty leader
smiled
To see with what a bold and buoyant air
The lowliest footman marched before
him there,
Till his proud head he lifted to the sun,
And his heart leaped as at a victory won
That self-same hour, o'er which bright-
hovering shone
The steadfast image of an ivory throne.

But the Queen's host by skilful cham-
pions led,
Its powers meanwhile concentred to a
head,

Lay, an embattled force with wary
eye,
Ready to ward or strike whene'er the
cry
Of coming foemen on their ears should
fall,
Nigh the huge towers which guard the
capital.

Not long their watch: one bluff October
day,
There rose a blare of trumpets far away,
And sound of thronging hoofs which
muffled came,
Borne on the wind, like the dull noise of
flame
Half stifled in dense woodlands; then
the wings
Of the Queen's host, as each swift section
flings
The imperial banner proudly fluttering
out,
Spread from the royal centre.   Hark! a
shout,
As from those thousand hearts in one
great soul
Sublimely fused, rose thunder-deep, to
roll,
In wild acclaim, far down the quivering
van;
And wilder still the heroic tumult ran
From front to rear, when through her
palace gate,
Daphles, in unaccustomed martial state,
A keen spear shimmering in its silver
hold,
And on her brow the Argive crown of
gold,
Flashed like a sunbeam on her warriors'
sight.
Girt by her generals, on a neighboring
height
She reined her Lybian courser, while the
air
Played with the bright waves of her
meteor hair,
And on her lovely April face the tide
Of varied feeling — now a jubilant
pride

In those strong arms and stronger hearts
   below,
And now a prescient fear did ebb and
   flow,
Its sensitive heaven transforming mo-
   mently.
But soon the foeman's cohorts, like a
   sea,
With waves of steel, and foam of snow-
   white plumes,
Slowly emerged from out the forest
   glooms,
In splendid pomp and antique pageantry.
An ominous pause! And then the
   trumpets high
Sounded the terrible onset, and the field
Rocked as with earthquake, and the
   thick air reeled
With clangors fierce from echoing hill to
   hill.

Bloody but brief the contest! All the
   skill
Of Doracles against the steadfast will
Planted by love in faithful hearts that
   day
Frothed like an idle tide that slips away
From granite walls! His knights their
   furious blows
Discharged on what seemed statues
   whose repose
Was iron, or their fated coursers hurled
On spears unbent as bases of a world!
Meanwhile the whole dread scene did
   Daphles view
With anguished, tearless eyes. But
   when she knew
The victory hers, down the hill-slopes
   she urged
Her restless steed, where still but faintly
   surged
The last worn waves of tumult; there
   her bands
Of conquering captains she with fervent
   hands
And o'erfraught swelling breast did
   proudly greet;
Yet her pale face was touched with pity
   sweet

While the chained rebels passed her
   worn and sore
With ghastly wounds, and shivering in
   their gore.
But when, untamed, uncowed, in 'midst
   of these,
The grand, defiant form of Doracles
Rose like a god discrowned, her wan
   cheeks flushed,
And through her heart a quick, hot tor-
   rent rushed
Of undefined, mysterious sympathy.
Viewing that haughty brow, that unbent
   knee,
"O kingly head!" she thought, "too
   well I know
How bitter-keen to him the signal blow
This day hath dealt! O kingly resolute
   eyes,
Shrining the sov'ran soul! 'twere surely
   wise
To change their glance of cold vindictive
   gloom
To grateful light, and make what seemed
   a doom
Heavy as death, the clouded path to
   fame,
Lordship, and honor!" Ah, but pity
   came
To crown admiring kindness with a
   flame
Of subtler life; for he, the vanquished
   one,
On whom that day his fate's malignant
   sun
Had set in storms, that night would
   slumber, kissed
By a fair phantom girt with golden
   mist,
A new-born delicate love, but dimly
   guessed
Even in the pure depths of the maiden
   breast,
Whence the sweet sylph had 'scaped her
   unaware.
But when the evening silence drew
   anear,
And round about the borders of the
   world

The second night since that great con-
test furled
Its brooding shades, the young Queen,
all alone,
Paused by the dungeon floor whereon
were thrown,
At listless length, the limbs of Doracles.
"How, how," she murmured, "may I
best appease
His stricken pride, or touch to tender
calm
His fevered honor? with what healing
balm
Allay the smart wherewith his spirit
groans?"
Perplexed, and yearning, on the dismal
stones
Without the prison door she walked
apart,
Love, doubt, and shame, all struggling
in her heart,
Till the large flood of mingled love and
woe
Rose to her snowy eyelids and did flow
In soft refreshing tears like spring-tide
showers;
Then, bright and blushing as the moss-
rose bowers
Of dewy May, she pushed the huge grate
back,
And through the dusky glooms, the
shadows black
Dawned glowingly! Next for a moment
she
Stood in a timid, strange uncertainty,
Changing from rosy red to deathly white;
When, as a Queen sustained by true
love's right,
She spake in mild, pure, steadfastness
of soul:
"I come, O Doracles, with no mean
dole
Of transient pity, but to show thee how
Thy mistress would exalt the abasèd
brow
Of one who knows her not!" There-
with she freed
His fettered limbs, or yet his brain could
heed

Or comprehend her mercy's cordial
scope:
His soul had shrunk too low for dreams
of hope,
Such swift misfortunes smote him: still,
when all
The Queen's fair meaning on his mind
did fall,
The locked and frozen sternness of his
look
Broke up, as breaks the death-cold win-
try brook
Its icy spell at noonday; yet his face
Was lighted not by thankful, reverent
grace,
But flashed an evil triumph where he
stood
Spurning his unloosed chains. In such
base mood,
One eager foot pressed on the dungeon
stair,
"What terms," he asked, "O Queen,
demand'st thou here?
I pledge thee faith!" Silent were
Daphles' lips,
And all her gentle hopes by swift eclipse
Were darkened. With a deathly smile
she signed
The chief farewell, as one who scorned
to bind
Her mercy with set terms. He turned
to go,
Self-centred, callous, dreaming not how
low
Her heart had sunk at each cold, shallow
word
With which his barren nature, faintly
stirred
By ruth, or love, or pardon, dared repay
Her matchless mercy. On his unchecked
way
He turned to go, when, with one shud-
dering sob,
And deep-drawn, plaintive breath,
which seemed to rob
Life of its last dear hope, the Queen
sank down,
Wrapped in a death-like trance. With
sullen frown,

And many a muttered oath, he raised
 her form,
Frail now as some pale lily by the storm
Wind-blown and beaten; for at woman's
 love
He could but vaguely guess, and no poor
 dove
Pierced by the woodman's shaft was less
 to him
Than this fair spirit struggling in the
 dim
And tortured twilight of unshared de-
 sire;
Nor could he part the pure romantic fire
Of such high passion from the lukewarm
 flame
That feebly burns in sordid hearts and
 tame,
Not of love's heat, but vacant flattery's
 born,
To feed his pride, yet stir the latent
 scorn
Of that rough manhood such hard na-
 tures know.
Waked from her trance, with wandering
 eyes and slow
The Queen looked round, but dimly con-
 scious yet,
Until at last her faltering glance was set
On Doracles, to whom — that he might
 see
How a soft ruth to love's intensity
Had strangely grown — she laid her deep
 heart bare:
Then, with a sweet but nobly queen-like
 air,
She said, " O Doracles, in just return
For all this love and pity, which did
 yearn
To lift thee fallen, and to find thee, lost,
And slowly sickening underneath the
 frost
Of bleak despair, I well might ask of
 thee
Thy heart, with all its rarest freight in
 fee,
Save that I feel my virgin fame and life
Must count as pure, when thou hast
 made me wife,

Though but a wife in state and name
 alone.
Behold, O chief! I proffer, too, my
 throne,
Not as thy freedom's sole condition
 given,
But that men's eyes and scornful
 thoughts be driven
Away from what in me may seem as
 ill,
If — if — perchance, thou shouldst reject
 me still.''
At which hard word she droops her head,
 and sighs,
While patient tears bedew her downcast
 eyes.

Now, with sly semblance of a soul at
 ease,
Her liberal proffer crafty Doracles
Freely embraced. They passed the
 prison-bound,
And that same day with silver-ringing
 sound
Of trump and cymbal, the state heralds
 cried
Abroad through all the city, far and
 wide,
The Queen's vast pardon; whereupon
 her court, —
Nobles and dames, — each quaintly gor-
 geous sport,
Known in the old time, bold or debon-
 air,
With feasts, and mimic strifes, and pa-
 geants rare,
Did hold in honor of their sovereign's
 choice;
A choice none there would question! Not a voice,
Gentle or simple, but was raised to bless,
And pray the kindly gods for happiness
And peace on both! Meanwhile the
 thrall made king,
Albeit a secret anger still would wring
His thankless soul, in princely fashion
 took
The general homage, nor by word or
 look

Betrayed the festering consciousness
   within:
So gracious seemed he, Daphles' hopes
   begin
To wake, and whisper fond, sweet, fool-
   ish words
Close to her heart, that flutters like a
   bird's
Wooed in the spring-dawn: yet, alas!
   alas!
For joy that dies, and dreamy hopes that
   pass
To nothingness! In 'midst of this, her
   trust,
Came a swift blow which smote her to
   the dust;
News that her ingrate love had basely
   fled,
Whither none knew. Scarce had this
   shaft been sped
From fate's unerring bow, than swift
   again
Hurtled a second steeped in poisoned
   pain;
For now the whole dark truth came
   sternly out:
Leagued with her bitterest foes, a savage
   rout
Of mountain-robbers o'er the frontier
   land,
He unto whom she proffered heart and
   hand,
Kingdom and crown, had bared his
   treacherous blade,
And of the great and just gods unafraid,
Upreared his standard 'neath the blood-
   red star,
And raised once more the incarnate
   curse of war!
So from that day all gladness left the
   heart
Of broken Daphles; she would muse
   apart
From court and friends, her once blithe
   footsteps slow,
Her once proud head bowed down, and
   such wild woe
Couched in the clouded depths of mourn-
   ful eyes

That few could mark her misèry but
   with sighs
Deep almost as her own. At last, she
   wrote
(For still her soul hailed, watery and re-
   mote,
One beam of hope) a missive tender-
   sweet,
Charmed with such pathos, to her deli-
   cate feet
It might have lured a spirit, nigh to
   death,
And straight imbued with warm compas-
   sionate breath
A heart as cold as spires of Arctic
   ice!

Ah, futile hope! Ah, fond and vain de-
   vice!
Not all the pleading eloquence of wrong,
Veiling its wounds, and golden-soft as
   song
Trilled by the brown Sicilian nightin-
   gales,
In dusky nooks of melancholy vales,
Could melt the granite will of Doracles.
Each tender line she sent him did but
   tease
And sting his obdurate temper into
   hate,
As if the deep harmonious terms that
   wait
On truest love, were wasp-like, poisoned
   things:
Her timorous hints, her sweet imagin-
   ings,
Far thoughts, and dreams evanishing,
   but high,
Filled with the maiden dews of sanctity,
He crushed, as one might crush in mad-
   dened hours
The fairest of the sisterhood of flowers;
No further answer made he than could
   be
Couched in brief terms of cold discourt-
   esy,
Holding *all* love — the noblest love on
   earth —
Of lesser moment than an insect's birth,

Buzzing its life out 'twixt the dawn and
dark.
That letter stifled the last healthful spark
Of the Queen's flickering reason, turned
her wit
To wild and errant courses, sadly lit
By wandering stars, and orbs of fantasy.
Deeming that she full soon must sink
and die,
Daphles, still true to that one dominant
thought
And firm affection which such ill had
brought,
Summoned her learned scribes and bade
them draw
After strict form and precedents of law,
Her solemn testament; whereby she gave
Her throne to Doracles, whene'er the
grave
Closed o'er her broken heart and hum-
bled head.
But now her chiefs and nobles, hard be-
stead
By circumstance, and dreading much
lest he,
The renegade, and rebel, who did flee
From love to league with license, yet
should sway
The honored Argive sceptre, on a day
Called forth to solemn council and debate
Lords, liegemen, ministers, to save the
state
From threatened tyranny and upstart
rule:
Thereto the wan Queen, powerless now
to school
Features or mind to subjugation meet,
Came weakly tottering; in her lofty seat
She sank bewildered, listless; all could
mark
Beneath her languid eyes the hollows
dark,
And — save that sometimes as she slowly
turned
Her wasted form, the fires of fever
burned,
Death's prescient blazon, on each sunken
cheek —
Her face was pallid as a cold white streak

Of wintry moonlight on Siberian snows;
Her quivering mouth and chill con-
tracted brows
Bespoke an inward torture, while from
all
The shrewd debate within that council
hall
Her dim thoughts wandered vaguely,
lost and dumb.
But when her pitying maidens round her
come,
And gently strive on her drooped head to
place
The self-same laurel garland which did
grace
Her warm, white temples on that morn
of strife
And woeful victory, her sick brain seemed
rife
Once more with memories; in her hand
she pressed
The half-dead wreath, and o'er her
flowing vest
Strewed the plucked leaves those aimless
fingers tore
Unwittingly; which on the marble
floor,
Down fluttering, one by one, lay blurred
and dead,
Like the sere hopes her withered heart
had shed,
Smitten of love; for now she touched
the close
Of the soul's dreamy autumn, and the
snows
Of winter soon would clasp her eyelids
cold.
Yea, soon, too soon! for while her fin-
gers fold
The garland loosely, and in fitful grief
She still would strip the circlet, leaf by
leaf,
Till now one-half the wreath is plucked
and bare,
She lifts her dim eyes, hearkening, as
though 'ware
Of mystic voices calling on her name;
Therewith her cheek, whence the quick,
fevered flame

Had quite pulsed out, with one last
  quiver, she
Drops on the cushioned dais, passively;
For death, more kind than love, hath
  brought her peace.

Long was it ere her stricken realm could
  cease
To mourn for Daphles; yet her burial
  rites,
With all their mournful pomp, their
  sombre sights
Funereal, scarce were passed, when her
  last will,
Despite its humbling terms, which ran-
  kled still
In all men's minds, her faithful courtiers
  sent,
With news of that most sudden, sad
  event
Which made him king, to restless Dor-
  acles.
What recked he then that to its bitterest
  lees
A pure young soul had quaffed of mis-
  ery's cup,
And after, death's? "My star," he
  thought, "flames up,
Fronting the heights of empire! All is
  well!"
Thereon, impelled by keen desire to
  dwell
In his new realm, with reckless haste he
  rode
From town to town, till now the grand
  abode,
The palace of the royal Argive race,
Did rise before him in its lofty place,
O'erlooking leagues of golden fields and
  streams,
Fair hills and shadowy vineyards, by
  great teams
Of laboring oxen rifled morn by morn,
Till the bared, tremulous branches swung
  forlorn
'Gainst the red flush of autumn's sunset
  sky.
Housed with rich state therein, full re-
  gally

The king his sovereign life and course
  began,
Striving at one swift bound to reach the
  van
Of princely fame; his rare magnificence
Of feasts, shows, pageants, and high
  splendors, whence
The wondering guests all dazzled went
  their way,
Grew to a world-wide proverb for dis-
  play
And costly lavishness. Yet one there
  was
O'er whose gray head these days of pomp
  did pass
Like purpling shadows o'er the faded
  grass:
Wit touched him not to smiles, gay mu-
  sic's flow
Fell powerless on his closed heart's secret
  woe,
While at their feasts silent he sat, and
  grim.
Ofttimes the king a cold glance cast on
  him,
As one who marred their mirthful rev-
  elry,
And in the boisterous spring-tide of their
  glee
Rose like a boding phantom! More and
  more
He felt a vague, dim trouble at the core
Of his rude nature stirred, whene'er he
  saw
Phorbas draw near; something akin to
  awe,
If not to dread, for this old man did
  stand
Chiefest of Daphles' mourners in her
  land,
As chief of her life's friends, ere that
  black doom
Stole from her heart its joy, her cheek
  its bloom.

Just where the mellowed rays of noon-
  day light
Streamed through the curtained gloom,
  obscurely bright,

"Leagues of golden fields and streams,
Fair hills and shadowy vineyards, by great teams
Of laboring oxen rifled morn by morn."

Which wrapped the great art-galleries
   richly round,
There hung, 'mid many a stately por-
   trait, bound
In frames of costly ivory, carved and
   wrought,
A picture, which the king's eyes oft had
   sought
With anxious wonder; for day following
   day
Would Phorbas, mutely sorrowing, make
   delay
Going or coming from the council-hall
To view that muffled mystery on the
   wall.
Over it flowed a veil of silvery hue,
With here and there fine threads of gold
   shot through
The delicate woof; and whoso chanced
   to turn
A glance thereon, would feel his spirit
   burn
To pierce the jealous veil whose folds
   might hide
Some priceless marvel. Now, at high
   noontide
Of one calm autumn day, the king again
Met Phorbas — his worn features drawn
   with pain,
And in his eyes the sharp salt-rheum of
   age —
Still poring on the picture! "Thou a
   sage!"
Sneered Doracles, "yet idly bent, for-
   sooth,
On vaporing fancies?" Then, more
   harsh, "The truth!
The *truth*, old man! What strong spell
   drags thee here?
(Some charm, methinks, 'twixt passion
   and despair:)
Morn after morn, forcing thine eyes to
   stray
O'er yon blank mystery? Prythee,
   Phorbas, say
What image lurks beneath that glimmer-
   ing shroud?
Perchance the last king's? Well! am I
   less proud

And princely wise than he? Or art thou
   bold
To deem *me* all unworthy to behold
My brave forerunner?" Thereupon he
   knit
His rugged brows, the while his soul was
   lit
To keen, impatient wrath. With trem-
   bling hands —
But not for fear — Phorbas unloosed the
   bands,
Studded with diamond points. which
   clasped the veil
Close to its place. The startled prince
   grew pale,
As there, in all her fresh young grace,
   did shine
The face of Daphles, with a smile di-
   vine,
Into arch dimples rippling joyfully!
Some faintly-pensive memory seemed to
   vie
With deeper feelings, in the low, quick
   tone
Wherewith the king spake, whispering
   to his own
Half-wakened heart, — "Certes, it could
   not be,
That she, who owned the glorious face I
   see,
Bright with all brightness of a young
   delight,
Yet pined and withered 'neath the fatal
   night
Of starless grief!" To which, "Thy
   pardon, sire,"
The old man said, "but ere my life's
   low fire
Hath quite gone out, I fain would free
   my soul
Of that which long hath borne me care
   and dole;
So, sovereign lord, list to the tale I tell!"
And therewithal did Phorbas deem it
   well
To show how Daphles' darkened life did
   wane ;
How love, first touched by doubt, soon
   changed to pain,

And, last, blank desolation, whose wild
    stress
Wrecked and made bare her perfect
    loveliness,
O'erwhelming wit with beauty. "Still,"
    said he,
" O sire! to her last hour most tenderly
She spake of thee, her twilight reason
    set
On the sole thought, '*My love may love
    me yet :*
*For man's love comes with knowledge,
    so I deem,*
Slow-hearted man's !' Ah, heaven! she
    could not dream,
But *thy* name filled her dreams. When
    madness stole
Like a dread mist about her, and her
    soul,
Wound in its viewless cerement-folds
    accursed —— "
" Madness!" the king cried in a sharp
    outburst
Of wild amazement: " madness! *I* have
    known
The mad impatience of a will o'ergrown,
When sternly thwarted in its fiery
    zeal,
But dreamed not how these fairy creat-
    ures feel,
These soft, frail-natured women, if, per-
    chance,
Love turn on them a cold or lukewarm
    glance
Of brief denial!" Then the impatient
    red,
In a swift flood, — but not of anger, —
    spread
O'er the king's face; convulsed it seemed,
    and stern.
But when from garrulous Phorbas he did
    learn
How the queen's laurel wreath half bare
    became,
The hot blood ebbed, and o'er its waning
    flame
Coursed the first tear his warrior-soul
    had shed.
Nor could he rouse again the lustihead

Of ruder thoughts, but, thickly mutter-
    ing, laid
On the fair portrait of the sovereign
    maid
A reverent hand; from 'midst the painted
    dome
Of the great gallery forth he bore it
    home
Unto the secret chamber of his rest;
There next his couch he placed the beau-
    teous guest;
There feasted on its sweetness; and since
    naught
Of public import now did claim his
    thought,
No fierce war threatened, no shrewd trea-
    ties pressed,
Strangely the picture mastered him; it
    grew,
As days, then weeks, and seasons, o'er
    him flew,
A part, an inmost essence of all life,
Which touched to joy or thrilled to
    shuddering strife
The soul's deep-seated issues: yet, at last,
Stronger the fierce strife waxed; the bliss
    was passed;
And, wheresoe'er the king went, night
    or day,
One haunting phantom barred his
    doomèd way!

But ere he reached the worst wild stage
    of woe,
Through many a change of passion, swift
    or slow,
The king passed downward, nearing
    treacherous death;
And thus it happed, our old-world legend
    saith:

The more he gazed on Daphles' blooming
    face,
All flushed with happy youth and Hebe
    grace,
The more her marvellous image seemed
    alive;
He saw, or dreamed he saw, the warm
    blood strive,

In ruddier tide, with conscious hues to
　dye
Her lovely brow and swanlike neck, or
　vie
With Syrian roses on her cheeks of
　flame;
The more he gazed, the more her lips
　became
Instinct with timorous motion, till a
　sigh,
New-born of honeyed love unwittingly,
Seemed hovering like a murmurous fairy-
　bee
About their rich, half-parted comeli-
　ness:
What slight breath softly stirs the truant
　tress,
Which like a waif of sunset light did
　rest
In wandering golden lustre on her
　breast?
And what dear thought her bosom gra-
　ciously
Heaves into gentle billows, like a sea
Moon-kissed, and whispering? Thus
　the king would task
Long hours with doting questions, when
　the mask
Of dull state forms and ceremonial
　play
With wearied brain and hand was cast
　away,
And he a dead maid's crafty image
　turned
To breathing life, and blissful love that
　burned
From her wild pulses and fond heart to
　his,
And on her mouth he pressed a bride-
　groom's kiss.

Then the sweet spell was broken; con-
　science spoke;
And in her burning depths pale memory
　woke.
Even in that gentle shape his cold self-
　will
Had strangely turned, and wrought him
　direful ill;

Distempered, moody, sometimes nigh
　distraught
With ceaseless pressure of one harrow-
　ing thought,
He grew, and hapless thrills of lonely
　pain;
Her picture, imaged on his heart and
　brain,
Ruled all his tides of being, as the moon
Draws changeful seas; now in a clear
　high noon
Of memories bitter-sweet his soul would
　swim,
Anon to sink in turbulent gulfs and dim
Of wild regret, or as the dead to lie
Locked in a mute, life-withering leth-
　argy.
Creator sweet of all his fortunes high,
Oh, that in Hades she could hear his
　cry
Remorseful, and come back in pitying
　guise
To ease his grief and calm his tortured
　sighs!
A thousand, thousand times this wild
　desire
Would wake, and surge through all his
　veins like fire:
Followed, alas, too soon, by such deep
　sense
Of powerless will, and mortal impotence,
As in red hurry up from soul to cheeks
Runs rioting, and ever harshly seeks
To drag them into gaunt, gray lines of
　care!
Months sped eventless, with his dark
　despair
Grown darker; till, one sad November
　morn,
Set to the rhythmic wail of winds for-
　lorn,
They found, just where the morning's
　shadowy gloom
Had gathered deepest in the prince's
　room,
His prostrate body, cold and turned in
　part
Upwards,—the blade's hilt glittering
　o'er his heart,

Where his own mad right arm had sent
    it home.
Beneath him, in soft-tinted, fadeless
    bloom,
Beneath him smiled the portrait he had
    torn
Madly from off the wall, his wan face
    borne
Next the clear brightness of that life-
    like one
For whose fair sake he lay, at last un-
    done;
But whose glad smile, could *she* have
    lived that hour,
Had waned and withered inward, like a
    flower
The storm-wind blights, at stern re-
    venge, like this,
Of love's cold scorn and passion's unpaid
    kiss.

AËTHRA.

IT is a sweet tradition, with a soul
Of tenderest pathos! Hearken, love! —
    for all
The sacred undercurrents of the heart
Thrill to its cordial music:
                    Once, a chief,
Philantus, king of Sparta, left the stern
And bleak defiles of his unfruitful
    land —
Girt by a band of eager colonists —
To seek new homes on fair Italian
    plains.
Apollo's oracle had darkly spoken:
" *Where'er from cloudless skies a*
    plenteous shower
Outpours, the Fates decree that ye should
    pause
And rear your household deities! "
    Racked by doubt
Philantus traversed with his faithful
    band
Full many a bounteous realm; but still
    defeat
Darkened his banners, and the strong-
    walled towns

His desperate sieges grimly laughed to
    scorn!
Weighed down by anxious thoughts, one
    sultry eve
The warrior — his rude helmet cast
    aside —
Rested his weary head upon the lap
Of his fair wife, who loved him ten-
    derly;
And there he drank a generous draught
    of sleep.
She, gazing on his brow all worn with
    toil
And his dark locks, which pain had
    silvered over
With glistening touches of a frosty
    rime,
Wept on the sudden bitterly; her
    tears
Fell on his face, and, wondering, he
    woke.
" O blest art thou, my Aëthra, *my clear*
    sky,"
He cried exultant, " from whose pitying
    blue
A heart-rain falls to fertilize my fate:
Lo! the deep riddle's solved — the gods
    spake truth! "

So the next night he stormed Tarentum,
    took
The enemy's host at vantage, and o'er-
    threw
His mightiest captains. Thence with
    kindly sway
He ruled those pleasant regions he had
    won, —
But dearer even than his rich demesnes
The love of her whose gentle tears un-
    locked
The close-shut mystery of the Oracle!

RENEWED.

WELCOME, rippling sunshine!
    Welcome, joyous air!
Like a demon shadow
    Flies the gaunt despair!

Heaven, through heights of happy calm,
Its heart of hearts uncloses,
To win earth's answering love in balm,
Her blushing thanks — in roses!

Voices from the pine-grove,
Where the pheasant's drumming,
Voices from the ferny hills
Alive with insect humming;

Voices low and sweet
From the far-off stream,
Where two rivulets meet
With the murmur of a dream;
Voices loud and free
From every bush and tree,
Of sportive forest bards outpouring songs of gladness;
But over them still
With its passionate trill,
The mock-bird's jocund madness!

"Voices low and sweet
From the far-off stream."

Deep down the swampy brake
Even the poison-snake,
Uncoiled and basking in the noontide splendor,
May feel, perchance on this auspicious day
(All dark clouds rolled away),
Through his stagnant blood,
Warmed by the sunlight flood
A faint, far sense,
Coming he knows not whence,
Of dim intelligence, —
The thinnest conscious thrill that human is, and tender!

Look! where on luminous wing
The ether's stately king,

The lone sea-eagle, circling proud and slow,
Towers in the sapphire glow;
From out whose dazzling beam,
His resonant scream;
Heard even here, — a note of fierce desire, —
Hushes to silent awe the sylvan choir.
Till bird and note in airy deeps updrawn
Are melting toward the dawn!

And hear! O! hear!
No longer wildly terrible and drear,
But as if merry pulses timed their beating,
The frolic sea-waves near,

Dancing along like happy maidens
　　playing
When blithe love goes " a-Maying,"
And wreaking on the shore their pant-
　　ing blisses
　　In coy impulsive kisses;
Whilst he — poor dullard — cannot catch
　　nor hold them,
Nor in his massive, earthen arms en-
　　fold them,
The laughing virgin waves, so archly,
　　swiftly fleeting!
　　This subtle atmosphere,
　　So magically clear,
Melts, as it were upon my eager lip;
From some invisible goblet of delight
Idly I sip and sip
A wine so warm and golden
(From some enchanted bin the wine
　　was stolen),
　　A wine so sweet and rare,
　　Methinks a nobler birth
　　Illuminates the earth,
And in my heart I hear a fairy singing;
Yet well I know 'tis but my soul renewed,
　　Reborn and bright,
From grief and grief's malignant soli-
　　tude!
　　Yet well I know, Joy is the Ganymede,
　　Who in my yearning need,
　　Turns to a cordial rich the balmy air;
And 'tis but Hope's, divinest Hope's
　　return,
Which makes my inmost spirit throb
　　and burn,
　　And Hope's triumphant song,
　　So sweet and strong,
That all creation seems with that weird
　　music ringing!

———◆———

KRISHNA AND HIS THREE HAND-MAIDENS.

AND where he sat beneath the mystic
　　stars,
Nigh the twin founts of Immortality,
That feed fair channels of the Stream
　　of Trance, —

To Krishna once his three handmaidens
　　came,
Asking a boon: " O king! O lord!" they
　　said,
" Test thou thy servants' wisdom; long
　　in dreams,
Born of the waters of thy Stream of
　　Trance,
Have we, thy fond handmaidens wan-
　　dered free,
And lapped in airiest wreaths of fantasy;
Now would we, viewless, bearing each
　　some gift
From thee, our father, seek the world of
　　man,
The world of man and pain, which
　　whoso leaves
Better or brighter, for thy gift bestowed
Most worthily, shall claim thy just re-
　　ward,
The Crown of Wisdom!" Krishna
　　heard, and gave
To each one tiny drop of diamond dew,
Drawn from the founts that feed the
　　Stream of Trance,
Wherewith, on waftage of miraculous
　　winds,
Breathing full south, they sought the
　　world of man,
The world of man and pain, that shrank
　　in drought,
Palsied and withered, like an old man's
　　face
Death-smitten.

　　　　And the first handmaiden saw
A monarch's fountain, sparkling in the
　　waste,
Glowing and fresh, though all the land
　　was sick,
Gasping for rain, and famished thou-
　　sands died:
" O brave," she said, " O beautiful
　　bright waves!
Like calls to like;" and so her dewdrop
　　glanced,
And glittered downward as a fairy star
Loosed from a tress of Cassiopeia's hair,
Down to the glorious fountain of the king.

Over the passionless bosom of the
    sea,
The Indian Sea, cerulean, crystal-clear,
And calm, the second handmaid, hover-
    ing, viewed —
Far through the tangled sea-weed and
    cool tides
Pulsing 'twixt coral branches — the wide
    lips
Of purpling shells that yearned to clasp
    a pearl:
So where the oyster, blindly reared,
    awaits
Its priceless soul — she lets the dewdrop
    fall,
Thenceforth to grow a jewel fit for
    courts,
And shine on swanlike necks of haughty
    queens!

But Krishna's third handmaiden scarce
    had felt
The fume from parchèd plains that made
    the air
As one vast caldron of invisible fire,
Than casting downward pitiful eyes, she
    saw,
Crouched in the brazen cere of that red
    heat,
A tiny bird — a poor, weak, suffering
    thing
(Its bright eyes glazed, its limbs con-
    vulsed and prone), —
Dying of thirst in torture: "Ah, kind
    Lord
Krishna," his handmaid murmured,
    "speed thy gift,
Best yielded here, to soothe, perchance
    to save
The lowliest mortal creature cursed with
    pain!"
Gently she shook the dewdrop from her
    palm
Into the silent throat that thirst had
    sealed,
Soon silent, sealed no more, — for, lo!
    the bird
Fluttered, arose, was strengthened, and
    through calms

Of happy ether, echoing fair and far,
Rang the charmed music of the nightin-
    gale.

And so, where crowned beneath the
    mystic stars,
Nigh the twin founts of immortality,
Krishna, the father, saw what ruth was
    hers,
And, smiling, to his wise handmaiden's
    rule
Gave the great storm-clouds and the
    mists of heaven,
Till at her voice the mighty vapors
    rolled
Up from the mountain-gorges, and the
    seas,
And cloudland darkened, and the grate-
    ful rain,
Burdened with benedictions, rushed and
    foamed
Down the hot channels, and the foliaged
    hills,
And the frayed lips and languid limbs
    of flowers;
And all the woodlands laughed, and
    earth was glad!

UNDER THE PINE.

TO THE MEMORY OF HENRY TIMROD.

THE same majestic pine is lifted high
    Against the twilight sky,
The same low, melancholy music grieves
    Amid the topmost leaves,
As when I watched, and mused, and
    dreamed with him,
    Beneath these shadows dim.

O Tree! hast thou no memory at thy
    core
    Of one who comes no more?
No yearning memory of those scenes
    that were
    So richly calm and fair,
When the last rays of sunset, shimmer-
    ing down,
    Flashed like a royal crown?

And he, with hand outstretched and
　　eyes ablaze,
　Looked forth with burning gaze,
And seemed to drink the sunset like
　　strong wine,
　Or, hushed in trance divine,
Hailed the first shy and timorous glance
　　from far
　Of evening's virgin star ?

O Tree! against thy mighty trunk he
　　laid
　His weary head; thy shade
Stole o'er him like the first cool spell of
　　sleep:
　It brought a peace *so* deep
The unquiet passion died from out his
　　eyes,
　As lightning from stilled skies.

And in that calm he loved to rest, and
　　hear
　The soft wind-angels, clear
And sweet, among the uppermost
　　branches sighing:
　Voices he heard replying
(Or so he dreamed) far up the mystic
　　height,
　And pinions rustling light.

O Tree! have not his poet-touch, his
　　dreams
　So full of heavenly gleams,
Wrought through the folded dullness of
　　thy bark,
　And all thy nature dark
Stirred to slow throbbings, and the flut-
　　tering fire
　Of faint, unknown desire ?

At least to me there sweeps no rugged
　　ring
　That girds the forest-king
No immemorial stain, or awful rent
　(The mark of tempest spent),
No delicate leaf, no lithe bough, vine-
　　o'ergrown,
　No distant, flickering cone,

But speaks of him, and seems to bring
　　once more
　The joy, the love of yore;
But most when breathed from out the
　　sunset-land
　The sunset airs are bland,
That blow between the twilight and the
　　night,
　Ere yet the stars are bright;

For then that quiet eve comes back to
　　me,
　When, deeply, thrillingly,
He spake of lofty hopes which vanquish
　　Death;
　And on his mortal breath
A language of immortal meanings hung,
　That fired his heart and tongue.

For then unearthly breezes stir and
　　sigh,
　Murmuring, " Look up ! 'tis I:
Thy friend is near thee! Ah, thou
　　canst not see!"
　And through the sacred tree
Passes what seems a wild and sentient
　　thrill —
　Passes, and all is still! —

Still as the grave which holds his tran-
　　quil form,
　Hushed after many a storm, —
Still as the calm that crowns his marble
　　brow,
　No pain can wrinkle now, —
Still as the peace — pathetic peace of
　　God —
　That wraps the holy sod,

Where every flower from our dead min-
　　strel's dust
　Should bloom, a type of trust, —
That faith which waxed to wings of
　　heavenward might
　To bear his soul from night, —
That faith, dear Christ! whereby we
　　pray to meet
　His spirit at God's feet!

A DREAM OF THE SOUTH WINDS.

O FRESH, how fresh and fair
Through the crystal gulfs of air,
The fairy South Wind floateth on her
    subtle wings of balm!
And the green earth lapped in bliss,
To the magic of her kiss
Seems yearning upward fondly through
    the golden-crested calm!

From the distant Tropic strand,
Where the billows, bright and bland,
Go creeping, curling round the palms
    with sweet, faint undertune
From its fields of purpling flowers
Still wet with fragrant showers,
The happy South Wind lingering sweeps
    the royal blooms of June.

All heavenly fancies rise
On the perfume of her sighs,
Which steep the inmost spirit in a lan-
    guor rare and fine,
And a peace more pure than sleep's
Unto dim, half-conscious deeps,
Transports me, lulled and dreaming, on
    its twilight tides divine.

Those dreams! ah me! the splendor,
So mystical and tender,
Wherewith like soft heat-lightnings
    they gird their meaning round,
And those waters, calling, calling,
With a nameless charm enthralling,
Like the ghost of music melting on a
    rainbow spray of sound!

Touch, touch me not, nor wake me,
Lest grosser thoughts o'ertake me,
From earth receding faintly with her
    dreary din and jars, —
What viewless arms caress me?
What whispered voices bless me,
With welcomes dropping dewlike from
    the weird and wondrous stars?

Alas! dim, dim, and dimmer
Grows the preternatural glimmer
Of that trance the South Wind brought
    me on her subtle wings of balm,

For behold! its spirit flieth,
And its fairy murmur dieth,
And the silence closing round me is a
    dull and soulless calm!

IN THE MIST.

MORE fearful grows the hillside way,
    The gloom no softening breeze hath
      kissed!
I glance far upward to the day,
But scarce can catch one faltering ray
    From out the mist!

Ah, heaven! to think youth's morning
    prime,
    All flushed with rose and amethyst,
Its tender loves, its hopes sublime,
Should shrink to this dull twilight-time
    Of cold and mist!

No tranquil evening hour descends,
    When peace with memory holds her
      tryst,
But doubt with prescient terror blends,
And grief her mournful curfew sends
    Along the mist!

Weird shapes and wild, stalk strangely
    by,
    And say, what bodeful voices hissed
Where yonder blasted pine-trunks lie?
What mystic phantoms shuddering fly
    Far down the mist?

Dark omens all! they bid me stay,
    Unsheathe resolve, pause, strive, re-
      sist
That poisonous charm which haunts my
    way;
Alas! the fiend, more bold than they,
    Still rules the mist!

And now from gulfs of turbulent gloom
    A torrent's threatening thunder;—
      list!
That ravening roar! that hungry boom!
Down, down I pass to meet my doom
    Within the mist!

A SUMMER MOOD.

"Now, by my faith a gruesome mood, for
summer!" — THOMAS HEYWARD (1597).

AH, me! for evermore, for evermore
    These human hearts of ours must
        yearn and sigh,
While down the dells and up the mur-
      murous shore
    Nature renews her immortality.

The heavens of June stretch calm and
      bland above,
    June roses blush with tints of Orient
        skies,
But we, by graves of joy, desire, and
      love,
    Mourn in a world which breathes of
        Paradise!

The sunshine mocks the tears it may
      not dry,
    The breezes — tricksy couriers of the
        air —
Child-roisterers winged, and lightly flut-
      tering by —
    Blow their gay trumpets in the face
        of care;

And bolder winds, the deep sky's pas-
      sionate speech,
    Woven into rhythmic raptures of de-
       sire,
Or fugues of mystic victory, sadly reach
    Our humbled souls, to rack, not raise
        them higher!

The field-birds seem to twit us as they
      pass
    With their small blisses, piped so clear
       and loud;
The cricket triumphs o'er us in the grass,
    And the lark, glancing beamlike up
       the cloud,

Sings us to scorn with his keen rhapso-
      dies;
    Small things and great unconscious
       tauntings bring

To edge our cares, whilst we, the proud
      and wise,
    Envy the insect's joy, the birdling's
       wing!

And thus for evermore, till time shall
      cease,
    Man's soul and Nature's — each a sep-
      arate sphere —
Revolve, the one in discord, one in
      peace,
    And who shall make the solemn mys-
       tery clear?

MIDNIGHT.

The Moon, a ghost of her sweet self,
    And wading through a watery cloud,
    Which wraps her lustre like a shroud,
Creeps up the gray, funereal sky,
    Wearily! how wearily!

The Wind, with low, bewildered wail
    A homeless spirit, sadly lost,
    Sweeps shuddering o'er the pallid
      frost,
And faints afar, with heart-sick sigh,
    Drearily! how drearily!

And now a deathly stillness falls
    On earth and heaven, save when the
      shrill,
    Malignant owl o'er heath and hill
Smites the wan silence with a cry,
    Eerily! how eerily!

THE BONNY BROWN HAND.

OH, drearily, how drearily, the sombre
      eve comes down!
    And wearily, how wearily, the seaward
      breezes blow!
But place your little hand in mine — so
      dainty, yet so brown!
    For household toil hath worn away its
      rosy-tinted snow;

"The Moon, a ghost of her sweet self, ..
Creeps up the gray, funereal sky,
Wearily! how wearily."

But I fold it, wife, the nearer,
And I feel, my love, 'tis dearer
Than all dear things of earth,
As I watch the pensive gloaming,
And my wild thoughts cease from
    roaming,
And birdlike furl their pinions close be-
    side our peaceful hearth:
Then rest your little hand in mine, while
    twilight shimmers down, —
That little hand, that fervent hand, that
    hand of bonny brown, —
The hand that holds an honest heart,
    and rules a happy hearth.

Oh, merrily, how merrily, our children's
    voices rise!
And cheerily, how cheerily, their tiny
    footsteps fall!
But, hand, you must not stir awhile, for
    there our nestling lies,
Snug in the cradle at your side, the
    loveliest far of all;
And she looks so arch and airy,
So softly pure a fairy, —
She scarce seems bound to earth;
And her dimpled mouth keeps
    smiling,
As at some child fay's beguiling,
Who flies from Ariel realms to light her
    slumbers on the hearth.
Ha, little hand, you yearn to move, and
    smooth the bright locks down!
But, little hand, — but, trembling hand,
    — but, hand of bonny brown,
Stay, stay with me! — she will not flee,
    our birdling on the hearth.

Oh, flittingly, how flittingly, the parlor
    shadows thrill,
As wittingly, half wittingly, they seem
    to pulse and pass!
And solemn sounds are on the wind that
    sweeps the haunted hill,
And murmurs of a ghostly breath from
    out the graveyard grass.
Let me feel your glowing fingers
In a clasp that warms and lingers
With the full, fond love of earth,

Till the joy of love's completeness
In this flush of fireside sweetness,
Shall brim our hearts with spirit-wine,
    outpoured beside the hearth.
So steal your little hand in mine, while
    twilight falters down, —
That little hand, that fervent hand, that
    hand of bonny brown, —
The hand which points the path to
    heaven, yet makes a heaven of
    earth.

SONNETS.

THE COTTAGE ON THE HILL.

On a steep hillside, to all airs that blow,
Open, and open to the varying sky,
Our cottage homestead, smiling tran-
    quilly,
Catches morn's earliest and eve's latest
    glow;
Here, far from worldly strife, and
    pompous show,
The peaceful seasons glide serenely by,
Fulfil their missions, and as calmly die,
As waves on quiet shores when winds
    are low.
Fields, lonely paths, the one small glim-
    mering rill
That twinkles like a wood-fay's mirth
    ful eye,
Under moist bay-leaves, clouds fantas-
    tical
That float and change at the light
    breeze's will, —
To me, thus lapped in sylvan luxury,
Are more than death of kings, or
    empires' fall.

NOVEMBER.

Within the deep-blue eyes of Heaven a
    haze
Of saddened passion dims their tender
    light,
For that her fair queen-child, the Sum-
    mer bright,

Lies a wan corse amidst her mouldering
　　bays:
The sullen Autumn lifts no voice of
　　praise
To herald Winter's cold and cruel
　　might,
But winds foreboding fill the desolate
　　night,
And die at dawning down wild wood-
　　land ways:
The sovereign sun at noonday smileth
　　cold,
As through a shroud he hath no power
　　to part,
While huddled flocks crouch listless
　　round their fold;
The mock-bird's dumb, no more with
　　cheerful dart
Upsoars the lark through morning's
　　quivering gold,
And dumb or dead, methinks, great
　　Nature's heart!

SYLVAN MUSINGS. — IN MAY.

COUCHED in cool shadow, girt by
　　billowy swells
Of foliage, rippling into buds and
　　flowers,
Here I repose o'erfanned by breezy
　　bowers, —
Lulled by a delicate stream whose
　　music wells
Tender and low through those luxuriant
　　dells,
Wherefrom a single broad-leaved chest-
　　nut towers; —
Still musing in the long, lush, languid
　　hours, —
As in a dream I heard the tinkling
　　bells
Of far-off kine, glimpsed through the
　　verdurous sheen,
Blent with faint bleatings from the dis-
　　tant croft, —
The bee-throngs murmurous in the
　　golden fern,
The wood-doves veiled by depths of
　　flickering green, —

And near me, where the wild "queen
　　fairies" * burn,
The thrush's bridal passion, warm and
　　soft!

POETS.

SOME thunder on the heights of song,
　　their race
Godlike in power, while others at their
　　feet
Are breathing measures scarce less
　　strong and sweet
Than those which peal from out that
　　loftiest place;
Meantime, just midway on the mount,
　　his face
Fairer than April heavens, when storms
　　retreat,
And on their edges rain and sunshine
　　meet,
Pipes the soft lyrist lays cf tender
　　grace;
But where the slopes of bright Parnassus
　　sweep
Near to the common ground, a various
　　throng
Chant lowlier measures, — yet each tune-
　　ful strain
(The silvery minor of earth's perfect
　　song)
Blends with that music of the topmost
　　steep,
O'er whose vast realm the master min-
　　strels reign!

SONNET.

BEHOLD! how weirdly, wonderfully
　　grand
The shades and colors of yon sunset sky!
Rare isles of light in crimson oceans lie,
Whose airy waves seem rippling, bright
　　and bland,
Up the soft slopes of many a mystic
　　strand, —

---

* "Queen fairy," the name given popularly
to an exquisite Southern wild flower.

While luminous capes, and mountains
    towering high
In golden pomp and proud regality,
O'erlook the frontier of that fairy land,
But now, in transformations swift and
    strange
The vision changes! Castles glittering
    fair,

And sapphire battlements of loftiest
    range
Commingle with vast spire and gorgeous
    dome,
Round which the sunset rolls its purpling
    foam,
Girding this transient Venice of the
    air.

"Upveiled in yonder dim ethereal sea,
Its airy towers the work of phantom spells,
A viewless belfry tolls its wizard bells."

THE PHANTOM BELLS.

UPVEILED in yonder dim ethereal sea,
Its airy towers the work of phantom
    spells,
A viewless belfry tolls its wizard bells,
Pealed o'er this populous earth perpet-
    ually.
Some hear, some hear them not; but
    aye they be

Laden with one strange note that sinks
    or swells,
Now dread as doom, now gentle as fare-
    wells,
Time's dirge borne ever toward eternity.
Each hour its measured breath sobs out
    and dies,
While the bell tolls its requiem, —
    "*Passing, past,*"—
The sole sad burden of their long refrain.

Still, with those hours each pang, each
　　pleasure flies,
Brief sweet, brief bitter, — all our days
　　are vain,
Knolled into drear forgetfulness at last.

THE LIFE-FOREST.

In springtime of our youth, life's pur-
　　pling shade,
Foliage and fruit, do hang so thickly
　　round,
We seem glad tenants of enchanted
　　ground,
O'er which for aye dream-whispering
　　winds have played.
Then summer comes, her full-blown
　　charm is laid
On all the forest aisles; from bound to
　　bound
Floats woodland music, and the silvery
　　sound
Of fountains babbling to the golden
　　glade.
Next, a chill breath, the breath of Au-
　　tumn's doom
Strips the fair sylvan branches, one by
　　one,
Till the bare landscape broadens to our
　　view;
Behind, black tree boles blot the twilight
　　blue,
Before, unfoliaged, bald of light and
　　bloom,
Our pathway darkens towards the dark-
　　ening sun!

CLOUD FANTASIES.

Wild, rapid, dark, like dreams of threat-
　　ening doom,
Low cloud-racks scud before the level
　　wind;
Beneath them, the bare moorlands,
　　blank and blind,
Stretch, mournful, through pale lengths
　　of glimmering gloom;
Afar, grand mimic of the sea waves'
　　boom,

Hollow, yet sweet as if a Titan pined
O'er deathless woes, yon mighty wood,
　　consigned
To autumn's blight, bemoans its
　　perished bloom;
The dim air creeps with a vague shud-
　　dering thrill
Down from those monstrous mists the
　　sea-gale brings,
Half formless, inland, poisoning earth
　　and sky;
Most from yon black cloud, shaped like
　　vampire wings
O'er a lost angel's visage, deathly-still,
Uplifted toward some dread eternity.

SONNET.

I fear thee not, O Death! nay, oft I pine
To clasp thy passionless bosom to mine
　　own,
And on thy heart sob out my latest
　　moan,
Ere lapped and lost in thy strange sleep
　　divine;
But much I fear lest that chill breath of
　　thine
Should freeze all tender memories into
　　stone, —
Lest ruthless and malign Oblivion
Quench the last spark that lingers on
　　love's shrine:
O God! to moulder through dark, date-
　　less years,
The while all loving ministries shall
　　cease,
And time assuage the fondest mourner's
　　tears!
Here lies the sting! — this, *this* it is to die!
And yet great nature rounds all strife
　　with peace,
And life or death, each rests in mystery!

SONNET.

Of all the woodland flowers of earlier
　　spring,
These golden jasmines, each an air-hung
　　bower,

Meet for the Queen of Fairies' tiring
    hour,
Seem loveliest and most fair in blossom-
    ing;
How yonder mock-bird thrills his fer-
    vid wing
And long, lithe throat, where twinkling
    flower on flower
Rains the globed dewdrops down, a dia-
    mond shower,
O'er his brown head poised as in act to
    sing;
Lo! the swift sunshine floods the flowery
    urns,
Girding their delicate gold with match-
    less light,
Till the blent life of bough, leaf, blossom,
    burns;
Then, then outbursts the mock-bird clear
    and loud,
Half-drunk with perfume, veiled by ra-
    diance bright,
A star of music in a fiery cloud!

FIRE-PICTURES.

O! THE rolling, rushing fire!
    O! the fire!
How it rages, wilder, higher,
Like a hot heart's fierce desire,
Thrilled with passion that appalls us,
Half appalls, and yet enthralls us,
    O! the madly mounting fire!

Up it sweepeth,—wave and quiver,—
Roaring like an angry river,—
    O! the fire!
Which an earthquake backward turneth,
Backward o'er its riven courses,
Backward to its mountain sources,
While the blood-red sunset burneth,
Like a God's face grand with ire,
    O! the bursting, billowy fire!

Now the sombre smoke-clouds thicken
To a dim Plutonian night;—
    O! the fire!
How its flickering glories sicken,

Sicken at the blight!
Pales the flame, and spreads the vapor,
Till scarce larger than a taper,
Flares the waning, struggling light:
O! thou wan, faint-hearted fire,
    Sadly darkling,
    Weakly sparkling,
    Rise! assert thy might!
    Aspire! aspire!

At the word, a vivid lightning,
Threatening, swaying, darting, bright-
    ening,
Where the loftiest yule-log towers, —
    Bursts once more,
Sudden bursts the awakened fire;
    Hear it roar!
Roar, and mount high, high, and higher,
    Till beneath,
Only here and there a wreath
Of the passing smoke-cloud lowers, —
    Ha! the glad, victorious fire!

    O! the fire!
    How it changes,
    Changes, ranges
Through all phases fancy-wrought,
Changes like a wizard thought;
See Vesuvian lavas rushing
'Twixt the rocks! the ground asunder
Shivers at the earthquake's thunder;
And the glare of Hell is flushing
Startled hill-top, quaking town;
Temples, statues, towers go down,
While beyond that lava flood,
Dark-red like blood,
I behold the children fleeting
Clasped by many a frenzied hand;
What a flight, and what a meeting,
On the ruined strand!

    O! the fire!
Eddying higher, higher, higher
From the vast volcanic cones;
O! the agony, the groans
Of those thousands stifling there!
" Fancy," say you? but how near
Seem the anguish and the fear!
Swelling, turbulent, pitiless fire:

'Tis a mad northeastern breeze
Raving o'er the prairie seas;
How, like living things, the grasses
Tremble as the storm-breath passes,
Ere the flames' devouring magic
Coils about their golden splendor,
          And the tender
Glory of the mellowing fields
To the wild destroyer yields;
Dreadful waste for flowering blooms,
Desolate darkness, like the tomb's,
Over which there broods the while,
Instead of daylight's happy smile,
A pall malign and tragic!

          Marvellous fire!
          Changing, ranging
Through all phases fancy-wrought,
Changing like a charmèd thought;
A stir, a murmur deep,
Like airs that rustle over jungle-reeds,
Where the gaunt tiger breathes but half
          asleep;
          A bodeful stir, —
And then the victim of his own pure
          deeds,
          I mark the mighty fire
Clasps in its cruel palms a martyr-saint,
          Christ's faithful worshipper;
One mortal cry affronts the pitying day,
One ghastly arm uplifts itself to heav-
          en —
When the swart smoke is riven, —
Ere the last sob of anguish dies away,
The worn limbs droop and faint,
And o'er those reverend hairs, silvery
          and hoary,
Settles the semblance of a crown of
          glory.

          Tireless fire!
          Changing, ranging
Through all phases fancy-wrought,
Changing like a Prótean thought;
Here's a glowing, warm interior,
A Dutch tavern, rich and rosy
With deep color, — sill and floor
Dazzling as the white seashore,
Where within his armchair cozy

Sits a toper, stout and yellow,
Blinking o'er his steamy bowl;
          Hugely drinking,
          Slyly winking,
As the pot-house Hebe passes,
With a clink and clang of glasses;
Ha! 'tis plain, the stout old fellow —
As his wont is — waxes mellow,
Nodding 'twixt each dreamy leer,
Swaying in his elbow chair,
Next to one, — a portly peasant, —
Pipe in hand, whose swelling cheek,
Jolly, rubicund, and sleek,
Puffs above the blazing coal;
While his heavy, half-shut, eyes
Watch the smoke-wreaths evanescent,
Eddying lightly as they rise,
Eddying lightly and aloof
Toward the great, black, oaken roof!

Dreaming still, from out the fire
Faces grinning and grotesque,
Flash an eery glance upon me;
Or, once more, methinks I sun me
On the breadths of happy plain
Sloping towards the southern main,
Where the inmost soul of shadow
          Wins a golden heat,
And the hill-side and the meadow
(Where the vines and clover meet,
Twining round the virgins' feet,
While the natural arabesque
Of the foliage grouped above them
Droops, as if the leaves did love them,
Over brow, and lips, and eyes)
Gleam with hints of Paradise!

          Ah! the fire!
          Gently glowing,
          Fairly flowing,
Like a rivulet rippling deep
Through the meadow-lands of sleep,
Bordered where its music swells,
By the languid lotos-bells,
And the twilight asphodels;
Mingled with a richer boon
Of queen-lilies, each a moon,
Orbèd into white completeness;
O! the perfume! the rare sweetness

"Countless coruscations glimmer,
Glow and darken, wane and shimmer, . . .
By mysterious currents stirred
Of great winds."

Of those grouped and fairy flowers,
Over which the love-lorn hours
Linger, — not alone for them,
Though the lotos swings its stem
With a lulling stir of leaves,—
Though the lady-lily waves,
And a silvery undertune
From some mystic wind-song grieves
Dainty sweet amid the bells
Of the twilight asphodels;
But because a charm more rare
Glorifies the mellow air,
In the gleam of lifted eyes,
In the tranquil ecstasies
Of two lovers, leaf-embowered,
Lingering there,
Each of whose fair lives hath flowered,
Like the lily-petals finely,
Like the asphodel divinely.

Titan arches!
Titan spires!
Pillars whose vast capitals
Tower toward Cyclopean halls,
And whose unknown bases pierce
Down the nether universe;
Countless coruscations glimmer,
Glow and darken, wane and shimmer,
'Twixt majestic standards, swooping, —
Like the wings of some strange bird
By mysterious currents stirred
Of great winds, — or darkly drooping,
In a hush sublime as death,
When the conflict's quivering breath
Sobs its gory life away,
At the close of fateful marches,
On an empire's natal day:
Countless coruscations glimmer,
Glow and darken, wane and shimmer,
Round the shafts, and round the walls,
Whence an ebon splendor falls
On the scar-seamed, angel bands, —
(Desolate bands!)
Grasping in their ghostly hands
Weapons of an antique rage,
From some lost, celestial age,
When the serried throngs were hurled
Blasted to the under world:
Shattered spear-heads, broken brands,

And the mammoth, moonlike shields,
Blazoned on their lurid fields,
With uncouth, malignant forms,
Glowering, wild,
Like the huge cloud-masses piled
Up a Heaven of storms!

.   .   .   .   .

Ah, the faint and flickering fire!
Ah, the fire!
Like a young man's transient ire,
Like an old man's last desire,
Lo! it falters, dies!
Still, through weary, half-closed lashes,
Still I see,
But brokenly, but mistily,
Fall and rise,
Rise and fall,
Ghosts of shifting fantasy;
Now the embers, smouldered all,
Sink to ruin; sadder dreams
Follow on their vanished gleams;
Wailingly the spirits call,
Spirits on the night-winds solemn,
Wraiths of happy Hopes that left me;
(Cruel! why did ye depart ?)
Hopes that sleep, their youthful riot
Mergèd in an awful quiet,
With the heavy grief-moulds pressed
On each pallid, pulseless breast,
In that graveyard called THE HEART,
Stern and lone.
Needing no memorial stone,
And no blazoned column:
Let them rest!
Let them rest!
Yes, 't is useless to remember
May-morn in the mirk December;
Still, O Hopes! because ye were
Beautiful, and strong, and fair,
Nobly brave, and sweetly bright,
Who shall dare
Scorn me, if through moistened lashes,
Musing by my hearthstone blighted,
Weary, desolate, benighted, —
I, because those sweet Hopes left me,
I, because my fate bereft me,
Mourn my dead,
Mourn, — and shed
Hot tears in the ashes ?

AN ANNIVERSARY.

O Love, it is our wedding day!
　This morn,—how swift the seasons
　　flee!—
A virgin morn of cloudless May,
　You gave your loyal hand to me,
Your dainty hand, clasped sweet and sure
As Love's sweet self, for evermore!

O Love, it is our wedding-day,
　And memory flies from now to then;
I mark the soft heat-lightning play
　Of blushes o'er your cheek again,
And shy but fond foreshadowings rise
Of tranquil joy in tender eyes.

O Love, it is our wedding-day;
　The very rustling of your dress,
The trembling of your arm that lay
　On mine, with timorous happiness,
Your fluttered breath and faint foot-
　　fall,—
Ah, sweet, I hear, I see them all!

O Love, it is our wedding-day,
　And backward Time's strange current
　　rolls,
Till life's and love's auspicious May
　Once more is blooming in our souls,
And larklike, swell the songs of hope,
Your blissful bridal horoscope.

O Love, it is our wedding-day,—
　Yet say, did those fair hopes but sing,
Lapped in the tuneful morn of May,
　To die or droop on faltering wing,
When noontide heats and evening
　　chills
Made pale the flowers and veiled the
　　hills?

O Love, it is our wedding-day,
　And none of those glad hopes of
　　youth,
Thrilled to its height, outpoured a lay
　To match our future's simple truth:
Though deep the joy of vow and shrine,
Our wedded calm is more divine!

O Love, it is our wedding-day!
　Life's summer, with slow-waning
　　beam,
Tints the near autumn's cloud-land gray
　To softness of a fairy dream,
Whence peace by musing pathos kissed,
Smiles through a veil of golden mist.

O Love, it is our wedding-day;
　The conscious winds are whispering
　　low
Those passionate secrets of the May
　Fraught with your kisses long ago;
Warm memories of our years remote
Are trembling in the mock-bird's throat.

O Love, it is our wedding-day,—
　And not a thrush in woodland bowers,
And not a rivulet's silvery lay,
　Nor tiny bee-song 'mid the flowers,
Nor any voice of land or sea,
But deepens love to ecstasy!

Our wedding-day! The soul's noontide!
　In these rare words at watchful rest
What sweet, melodious meanings hide
　Like birds within one balmy nest,
Each quivering with an impulse strong
To flood all heaven and earth with song!

———◇———

FROM THE WOODS.

Why should I, with a mournful, mor-
　　bid spleen,
Lament that here, in this half-desert
　　scene,
　My lot is placed?
At least the poet-winds are bold and
　　loud,—
At least the sunset glorifies the cloud,
　And forests old and proud
Rustle their verdurous banners o'er the
　　waste.

Perchance 'tis best that I, whose Fate's
　　eclipse
Seems final,—I, whose sluggish life-
　　wave slips
　Languid away,—

Should here, within these lowly walks,
  apart
From the fierce throbbings of the pop-
  ulous mart,
    Commune with mine own heart,
While Wisdom blooms from buried
  Hope's decay.

Nature, though wild her forms, sus-
  tains me still;
The founts are musical, — the barren
  hill
    Glows with strange lights;
Through solemn pine-groves the small
  rivulets fleet
Sparkling, as if a Naiad's silvery feet
    In quick and coy retreat,
Glanced through the star-gleams on calm
  summer nights;

And the great sky, the royal heaven
  above,
Darkens with storms or melts with
  hues of love;
    While far remote,
Just where the sunlight smites the
  woods with fire,
Wakens the multitudinous sylvan
  choir;
    Their innocent love's desire
Poured in a rill of song from each har-
  monious throat.

My walls are crumbling, but immortal
  looks
Smile on me here from faces of rare
  books:
    Shakspeare consoles
My heart with true philosophies; a
  balm
Of spiritual dews from humbler song
  or psalm
    Fills me with tender calm,
Or through hushed heavens of soul Mil-
  ton's deep thunder rolls!

And more than all, o'er shattered
  wrecks of Fate,
The relics of a happier time and state,
    My nobler life

Shines on unquenched! O deathless
  love that lies
In the clear midnight of those passion-
  ate eyes!
    Joy waneth! Fortune flies!
What then? Thou still art here, soul of
  my soul, my Wife!

DOLCE FAR NIENTE.

LET the world roll blindly on!
Give me shadow, give me sun,
And a perfumed eve as this is:
    Let me lie,
      Dreamfully,
When the last quick sunbeams shiver
Spears of light athwart the river,
And a breeze, which seems the sigh
Of a fairy floating by,
    Coyly kisses
Tender leaf and feathered grasses;
Yet so soft its breathing passes,
These tall ferns, just glimmering o'er me,
Blending goldenly before me,
    Hardly quiver!

I have done with worldly scheming,
Mocking show and hollow seeming!
    Let me lie
      Idly here,
Lapped in lulling waves of air,
Facing full the shadowy sky.
Fame! — the very sound is dreary, —
Shut, O soul! thine eyelids weary,
For all nature's voices say,
"'Tis the close — the close of day,
Thought and grief have had their sway:"
Now Sleep bares her balmy breast, —
    Whispering low
(Low as moon-set tides that flow
Up still beaches far away;
While, from out the lucid West,
Flutelike winds of murmurous breath
Sink to tender-panting death),
" On my bosom take thy rest;
(Care and grief have had their day!)
'Tis the hour for dreaming,
Fragrant rest, elysian dreaming!"

CAMBYSES AND THE MACROBIAN BOW.

ONE morn, hard by a slumberous stream-
　　let's wave,
The plane-trees stirless in the unbreath-
　　ing calm,
And all the lush-red roses drooped in
　　dream,
Lay King Cambyses, idle as a cloud
That waits the wind,—aimless of thought
　　and will, —
But with vague evil, like the lightning's
　　bolt
Ere yet the electric death be forged to
　　smite,
Seething at heart.　His courtiers ringed
　　him round,
Whereof was one who to his comrades'
　　ears,
With bated breath and wonder-archèd
　　brows,
Extolled a certain Bactrian's matchless
　　skill
Displayed in bowcraft: at whose mar-
　　vellous feats,
Eagerly vaunted, the King's soul grew
　　hot
With envy, for himself erewhile had been
Rated the mightiest archer in his realm.
Slowly he rose, and pointing southward,
　　said,
"Seest thou, Prexaspes, yonder slender
　　palm,
A mere wan shadow, quivering in the
　　light,
Topped by a ghastly leaf-crown? Pri-
　　thee, now,
Can this, thy famous Bactrian, standing
　　here,
Cleave with his shaft a hand's breadth
　　marked thereon?"
To which Prexaspes answered, "Nay,
　　my lord;
I spake of feats compassed by mortal
　　skill,
Not of gods' prowess." Unto whom,
　　the King:—
"And if myself, Prexaspes, made essay,

Think'st thou, wise counsellor, I too
　　should fail?"
"Needs must I, sire," —albeit the court-
　　ier's voice
Trembled, and some dark prescience
　　bade him pause, —
"Needs must I hold such cunning more
　　than man's;
And for the rest, I pray thy pardon,
　　King,·
But yester-eve, amid the feast and dance,
Thou tarried'st with the beakers over-
　　long."

The thick, wild, treacherous eyebrows of
　　the King,
That looked a sheltering ambush for ill
　　thoughts
Waxing to manhood of malignant acts,
These treacherous eyebrows, pent-house
　　fashion, closed
O'er the black orbits of his fiery eyes, —
Which, clouded thus, but flashed a dead-
　　lier gleam
On all before him: suddenly as fire,
Half choked and smouldering in its own
　　dense smoke,
Bursts into roaring radiance and swift
　　flame,
Touched by keen breaths of liberating
　　wind, —
So now Cambyses' eyes a stormy joy
Stormily filled; for on Prexaspes' son,
His first-born son, they lingered, — a fair
　　boy
('Midmost his fellow-pages flushed with
　　sport),
Who, in his office of King's cupbearer,
So gracious and so sweet were all his
　　ways,
Had even the captious sovereign seemed
　　to please;
While for the court, the reckless, revel-
　　ling court,
They loved him one and all:
"Go," said Cambyses now, his voice a
　　hiss,
Poisonous and low, "go, bind my dainty
　　page

To yonder palm-tree; bind him fast and
    sure,
So that no finger stirreth; which being
    done,
Fetch me, Prexaspes, the Macrobian
    bow."

Thus ordered, thus accomplished, fast
    they bound
The innocent child, the while that mam-
    moth bow,
Brought by the spies from Ethiopian
    camps,
Lay in the King's hand; slowly, sternly
    up,
He reared it to the level of his sight,
Reared, and bent back its oaken massive-
    ness
Till the vast muscles, tough as grape-
    vines, bulged
From naked arm and shoulder, and the
    horns
Of the fierce weapon groaning, almost
    met,
When, with one lowering glance askance
    at him, —
His doubting satrap, — the King coolly
    said,
"Prexaspes, look, my aim is at the
    heart!"

Then came the sharp twang and the
    deadly whirr
Of the loosed arrow, followed by the dull,
Drear echo of a bolt that smites its mark;
And those of keenest vision shook to
    see
The fair child fallen forward across his
    bonds,
With all his limbs a-quivering. Quoth
    the King,
Clapping Prexaspes' shoulder, as in glee,
"Go thou, and tell me how that shaft
    hath sped!"
Forward the wretched father, step by
    step,
Crept, as one creeps whom black Hadèan
    dreams,
Visions of fate and fear unutterable,

Draw, tranced and rigid, towards some
    definite goal
Of horror; thus he went, and thus he
    saw
What never in the noontide or the night,
Awake or sleeping, idle or in toil,
'Neath the wild forest or the perfumed
    lamps
Of palaces, shall leave his stricken sight
Unblasted, or his spirit purged of woe.

Prexaspes saw, yet lived; saw, and re-
    turned
Where still environed by his dissolute
    court,
Cambyses leaned, half scornful, on his
    bow:
The old man's face was riven and white
    as death;
But making meek obeisance to his King,
He smiled (ah, *such* a smile!) and feebly
    said,
"What *am* I, mighty master, what am *I*,
That I durst question my lord's strength
    and skill ?
His arrows are like arrows of the god,
Egyptian Horus, — and for proof, — but
    now,
I felt a child's heart (once a child was
    mine,
'Tis my Lord's now and Death's), all
    mute and still,
Pierced by his shaft, and cloven, ye
    gods! in twain!"

Then laughed the great King loudly, till
    his beard
Quivered, and all his stalwart body
    shook
With merriment; but when his mirth
    was calmed,
"Thou art forgiven," said he, "forgiv-
    en, old man;
Only when next these Persian dogs shall
    call
Cambyses drunkard, rise, Prexaspes,
    rise!
And tell them how, and to what purpose,
    once,

Once, on a morn which followed hot and
　　wan
A night of monstrous revel and de-
　　bauch,
Cambyses bent this huge Macrobian
　　bow.''

---◇---

BY THE AUTUMN SEA.

FAIR as the dawn of the fairest day,
Sad as the evening's tender gray,
By the latest lustre of sunset kissed,
That wavers and wanes through an am-
　　ber mist,
There cometh a dream of the past to me,
On the desert sands, by the autumn sea.

All heaven is wrapped in a mystic veil,
And the face of the ocean is dim and
　　pale,
And there rises a wind from the chill
　　northwest,
That seemeth the wail of a soul's unrest,
As the twilight falls, and the vapors
　　flee
Far over the wastes of the autumn sea.

A single ship through the gloaming
　　glides
Upborne on the swell of the seaward
　　tides;
And above the gleam of her topmost
　　spar
Are the virgin eyes of the vesper-star
That shine with an angel's ruth on me,
A hopeless waif, by the autumn sea.

The wings of the ghostly beach-birds
　　gleam
Through the shimmering surf, and the
　　curlew's scream
Falls faintly shrill from the darkening
　　height;
The first weird sigh on the lips of Night
Breathes low through the sedge and the
　　blasted tree,
With a murmur of doom, by the autumn
　　sea.

Oh, sky-enshadowed and yearning main,
Your gloom but deepens this *human*
　　pain;
Those waves seem big with a nameless
　　care,
That sky is a type of the heart's despair,
As I linger and muse by the sombre lea,
And the night shades close on the au-
　　tumn sea.

---◇---

THE WIFE OF BRITTANY.

[Suggested by the Frankeleine's Tale of
　　Chaucer.]

PROEM.

TRUTH wed to beauty in an antique
　　tale,
Sweet-voiced like some immortal night-
　　ingale,
Trills the clear burden of her passsionate
　　lay,
As fresh, as fair as wonderful to-day
As when the music of her balmy tongue
Ravished the first warm hearts for whom
　　she sung.

Thus, when the early spring-dawn buds
　　are green,
Glistening beneath the sudden silvery
　　sheen
Of glancing showers; while heaven with
　　bridegroom-kiss
Wakens the virgin earth to bloom and
　　bliss,
Enamored breathing and soft raptures
　　born
About the roseate footsteps of the morn,
An old-world song, whose breezy music
　　pours
Through limpid channels 'twixt en-
　　chanted shores,
Steals on me wooingly from that far
　　time
When tuneful Chaucer wrought his
　　lusty rhyme
Into rare shapes and fancies and delight,
For May winds blithely blew, and haw-
　　thorn flowers were bright.

"There cometh a dream of the past to me,
On the desert sands by the autumn sea."

O brave old poet! genius frank and
   bold!
Sustain me, cherish and around me
   fold
Thine own hale, sun-warm atmosphere
   of song,
Lest I, who touch thy numbers, do thee
   wrong;
Speed the deep measure, make the mean-
   ing shine
Ruddy and high with healthful spirit
   wine,
Till to attempered sense and quickening
   ears
My strain some faint harmonious echo
   bears
From that rich realm wherein thy cor-
   dial art
Throbbed with its pulse of fire 'gainst
   youthful England's heart.

THE STORY.

WHERE the hoarse billows of the north-
   land Sea
Sweep the rude coast of rockbound Brit-
   tany,
Dwelt, ages since, a knight whose war-
   rior-fame
Might well have struck all carpet-knights
   with shame;
Vowed to great deeds and princely man-
   hood, he
Burgeoned the topmost-flower of chiv-
   alry;
Yet gentle-hearted, nursed one delicate
   thought
Fixed firm in love: with anxious pain he
   sought
To serve his lady in the noblest wise,
And many a labor, many a grand em-
   prise
He wrought ere that sweet lady could be
   won.
She was a maiden bright-aired as the
   sun,
And graceful as the tall lake-lilies are
Flushed 'twixt the twilight and the ves-
   per-star;.

But born to such rare state and sover-
   eignty,
He hardly durst before her bend the
   knee
In passion's ardor and keen heart dis-
   tress;
Still, at the last, his loyal worthiness
And mild obeisance, his observance
   high
Of manly faith, firm will, and constancy
Aroused an answering pity to his
   sighs,
Till pity, grown to love, beamed forth
   from genial eyes.

Thus with pure trust, and cheerful calm
   accord,
She made this gentle suitor her soul's
   lord;
And he, that thence their happy fates
   should stray
Through pastures beauteous as the fields
   of May,
Swore of his own free mind to use the
   right
Her mercy gave him, with no churlish
   might,
Nor e'er in wanton freaks of mastery,
Ire-bred perverseness, or sharp jeal-
   ousy,
Vex the clear-flowing current of her
   days.
She thanked him in a hundred winning
   ways:
" And I," she said, " will be thy loyal
   wife;
Take here my vows, my solemn troth
   for life. "

On a June morning, when'the verdurous
   woods
Flushed to the core of dew-lit solitudes,
Murmured almost as with a human
   feeling,
Tenderly, low, to frolic breezes stealing
Through dappled shades and depths of
   dainty fern,
Crushed here and there by some low-
   whimpering burn,

These twain were wedded at a forest
　　shrine.
O saffron-vested Hymen the divine!
Did aught of gloom or boding shadow
　　weigh
Upon thy blushing consciousness that
　　day ?
No! thy frank face breathed only hope
　　and love;
Earth laughed in wave and leaf, all
　　heaven was fair above.

Home to the land wherein the knight
　　was born
Blithely they rode upon the morrow-
　　morn,
Not far from Penmark; there they lived
　　in ease
And solace of matured felicities,
Until Arviragus whose soul of fire
Not even fruition of his love's desire
Could fill with languorous idlesse, cut
　　the tie,
Which bound to silken dalliance sud-
　　denly,
Sailing the straits for England's war-
　　torn strand,
There ampler bays to pluck from vic-
　　tory's " red right hand. "

But Iolene, fond Iolene, whose heart
Can beat no longer, lonely and apart
From him she loves, save with a sicken-
　　ing stress
Of fear o'erwrought and brooding ten-
　　derness,
Mourns for his absence with soul-weary-
　　ing plaint,
Slow, pitiful tears and midnight mur-
　　murings faint,
And thus the whole world sadly sets at
　　naught.
Meanwhile her friends, who guess what
　　canker-thought
Preys on her quiet, with a mild essay
Strive to subdue her passion's torturing
　　sway:
" Beware! beware, sweet lady, thou wilt
　　slay

Thy reason! nay thy very life's at stake!
By love, and love's dear pleadings, for
　　his sake
Who yearns to clasp thee scathless to
　　his breast,
We pray thee, soothe these maddening
　　cares to rest!' '

Even as the patient graver on a stone,
Laboring with tireless fingers, sees anon
The shape embodying his rare fancies
　　grow
And lighten, thus upon her stubborn woe
Their tireless comforts wrought, until a
　　trust,
Clear-eyed and constant, raised her
　　from the dust
And ashy shroud of sorrow; her despair
Gave place to twilight gladness and soft
　　cheer
Confirmed ere long by letters from her
　　love:
" Dear Iolene! " he wrote, " thou tender
　　dove
That tremblest in thy chilly nest at
　　home,
Prithee embrace meek patience till I
　　come.
Lo, the swift winds blow freshening o'er
　　the sea,
From out the sunset isles I speed to rest
　　with thee!' '

The knight's ancestral home stood grim
　　and tall
Beyond its shadowy moat and frowning
　　wall;
It topped a gradual summit crowned
　　with fir,
Green murmurous myrtle, and wild
　　juniper,
Fronting a long, rude, solitary strand,
Whereon the earliest sunbeam, like a
　　hand
Of tremulous benediction, rested bland,
And warmly quivering; o'er the wave-
　　worn lea
Gleamed the broad spaces of the open
　　sea.

Now often, with her pitying friends
    beside,
She walked the desolate beach and
    watched the tide,
Forth looking through unconscious tears
    to view
Sail after sail pass shimmering o'er the
    blue;
And to herself, ofttimes, "Alas!" said
    she,
" Is there no ship, of all these ships I see,
Will bring me home my lord ? Woe, woe
    is me!
Though winds blow fresh, and sea-birds
    skim the main,
Thou still delay'st, my liege! Ah, *wilt*
    thou come again ? "

Sometimes would she, half-dreaming, sit
    and think,
Casting her dark eyes downward from
    the brink;
And when she saw those grisly rocks
    beneath,
Round which the pallid foam, in many
    a wreath
White as the lips of passion, faintly
    curled,
Her thoughts would pierce to the drear
    under-world,
'Mid shipwrecks wandering, and
    bleached bones of those
O'er whom the unresting ocean ebbs and
    flows;
And though the shining waters hushed
    and deep,
Might slumber like an innocent child
    asleep,
From out the North her prescient fancy
    raised
Huge ghostlike clouds, and spectral
    lightnings blazed
I' th' van of phantom thunder, and the
    roar
Of multitudinous waters on the shore,
Heard as in dreadful trance its billowy
    swells
Blent with the mournful tone of far
    funereal bells!

Her friends perceiving that this seaside
    walk,
Though gay and jovial their unstudied
    talk,
But dashed her dubious spirits, kindly
    took
And led her where the blossom-bordered
    brook
Babbled through woodlands, and the
    limpid pool
Lay crouched like some shy Naiad in
    the cool
Of mossy glades; or when a tedious
    hour
Pressed on her with its dim, lethargic
    power,
They wooed her with glad games or
    jocund song,
Till the dull demon ceased to do her
    wrong.

So, on a pleasant May morn, while the
    dew
Sparkled on tiny hedgerow-flowers of
    blue,
Passing through many a sun-brown orch-
    ard-field,
They reach a fairy pleasaunce, which
    revealed
Such prospects into breezy inland
    vales,
The natural haunt of plaining nightin-
    gales,
Such verdant, grassy plots, through
    which there rolled
A gleeful rivulet glimpsing sands of
    gold,
And winding slow by clumps of plumèd
    pines,
Rich realms of bay, and gorgeous jas-
    mine-vines,
That none who strayed to that fair
    flowery place
Had paused in wonder if its sylvan
    grace,
Embodied, beauteous, with an arch em-
    brace
Had stopped, and smiling, kissed them
    face to face.

A buoyant, blithesome company were
    they,
Grouped round the pleasaunce on that
    morn of May;
Wit, song, and rippling laughter, and
    arch looks
That might have lured the wood-gods
    from their nooks,
Echoed and flashed like dazzling arrows
    tipped
With amorous heat; and now and then
    there slipped
From out the whirling ring of jocund
    girls,
Wreathing white arms and tossing wan-
    ton curls,
Some maiden who with momentary mien
Of coy demureness bent o'er Iolene,
And whispered sunniest nothings in her
    ear.

First 'mid the brave gallants assembling
    there
Aurelian came, a squire of fair degree,
Tall, vigorous, handsome, his whole air
    so free,
Yet courteous, and such princely sweet-
    ness blent
With every well-timed, graceful compli-
    ment,
That sooth to speak, where'er Aurelian
    went,
To turbulent tilt-yard and baronial hall,
Sporting afield or at high festival,
Favor, like sunshine, filled his heart and
    eyes.

Thus nobly gifted, high-born, opulent,
    wise,
One hidden curse was his: for troublous
    years,*
Secretly, swayed in turn by hopes and
    fears,

* We are to suppose that Aurelian had seen
Iolene previous to her marriage, and that cir-
cumstances had prevented his becoming inti-
mate with her, or in any way prosecuting his
suit honestly and frankly.

And all unknown to her, his heart's
    desire,
This youth had loved with wild, deliri-
    ous fire,
The lonely, sad, unconscious Iolene.
He durst not show how love had brought
    him teen,
Nor prove how deep his passion's inward
    might;
Thinking, half maddened, on her absent
    knight;
Save that the burden of a love-lorn
    lay
Would somewhat of his stifled flame
    betray,
But in those vague complainings poets
    use,
When charging Love with outrage and
    abuse
Of his all-potent witchery. "Ah," said
    he,
"I love, but ever love despondently;
For though one vision haunts me, and I
    burn
To hold that dream incarnated, I yearn
In vain, in vain; love breathes no bland
    return!"

Thus only did Aurelian strive to show
What pangs of hidden passion worked
    below
The surface calmness of his front serene;
Unless perhaps he met his beauteous
    Queen,
Scarce brightening at the banquet or the
    dance;
When, with a piercing yet half-piteous
    glance,
His eyes would search, then strangely
    shun her face,
As one condemned, who fears to sue for
    grace.

But on this self-same day, when home-
    ward bound,
Her footsteps sought the loneliest path
    that wound
Through tangled copses to the upland
    ground

And orchard close, — her fair compan-
    ions kissed
With tearful thanks, and all kind friends
    dismissed, —
Aurelian, who the secret pathway knew,
Through the dense growth and shrouded
    foliage drew
Near the pale Queen, the lady of his
    dreams:
The evening's soft, pathetic splendor
    streams
O'er her clear forehead and her chestnut
    hair,
All glorified as in celestial air;
But the dark eyes a wistful light con-
    fessed,
And some soft murmuring fancies heaved
    her breast
Benignly, like enamored tides that rise
And sink melodious to the west wind's
    sighs.

He gazed, and the long passion he had
    nursed,
Impetuous, sudden, unrestrained, o'er-
    burst
All bounds of custom and enforced re-
    straint:
"O lady, hear me: I am deadly faint,
Yet wild with love! such love as forces
    man
To beard conventions, trample on the
    ban
Of partial laws, spurn with contemptuous
    hate
Whate'er would bar or blight his bliss-
    ful fate,
And in the feverous frenzy of his zeal,
Even from the shrinking flower he dotes
    on, steal
Blush, fragrance, and heart-dew! For-
    give! forgive!
What! have I dared to tell thee this, to
    live
For aye hereafter in thy cold regard?
Yet veil thy scorn; nor make more cold
    and hard
The anguished life now cowering at thy
    feet."

As o'er a billowy field of ripened wheat
One sees perchance the spectral shadows
    meet,
Cast by a darkened heaven whose lower-
    ing hush
Broods, thunder-charged, above its gold-
    en flush, —
So, a dark wonder, a sublime suspense,
Of gathering wrath at this wild inso-
    lence,
Dimmed the mild glory of her brow and
    lips;
Her beauty, more majestic in eclipse,
Shone with that awful lustre which of
    old,
In the gods' temples and the fanes of
    gold,
Blazed in the Pythia's face, and shook
    her form
With throes of baleful prophecy; a
    storm
She stood incarnate, in whose ominous
    gloom
Throbbed the red lightning on the verge
    of doom.

But as a current of soft air, unfelt
On the lower earth, is seen ere long to
    melt
The up-piled surge of tempests slowly
    driven
In scattered vapors through the deeps of
    heaven,
Thus a serener thought tenderly played
Across her spirit; its portentous shade,
Big with unuttered wrath and meanings
    dire,
Began with slow, wan pulsings to expire;
A far ethereal voice she seemed to
    hear
Luting its merciful accents in her ear,
Subtly harmonious: "Yea," she thought,
    "in truth,
A rage, a madness holds him, the poor
    youth
Is drunk with passion! Shall I, deeply
    blessed
By all love's sweets, its balm and trustful
    rest.

Crush the less fortunate spirit! utterly
Blight and destroy him, *all for love of
me?*
His hopes, if hopes he hath, must surely
die;
Still would I nip their blossoms tenderly,
With a slight, airy frost-bite of con-
tempt.
God's mercy, good Sir Squire, art thou
exempt
Of courtesy as of reason? What weird
spell
Doth work this madness in thee and
compel
Thy nobler nature to such base de-
spites?
Forsooth, thou'lt blush some day the
flower of knights,
Should this thy budding virtue wax and
grow
To natural consummation! Come! thy
flow
Of weak self-ruth might shame the veri-
est child,
A six years' peevish urchin; whimpering
wild,
And scattering his torn locks, because
afar
He sees and yearns to clasp, but cannot
clasp, a star!"

She ceased, with shame and pity weigh-
ing down
Her dovelike lids demurely, and a
frown
Just struggling faintly with as faint a
smile
(For the mute trembling squire still
knelt the while)
Round the arch dimples of her rosy
mouth;
Whereon, in fitful fashion, like the
South
Which sweeps with petulant wing a field
of blooms,
Then dies a heedless death 'mong gold-
en brooms
And lavish shrubbery, briefly she re-
sumes,

With quick-drawn breath, the courses
of her speech:
"Aurelian, rise! Behold'st thou yon-
der beach,
And the blue waves beyond? those
bristling rocks,
O'er which the chafed sea, in quick thun-
der-shocks,
Leaps passionate, panting through the
showery spray,
Roaring defiance to the calm-eyed day?
Ah, well, fantastic boy! I blithely
swear
When yon rude coast beneath us rises
clear
(Down to the farthest bounds of wild
Bretaigne),
Of that black rampart darkening sky
and main,
I'll pay thy vows with answering vows
again,
And be — God save the mark! — thy
paramour."

Her words struck keen and deep, even
to the core
Of the rash listener's soul; they seemed
to be
More fatal in their careless irony
Than if the levin bolt, hurled from
above,
Had slain at once his manhood and his
love.
What more he felt in sooth 'twere vain
to tell;
He only heard her whispering, "Fare-
thee-well,
And Heaven assoil thee of all sinful sor-
row!"
Then with a grace and majesty which
borrow
Fresh lustrous sweetness from an inward
stress
And hidden motion of chaste gentle-
ness,
She glideth like some beauteous cloud
apart;
Aurelian saw her pass with yearning
pangs at heart.

PART II.

Soul-epochs are there, when grief's piti-
less storm
O'erwhelms the amazèd spirit; when the
warm
Exultant heart whose hopes were brave
and high,
Shrinks in the darkness withering all
its sky:

Then, like a wounded bird by the rude
wind
Clutched and borne onward, tortured,
reckless, blind,
Too frail to struggle with that passion-
ate blast,
We take wild, wavering courses, and at
last
Are dashed, it may be, on the rocky
verge,

"Those bristling rocks,
O'er which the chafed sea, in quick thunder-shocks,
Leaps passionate, panting through the showery spray."

Or hurled o'er the unknown and perilous
surge
Of some dark doom, when, bruised and
tempest-tost,
We sink in turbulent eddies, and are
lost.

Urged by a mood thus desperate, care-
less what
Thenceforth befell him, from that hate-
ful spot,
The scene of such stern anguish and de-
spair,
Aurelian rushed, he knew not, recked
not, where.

All night he wandered in the forest drear,
Till on the pale phantasmal front of morn
The first thin flickering day-gleam
glanced forlorn,
Wan as the wraith of perished hopes,
the ghost
Of wishes long sustained and fostered
most,
Now gone for evermore. "O Christ!
that I,"
He muttered hoarsely, "might unsought
for lie
Here, in the dismal shadows and dank
grass,
And close my heavy eyelids, and so pass

With one brief struggle from the world
  of men,
Never to grieve or languish, — never
  again!
Never to sow live seeds of expectation
And joyous promise, to reap desolation;
But as the seasons fly, snow-wreathed, or
  crowned
With odorous garlands, rest in the mute
  ground,
Peaceful, oblivious, — a Lethéan cloud
Wrapped round my faded senses like a
  shroud,
And all earth's turmoil and its juggling
  show
Dead as a dream dissolved ten thousand
  years ago!"

Long, long revolving his sad thoughts he
  stood,
When gleefully from out the lightening
  wood
Came the sharp ring of horn and echoing
  steed;
A score of huntsmen, scouring at full
  speed,
Flashed like a brilliant meteor o'er the
  scene,
In royal pomp of glimmering gold and
  green;
Whereat, with wrathful gestures, 'neath
  the dome
Of the old wood he hastened towards his
  home,
Where day by day he grew more woeful-
  pale,
Calling on Heaven unheard to ease his
  bale.

Among his kinsfolk, many in hot haste,
To salve an unknown wound with balms
  misplaced,
Came the squire's brother, Curio, — a
  wise scribe,
Modest withal, and nobler than his tribe;
With heart as loving as his brain was
  wise:
He could not see with cold, indifferent
  eyes

Aurelian pass to madness or the grave,
While care and wit of man perchance
  might save;
So, pondering o'er what seemed a des-
  perate case,
At length there leapt into his kindling
  face
The flush of a bright thought.   "By
  Heaven!" cried he,
"O brother, there may still be hope for
  thee;
Therefore, take heart of grace, for what
  I tell
Doubtless preludes a health-inspiring
  spell;
And thou, released from this long, sor-
  rowful blight,
Shalt feel the stir of joy, and bless the
  morning light.

"Ten years — ten centuries sometimes
  they would seem —
Passed idly o'er me like a mystic's
  dream;
Ten years agone, when these dull locks
  of mine
Flowed round broad shoulders with a
  perfumed shine,
And life's clear glass o'erbrimmed with
  purpling wine,
I met in Orleans a shrewd clerk-at-law,
One all his comrades loved, yet viewed
  with awe,
To whom the deepest lore of antique
  ages,
The storèd secrets of old seers and
  sages
In Greece, or Ind, or Araby, lay
  bare;
From out the vacant kingdoms of the
  air,
He could at will call forth a hundred
  forms,
Hideous or lovely; the wild wrath of
  storms;
The zephyr's sweetness; bird, beast,
  wave, obeyed
The luminous signs his slender wand
  conveyed,

At whose weird touch men sick in flesh
or brain
Became their old, bright, hopeful selves
again.
Aurelian, rise! shake off this vile disease,
And ride with me to Orleans; an' it
please
God and our Lady, we may chance to
meet
Mine ancient comrade, who with deftest
feat
Of magic skill may cut the Gordian knot
That long hath bound, and darkly binds
thy lot.''

"But," said Aurelian, with a listless
turn
Of his drooped head, and wandering
eyes that burn
With a quick feverish brilliance, "dost
thou speak
Of thine own knowledge, when thou
bid'st me seek
This rare magician? Hast *thou* looked
on aught
Of all the mighty marvels he hath
wrought?"

"Yea! I bethink me how, one summer's
day,
He led me through the city gates, away
To the dark hollows 'neath a lonely hill:
So hushed the noontide, and so breath-
less-still
The drowsy air, the voice of one far
stream
Came like thin whispers murmuring in
a dream;
The blithesome grasshopper, his sense
half closed
To all his verdurous luxury, reposed
Pendent upon the quivering, spearlike
grain;
Steeped in the mellow sunshine's noise-
less rain,
All Nature slept; alone the matron
wren,
From the thick coverts of her thorny
den,

Teased the hot silence with her twitter-
ing low:
My inmost soul accordant, seemed to
grow
Languid and dumb within that mystic
place.
At length the Wizard's hand across my
face
Was waved with gentle motion; a vague
mist
Flickered before me, on a sudden kissed
To warmth and glory by an influence
bright;
The strangest glamour hovered o'er my
sight,
Wherethrough I saw, methought, a
palace proud,
Crowned by a lightning-veinèd thunder-
cloud,
Whose wreaths of vapory darkness
gleamed with eyes
Of multitudinous shifting fantasies;
Its pinnacles like diamond spars out-
shone
The starry splendors of an orient
zone;
And, leading towards its lordly entrance,
rose
Through slow gradations to its marbled
close,
White terraces where golden sunflowers
bloomed;
Above a ponderous portal archway
loomed,
High-columned, quaint, majestical: we
passed
Within that palace, gorgeous, wild, and
vast.
Ah! blessed saints! what wonders weirdly
blent
Did smite me with a hushed astonish-
ment!
A troop of monsters couchant lined our
path,
Their tawny manes and eyes of fiery
wrath
Erect and blazing; an unearthly roar
Of fury, shaking vaulted roof and
floor,

Burst from each savage, inarticulate
   throat,
In sullen echoings lost through halls and
   courts remote.

"At the far end of glimmering colon-
   nades
That gleamed gigantic through the dusky
   shades,
Two mighty doors swept backward noise-
   lessly;
There heaved beyond us a vast laboring
   sea;
Not vacant, for a stately vessel bore
Swift down the threatening tides that
   flashed before,
Thronged with black-bearded Titans,
   such as moved
In far-off times heroic, well-beloved
Of the old gods; there at his stalwart
   ease,
Shouldering his knotted club, great Her-
   cules
Towered, his fierce eyes touched to dewy
   light,
And rapt on Hylas, who, serenely bright,
With intense gaze uplifted, tranced and
   mute,
Heard, in ecstatic reverie, the lute
Of Orpheus plaining to the waves that
   bow
And dance subsiding round the blazoned
   prow;
Till the rude winds blew meekly, and
   caressed
The mimic golden fleeces o'er the crest
Of bard and warrior, on their secret quest
Bound to the groves of Colchis; and the
   bark,
Round which had frowned a threatening
   shape and dark,
Now seemed to thrill, like some proud,
   sentient thing
That glories in the prowess of its wing.
The gusty billows of that turbulent sea
Their wild crests smoothed, and slowly,
   pantingly,
Sunk to the quiet of a charmèd calm;
What odors Hesperéan, what rich balm

Freight the fair zephyrs, as they shyly
   run
O'er the lulled waters dimpling in the
   sun!
And murmurings, hark! soft as the long-
   drawn kiss
Pressed by a young god-lover in his
   bliss
On lips immortal, when the world was
   new;
And, lo! across the pure, pellucid
   blue,
A barge, with silken sails, whose beaute-
   ous crew,
Winged fays and Cupids, curl their
   sportive arms
O'er one, more lovely in her noontide
   charms
Than youngest nymphs of Paphos; fra-
   grant showers
Of freshening roses, all luxuriant flowers
That feed on eastern dews, their fairy
   bands
Scatter about her from white liberal
   hands;
While o'er the surface of the dazzling
   water,
Dark-eyed, mysterious, many an ocean
   daughter
Flashes a vanishing brightness on her
   way,
Half seen through tiny tinklings of the
   spray;
And music its full heart in airy falls
Outpours, like silvery cascades down the
   walls
Of haunted rocks, and golden cymbals
   ring,
And lutelike measures on voluptuous
   wing
Rise gently to the trancèd heavens, re-
   plying
From azure-tinted deeps in a low pas-
   sionate sighing.

"Then were all climes, all ages, wildly
   blended
On blood-red fields, wherefrom shrill
   shouts ascended

Of naked warriors, huge and swart of
 limb,
Mixed with the mailèd Grecians' omi-
 nous hymn,
Where mighty banners starlike waved
 and shone
'Mid cloven bucklers grandly; and
 anon
Marched the stern Roman phalanx, with
 a ring
And clash of spears, and lusty trum-
 peting,
And steeds that neighed defiance unto
 death,
And all war's dreadful pomp and hot,
 devouring breath.
Last, on a sudden, the whole tumult
 died,
The vision disappeared; pale, leaden-
 eyed,
Bewildered, on the enchanted floor I
 sank;
When next my wakening spirit faintly
 drank
Life's consciousness, within my lonely
 room
I sat, and round me drooped the dreary
 twilight gloom."

Enough, good brother! By the Holy
 Rood
Thy tale is medicinal! the black mood,
Which like a spiritual vulture seized
 and tore
My heart-strings, and imbued its beak
 in gore
Hot from the soul, beneath the golden
 spell
Of sovereign hope hath sought its native
 hell.
Then, ho! for Orleans!" At the word
 he sprung
Light to his feet; it seemed there scarcely
 hung
One trace of his long madness round
 him now,
So blithe his smile, so bright his kind-
 ling brow.
All day they rode till waning afternoon,

Through breezy copses, and the shad-
 owy boon
Of mightier woods, when, as the latest
 glance
Of sunset, like a level burnished lance,
Smote their steel morions, sauntering
 near the town,
With thoughtful mien, robed in his
 scholar's gown,
They met a keen-eyed man, ruddy and
 tall;
O'er his grave vest a beard of wavy
 fall
Flowed like a rushing streamlet, rippling
 down:
" Welcome!" he cried in mellow accents
 deep;
" The stars have warned me, and my
 visioned sleep
Foretold your mission, gentles. Curio,
 what!
Thine ancient, loving comrade quite
 forgot ?
Spur thy dull memory, gossip!"

 " By St. Paul!
The learned clerk, the gracious Artevall,
Or glamour's in it," shouted Curio;
 " yet
Thou look'st as hale, as young, as firmly
 set
In face and form, as if for thee old
 Time
Had stopped his flight. " A lofty glance,
 sublime
And swift as lightning, from the Magi-
 an's eye
Darted some latent meaning grave and
 high.
He spake not, but the twain he gently
 led
Where grassy pathways and fair meads
 were spread,
Skirting the city walls, till near them
 stood,
Fronting the gloomy boskage of a wood,
The wizard's lonely home, I need not
 pause
To tell how magic and the occult laws

Of sciences long dead that sage's
lore
Did in the spectral midnight hours ex-
plore.
Enough, that his strange spells a mar-
vel wrought
Beyond the utmost reach of credulous
thought.
At last he said, "Sir Squire, my task is
o'er;
Go when thou wilt, and view the Breton
shore,
And thou shalt see a wide unwrinkled
strand,
Smooth as thy lovely lady's delicate
hand,
Washed by a sea o'er which the halcyon
West
Broods like a happy heart whose dreams
are dreams of rest."

PART III.

Meanwhile Arviragus, a year before
Returned in honor from the English
shore,
Led with his faithful Iolene that
life
Harmonious, justly balanced, free from
strife,
Which crowns our hopes with a true-
hearted wife.

Ne'er dreamed he, as she laid her happy
head
Close to his heart, what cloud of shame
and dread
Gloomed o'er his placid roof-tree; but
content
To think how nobly his late toils had
spent
Their force beneath Death's gory drip-
ping brow
Through shocks of battle, a fresh laurel
bough
Plucking therefrom to flourish green
and high
About his war-worn temples' majesty,

Gladly from bloodshed, conflicts, and
alarms
Here rested in those white, encircling
arms,
And oft his strong heart thrilled, his
eyes grew dim,
To know, kind heaven! how deep her
love for him.

Thus month on month the cheerful days
went by,
Like carolling birds across an April sky,
A fairy sky undimmed by clouds or
showers.
But on a morning, while her favorite
flowers
Iolene tended, in the garden-walks
Pausing to clip dead leaves and prop the
stalks
Of drooping plants, herself more sweet
and fair
Than any flower, the brightest that
blushed there,
Her lord stole gently on her unaware;
His haughty grace all softened, he bowed
down
To kiss the stray curls of her locks of
brown,
Thick sown with threads of tangled,
glimmering gold:
"At need," he said, "thou canst be
calm and bold;
Therefore, thou wilt not yield to foolish
woe
If duty parts us briefly. Wife, I go
To scourge some banded ruffians who of
late
Assailed our peaceful serfs, and our es-
tate —
Thou knowest it well — northwest of
Penmark town,
Ravished with sword and fire. Thy
lord's renown,
Yea, and thy lord, were soon the scoff of
all,
If in his own fair fief such crimes befall
Unscourged of justice; so, dear love,
adieu!
Nor fear the end of that I have to do."

Thus spake the knight, who forthwith
  raised a shout,
And bade them bring his stalwart war-
  horse out;
When, on the sudden, a steed, tall, jet-
  black,
Led by a groom came whinnying down
  the track,
'Twixt the green myrtle hedges; at a
  bound
He vaulted in the selle; smilingly round
He turned to wave "farewell" with
  mailèd hand,
And then rode blithely down the sunlit
  land.

That evening, at the close of vesper
  prayer,
Wandering along through the still twi-
  light air,
Iolene, somewhat sad and sick in mind,
Met in her homeward pathway, low-re-
  clined
Beneath the blasted branches of an oak,
Aurelian, her wild lover of old days:
She started backward in a wan amaze.
But he, uprising calmly, bowed and
  spoke;
"Ha! thou recall'st me, lady? I had
  deemed
These bitter years which have so scarred
  and seamed
Whate'er of grace I owned in youthful
  prime,
Had razed me from thy memory. See a
  rime
Like that of age hath touched my locks
  to white;
Yet never once, — so help me heaven! —
  by night
Or day, in storm or brightness, hath my
  soul
Veered but a point from thee, its starry
  goal.
A mighty purpose doth itself fulfil,
Wise men have said. Lady! I love thee
  still,
And Love works marvels. Prithee come
  with me,

Ay, quickly come, and thou thyself shalt
  see
I am no falsehood-monger. Yea, come,
  come!"
His words, his sudden passion, smote her
  dumb,
And from her cheeks, those delicate gar-
  dens, wane
The rare twin roses, as when autumn
  rain,
Fatally sharp, sweeps o'er some doomed
  domain
Of matron blooms, and their rich colors
  fade
Like rainbows slowly dying, shade by
  shade,
Unto wan spectres of the flowers that
  were.
With languid head and thoughts of pre-
  scient fear,
Passively following where Aurelian
  guides,
She hears anon the surge and rush of
  tides
On the seashore, and feels the freshen-
  ing spray
Bedew her brow. "Lady, look forth,
  and say
If, to a love unquenched, unquenchable,
Eternal Nature yields not; its strong
  spell
Hath toiled for me, till the rocks rooted
  under
Those heaving waters have been rent
  asunder,
And the wide spaces of the ocean plain,
Down to the farthest bounds of wild
  Bretaigne,
Rise calmly glorious in the day-god's
  beam.
Look, look thy fill! it is no vanishing
  dream:
Lo! now I claim thy promise!"

A keen gleam
Shot its victorious radiance o'er his
  brow.
But she, bewildered, tremulous, shrink-
  ing low,

Her clinched hands pale even to the fin-
ger-tips,
Pressed on her blinded eyes and faltering
lips,
Sued in a voice like wailing wind that
breaks
From aspen coverts over lonely lakes,
In the shut heart of immemorial dells, —
A fitful, sobbing voice, whose anguish
swells,
Burdened with deep upyearning suppli-
cation,
Coldly across his evil exultation.
She pleads for brief delay, with frenzied
pain
Grasping at some dim phantom of the
brain,
Shadowing a vague deliverance. "As
thou wilt,"
He answered slowly. "Well I know the
guilt
Of broken vows can never rest on thee!
Pass by unhurt!" Mutely she turned to
flee,
Nor paused until her chambered privacy
She reached with panting sides, pallid as
death,
And gasping with short, anguished sobs
for breath.
"Caught am I, trapped like a poor flut-
tering bird,
Or dappled youngling from the innocent
herd
Lured to a pitfall! Yet such oath as *this*
Were surely void ? If not, he still shall
miss —
Whate'er betide — his long-expected
bliss!
Better pure-folded arms, and stainless
sleep
Where the gray-drooping willow-
branches weep,
Than meet a fate so hideous! Let me
think!
Others, — pure wives, brave virgins, on
the brink
Of shame and ruin, have struck home
and fled,
To find unending quiet with the dead."

Borne down as by a demon's hand which
pressed
Invisible, but stifling on her breast,
With brain benumbed, yet burning, and
a sense
Of utter, wearied, desperate impotence,
Her forlorn glance around the darkening
room
Roving in helpless search, from out the
gloom
Caught the blue glitter of a half-sheathed
blade,
A small but trenchant steel, whose lustre
played
Balefully bright, and like a serpent's
eye
Fixed on her with malign expectancy,
Drew her perforce towards Death, — that
death which seemed
The sole, stern means through which
her fame redeemed,
Should soar in spiritual beauty o'er the
tomb
Wherein might rest her body's moulder-
ing bloom.

Ah, me! the looks distraught, the
passionate care,
The whole wild scene, its misery and
despair,
Come back like scenes of yesterday.
Half bowed
Her queenly form, and the pent grief
allowed
A moment's freedom shakes her to the
core,
The inmost seat of reason. "All is
o'er,"
She murmurs, as her slender fingers feel
The deadly edge of the cold shimmering
steel.
At once her swift arm flashes to its
height,
While the poised death hangs quivering,
and her sight
Grows dazed and giddy: when from far,
so far
It sounded like the weird voice of a
star,

"He turned to wave 'farewell' with mailèd hand,
And then rode blithely down the sunlit land."

Muffled by distance, yet distinct and
    deep,
About her in the terrible silence creep
Accents that seize as with a bodily
    force
On her white arm suspended, and its
    course
To fatal issues, with arresting will
Hold rigid, till supine it drops and
    still,
Back to its drooping level, and a
    clang
Of the freed steel through all the cham-
    ber rang
Sharply, and something shuddered
    down the air
Like wings of baffled fiends passing in
    fierce despair.

A warning blent of prescient wrath and
    prayer
Those accents seemed, where through a
    palpable dread
Ran coldly shivering. "Pause, pause,
    pause!" they said;
"Bar not thy hopes 'gainst chance of
    happier fate!
The circuit vast which rounds life's dial-
    plate
Hath many lights and shades; its hand
    which lowers
So threatening *now*, may move to
    golden hours,
And thou on this sad time may'st look
    like one
Smiling on mortal woes from some
    unsetting sun."

Motionless, overcome by hushing awe,
She heard the mystic voice, and dreamed
    she saw,
Just o'er the dubious borders of the
    light,
A wavering apparition, scarce more
    bright
Than one faint moon-ray, through the
    misty tears
Of clouded evenings seen on breezeless
    mountain meres.

Mistlike it waned; but in her heart of
    hearts
The solemn counsel sank: with guilty
    starts,
She thought how near, through grief's
    bewildering blight,
How near to death, to death and shame,
    this night
Her reckless soul had strayed. Yet
    short-lived hope
Moved hour by hour through paths of
    narrowing scope,
As, day by day, her term of grace
    passed by,
Like phantom birds across a phantom
    sky;
Her lord still absent, and Aurelian
    bound
(For thus he wrote her) to one weary
    round,
Morn after morn, of pacings to and fro,
Within the wooded garden-walls below
The city's southward portals. "There,"
    said he,
"Each day, and all day long, impatiently
I wait thy will."
         As when in dewy spring,
'Mid the moist herbage closely nestling,
Ofttimes we see the hunted partridge
    cling,
Panting and scared, to the thick-cover-
    ing grass,
The while above her couch doth darkly
    pass
What seemeth the shadow of a giant
    wing,
And she, more lowly, with a cowering
    stoop,
Shivers, expecting the fell, fiery swoop
Of the gaunt hawk, that corsair of the
    breeze,
And feels beforehand his sharp talons
    seize
And rend her tender vitals; so at home,
Iolene, trembling at the stroke to come,
Touched by the lurid shadow of her
    doom,
Lingered; until, upon a sunny dawn,
Her lord returning, gayly up the lawn

Urged his blithe courser, and, dismount-
ing, came
Upon her, warmly glowing, all aflame
With hope and love. But as her dreary
eyes
Were turned on his, a quick, disturbed
surprise
And then a terror, smote him, and the
voice
All jubilant, full-breathed to say, "Re-
joice,
Our foes are slain!" clave stammering
in his throat.
But she, her loose, dishevelled locks
afloat
Round the fair-sloping shoulders, her
hands clasped
About his mailèd knees, brokenly gasped
Her anguish forth, and told her sorrow-
ful tale.
Dizzy and mute, and as the marble
pale
Whereon he leaned, unto the desperate
close
The knight heard all, locked in a cold
repose
More dread than stormiest passion; life
and strength
Seemed slowly ebbing from him, till at
length
His soul, like one that walks the fatal
sand
(Whose treacherous smoothness looks a
solid strand,
But tempts to ruin), felt all earth grow
dim,
And round him saw, as in a chaos,
swim
Joy's fair horizon melting in the
cloud.
But soon his stalwart will, rugged and
proud,
Woke lionlike to action; a swift flush
Rushed like a sunset river's reddening
glow
O'er the tempestuous blackness of his
brow,
Pregnant with thunder; through the dis-
mal hush,

His pitiless voice, sharp-echoing round
about
The clanging court, leaped like a falchion
out.

" Thou hast played with honor as a jug-
gler's ball;
God strikes thee from thy balance, and
the thrall
Art thou, henceforth, of one vainglorious
deed.
What! shall we plant with rash caprice
the seed
Of bitterness, nor look for some harsh
fruit
To spring untimely from its poisonous
root?
What! a lewd spark, a perfumed pop-
injay,
Dares in the broad-browed, honest gaze
of day,
To dash a foul thought, like the hideous
spray
Of Hell, right in thy forehead, — and
thy hand,
Which should have towered as if the
levin-brand
Of scorn and judgment armed it, but a
bland
Dismissal signs him! not one hint which
tells
Thy lord, meantime, what loathsome
secret dwells
Here, by his hearthstone, muffled up,
concealed,
And like a corse corrupting, till, revealed
By vengeful doom, its pestilent odor
steals
Outward, while all the wholesome blood
congeals
To a chill horror, and the air grows vile,
And even the blessed sun a death's-head
smile
Assumes in our distempered fantasy?
By Heaven! this withering curse which
hangs o'er thee,
O Iolene!" — but here his angry voice
Broke short, — " There is no choice," he
moaned, " no choice."

Yea, wife! may Christ adjudge me if I
    lie,
To endless, as now keen calamity,
But through this troublous gloom my
    mind discerns
One lonely light to guide us; lo, it burns
Lurid, yet clear, by whose fierce flame I
    see —
Ah, grief malign! ah, bitter destiny! —
As if God's own right hand the blazing
    pain
And fiery bale did stamp on soul and
    brain,
These terms of doom:
    Shame and despair for both,
Sorrow and heartbreak! Through all,
    keep thine oath,
Thou woman, self-involved, self-lost;
    and so
Face the black front of this tremendous
    woe!"

She bowed as if a blast of sudden wind,
Breathing full winter, smote her cold
    and blind;
Then as one wandering in a soul-eclipse,
Feebly she rose, and with her quivering
    lips
Kissed her pale lord, stifling one desolate
    cry.
Anon she moved around him noiselessly
Bent on the small, sweet offices of love;
And sometimes pausing, she would
    glance above
With tearless eyes, for solemn griefs like
    this,
Blighting at once both root and flowers
    of bliss,
Are arid as the desert, and in vain
Thirst for the cooling freshness of the
    rain,
Fitfully led from treasured nook to
    nook
Of her dear home, she walked with far-
    off look,
And absent fingers, plying household
    tasks:
Bravely her sunless wretchedness she
    masks

Through moments deemed unending
    while they passed —
When passed, a flickering point! Hark!
    The doomed hour at last!

. . . . .

An afternoon it was, stirless and calm:
From field and garden-close rare breaths
    of balm
Made the air moist and odorous. Nature
    lay
Divinely peaceful; only far away
In the broad zenith, a strange cloud
    unfurled
Its boding banner weirdly o'er the world;
Whilst Iolene, her veiled head sadly
    bowed,
Passed through the gay thorpe and its
    motley crowd,
To where a great wall towered this side
    a wood.
All things her mazed, chaotic fancy
    viewed
Looked dreamlike; even Aurelian lin-
    gering there,
To meet her in the shadiest forest-lair,
Gleamed ghostly dim, a dreadful ghost
    in sooth, —
For still a hideous trance appeared to
    press
Upon her and a nightmare helpless-
    ness,—
To whom she knelt in sad mechanic
    guise,
Pleading for mercy with such piteous
    eyes,
And such soft flow of self-bewailing
    ruth,
Aurelian felt his passion's quivering
    chords
Stilled at the touch of those pathetic
    words,
That glance of wild appealing agonies.
Stirred by his nobler nature's grave
    command
(That fair, indwelling angel sweet and
    grand,
Born to transmute the worn and blasted
    soil
Of sinful hearts by his celestial toil

To Eden places and the haunts of God),
He stooped, and, courteous, raised her
    from the sod,
And whispered closely in her eager
    ear
Words which his guardian genius smiled
    to hear;
Words of release, and balmy breathing
    cheer.
And while his softening gaze a grateful
    mist
Feelingly dimmed, with knightly grace
    he kissed
Her drooping forehead, and loose tresses
    thrown
In rippling waves adown the heaving
    zone;
Once, twice, he kissed her thus, with
    reverence meek;
But when her brimming eyes uplifted,
    seek
Aurelian now, with eloquent looks to
    tell
What tenderest words could not convey
    so well,
She only hears the tree-stems, tall and
    brown,
The golden leaves come faintly fluttering
    down,
And only hears the wind of sunset moan:
Midmost the twilight wood the lady
    stands alone.

Stung by his misery into frenzied mo-
    tion,
Her lord meantime beside the restless
    ocean
Roamed, hearkening to the mournful
    undertone
Of the sea's mighty heart, which touched
    his own,
O God, how sadly! when abruptly lift-
    ing
His furrowed brow, long fixed upon the
    shifting
And mimic whirlwinds of loose sand that
    flew
Hither and thither, as the brief winds
    blew

At fitful whiles from o'er the watery
    waste,
He saw, as if she spurned the earth in
    haste,
His gentle wife returning, with a
    face
Whereon there dwelt no shadow of dis-
    grace;
A face that seemed transfigured in the
    light
Of Paradise, it shone so softly bright.
Beautiful ever, round her now there
    hovered
A subtle, new-born glory, which discov-
    ered
A shape so dazzling, you had thought the
    plume
Of some archangel's pinion cast its
    bloom
About her, and the veil of heaven with-
    drawn,
She viewed the mystic streams, the
    sapphire dawn,
And heard the choirs celestial, tier on
    tier
Uptowering to the uttermost golden
    sphere,
Sing of a vanquished dread, a blest re-
    lease,
The effluence and the solemn charm of
    peace.

Evening closed round them; o'er the
    placid reach
Stretching far northward of the sea-girt
    beach,
They passed, while night's first planet in
    the sky
Faltered from out the stillness timidly,
And perfumed breezes rustled murmur-
    ing by,
'Twixt the grim headlands up the glens
    to die,
And white-winged sea-birds, with a long-
    drawn cry,
Which spake of homeward flight and
    billowy nest,
Glanced through the sunset down the
    wavering West.

Evening closed o'er them, mellowing
    into dark;
Along the horizon's edge, a tiny spark,
Dull-red at first, but broadening to a
    white
And tranquil orb of silver-streaming
    light,
Slowly the Night Queen fair her heaven
    ascends:
The outlines of those loving forms she
    blends
Into one luminous shade, which seems
    to float,
Mingle and melt in shining mists remote;
Type of two perfect lives, whose single
    soul
Outbreathes a cordial music, sweet and
    whole,
One will, one mind, one joy-encircled
    fate,
And one winged faith that soars beyond
    the heavenly gate.

My song, which now hath long flowed
    unperplexed
Through scenes so various, calm as
    heaven, or vexed
By gusty passion, reaches the lone shore,
Ghostlike and strange, of silence and old
    dreams;
Far-off its weird and wandering whisper
    seems
Like airs that faint o'er untracked oceans
    hoar
On haunted midnights, when the moon
    is low.
And now 'tis ended: long, yea, long
    ago,
Lost on the wings of all the winds that
    blow,
The dust of these dead loves hath passed
    away;
Still, still, methinks, a soft, ethereal
    ray
Illumes the tender record, and makes
    bright
Its heart-deep pathos with a marvellous
    light,

So that whate'er of frenzied grief and
    pain
Marred the pure currents of the crystal
    strain,
Transfigured shines through fancy's mel-
    lowing trance,
Touching with golden haze the quaint
    old-world romance.

NOTE. — Of "The Frankleines Tale," the plot of which has been followed in "The Wife of Brittany," Richard Henry Horne, the author of "Orion," says: "It is a noble story, perfect in its moral purpose, and chivalrous self-devotion to a feeling of truth and honor; but it would have been more satisfactory in an intellectual sense had a distinction been made between a sincere pledge of faith and a 'merry bond!'"

THE RIVER.

["Man's life is like a river, which likewise hath its seasons or phases of progress: first, its spring rise, gentle and beautiful; next, its summer, of eventful maturity, mixed calm, and storm, followed by autumnal decadence, and mists of winter, after which cometh the all-embracing sea, type of that mystery we call eternity!"]

UP among the dew-lit fallows
    Slight but fair it took its rise,
And through rounds of golden shallows
    Brightened under broadening skies;
While the delicate wind of morning
    Touched the waves to happier grace,
Like a breath of love's forewarning,
    Dimpling o'er a virgin face, —
Till the tides of that rare river
    Merged and mellowed into one,
Flashed the shafts from sundawn's quiver
    Backward to the sun.

Royal breadths of sky-born blushes
    Burned athwart its billowy breast, —
But beyond those roseate flushes
    Shone the snow-white swans at rest;
Round in graceful flights the swallows
    Dipped and soared, and soaring sang,
And in bays and reed-bound hollows,
    How earth's wild, sweet voices rang!

Till the strong, swift, glorious river
　Seemed with mightier pulse to run,
Thus to roll and rush forever,
　Laughing in the sun.

Nay; a something born of shadow
　Slowly crept the landscape o'er, —
Something weird o'er wave and meadow,
　Something cold o'er stream and shore;
While on birds that gleamed or chanted,
　Stole gray gloom and silence grim,
And the troubled wave-heart panted,
　And the smiling heavens waxed dim,
And from far strange spaces seaward,
　Out of dreamy cloud-lands dun,
Came a low gust moaning leeward,
　Chilling leaf and sun.

Then, from gloom to gloom intenser,
　On the laboring streamlet rolled,
Where from cloud-racks gathered denser,
　Hark! the ominous thunder knolled!
While like ghosts that flit and shiver,
　Down the mists, from out the blast,
Spectral pinions crossed the river, —
　Spectral voices wailing passed!
Till the fierce tides, rising starkly,
　Blended, towering into one
Mighty wall of blackness, darkly
　Quenching sky and sun!

Thence, to softer scenes it wandered,
　Scents of flowers and airs of balm,
And methought the streamlet pondered,
　Conscious of the blissful calm;
Slow it wound now, slow and slower
　By still beach and ripply bight,
And the voice of waves sank lower,
　Laden, languid with delight;
In and out the cordial river
　Strayed in peaceful curves that won
Glory from the great Life-Giver,
　Beauty from the sun!

Thence again with quaintest ranges,
　On the fateful streamlet rolled
Through unnumbered, nameless changes,
　Shade and sunshine, gloom and gold,

Till the tides, grown sad and weary,
　Longed to meet the mightier main,
And their low-toned *miserere*
　Mingled with his grand refrain;
Oh, the languid, lapsing river,
　Weak of pulse and soft of tune, —
Lo! the sun hath set forever,
　Lo! the ghostly moon!

But thenceforth through moon and star-
　　light
Sudden-swift the streamlet's sweep;
Yearning for the mystic far-light,
　Pining for the solemn deep;
While the old strength gathers o'er it,
　While the old voice rings sublime,
And in pallid mist before it,
　Fade the phantom shows of time, —
Till with one last eddying quiver,
　All its checkered journey done,
Seaward breaks the ransomed river,
　Goal and grave are won!

———◇———

THE STORY OF GLAUCUS THE THESSALIAN.*

TO ———

List to this legend, which an antique
　　poet
Hath left among the musty tomes of eld,
Like a flushed rosebud pressed between
　　the leaves
Of some worn, dark-hued volume. What
　　a light
Of healthful bloom about it! What an
　　air
Seems breathing round its delicate petals
　　still!
Wilt thou not take it, lady, — thou,
　　whose face
Is lovely as a lost Arcadian dream, —
And place it next thy heart, and keep it
　　fresh
With balmy dews thy gentle spirit sends

---

* The elements of this story are to be found
in Apollonius Rhodius, and Leigh Hunt has
embodied them in a graceful prose legend.

"On the fateful streamlet rolled
Through unnumbered, nameless changes,
Shade and sunshine, gloom and gold."

Up to the deep founts of the tenderest
    eyes
That e'er have shone, I think, since in
    some dell
Of Argos and enchanted Thessaly,
The poet, from whose heart-lit brain it
    came,
Murmured this record unto her he loved ?

THE STORY.

Glaucus, a young Thessalian, while the
    dawn
Of a fresh spring-tide brightened copse
    and lawn,
Sauntered, with lingering steps and
    dreamy mood,
Adown the fragrant pathway of a wood
Which skirted his small homestead
    pleasantly, —
And there he saw a tall, majestic tree,
An oak of untold summers, whose broad
    crown,
Quivering as if in some slow agony,
And trembling inch by inch forlornly
    down,
Threatened, for want of a kind propping
    care,
To leave its breezy realm of golden air,
And from its leafy heights, with shriek
    and groan,
Like some proud forest empire over-
    thrown,
Measure its vast bulk on the greensward
    lone.

Glaucus beheld and pitied it. He saw
The approaching ruin with a touch of
    awe,
No less than genial sympathy,— for men,
In those old times, pierced with a wiser
    ken
To the deep soul of Nature, and from
    thence
Drew a serene and mystic influence,
Which thrilled all life to music. There-
    fore he
Called on his slaves, and bade them prop
    the tree.

Musing he passed to a still lonelier place
In the dim forest, by this act of grace
Lightened and cheered, when, from the
    copse-wood nigh,
There dawned upon his vision suddenly
A shape more fair and lustrous than the
    star
Which rides o'er Cloudland on her
    sapphire car
When vesper winds are fluting solemnly.
" Glaucus," she said, in tones whose
    liquid flow,
Mellow, harmonious, passionately low,
Stole o'er his spirit with a strange, wild
    thrill,
" I am the Nymph of that fair tree thy
    will
Hath saved from ruin; but for thee my
    breath
Had vanished mistlike, — my glad eyes
    in death
Been sealed for evermore. Yes! but for
    thee
I must have lost that half-divinity
Whose secret essence, spiritually fine,
Hath warmed my veins like Hebe's
    heavenly wine.
No more, no more amid my rippling hair
Could I have felt soft fingers of the
    air
Dallying at dawn or twilight, — on my
    cheek
Have felt the sun rest with a rosy streak,
Pulsing in languor; nor with pleasant
    pain
Drooped in the cool arms of the loving
    Rain,
That wept its soul out on my bosom fair.
But now, in long, calm, blissful days
    to be,
This life of mine shall lapse deliciously
Through all the seasons of the boun-
    teous year;
Beneath my shade mortals shall sit, and
    hear
Benignant whispers in the shimmering
    leaves;
And sometimes, upon warm and odorous
    eves,

Lovers shall bring me offerings of sweet
    things, —
Honey and fruit, — and dream they mark
    the wings
Of Cupids fluttering through the oak-
    boughs hoar.
All this I owe thee, Glaucus, — all, and
    more!
Ask what thou wilt! — thou shalt not
    ask in vain!''

Then Glaucus, gazing in her glorious
    eyes,
And rallying from his first unmanned
    surprise,
Emboldened, too, by her soft looks,
    which drew
A spell about his heart like fire and dew
Mingled and melting in a love-charm
    bland, —
And by the twinkling of her moon-white
    hand,
That seemed to beckon coyly to her side,
And by her maiden sweetness deified,
And something that he deemed a dear
    unrest
Heaving the unveiled billows of her
    breast —
(As if her preternatural part, as free
And wild as any nursling of the lea,
Yearned wholly downward to human-
    ity) —
Emboldened thus, I say, Glaucus re-
    plied:
"O fairest vision! be my love, — my
    bride!''

Over her face there passed an airy flush,
The roseate shade, the twilight of a
    blush,
Ere the low-whispering answer pensively
Stirred the dim silence in its trancèd
    hush.
"Thy suit is granted, Glaucus! though,
    perchance
A peril broods o'er this, thy bright ro-
    mance,
Like a lone cloudlet o'er a lake that's
    fair.

When the high noon, flaunting so hotly
    now
Fades into evening, thou may'st meet
    me here,
Just in the cool of this rill-shadowing
    bough;
My favorite bee, my fairy of the flowers,
Shall bid thee come to that pure tryst of
    ours.''

Who now so proud as Glaucus? "I have
    won,''
Lightly he said, "the marvellous ben-
    ison
Of love from her in whose soft-folding
    arms
Gods might forget Elysium! O! her
    charms
Are perfect, — perfect heaven and per-
    fect earth,
Blest and commingled in one exquisite
    birth
Of beauty, — and for me! I know not
    why,
But rosy Eros ever seems to fly
Gayly before me, armed for victory,
In every pleasant love-strife!'' On this
    theme
Deeply he dwelt, till a vain self-esteem
Obscured his worthier spirit. Thus he
    went
Out from the haunted wood, his nature
    toned
Down to the common daylight, disen-
    zoned
Of all its rare, ethereal ravishment.

Still in this mood, he sought the neigh-
    boring town,
Met with some gay young comrades, and
    sat down
To dice and wassail. All that morn he
    played,
And quaffed, and sang, and feasted, till
    the shade
Of evening o'er earth's forehead cast a
    gloom;
And still he played, when on his ear the
    boom

Of a swift, shining, yellow-breasted bee
Rung out its small alarum. Teasingly
The insect hummed about him, went and
came,
And like a tiny hell of circling flame
And discord seemed to Glaucus, who at
last
Struck at the wingèd torment testily.
The bee — poor go-between! — in either
thigh
Cruelly maimed, with feeble flutterings,
passed
Back to its home amid the foliaged
bloom.

At length, in two most fortunate throws,
the game
Was won by Glaucus! With triumphant
smile
He seized and pocketed a glittering pile
Of new sestertii. "Ay! 'tis e'er the
same,"
He muttered; "dice or women, I *must*
win!
But hold! — by Venus! 'twere a burning
sin,
And false to my fond wild flower of the
wood
Longer to dally here. O Fortune! good,
Kind mistress, speed me still! Would
that each heel
Were plumed like happy Hermes'!"
His late zeal
Spurred the youth onward to the place
of tryst, —
One final burst of sunset — amethyst,
Ruby, and topaz — blazed among the
boughs,
Whence a sad voice, — "*Breaker of
solemn vows,
What dost thou here? Thine hour has
past for aye!*"
Glaucus, with startled eyes, peered
through the sway
Of moistened fern and thicket, but his
view
Rested alone on vacancy, or caught,
Swift as the shifting glamour of a
thought,

Only the golden and evanishing ray,
Which, softened by cool sparkles of the
dew,
Flashed through the half-closed lids of
weary Day.

"Here am I," said the voice, so sadly
sweet,
The listener thrilled even to his pausing
feet, —
"Here, right before thee, Glaucus!"
Yet again
The youth with straining eyeballs and
hot brain,
Searched the dense thickets, — it was all
in vain.
"Alas! alas!" (and now a tremulous
moan
Sobbed through the voice, like a faint
minor tone
In mournful human music) — "thou
canst see
My face no more, for sternly, drearily,
A wildering cloud of sense, that shall
not rise,
Hath come between me and thy darken-
ing eyes.
O shallow-hearted! nevermore on thee
Shall visions of that finer world above
Dawn from the chaste auroras of their
love;
But common things, seen in a funeral
haze
Of earthiness, and sorrow, and mistrust,
Weigh the soul down, and soil its hopes
with dust;
A hand like Fate's with cruel force shall
press
Thy spirit backward into heaviness.
And the base realm of that forlorn abyss
Wherein the serpent Passions writhe and
hiss
In savage desolation! Blind, blind,
blind
Art thou henceforth in heart, and hope,
and mind!
For he to whom my messenger of joy
And soothing promise only brought
annoy

And sharp disquiet in his low-born
	lust, —
What, what to him *Ideal Beauty's*
	kiss,
The charm of lofty converse in the
	dells,
Of divine meetings, musical farewells,
And glimpses through the flickering
	leaves at night
Of such fair mysteries in awe-hushing
	light
That even I, who in these forests
	dwell
Purely with innocent creatures, unto
	whom
All Nature opes her innermost heart of
	bloom
And blessedness, by some majestic
	spell
Uplifted unto realms ineffable,
Faint almost in the splendor large and
	clear ?
The winds have ceased their murmur-
	ings, — on my ear
The rill-songs melt to threads of delicate
	tune,
And every small mote dancing in the
	moon
Expands, and brightens to a spiritual
	eye,
Luring me up to Immortality.
O! then my earthly nature, loosening
	slips
Down like a garment, and invisible
	lips
Whisper the secrets of their happier
	sphere!
This bliss, O youth! my soul had shared
	with one
Worthy the gift! Alas! *thou* art not he!"

The voice died off toward the waning
	sun!
Glaucus looked up, — the gaunt, gray
	forest trees
Seemed to close o'er him like a vault of
	stone.
"*Just Gods !*" he sighed, "*I am indeed
	alone !*"

THE NEST.

AT the poet's life-core lying
	Is a sheltered and sacred nest,
Where, as yet, unfledged for flying,
	His callow fancies rest:

Fancies, and thoughts, and feelings,
	Which the mother Psyche breeds,
And passions whose dim revealings
	But torture their hungry needs.

Yet, — there cometh a summer splendor
	When the golden brood wax strong,
And, with voices grand or tender,
	They rise to the heaven of song.

———◆———

NOT DEAD.

TO J. A. D.

HERE, at the sweetest hour of this sweet
	day,
	Here in the calmest woodland haunt
		I know,
Benignant thoughts around my memory
	play,
	And in my heart do pleasant fancies
		blow,
	Like flowers turned to thee, radiant
		and aglow,
Flushed by the light of times forever
	fled,
Whose tender glory pales, but is not
	dead.

The warm south wind is like thy gener-
	ous breath,
	Laden with kindly words of gentle
		cheer,
And every whispering leaf above me
	saith,
	She whom thou dream'st so distant
		hovers near;
	Her love it is that thrills the sunset air
With mystic motions from a time that's
	fled,
Long past and gone, in sooth, — but,
	oh! not dead!

The drowsy murmur of cool brooks
    below;
  The soft, slow clouds that seem to *muse*
    on high;
Love-notes of hidden birds, that come
    and go,
  Making a sentient rapture of the sky;
  All the rare season's peaceful sorcery,
These hints of cordial joys forever
    fled,
Joys past, indeed, and yet they are not
    dead:

Far from the motley throng of sordid
    men,
  From fashion far, mean strife and
    frenzied gain,
In those dear days through many a
    mountain glen,
  By mountain streams, and fields of
    rippling grain,
  We roamed untouched by Passion's
    feverish pain,
But quaffing Friendship's tranquil
    draughts instead,
Its waters clear whose sweetness is not
    dead!

Above that nook of fair remembrance
    stands
  A dove-eyed Faith, that falters not,
    nor sleeps;
No flowers of Lethe droop in her white
    hands,
  And if the watch that steadfast angel
    keeps
  Be pensive and some transient tears
    she weeps,
They are but tears a fond regret may
    shed
O'er twilight joys which fade, but are
    not dead!

Not dead! not dead! but glorified and
    fair,
  Like yonder marvellous cloudland
    floating far
Between the mellowing sunset's amber
    air

And the mild lustre of eve's earliest
    star,
  Oh, such, so pure, so bright, these
    memories are!
Earth's warmth and Heaven's serene
    around them spread,
They pass, they wane, but, sweet! they
    are not dead!

SONNET.

Hast thou beheld a landscape dull and
    bare,
  On which, at times, a flying gleam was
    shed
  From some shy sunbeam shifting over-
    head,
That made the scene for one brief mo-
    ment fair?
Such is the light, so transient, flickering,
    rare,
  Which, from fate's sullen heavens
    above me spread,
  Hath flushed the path my weary foot-
    steps tread,
And lent to darkness glimpses of sweet
    cheer.
Alas! alas! that I, whose soul doth burn
    With such deep passion for a steadfast
    bliss,
Must bend forever o'er hope's burial urn,
    And greet even love with a half-
    mournful kiss!
  In sooth, what stern, malignant doom
    is this?
Joy! delicate Ariel! ah! return! return!

MARGUERITE.

She was a child of gentlest air,
Of deep-dark eyes, but golden hair,
And, ah! I loved her unaware,
        Marguerite!

She spelled me with those midnight eyes,
The sweetness of her naïve replies,
And all her innocent sorceries,
        Marguerite!

The fever of my soul grew calm
Beneath her smile that healed like balm,
Her words were holier than a psalm,
          Marguerite!

But 'twixt us yawned a gulf of fate,
Whose blackness I beheld, — too late.
*O Christ! that love should smite like
          hate.*
          Marguerite!

She did not wither to the tomb,
But round her crept a tender gloom
More touching than her earliest bloom,
          Marguerite!

The sun of one fair hope had set,
A hope she dared not all forget,
Its twilight glory kissed her yet, —
          Marguerite!

And ever in the twilight fair
Moves with deep eyes and golden hair
The child who loved me unaware!
          Marguerite!

—◇—

APART.

COME not with empty words that say,
" Your strength of manhood wastes
          away
In long, ignoble, fruitless years!"
I live apart from pain and tears,
Wherewith the ways of men are sown,
Nor dwell I loveless and alone;
One tender spirit shares my days,
One voice is swift to yield me praise,
One true heart beats against my own!
What more, what more could man desire
Than love that burns a steadfast fire
And faith that ever leads him higher
Along the path which points to peace ?

Oh, far and faint I hear the din
Of battle-blows, and mortal sin
From out the stir and press of life;
Those hollow muffled sounds of strife

Seem rolled from thunder-clouds up-
          curled
About a dim and distant world;
Below me, in the sunless gloom;
But round my brow the amaranths
          bloom
Of sober joy with heart's-ease furled;
For more, what more can man desire
Than love that burns a steadfast fire,
And faith that ever leads him higher,
Where all the jars of earth shall cease ?

A present glory haunts my way,
A promise of diviner day
Illumes the flushed horizon's verge;
And fainter, farther still, the surge
Of buffeting waves that beat and roar
Up the dim world's tempestuous shore
Beneath me in the moonless airs;
Alas, its passions, sorrows, cares!
Alas, its fathomless despairs!
Yet dreams, vague dreams, they seem to
          me,
On these clear heights of liberty,
These summits of serene desire, —
Whence love ascends, a quenchless fire.
And sweet faith ever leads me higher
To pearly paths of perfect peace!

—◇—

THE LOTOS AND THE LILY.

The little poems which follow were sug-
gested by an oriental idea developed in Alger's
" Specimens of Eastern Poetry." The moon
is strangely spoken of as masculine.

THE LOTOS.

DROOPING in the sunlit streams,
We are wrapped all day in dreams;

Morn and noon and evening light
Robed for us in garbs of night.

Only when the moon appears
Through a silvery mist of tears,

From the waters dark and still,
We arise to drink our fill

Of the tender love he sheds
On our fair enamored heads.

Ah! no longer wrapped in dreams,
How we pant beneath his beams!

How, with breath of softest sighs,
We unclose our yearning eyes,

And our snowy necks in pride
Curve about the glittering tide!

Warmth for warmth and kiss for kiss,
All our pulses burn with bliss,

Till revealed our inmost charms
Glowing in the night-god's arms.

"View us, white robed lilies,
We, whose beauty's rareness
Sleeps until the bridegroom sun
Woos our virgin fairness."

THE LILY.

VIEW us, white-robed lilies,
  We whose beauty's rareness
Sleeps until the bridegroom Sun
  Woos our virgin fairness.

Then, our bosoms baring,
  'Neath his ardent kisses,
Stem, and leaf, and delicate heart
  Trembling into blisses,

The full, fervid godhead
  Thrills our being tender,
And our happy souls expand
  In ecstatic splendor.

Thus all, *all* we yield him
  Of our shrinèd sweetness, —
All that maiden warmth may grant
  To true love's completeness,

WINDLESS RAIN.

THE rain, the desolate rain!
  Ceaseless, and solemn, and chill!
How it drips on the misty pane,
  How it drenches the darkened sill!
O scene of sorrow and dearth!
  I would that the wind awaking
To a fierce and gusty birth,
    Might vary this dull refrain
    Of the rain, the desolate rain:
For the heart of heaven seems breaking
In tears o'er the fallen earth,
    And again, again, again
    We list to the sombre strain,
The faint, cold monotone —
  Whose soul is a mystic moan —
Of the rain, the mournful rain,
  The soft, despairing rain!

The rain, the murmurous rain!
  Weary, passionless, slow,
'Tis the rhythm of settled sorrow,
  'Tis the sobbing of cureless woe!
And all the tragic of life,
  The pathos of Long-Ago,
    Comes back on the sad refrain
    Of the rain, the dreary rain,
Till the graves in my heart unclose,
  And the dead that its depths enfold,
From a solemn and weird repose
    Awake, — but with eyelids cold,
And voices that melt in pain
On the tide of the plaintive rain,
  The yearning, hopeless rain,
The long, low, whispering rain!

———◇———

"IN UTROQUE FIDELIS."

ALONG the woods the whispering night-
    airs swoon,
  A single bird-note dies adown the trees,
Clear, pallid, mournful, droops the sum-
    mer moon,
    Dipped in the foam of cloudland's
      phantom seas; —
    Soundless they heave above
The dim, ancestral home that holds my
    love.

How breathless still! A mystic glamour
    keeps
Calm watch and ward o'er this weird,
    drowsy hour:
Yon heaven's at peace, the earth be-
    nignly sleeps;
  And thou, thou slumberest too, my
      woodland flower, —
    Fair lily steeped in light
And happy visions of the marvellous
    night!

I waft a sigh from this fond soul to
    thine, —
  A little sigh, yet honey-laden, dear,
With fairy freightage of such hopes di-
    vine
  As fain would flutter gently at thine
    ear,
    And, entering, find their way
Down to the heart so veiled from me by
    day.

In dreams, in dreams, perchance, thou
    art not coy;
  And one keen hope more bold than all
    the rest
May touch thy spirit with a tremulous
    joy,
  And stir an answering softness in thy
    breast:
    O sleep! O blest eclipse!
What murmured word is faltering at her
    lips?

Awake for one brief moment, genial
    South:
  Breathe o'er her slumbers, — waft that
    word to me,
Warm with the fragrance of her rosebud
    mouth,
  Enwreathed in smiles of dreamful fan-
    tasy:
    Come, whisper, low and light,
The name which haunts her maiden
    trance to-night.

Still, breathless-still! No voice in earth
    or air:
  I only know my delicate darling lies,

A twilight lustre glimmering in her
  hair,
  And dews of peace within her languid
  eyes:
  Yea, only know that I
Am called from love and dreams, per-
  haps to die, —

Die when the heavens are thick with
  scarlet rain,
  And every time-throb's fated: even
  there
Her face would shine through mists of
  mortal pain,
  And sweeten death, like some incar-
  nate prayer:
  Hark! 'tis the trumpet's swell!
O love! O dreams! farewell, farewell,
  farewell!

---◆---

NATURE, BETROTHED AND WEDDED.

HAVE you not noted how in early spring,
From out the forests, past the murmur-
  ing brooks,
O'er the hillsides, Nature, with airy
  grace,
Like some fair virgin, touched by lights
  and shades,
Glides timidly, a veil of golden mist
About her brows, and budding bosom
  draped
In maiden coyness? She's a bride be-
  trothed
Unto that mystic god, who comes from
  far,
Rich Orient lands upon the winds of
  June,
That bear him like swift ardors, winged
  with fire;
And when, on some calm, lustrous morn,
  her lord
Uplifts the golden veil, and weds to hers
The quickening warmth of ripe, immor-
  tal lips,
How the broad earth leaps into raptured
  life,
And thrills with music!

Then a queenly spouse
Raised unto fruitful empire, through all
  hours
Of bounteous summer, she walks proudly
  on,
Shining with blissful eyes of matronhood,
Till, at the last, autumn, with reverent
  hand,
Doth crown her with such full, com-
  pleted joy,
Such wealth of sovereign beauty, she
  once more
About her brows and sumptuous bosom
  folds
That golden veil, — not in the tremulous
  fear
Of maiden coyness now, but lest rash
  men,
Drawn by her awful loveliness, should
  dare
To gaze too closely on it, and thus fall,
Smitten and blind, at her imperial feet!

---◆---

CHLORIS.

WHAT time the rosy-flushing West
  Sleeps soft on copse and dingle,
Wherein the sunset shadows rest,
  Or richly float and mingle;

When down the vale the wood-dove's tone
  Thrills in a cadence tender,
And every rare, ethereal mote
  Turns to a wingèd splendor.

Just as the mystic cloudlands ope,
  Far up their sapphire portal,
Fair as the fairest dream of Hope,
  Half goddess and half mortal,

I see that lovely genius rise,
  That child of Orient trances,
On whose sweet face the glory lies
  Of weird Hellenic fancies, —

Chloris! beneath whose procreant tread
  All earth yields up her sweetness, —
The violet's scent, the rose's red,
  The dahlia's orbed completeness,

And verdures on the myriad hills,
  The breath of her pure duty
Hath nursed to life by sparkling rills
  And foliaged nooks of beauty;

Till bloom and odor, blush and song,
  So fill earth's radiant spaces,
The fading touch of sin, or wrong,
  Leaves glad the weariest faces;

And so, through happy spring-tide dells,
  O'er mount, and field, and river,
Her zephyr's fairy clarion swells,
  Her footsteps glance forever!

———◆———

FORTUNIO.

A PARABLE FOR THE TIMES.

WHO at the court of Astolf, the great
    King,
King of a realm of firs, and icy floes,
Cold bright fiords, and mountains capped
    with clouds.
Who there so loved and honored as the
    knight,
The youthful knight Fortunio? Whence
    he came,
None knew, nor whom his kindred: at
    a bound
He passed all rivals moving towards the
    throne,
And stood firm-poised above them; yet
    with mien
So sweet it honeyed envy, and sur-
    prised
The bitterest railers into complaisance!
Low-voiced and delicate-featured, with
    a cheek
As soft as peach down, or the golden
    dust
Shrined in a maiden lily's heart of
    hearts,
Yet a stern will bent bowlike, with the
    shaft
Of some keen purpose swiftly drawn to
    head,
Or launched unerring at its lofty mark,

Rose thrilled with action, or high strung
    at aim,
Beneath his jewelled doublet! While
    the hand
So warm, so white, and wont to press
    the palm
In palpitating clasp of fair sixteen,
Could wield the ponderous battle-axe,
    or flash
The lightning rapier in the foeman's
    eyes.
Prince of the tourney and the dance
    alike,
War's fiercer lists had seen his furrow-
    less brow
Flushed red with heat of battle, heard
    his voice
Shrilled clear beyond the clarions,
    mount and break
In larklike song far o'er the mists of
    blood,
Through victory's calmer heaven.
    Mixed love and fear,
With love ofttimes preponderant, girded
    him
Closely as with an atmosphere disturbed
Only by hints of thunder, ghosts of
    cloud.
But love, all love, love in her passionate
    eyes,
Love 'twixt the pure twin rosebuds of
    her mouth,
Love in the arch of brooding, beauteous
    brows,
And every wavering dimple wherein
    smiles
At hide-and-seek with sly, mock frown-
    ings played,—
All love was Freyla, though a princess
    she,
For this unknown Fortunio! Wildly
    beat
And burned her heart at each soft glance
    he gave,
Or softer word, albeit as yet unthrilled
By answering passion! Swiftly flew her
    dreams
Birdlike on balmy winds **of fancy**
    borne,

To bridal realms empurpled and di-
vine,—
Alas! but Scorn, that long had lurked
and spied
In ambush, shot its sudden bolts, and
brought
Those wingèd dreams transfixed to earth
and dead!

While Rage, Scorn's ally, in her father's
breast,
Clutched the sweet dreamer rudely,
dragged her soul
Into the garish glare of commonplace
(Soon to be lit by horror's lurid star!)
And so convulsed her tenderness with
threats,

"King of a realm of firs, and icy floes,
Cold bright fiords, and mountains capped with clouds."

That all her being seemed collapsed to fall
Crushed, as in moral earthquake: "Dot-
ing fool,"
Outshrieked the King, "dost dream
great Odin's blood
Could mix with veins plebeian? Purge
thy thoughts,
Unvirgined, vile, of sacrilegious sin!
But for this boy, our twelvemonth's
grace hath raised
So high, a moment's justice shall cast
down
To fathomless depths of ruin!"

Wherewithal
(Harping on justice still, though justice
slept)
The King decreed, "This youth Fortu-
nio dies!"
So, on a bright spring morn, the knight
stood up,
Fronting the royal doomsmen, with a
face
Sublimely calm; they tore his bravery
off,
His jewelled vest and knighthood's
golden spurs,

And bared his heart to catch the arrowy
hail,—
When lo! beneath those rough, disrob-
ing hands,
*The dangerous, lewd seducer, coyly
bowed,*
*Outbeamed a virgin beauty chaste and
fair!*

The King, beholding, started, and then
smiled:
"Thou wanton madcap," said he, "go
in peace!'"

O cordial eyes, the brown eyes and the
blue,
Or ye dark eyes, with deeps like mid-
night heavens,
Where unimagined worlds of thought
and love
Shine starlike, would ye quench your
glorious rays
In the low levels of the lives of men?
O gracious souls of women tender-sweet,
And luminous with goodness, would ye
soil
Your nascent angel-plumage in the stye
Of sordid worldliness? Be warned, be
warned!
Set not the frail spears of your rash
caprice
In rest against great Nature's pierceless
shield;
Strive not to grasp monopolies impure,
Man's fated heritage. Be warned, be
warned!
For surely as yon bright sun dawns and
dies,
And sure as Nature, all immutable,
Year after year completes her mystic
round
Through law's vast orbit,—so ye des-
perate Fair,
Arrayed against the eternal force of God,
Must fall discomfited, and like that
knight,
The false Fortunio, rest your claims at
last,
Not on deft spells of simulated power,

But on the soft white bosom which
enspheres
The sacred charms of perfect woman-
hood!

———◆———

A *FEUDAL PICTURE.*

[SCENE — The Corridor of a Palace. PER-
SONS — A young Knight and his Mentor.
TIME — The Fourteenth Century.]

MENTOR.

WITH what a grace she passed us by
just now!
Her delicate chin half raised, her cordial
brow
A cloudless heaven of bland benignities!
What tempered lustre too in her dove's
eyes,
Just touched to archness by the eye-
brow's curve,
And those quick dimples which the
mouth's reserve
Stir and break up, as sunlit ripples
break
The cool, clear calmness of a mountain
lake!
A woman in whom majesty and sweet-
ness
Blend to such issues of serene complete-
ness,
That to gaze on her were a prince's
boon!
The calm of evening, the large pomp of
noon,
Are hers; soft May morns melting into
June,
Hold not such tender languishments as
those
Which steep her in that dew-light of
repose,
That floats a dreamy balm around the
full-blown rose: —
And yet, 'tis not her beauty, though so
bright
(Clear moon-fire mixed with sun-flame),
nor the light,
Transparent charm we feel so exquisite,

Whereby she's compassed as a wizard
    star
By its own life-air! 'tis not one, nor all
Of these, whereby we're mastered, Sir,
    and fall
Slavelike before her: doubtless such
    things *are*
Potent as spells, — still there's a some-
    thing fine,
Subtler than hoar-rime in the faint
    moonshine,
More potent yet! — an undefinèd art,
'Twere vain to question: your whole
    being, heart,
Brain, blood, seem lapsing from you,
    fired and fused
In hers, — a terrible power, and if
    abused ——
But by St. Peter! 'tis not safe to talk
Of yon weird woman! turn now! watch
    her walk
'Twixt the tall tiger-lilies, — there's a
    free,
Brave grace in every step, — but still to
    me,
It hath — I know not what — of covert-
    ness,
Cunning, and cruel purpose! can you
    guess
The picture it brings up? — a lonely
    rock
From which a young Bedouin guards his
    flock,
In the swart desert: — there's a tawny
    band,
A curved and tangled pathway of loose
    sand,
Winding above him; — the tranced airs
    make dim
His slumberous senses! — his great
    brown eyes swim
In th' mist of dreams, when gliding
    with mute tread
Forth from the thorn-trees, o'er his
    nodding head,
Moves a lithe-bodied panther; — (God!
    how fair
The beast is, with her moony-spotted
    hair,

And her deft desert paces!) — one breath
    more!
And you'll behold the spouting of fresh
    gore,
Heart blood that's human! — can aught
    save him now? —
Hist! the sharp crackle of a blasted
    bough,
Whence flies a huge hill-eagle, rustling
O'er the boy's forehead his vast breadths
    of wing,
And sweeping as a half-seen shade,
    'twould seem,
Betwixt his startled spirit, and its
    dream;
He's roused! espies his danger! at a
    bound
Leaps into safety where the low-set
    ground
Is buttressed 'neath two giant crags
    thereby
(Now hark ye! 'tis no pictured phantasy,
This scene, my Anslem! but all's true
    and clear
Before me, though full many a weary
    year
Has waxed and waned since then):
My meaning prithee? foolish youth, be-
    ware!
There's treachery lurking in the gay
    parterre,
As in the hoary desert's silentness,
And dreams with danger, death per-
    chance behind,
May lull young sleepers in the perfumed
    wind,
Which hardly lifts the tiniest truant
    tress
It toys with coyly, of a woman's
    hair:
Our sternest fates have risen in forms as
    fair,
As — let us say for lack of similes, —
As, hers, who bends now with such
    gracious ease,
O'er her rich tulip-beds!
               Were I the bird,
Wert thou the shepherd Anslem of my
    tale,

(And that thou hast not hearkened, boy,
    unstirred
Is clear, albeit thou need'st not wax so
    pale),
What would true wisdom whisper, now
    'tis done,
My warning, and thy day-dream in the
    sun ?
What! why, her mandate's plain: I hear
    her say,
    Young Knight! 'to horse! leave the
      Queen's Court to-day!'"

THE WARNING.

PATIENCE! I yet may pierce the rind
Wherewith are shrewdly girded round
The subtle secrets of his mind:
A dark, unwholesome core is bound
Perchance within it! Sir, you see,
Men are not what they *seem* to be!

A candid mien and plausible tongue!
A bearing calmly frank and fair,
The tear ('twould seem) by pity wrung,
All these are his, but still, beware!
A something strange, false, unbegot
Of virtue, whispers, trust him not:
But yesterday, his mask (I know
He wears one), for a moment's space,
By chance dropped off and swift below
The smile just waning on his face,
I caught a look, flashed sudden, keen
As lightning, which he deemed unseen.

I will not pause to tell thee what
That look betrayed! enough I think,
To smite the spirit cold and hot,
By turns, and make one inly shrink
From contact with a soul that keeps
Such wild-fire smouldering in its deeps:
So friend, be warned! he is not one
Thy youth should trust, for all his
    smiles,
Frank foreheads, genial as the sun,
May hide a thousand treacherous wiles,
And tones, like music's honeyed flow,
May work (God knows!) the bitterest
    woe!

DRIFTING.

I HAVE settled at last in a sombre nook,
In the far-off heart of the Norland
    hills,
There's a dark pine forest before my
    gates,
And behind is the voice of rills
That murmur all day, and murmur all
    night,
Through the tangled copses green and
    lone,
Where, couched in the depths of the
    shadowy leaves,
The wood-dove makes her moan.

My home is a castle ancient and worn,
With hoary walls, and with crumbling
    floors,
And the burglar-winds their entrance
    force
Through the cobwebbed panes and
    doors.
I can hardly say that a roof is mine,
For whene'er the mountain tempests
    rise,
A deluge is poured through its countless
    rents,
Wide open to air and skies!

Ah! Nature alone keeps a wholesome
    mien,
In the midst of a squalor wildly bare,
And I draw sometimes from her bounte-
    ous breast
Brief balms for the heart's despair:
All *human* friends that were loyal have
    died,
And the false and treacherous only
    stay,
To poison the soul with their serpent
    tongues
In my fortune's dull decay!

Distant and dim in the perishing past
Grow the joys that made its springtime
    sweet,
And the last of the saving angels —
    Hope —

Hath spurned my lot with her shining
  feet;
Ambition is dead, and if love survives,
Her lip, it is pale, and her eyes forlorn
As beams of the waning stars that
  melt
In a clouded winter's morn.
I have met my fate as a man should meet
What cannot be vanquished, nor put
  aside,
I have striven with spirit and force to
  stem
Its rushing and mighty tide;
But the godlike nerve, and the iron will,
They were not granted to me, I say,
And therefore a waif on an angry sea,
I am drifting, drifting away!

Ay! drifting, and drifting, and drifting
  away,
Not a hand upraised, nor a cry for aid;
And hoarser the voice of the storm-wind
  swells,
And darker the wild night-shade;
There are breakers ahead that will crush
  me soon,
How much, O God! do thy creatures
  bear!
I marvel if somewhere, in heaven or
  hell,
This riddle of life grows clear!

SONNETS.

LEIGH HUNT.

" Leigh Hunt *loves everything;* he catches
the sunny side of everything, and — except a
few polemical antipathies — finds everything
beautiful." — HENRY CRABB ROBINSON.

DESPITE misfortune, poverty, the dearth
Of simplest justice to his heart and
  brain,
This gracious optimist lived not in vain;
Rather, he made a partial Heaven of
  Earth;
For whatsoe'er of pure and cordial birth
In body or soul dawned on him, he was
  fain

To bless and love, as an immortal gain
A thing divine, of fair immaculate
  worth: —
The clearest, cleanest nature given to
  man
In these, our latter days, methinks was
  his,
With instincts which alone did bring
  him bliss;
All life he viewed as one long, luminous
  plan
Wherein God's love and wisdom meet
  and kiss, —
His sole brave creed, the creed Samari-
  tan!

SOUL-ADVANCES.

HE, who with fervent toil and will aus-
  tere,
His innate forces and high faculties
Develops ever, with firm aim, and wise,
He *only* keeps his spiritual vision clear;
To him earth's treacherous shadows
  shift and veer
Like idle mists o'ercrowding windless
  skies,
Where through ofttimes to purged and
  prayerful eyes,
The steadfast heavens seem beckoning
  calm and near:
Still o'er life's rugged heights, with many
  a slip,
And painful pause he journeys, and sad
  fall,
Toward death's dark strand, washed by
  a mystic sea;
There her worn cable straining to be
  free,
He sees, and enters Faith's majestic ship,
To sail — *where'er the voice of God may
  call!*

CAROLINA.

THAT fair young land which gave me
  birth is dead!
Lost as a fallen star that quivering dies
Down the pale pathway of autumnal
  skies,

A vague faint radiance flickering where
   it fled;
All she hath wrought, all she hath
   planned or said,
Her golden eloquence, her high emprise
Wrecked, on the languid shore of Lethe
   lies,
While cold Oblivion veils her piteous
   head:*
O mother! loved and loveliest! debonair
As some brave queen of antique chiv-
   alries.
Thy beauty's blasted like thy desolate
   coasts ; —
Where now thy lustrous form, thy shin-
   ing hair ?
Where thy bright presence, thine impe-
   rial eyes ?
Lost in dim shadows of the realm of
   Ghosts!

SONNET.

IN yonder grim, funereal forest lies
A foul lagoon, o'erfilmed by dust and
   slime,
Hidden and ghastly, like a thought of
   crime
In some stern soul kept secret from
   men's eyes:
But if perchance a healthful breeze
   should rise,
And part those stifling boughs, sweet
   morning's prime,
And the fair flush of evening's cordial
   clime,
Reflect therein the calmly glorious skies:

Is't so with man ? holds not the dark-
   ened breast,
Turbid, corrupt, o'ergrown by worldli-
   ness,
One little spot whereon love's smile may
   rest ?
Lo ! a pure impulse breathes, the sin-
   clouds part,
The grief-defilements melt in hopes that
   bless,
And pour God's quickening sunshine on
   the heart!

———◆———

ODE TO SLEEP.

BEYOND the sunset, and the amber sea
To the lone depths of Ether, cold and
   bare,
Thy influence, soul of all tranquillity,
Hallows the earth and awes the reverent
   air;
Yon laughing rivulet quells its silvery
   tune,
The pines, like priestly watchers tall and
   grim,
Stand mute, against the pensive twi-
   light dim,
Breathless to hail the advent of the
   moon;
From the white beach the ocean falls
   away
Coyly, and with a thrill; the sea-birds
   dart
Ghostlike from out the distance, and
   depart

---

* This may be esteemed an *exaggeration :* but really it is the sober and melancholy truth. The fame of the great statesmen and orators, for example, who once flourished in South Carolina, and made her name illustrious from one end of the Union to the other, is fast becoming a mere shadowy tradition. With a single exception, their works have never been collected for publication, nor have their lives been written, unless in the most fragmentary and imperfect fashion. The period during which these things might have been rightly done has forever passed.

Thus, over their genius and performances, as over their native State, — the Carolina of old, —oblivion, day by day, is more darkly gathering. If elements of a new political birth exist in that unfortunate section, they are *now* hopelessly confused and chaotic!

While the Past recedes, becoming momently more ghostly and phantasmal, the Future is wrapped in thick clouds and darkness! Where, indeed, is the prophet or son of a prophet who can predict the nature of that new polity destined to rise from the old institutions and the defunct civilization ?

With a gray fleetness, moaning the dead
    day;
The wings of Silence overfolding space,
Droop with dusk grandeur from the
    heavenly steep,
And through the stillness gleams thy
    starry face,
    Serenest Angel — Sleep!

Come! woo me here, amid these flowery
    charms,
Breathe on my eyelids; press thy odor-
    ous lips
Close to mine own, enwreathe me in
    thine arms,
And cloud my spirit with thy sweet
    eclipse;
No dreams! no dreams! keep back the
    motley throng, —
For such are girded round with ghastly
    might,
And sing low burdens of despondent
    song,
Decked in the mockery of a lost de-
    light;
I ask oblivion's balsam! the mute peace
Toned to still breathings, and the gen-
    tlest sighs,
Not music woven of rarest harmonies
Could yield me such elysium of release:
The tones of earth are weariness, — not
    only
'Mid the loud mart, and in the walks of
    trade,
But where the mountain Genius broodeth
    lonely,
In the cool pulsing of the sylvan shade;
Then, bear me far into thy noiseless land,
Surround me with thy silence, deep on
    deep,
    Until serene I stand
Close by a duskier country, and more
    grand,
Mysterious solitude, than thine, O Sleep!

As he whose veins a feverous frenzy
    burns,
Whose life-blood withers in the fiery
    drought,

Feebly, and with a languid longing,
    turns
To the spring breezes gathering from the
    South,
So, feebly, and with languid longing, I
Turn to thy wished Nepenthe, and im-
    plore
The golden dimness, the purpureal gloom
Which haunt thy poppied realm, and
    make the shore
Of thy dominion balmy with all bloom:
In the clear gulfs of thy serene profound,
Worn passions sink to quiet, sorrows
    pause,
Suddenly fainting to still-breathèd
    rest;
Thou own'st a magical atmosphere,
    which awes
The memories seething in the turbulent
    breast;
Which muffling up the sharpness of all
    sound
Of mortal lamentation, — solely bears
The silvery minor toning of our woe,
All mellowed to harmonious under-
    flow,
Soft as the sad farewells of dying
    years, —
Lulling as sunset showers that veil the
    west,
    And sweet as Love's last tears
When overwelling hearts do mutely
    weep:
O griefs! O wailings! your tempestuous
    madness,
Merged in a regal quietude of sadness,
Wins a strange glory by the streams of
    sleep!

Then woo me here amid those flowery
    charms,
Breathe on my eyelids, press thy odor-
    ous lips,
Close to mine own, — enfold me in thine
    arms,
And cloud my spirit with thy sweet
    eclipse;
And while from waning depth to depth
    I fall,

Down lapsing to the utmost depths of
    all,
Till wan forgetfulness obscurely steal-
    ing,
Creeps like an incantation on the soul,
And o'er the slow ebb of my conscious
    life
Dies the thin flush of the last conscious
    feeling,
And like abortive thunder, the dull roll
Of sullen passions ebbs far, far away, —
O Angel! loose the chords which cling
    to strife,
Sever the gossamer bondage of my
    breath,
And let me pass gently as winds in
    May,
From the dim realm which owns thy
    shadowy sway,
To thy diviner sleep, O sacred death!

SONG.

O! TO be
By the sea, the sea!
While a brave nor'wester's blowing,
    With a swirl on the lee,
    Of cloud-foam free,
And a spring-tide deeply flowing!
    With the low moon red and large,
    O'er the flushed horizon's marge,
And a little pink hand in mine,
On the sands in the long moonshine!

O! to be
By the sea, the sea!
With the wind full west and dying,
    With a single star
    O'er the misty bar,
And the dim waves dreamily sighing!
    O! to be there, but there'
    With my sweet love nestling near!
Near, near, till her heart-throbs blend
    with mine,
Through the balmy hush of the night's
    decline,
On the glimmering beach, in the soft
    star-shine!

HOPES AND MEMORIES.

OUR hopes in youth are like those rose-
    ate shadows
Cast by the sunlight on the dewy grass
When first the fair morn opes her sap-
    phire eyes;
They seem gigantic and yet graceful
    shades,
Touched with bright color. As our sun
    of life
Rises towards meridian, less and less
Grow the bright tremulous shadows, till
    at last,
In the hot dust and noontide of our day,
They glimmer to blank nothingness.
    Again,
That grand climacteric passed, the shad-
    ows gleam
Bright still, perchance (if our past deeds
    be pure), —
Bright still, but all reversed! Eastward
    they point,
Lengthening and lengthening ever
    toward the dawn;
For hopes have then grown memories, whose
    strange life
Deepens and deepens as the sunset dies.

WIDDERIN'S RACE.

AUSTRALIAN.

[The incidents of the following sketch will
be found in "The Recollections of Geoffrey
Hamlyn," by Henry Kingsley.]

"A HORSE amongst ten thousand! on
    the verge,
The extremest verge of equine life he
    stands;
Yet mark his action, as those wild young
    colts
Freed from the stock-yard gallop whin-
    nying up;
See how he trots towards them, — nose
    in air,
Tail arched, and his still sinewy legs
    out-thrown

"Our hopes in youth are like those roseate shadows
Cast by the sunlight on the dewy grass."

In gallant grace before him! A brave
   beast
As ever spurned the moorland, ay, and
   more,
He bore me once,—such words but smite
   the truth,
I' the outer ring, while vivid memory
   wakes,
Recalling now, the passion and the
   pain, —
He bore me once from earthly hell to
   heaven!

" The sight of fine old Widderin (that's
   his name,
Caught from a peak, the topmost rugged
   peak
Of tall Mount Widderin, towering to
   the North
Most like a steed's head, with full nos-
   trils blown,
And ears pricked up), — the sight of
   Widderin brings
That day of days before me, whose
   strange hours
Of fear and anguish, ere the sunset,
   changed
To hours of such content and full-veined
   joy,
As Heaven can give our mortal lives but
   once.

" Well, here's the story: While yon bush-
   fires sweep
The distant ranges, and the river's voice
Pipes a thin treble through the heart of
   drought,
While the red heaven like some huge
   caldron's top
Seems with the heat a-simmering, better
   far
In place of riding tilt 'gainst such a sun,
Here in the safe veranda's flowery gloom,
To play the dwarfish Homer to a song,
Whereof myself am hero :

         " Two decades
Have passed since that wild autumn-time
   when last

The convict hordes from near Van Die-
   men, freed
By force or fraud, swept, like a blood-
   red fire,
Inland from beach to mountain, bent on
   raid
And rapine; fiends o' th' lowest pit, they
   spared
Nor sex, nor age, nor infancy; the vul-
   ture
Followed their track, and a black smoke
   like hell's
Hung its foul reek above each home
   accursed,
Sacked by their greed, or ravished by
   their lust.
Their crimes were monstrous, weird,
   unutterable,
Not to be hinted, save in awe-struck
   whispers
Dropped by dark hearthstones, far from
   maidens' ears,
In the blank silent midnight! all the
   land
Uprose to seek, confront and decimate
These devils spawned of Tophet; but
   their bands
At the first bruit of battle, the first clang
Of sabres girding honest loins, and
   champ
Of horse-bits held by manly hands that
   burned
To smite them, hip and thigh, — fled,
   disappeared,
And crouched in hiding, wheresoe'er the
   earth,
By wave and hill-side, forest, and bleak
   tarn,
Vouchsafed to shield them; as the time
   rolled on,
Our fears grew lighter, and all dread was
   quelled,
When on a morning, 'mid the outmost
   reefs
Of rough Cape Bolling, our chief herds-
   man found
The carcass of a huge boat overturned,
All stoven, and firmly wedged between
   the jaws

Of monster rocks, whereby three bodies
     lay,
Splashing and gurgling in the refluent
     tides,
Well known as corses of three desperate
     men,
The outlaws' leaders; thereupon 'twas
     deemed, —
And all must own with fairest likelihood,
That glutted by their vengeance, or
     spurred on
By hopes of rapine, beckoning other-
     where, —
The whole foul crew embarking, had
     been seized
By wind and wave, God's executioners,
The pitiless doomsmen of the wrath of
     Heaven, —
And so, crushed out of being, and
     made less
Than the vile seaweed dabbling in the
     surf.

"Thenceforth, our caution cooled;
     save here and there,
At critical mountain-passes, or lone
     caves,
And sheltered inlets of the wild south-
     west,
No sentinels watched; and wherefore
     should they watch?
The storm had threatened, broken and
     was passed!

"So, in late autumn, — 'twas a mar-
     vellous morn,
With breezes from the calm snow-river
     borne
That touched the air, and stirred it into
     thrills,
Mysterious and mesmeric, a bright mist
Lapping the landscape like a golden
     trance,
Swathing the hilltops with fantastic
     veils,
And o'er the moorland-ocean quivering
     light
As gossamer threads drawn down the
     forest aisles

At dewy dawning, — on this marvellous
     morn,
I, with four comrades, in this self-same
     spot,
Watched the fair scene, and drank the
     spicy airs,
That held a subtler spirit than our wine,
And talked and laughed, and mused in
     idleness,
Weaving vague fancies, as our pipe-
     wreaths curled
Fantastic, in the sunlight! I, with
     head
Thrown back, and cushioned snugly,
     and with eyes
Intent on one grotesque and curious
     cloud,
Puffed upward, that now seemed to
     take the shape
Of a Dutch tulip, now a Turk's face
     topped
By folds on folds of turban limitless, —
Heard suddenly, just as the clock
     chimed one,
To melt in musical echoes up the hills,
Quick footsteps on the gravelled path
     without, —
Steps of the couriers of calamity, —
So my heart told me, ere with
     blanched regards,
Two stalwart herdsmen on our thresh-
     old paused,
Panting, with lips that writhed, and
     awful eyes;
A breath's space in each other's eyes we
     glared,
Then, swift as interchange of lightning
     thrusts
In deadly combat, question and reply
Clashed sharply, 'What! the Rangers?'
     'Ay, by Heaven!
And loosed in force, — the hell-hounds!'
     'Whither bound?'
I stammered, hoarsely. 'Bound,' the
     elder said,
'Southward! — four stations had they
     sacked and burnt,
And now, drunk, furious ———' but I
     stopped to hear

No more; with booming thunder in
  mine ears,
And blood-flushed eyes, I rushed to
  Widderin's side,
Drew tight the girths, upgathered curb
  and rein,
And sprang to horse ere yet our laggard
  friends,
Now trooping from the green veranda's
  shade,
Could dream of action!

      "Love had winged my will,
For to the southward, fair Garoopna
  held
My all of hope, life, passion; she whose
  hair
(Its tiniest strand of waving, witch-like
  gold)
Had caught my heart, entwined, and
  bound it fast,
As 'twere some sweet enchantment's
  heavenly net!

" I only gave a hand-wave in farewell,
Shot by, and o'er the endless moorland
  swept
(Endless it seemed, as those weird,
  measureless plains,
Which in some nightmare vision, stretch
  and stretch
Towards infinity!) like some lone ship
O'er wastes of sailless waters; now, a
  pine,
The beacon pine gigantic, whose grim
  crown
Signals the far land-mariner from
  out
Gaunt boulders of the gray-backed Organ
  hill,
Rose on my sight, a mistlike, wavering
  orb,
The while, still onward, onward, on-
  ward still,
With motion winged, elastic, equable,
Brave Widderin cleaved the air tides,
  tossed aside
The winds as waves their swift, invisible,
  breasts,

Hissing with foamlike noise when
  pressed and pierced
By that keen head and fiery-crested
  form!

" The lonely shepherd guardian on the
  plains,
Watching his sheep through languid
  half-shut eyes,
Looked up, and marvelled, as we passed
  him by,
Thinking perchance it was a glorious
  thing,
So dressed, so booted, so caparisoned,
To ride such bright blood-coursers unto
  death!
Two sun-blacked natives, slumbering in
  the grass,
Just rose betimes to 'scape the trampling
  hoofs,
And hurled hot curses at me as I sped;
While here and there, the timid kanga-
  roo
Blundered athwart the mole-hills, and
  in puffs
Of steamy dust-cloud vanished like a
  mote!

" Onward, still onward, onward, onward
  still!
And lo! thank Heaven, the mighty Or-
  gan hill,
That seemed a dim blue cloudlet at the
  start,
Hangs in aërial, fluted cliffs aloft,
And still as through the long, low glacis
  borne,
Beneath the gorge borne ever at wild
  speed,
I saw the mateless mountain eagle wheel
Beyond the stark height's topmost pin-
  nacle;
I heard his shriek of rage and ravin die
Deep down the desolate dells, as far be-
  hind
I left the gorge and far before me swept
Another plain, tree-bordered now, and
  bound
By the clear river gurgling o'er its bed.

" By this, my panting, but unconquered
 steed
Had thrown his small head backward,
 and his breath
Through the red nostrils burst in labored
 sighs;
I bent above his outstretched neck, I
 threw
My quivering arms about him, murmur-
 ing low,
' Good horse! brave heart! a little longer
 bear
The strain, the travail; and thenceforth
 for thee
Free pastures all thy days, till death
 shall come!
Ah, many and many a time, my noble
 bay,
Her lily hand hath wandered through
 thy mane,
Patted thy rainbow neck, and brought
 thee ears
Of daintiest corn from out the farm-
 house loft,—
Help, help, to save her now!'

   " I'll vow the brute
Heard me and comprehended what he
 heard!
He shook his proud crest madly, and his
 eye
Turned for a moment sideways, flashed
 in mine
A lightning gleam, whose fiery language
 said,
' I know my lineage, will not shame my
 sire.
My sire, who rushed triumphant 'twixt
 the flags,
And frenzied thousands, when on Epsom
 downs
Arcturus won the Derby! — no, nor
 shame
My granddam, whose clean body, half
 enwrought
Of air, half fire, through swirls of desert
 sand
Bore Shïek Abdallah headlong on his
 prey!'"

" At last came forest shadows, and the
 road
Winding through bush and bracken, and
 at last
The hoarse stream rumbling o'er its
 quartz-sown crags.

" No, no! stanch Widderin! pause not
 now to drink;
An hour hence, and thy dainty nose
 shall dip
In richest wine, poured jubilantly forth
To quench thy thirst, my beauty! but
 press on,
Nor heed these sparkling waters. God!
 my brain's
On fire once more! an instant tells me
 all:
All! — life or death, — salvation or de-
 spair! —
For yonder, o'er the wild grass-matted
 slope
The house stands, or it stood but yester-
 day.

" A Titan cry of inarticulate joy
I raised, as calm and peaceful in the sun,
Shone the fair cottage, and the garden-
 close,
Wherein, white-robed, unconscious, sat
 my Love
Lilting a low song to the birds and flow-
 ers.
She heard the hoof-strokes, saw me,
 started up,
And with her blue eyes wider than their
 wont,
And rosy lips half tremulous, rushed to
 meet
And greet me swiftly. ' Up, dear Love!'
 I cried,
' The Convicts, the Bush-Rangers! — let
 us fly!'
Ah, then and there you should have seen
 her, friend,
My noble beauteous Helen! not a tear,
Nor sob, and scarce a transient pulse-
 quiver,
As, clasping hand in hand, her fairy foot

Lit like a small bird on my horseman's
    boot,
And up into the saddle, lithe and light,
Vaulting she perched, her bright curls
    round my face!

"We crossed the river, and, dismount-
    ing, led
O'er the steep slope of blended rock and
    turf,
The wearied horse, and there behind a
    Tor
Of castellated bluestone, paused to
    sweep

With young keen eyes the broad plain
    stretched afar,
Serene and autumn-tinted at our feet:
'Either,' said I, 'these devils have gone
    East,
To meet with bloodhound Desborough
    in his rage
Between the granite passes of Luxorme,
Or else, — dear Christ! my Helen, low!
    stoop low!'
(These words were hissed in horror, for
    just then,
'Twixt the deep hollows of the river-
    vale,

"No, no! stanch Widderin! pause not now to drink."

The miscreants, with mixed shouts and
    curses, poured
Down through the flinty gorge tumultu-
    ously,
Seeming, we thought, in one fierce
    throng to charge
Our hiding-place.) I seized my Widder-
    in's head,
Blindfolding him, for with a single neigh
Our fate were sealed o' th' instant! As
    they rode,
Those wild, foul-languaged demons, by
    our lair,
Scarce twelve yards off, my troubled
    steed shook wide
His streaming mane, stamped on the
    earth, and pawed

So loudly that the sweat of agony rolled
Down my cold forehead; at which point
    I felt
My arm clutched, and a voice I did not
    know,
Dropped the low murmur from pale,
    shuddering lips,
'O God! if in those brutal hands I
    fall,
Living, look not into your mother's face
Or *any* woman's more!'

        "What time had passed
Above our bowed heads, we pent, pin-
    ioned there
By awe and nameless horror, who shall
    tell?

Minutes, perchance, by mortal measurement,
Eternity by heart-throbs! — when at
　　length
We turned, and eyes of mutual wonder
　　raised,
We gazed on alien faces, haggard, worn,
And strange of feature as the faces
　　born
In fever and delirium! Were we
　　saved ?
We scarce could comprehend it, till,
　　from out
The neighboring oak-wood, rode our
　　friends at speed,
With clang of steel and eyebrows bent in
　　wrath.
But warned betimes, the wily ruffians
　　fled
Far up the forest-coverts, and beyond
The dazzling snow-line of the distant
　　hills,
Their yells of fiendish laughter pealing
　　faint,
And fainter from the cloudland, and the
　　mist
That closed about them like an ash-gray
　　shroud:
Yet were these wretches marked for
　　imminent death:
The next keen sunrise pierced the
　　savage gorge,
To which we tracked them, where,
　　mere beasts at bay,
Grimly they fought, and brute by brute
　　they fell.''

OCTOBER.

AFAR from the city, its cark and care, —
Thank God! I am cosily seated here,
　　On this night of hale October, —
While the flames leap high on the roaring hearth,
And voices, the dearest to me on earth,
Ring out in the music of household
　　mirth,
　　For the time is blithe October!

There's something, — but *what* I can
　　scarce divine, —
Perchance 'tis the breath like a potent
　　wine,
　　Of the cordial, clear October,
Which makes, when the jovial month
　　comes round,
The life-blood bloom, and the pulses
　　bound,
And the soul spring forth like a monarch
　　crown'd, —
　　God's grace on the brave October!

Come, sweetheart! open your choicest
　　bin,
For who, I would marvel, could deem it
　　sin,
　　On this night of keen October,
To quaff one health to his ruddy cheer,
On the golden edge of the waning year,
To his eyes so bright, and his cheeks so
　　clear,
　　Our bluff " King Hal," — October ?

Away with Rhenish and light champagne !
'Tis not in these we must pledge the
　　reign
　　Of the stout old lord, — October;
But in mighty stoups of the " mountain
　　dew,"
With " beads " like tears in an eye of
　　blue,
But tears of a laughter, sound and
　　true,
　　As thine honest heart, October!

He brought me love and he brought me
　　health,
He brought me *all* but the curse of
　　wealth,
　　This kindly and free October;
And forever and aye I will bless his
　　name,
While his winds blow fresh, and his
　　sunsets flame,
And the whole earth burns with his
　　crimson fame,
　　This prince of the months, — October !

WILL.

YOUR face, my boy, when six months
    old,
We propped you laughing in a chair,
And the sun-artist caught the gold
    Which rippled o'er your waving hair!
And deftly shadowed forth the while
That blooming cheek, that roguish
    smile,
    Those dimples seldom still:
The tiny, wondering, wide-eyed elf!
Now, *can* you recognize yourself
    In that small portrait, Will?

I glance at it, then turn to you,
    Where in your healthful ease you
    stand,
No beauty, — but a youth as true,
    And pure as any in the land!
For Nature, through fair sylvan ways,
Hath led and gladdened all your days,
    Kept free from sordid ill;
Hath filled your veins with blissful fire,
And winged your instincts to aspire
    Sunward, and Godward, Will!

Long-limbed and lusty, with a stride
    That leaves me many a pace behind,
You roam the woodlands, far and wide,
    You quaff great draughts of country
    wind;
While tree and wildflower, lake and
    stream,
Deep shadowy nook, and sunshot gleam,
    Cool vale and far-off hill,
Each plays its mute mysterious part,
In that strange growth of mind and heart
    I joy to witness, Will!

"Can this tall youth," I sometimes
    say,
    "Be mine? *my son?*" it surely seems
Scarce further backward than a day,
    Since watching o'er your feverish
    dreams
In that child-illness of the brain,
I thought (O Christ, with what keen
    pain!)

Your pulse would soon be still,
That all your boyish sports were o'er,
And I, heart-broken, nevermore
    Should call, or clasp you, Will!

But Heaven was kind, death passed you
    by;
    And now upon your arm I lean,
My second self, of clearer eye,
    Of firmer nerve, and steadier mien;
Through you, methinks, my long-lost
    youth
Revives, from whose sweet founts of truth
    And joy, I drink my fill:
I feel your every heart-throb, know
What inmost hopes within you glow,
    One soul's between us, Will!

Pray Heaven that this be always so!
    That ever on your soul and mine
Though my thin locks grow white as
    snow,
    The self-same radiant trust may shine;
Pray that while this, my life, endures,
It aye may sympathize with yours
    In thought, aim, action still;
That you, O son (till comes the end),
In me may find your comrade, friend,
    And *more* than father, Will!

——◆——

HERE AND THERE.*

HERE the warm sunshine fills
Like wine of gods the deepening, cup-
    shaped dells,
Embossed with marvellous flowers; the
    happy rills
Roam through the autumnal fields whose
    rich increase
Of gathered grain smiles under heavens
    of peace;
    While many a bird-song swells
From glades of neighboring woodlands,
    cool and fair, —
    Content and peace are *here.*

---

* Written during the war between France
and Germany.

There the wild battle's wrath
Thunders from castled height to storied
plain,
Ploughs with red lightning-bolts its terri-
ble path,
And sows the abhorrent seeds of blood
and death,
Blown far on Desolation's tameless
breath,
While for autumnal grain
Time reaps the harvest of a bleak de-
spair, —
God's curse consumes them *there*.

Here jovial children play
Beneath the latest vine-leaves; innocent
kings,
And blissful queens, — on them the ma-
tron Day,
Like a sweet mother drops her kisses
light;
The very clouds some secret joy makes
bright,
And round us clings and clings,
With Ariel arms, the season's influence
rare, —
Heaven's heart beats near us *here*.

There love bemoans its lost,
Countless as seaside sands; all joys of
life
Rest locked and stirless in the blood-red
frost;
Ye drums, roll out, shrill clarions, peal
your parts!
Ye cannot drown the wail of broken
hearts,
Nor still that spiritual strife
Which thrills through Victory's voice
its death-notes drear, —
Dear Christ, soothe, save them *there*.

———◇———

WELCOME TO WINTER.

Now, with wild and windy roar,
Stalwart Winter comes once more, —
O'er our roof-tree thunders loud,
And from edges of black cloud

Shakes his beard of hoary gold,
Like a tangled torrent rolled
Down the sky-rifts, clear and cold!

Hark! his trumpet summons rings,
Potent as a warrior-king's;
Till the forces of our blood
Rise to lusty hardihood,
And our summer's languid dreams
Melt, like foam-wreaths, down the
streams,
When the fierce northeasters roll,
Raving from the frozen pole.

Nobler hopes and keener life,
Quicken in his breath of strife;
Through the snow-storms and the sleet
On he stalks with armèd feet,
While the sounding clash of hail
Clanging on his icy mail,
Stirs whate'er of generous might
Time hath left us in his flight,
And our yearning pulses thrill
For some grand achievement still!

Lord of ice-bound sea and land,
Let me grasp thy kingly hand,
And from thy great heart and bold,
Hecla-warm, though all is cold
Round about thee, catch the fire
Of my lost youth's brave desire;
Let me, in the war with wrong,
Like thy storms, be swift and strong,
Gloomy griefs, and coward cares
Broods of 'wildering, dark despairs,
Making all life's glory dim,
Let me rend them, limb from limb,
As the forest-boughs are rent
When thou wak'st the firmament,
And with savage shriek and groan,
All the wildwood's overthrown!

———◆———

TO MY MOTHER.

Like streamlets to a silent sea,
These songs with varied motion
Flow from bright fancy's uplands free,
To Lethe's clouded ocean;

They lapse in deepening music down
　The slopes of flower-lit meadows,
Nor dream, poor songs! how near them
　　　frown
　Oblivion's rayless shadows!

Yet though of brief and dubious life,
　All wed to incompleteness, —
The voices of these lays are rife
　With frail and fleeting sweetness;
One chord to make more full the strain,
　One note I may not smother,
Is echoed in the heart's refrain
　Which holds thy name, my mother!

To thee my earliest verse I brought,
　All wreathed in loves and roses,
Some glowing boyish fancy, fraught
　With tender May-wind closes;
Thou did'st not taunt my fledgling song,
　Nor view its flight with scorning:
" The bird," thou saidst, " grown fleet
　　　and strong,
　Might yet outsoar the morning!' "

Ah me! between that hour and this,
　Eternities seem flowing;
O'er hapless graves of youth and bliss
　Dark cypress boughs are growing;
Our Fate hath dimmed with base alloy
　The rich, pure gold of pleasure,
And changed the choral chant of joy
　To care's heart-broken measure!

But through it all, — the blight, the pall,
　The stress of thunderous weather,
That God who keeps wild chance in
　　　thrall
　Hath linked our lots together;
So, hand in hand, we sail the gloom,
　Faith's mystic plummet casting
To sound the ways which end in bloom
　Of Edens everlasting!

I bless thee, Dear, with reverent
　　　thought!
　Pale face, and tresses hoary,
Whose every silvery thread hath caught
　Some hint of heavenly glory; —

To thee, with trust assured, sublime,
　Death's angel-call that waitest,
To thee, as once my earliest rhyme,
　Lo! now, I bring — my latest!

———◆———

SONNETS.

ILLEGITIMATE.

THE maiden Spring came laughing down
　　the dales,
Her fair brows arched, and on her rose-
　　bud mouth,
The balm and beauty of the lustrous
　　South;
Through soft green fields, from hills to
　　happy vales,
She tripped, her small feet twinkling in
　　the sun,
Her delicate finger raised with girlish
　　mirth,
Pointed at graybeard Winter, who, in
　　dearth,
Toiled toward his couch, his long day
　　labor done;
Ah no, not done! for hark! a sudden
　　wind,
Death-laden, sweeps from realms of arc-
　　tic sky,
And blurred with storm, the morn grows
　　crazed and blind;
Then Winter, mocking, backward turns
　　apace,
Where pallid Spring all vainly strives to
　　fly,
And with brute buffet scars her shrink-
　　ing face!

SONNET.

I CAST this sorrow from me like a
　　crown
Of bitter nettles, and unwholesome
　　weeds,
Nursed by cold night-dews, from malig-
　　nant seeds,
Ill Fortune sowed, when all the heaven
　　did frown;
Its loathsome round I trample deeply
　　down

In mire and dust, to burn my brain no
    more;
From off my brow I wipe the trickling
    gore;
While all about me, like keen clarions
    blown,
From breezy dells, and golden heights
    afar,
Their stern *reveillé* the wild March
    winds sound;
They wake an answering passion in my
    soul,
Whence, marshalled as brave warriors,
    taking ground
For noblest conflict, freed from doubt or
    dole,
Great thoughts uprising front Hope's
    morning star!

**VERNAL PICTURES (WITHOUT AND
        WITHIN).**

AMID fresh roses wandering, and the
    soft
And delicate wealth of apple-blossoms
    spread
In tender spirals of blent white and red,
Round the fair spaces of our blooming
    croft,
This morn I caught the gurgling note,
    so oft
Heard in the golden spring-tides that are
    dead, —
The swallow's note, murmuring of win-
    ter fled,
Dropped silverly from passionless calms
    aloft:
"O heart!" I said, "thy vernal depths
    unclose,
That mirror Nature's; warm airs, come
    and go
Of whispering ardors o'er thought's bud-
    ded rose,
And half-hid flowers of sweet philoso-
    phy;
While now upglancing, now borne swift
    and low,
Song like the swallow darts through fan-
    cy's sky."

THE MOUNTAIN OF THE LOVERS.*

I.

LOVE scorns degrees! the low he lifteth
    high,
The high he draweth down to that fair
    plain
Whereon, in his divine equality,
Two loving hearts may meet, nor meet
    in vain;
'Gainst such sweet levelling Custom
    cries amain,
But o'er its harshest utterance one bland
    sigh,
Breathed passion-wise, doth mount vic-
    torious still,
For Love, earth's lord, must have his
    lordly will.

II.

But ah! this sovereign will oft works
    at last
The deadliest bane, as happed erewhile
    to her,
Earl Godolf's daughter, many a century
    past:

---

* The most important feature in the land-
scape of this poem the old Chronicler persists
in designating as a mountain of "steep" and
"terrible" ascent; but that it could not have
been a mountain, and, despite certain obstacles
which made it dangerous for men on horse-
back, it might not even have been a *very* "ter-
rible" hill, is shown by the fact, that among
the crowd who reached the summit soon after
the catastrophe, were "old men," whom the
excitement of the time and scene would hardly
have sufficed to bear safely up were the Chron-
icler's expressions to be *literally* accepted.
To any man loaded as Oswald was, the ascent
of a comparatively moderate height would
prove a fearful trial; but in his case the atro-
cious cruelty of the experiment, and the life
and death issues involved, became so closely
associated in the spectators' minds with the
material scene of the tragedy, that the latter
was not unnaturally beheld through the mag-
nifying medium of pity and terror. Thus the
hill was elevated into a mountain! The old
Chronicler celebrates it as such. We follow
the old Chronicler — to the death!

She loved her father's low born forester,
About whose manful grace did breathe
    and stir
So clear a radiance, by soul-virtues cast,
He moved untouched of social blight or
    ban —
Nature's serene, true-hearted gentleman.

III.

Yet she alone of all the household saw
That softy soul beneath his serf's attire;
But of the ruthless Earl so great her
    awe,
Close, close she kept her spirit's veiled
    desire,
Nor outward shone one spark of hidden
    fire.
Too well she knew to what stern feudal
    law
She and her hapless Love perforce must
    yield,
If once this tender secret were re-
    vealed.

IV.

Yea! even by Oswald's self her covert
    flame
Undreamed of burned; proud stood she,
    coldly fair,
When, to report of woodcraft lore, he
    came
To the Earl's hall, and she was lingering
    there.
"Cold heart!" thought he; "who 'midst
    her liegemen, dare
Play as I played with death a desperate
    game
For her sweet sake? and yet, alas! and
    yet,
She scorns the service and disowns the
    debt."

V.

For sooth it was that one keen winter's
    night,
While slowly journeying homeward
    through a wood

Whose every deepest copse in moonshine
    bright
Glimmered from hoary trunk to frost-
    tipped bud,
On sire and child there burst a cry of
    blood,
Followed by hurrying feet, and the dread
    sight
Of scores of gray-skinned brutes — a
    direful pack
Of wolves half-starved that yelled along
    their track.

VI.

In vain his frantic team Earl Godolf
    smote,
With blended prayer and curse; nigh
    doom were they,
Riders and steeds, for now each ravening
    throat
Yawned like a foul tomb. On the bound-
    ing sleigh
The fierce horde gained, when from the
    silvery-gray,
Cold-branchèd glades outrang a bugle
    note,
With next a bowstring's twang, an
    arrowy whir,
As shaft on shaft the keen-eyed forester

VII.

Launched on the foe, each hurtling shaft
    a fate.
Then Oswald, 'twixt pursuers and
    pursued
Leapt, sword in hand, his eyes of fiery
    hate
Fixed on the baffled horde, whose doubt-
    ful mood
Changed to quick fear, they scoured
    adown the wood,
Their long gaunt lines, in fiend-like,
    vanquished state,
Fading with flash of blood-red orbs from
    far,
Till the last vanished like a baleful
    star!

VIII.

Now, by the mass! abrupt and brief, I
    ween,
The rude Earl's thanks for rescued limbs
    and life;
But not so graceless proved the fair
    Catrine,
As glancing backward to the field of
    strife
She flashed a smile with cordial meaning
    rife,
Which struck our sylvan hero (who did
    lean,
Pale, on his bow,) as 'twere the piercing
    gleam
Of some strange, sudden, half bewilder-
    ing dream.

IX.

Alack! the dream waxed not, but seemed
    to wane,
As if a cloudless sun but late arisen,
Back journeying, passed across the ethe-
    real plain,
And the fresh dawn it brought, died out
    in heaven;
For from that eve no subtlest signs were
    given,
As erst we said, that passion's blissful
    pain
Touched the maid's heart, or that her
    days were caught
In those fine meshes woven by love for
    thought.

X.

In Britain dwelt Earl Godolf, nigh the
    bounds
Of the Welsh marches; a wild rover he
In his hot youth, inured to strife and
    wounds
Through many a foray fierce by land and
    sea;
But, after years of bright tranquillity —
Years linked to love through pleasure's
    peaceful bounds —

So gently lapsed, the unmailed warrior's
    hand
Forgot almost the use of spear or brand.

XI.

A bride erewhile won by his dauntless
    blade
In a great sea fight — where his arm had
    slain
Some half score foemen — wan and half
    afraid,
Homeward he brought, whose every deli-
    cate vein
Pulsed the rich blood and tropic warmth
    of Spain;
But when pure wifehood crowned the
    noble maid,
Heart-fruits for him his beauteous lady
    bore,
Of whose strange sweets he had not
    dreamed before.

XII.

She strove his nature's ruggedness to
    smooth,
And in his bosom dropped a fruitful
    germ
Of those mild virtues given our lives to
    soothe,
And change their gusty solitude to warm
Beneficent calm, — divinest after storm.
Within him flowered a pallid grace of
    ruth,
Nor oft, as once, o'er bleeding breasts he
    trod
Straight to his purpose, blind to law and
    God.

XIII.

And in fair fulness of the ripened time,
Still gentler grew his dark, war-furrowed
    mien;
He quaffed the sunshine of a fairy clime,
Love charmed, hope gladdened, when,
    to crown the scene
Of transient bliss, there smiled a new
    Catrine —

"Every deepest copse in moonshine bright,
Glimmered from hoary trunk to frost-tipped bud. . . .
Scores of gray-skinned brutes—a direful pack
Of wolves half-starved that yelled along their track."

The loveliest babe e'er lulled by mother's
    rhyme —
Whose tiny fingers o'er her heart-strings
    played,
Making ineffable music where they
    strayed.

XIV.

Woe worth the end! for though the in-
    fant thrived
Slowly the hapless mother pined away;
Love to the last in pleading eyes sur-
    vived —
Those fond, fond eyes doomed to the
    churchyard clay,
Coffined, and shut from all blithe sights
    of day;
But Christ! in thee her stainless spirit
    lived,
Whose memory — a white star — should
    evermore
O'er her lord's paths have beamed to
    keep them pure.

XV.

Nathless, some souls there are by cruel
    loss
Stung, as with scourge of scorpions, to
    despair;
These will not seek the Christ, nor clasp
    His cross,
But, groping vaguely through sulphure-
    ous air,
Strike hands with Satan, in the murky
    glare
Of furious hell, whose billows rage and
    toss
About their tortured being, urged to
    curse
That mystic will which rules the uni-
    verse.

XVI.

Yea, such the Earl's; no cooling dew
    did fall
To heal his wound: 'gainst heaven and
    earth he turned,
Girt to his sense with one vast funeral
    pall;

And the sore heart within him writhed
    and burned
With baffled hope, and pain that madly
    yearned,
Vainly and madly, for dear love's recall.
No light o'ershone grief's ocean drear
    and black,
The while old passions thronged tumul-
    tuous back.

XVII.

So, his last state was worse than e'en his
    first;
Murder and rapine, pitiless greed, and
    ire
Raged wheresoe'er his raven banner
    burst,
'Mid shrieks and wails, and hollow roar
    of fire,
Which lapped the household porch and
    crackling byre;
He seemed demoniac in his aims ac-
    curst,
Wrath in his soul, and on his brow the
    sign
Of hell — a human scourge by power di-
    vine

XVIII.

For some mysterious end permitted
    still —
As many an evil thing our God allows
To range the world, and work its dread-
    ful will,
Whether in form of chiefs, with laurelled
    brows,
Or spies and traitors in the good man's
    house;
Or, it may be, some slow, infectious ill,
Untraced, and rising like a mist defiled
With poisonous odors on a lonely wild,

XIX.

Albeit no marsh is near, or steamy fen.
More monstrous year by year Earl Go-
    dolf's deeds
Flared in hell's livery on the eyes of men;
All growths of transient goodness
    checked by weeds,

Sin-bred; and, ah! *one* angel's bosom
    bleeds
To know she may not meet her love
    again;
And even the vales immortal seemed
    less sweet,
Because too pure for his crime-cumbered
    feet.

XX.

But, weal or woe, the world rolls
    blindly on,
While nature's charm, in child, and
    bird, and flower,
Works its rare marvels 'neath the noon-
    day sun,
And the still stars in midnight's slum-
    berous hour.
And so a human bud, through beam
    and shower,
Glad   play,   and   easeful   sleep — the
    orphaned one,
The beauteous babe — a sour old bel-
    dame's care,
Upflowered at length a matchless maid,
    and fair.

XXI.

Most fair to all but him to whom she owed
Her life and place in this bewildering
    world ;
For he, a changed man since that hour
    which showed
His wife's worn form in earthly cere-
    ments furled,
Cold scorn had launched, or captious
    passion hurled
At this sole offspring of his lone abode,
Till grown, alas! too early grave and
    wise,
She viewed her sire, in turn, with love-
    less eyes.

XXII.

Still in benignant arms did nature fold
Her favored child, and on her richly
    showered
All gifts of beauty; with long hair of
    gold

And lucid, languid eyes the maid she
    dowered,
And her enticing loveliness empowered
With charms to melt the wintriest tem-
    per's cold
Charms wrought of sunrise warmth,
    and twilight balm,
Passion's deep glow, and pity's saint-
    like calm.

XXIII.

Tall, lithe, and yielding as a young bay
    tree
Her perfect form; but 'neath its lissom
    grace
There lurked a latent strength keen
    eyes could see,
Drawn from her father's undegenerate
    race;
The dazzling fairness of her Saxon face,
Contrasted with the dark eyes' witchery,
Shone with such light as northern noon-
    days wake
Through the clear shadows of a moun-
    tain lake.

XXIV.

Her full blown flower of beauty lured
    ere long
Unnumbered suitors round her; these
    declare
Boldest report hath done the virgin
    wrong,
And past all power of words they deem
    her fair;
The kingdom's princeliest youth besiege
    her ear
And heart with ardent vows and amor-
    ous song;
Love, rank and wealth their splendid
    beams combine,
She the rare orb about whose path they
    shine.

XXV.

Still would she wed with none till rudely
    pressed
To the last boundary of her patience
    sweet;

No more she struggled in a yearning
    breast
To hide her passion, howsoe'er unmeet
For one high placed as she; her fervent
    feet
Oft bore her now where woodland flow-
    ers caressed
The grand old oaks, beneath whose shel-
    tering boughs
The lovers mused, or, whispering,
    breathed their vows.

XXVI.

But ere to such sweet pass their fates
    had led,
Or ere her thought unbosomed utterly,
To the rapt youth, in tremulous tones,
    she said,
"*I love thee,*" through full many a fine
    degree
Of feeling, touched by sad uncertainty,
That truth they neared, which, like a
    bird o'erhead,
Still faltering flew, till borne through
    shade and sun,
It nestled warm in two hearts made as
    one!

XXVII.

The truth, the fond conviction that all
    earth
Was less than naught — a mote, a van-
    ishing gleam,
Matched with the glow of that transcen-
    dent birth
Of love which wrapped them in his hap-
    piest dream;
Entrancèd thus, shut in by beam on beam
Of glory, is it strange but trivial worth
Their dazzled minds in transient doubts
    should see
Which some times crossed their keen fe-
    licity ?

XXVIII.

Their love awhile, like some smooth rivu-
    let borne
Through drooping umbrage of a lonely
    dell,

By clouds unvisited, by storms untorn,
Passed, rippling music; like a magic bell
Out rung by spirit hands invisible,
Each tender hour of meeting, eve or
    morn,
Above them, stole in rhythmic sweet-
    ness, blent
With rare fruition of supreme content.

XXIX.

But in the sunset tide of one calm day,
When, all unconscious at the place of
    tryst,
Beyond their wont they lingered; with
    dismay
They saw, begirt by gold and amethyst,
Of that rich time, gigantic in the midst
Of shimmering splendor, which did flash
    and play
About his form, and o'er his visage dire,
The wrathful Earl, midmost the sunset
    fire.

XXX.

No word he uttered, but his falchion
    drew,
Red with the slain boar's blood, and
    pointed grim
Where 'gainst the eastern heavens' slow-
    deepening blue
Uprose his castle turrets, tall and dim.
The maid's eyes close; she feels each
    nerveless limb
Sink nigh to swooning; but, heart-brave
    and true,
Clings to her Love, while from pale lips
    a sigh
Doth faintly fall, which means "*with
    him I die!*"

XXXI.

Gravely advancing, the Earl's stalwart
    hand
Rests on her shuddering shoulder; one
    quick glance,
Haughty and high, rife with severe com-
    mand,
On the 'mazed woodsman doth he dart
    askance,

Who doubtful bides, as one half roused
    from trance,
Striving to know on what new ground
    his stand
Thenceforth shall be; or if life's priceless
    all,
Put to the test just then, must rise or
    fall.

XXXII.

Fate wrought the issue! for as Oswald
    waits
Biding his time to smite, or else retreat,
With the maid's hand his own Earl
    Godolf mates,
And from the wood they pass with foot-
    steps fleet;
One tearful, backward look vouchsafed
    his sweet,
Just as the castle gates — those iron
    gates,
Heavy and stern, like Death's — were
    closed between
His burning vision and the lost Catrine.

XXXIII.

To heaven he raises wild despairing
    eyes,
But heaven responds not; then to earth
    returns
His baffled gaze from ranging the cold
    skies,
And earth but seems a place for burial
    urns;
In sooth, the whole creation mutely
    spurns
His prayer for aid; alas! what kind re-
    plies
Can woeful man from fair, dumb Nature
    draw
Locked in the grasp of adamantine Law ?

XXXIV.

Three morns thereafter, in the market
    place
Of the small town, from Godolf's castle
    wall
Distant, it might be, some twelve fur-
    longs' space,

Came, grandly robed, our Lord's high
    seneschal;
To all the lieges, with shrill trumpet
    call,
In name of his serene puissant grace
Godolf, the Earl; to all folk, bond or
    free,
With strident voice he read this foul de-
    cree:

XXXV.

"Whereas our virgin daughter, hight
    Catrine,
False to her noble race and lineage
    proud,
Hath owned her love for one of birth as
    mean
As any hind's who creeps among the
    crowd
Of common serfs, with cowering shoul-
    ders bowed —
Oswald by name — the whom ourselves
    have seen,
When least he deemed us nigh, his
    traitorous part
Press with hot wooing on the maiden's
    heart:

XXXVI.

"Let all men know hereby our will it is,
To-morrow morn their trial morn must
    be;
Either the serf shall win, and call her
    his,
Or both shall taste such bitter misery
As even in dreams the boldest soul would
    flee;
If lips unlicensed thus will meet and kiss,
Reason it seems that such unhallowed
    flame
Of love should end in agony and shame.

XXXVII.

"Therefore, the morrow morn shall view
    their doom
Accomplished; 'mid the ferns of Bolton
    Down,
Where Bolton Height doth catch the
    purpling bloom

Of early sunrise on his treeless crown,
We say to all — knight, burgher, squire
    and clown —
Just as the castle's morning bell shall
    boom
O'er the far hills, and brown moor's
    blossoming,
Come, and behold a yet undreamed-of
    thing.

XXXVIII.

"For then and there must Oswald bear
    aloft,
By his sole strength, unaided and alone,
The blameful maid, whose nature, grown
    too soft,
Durst thus betray our honor and her
    own;
Yet, if he gain the height, untamed, un-
    thrown,
All hands applaud him, and all plumes
    be doffed;
While for ourselves, we vow they both
    shall fare
Unharmed beyond our realm — we reck
    not where."

XXXIX.

So, as decreed, the next morn, calm and
    clear,
Witnessed, in many a diverse mode con-
    veyed,
A mixed and mighty concourse gathering
    near
The appointed height, some in rough
    frieze arrayed,
And some in gold; there blushed the
    downcast maid,
Urged to this cruel test, a passionate
    tear
Misting her view, as surged the living
    sea.
Behind her, his arms folded haughtily,

XL.

His comely head thrown back, his eyes
    on fire
With hot contempt, fixed on an armèd
    band

Which, stationed near him at the Earl's
    desire,
His every move o'erlooked, did Oswald
    stand,
Striving his rousèd anger to command,
And lift his clouded aspirations higher
Than thoughts revengeful. Hark! a
    deepening hum
On the crowd's verge — the trial hour
    has come!

XLI.

Divided, then, betwixt his ire and
    scorn,
Outspake the Earl, in tones of savage
    glee:
"Woodsman! essay thy task, for lo! the
    morn
Grows old, and I this wretched mum-
    mery
Would fain see ended."
            — With mien gravely free,
Clad in light garb, o'erwrought by hound
    and horn,
Oswald stood forth, nor quelled by frail
    alarms,
About the maiden clasped his reverent
    arms;

XLII.

And she, like some pure flower by May
    tide rain
Gracefully laden, turns her eyes apart
From the great throng, and, pierced by
    modest pain,
Veiled her sweet face upon her lover's
    heart;
Whereat the youth is seen to thrill and
    start,
While o'er his own face, calm and pale
    but now,
Rush the deep crimson waves from chin
    to brow;

XLIII.

Then do they ebb away, and leave him
    white
As the vexed foam on ocean's stormy
    swell,

Yet cool and constant in his manful
  might
As some stanch rock 'gainst which the
  tides rebel
In useless rage, with hollow, billowy
  knell;
Meanwhile advancing with sure steps
  and light,
He moves in measured wise to dare his
  fate
Beneath those looks of blended ruth and
  hate.

XLIV.

Stirred by his generous bravery, and the
  sight
Of such young lives — their love, hope,
  joyance set
On the hard mastery of yon terrible
  height,
Whose rugged slopes and sheer descent
  are wet
And slippery with the dews of dawning
  yet, —
Through the dense rout, which swayed
  now left, now right,
Low, inarticulate murmurs faintly ran,
And one keen, quivering shock from
  man to man.

XLV.

The watchful matrons sob, the virgins
  weep
Full tears, but all unheeded, as with
  slow,
Sure footfalls still he mounts the hostile
  steep
On to a point where two great columns
  show
Their rounded heads, crowned by the
  morning glow.
His task half done, a sigh, long, grateful,
  deep,
Breaks from his heaving heart; secure
  he stands,
A sunbeam glimmering on his claspèd
  hands,

XLVI.

And the glad lustre of his wind-swept
  locks
More radiant made thereby; his tall
  form towers
'Gainst the dark background, piled
  with rocks on rocks
Precipitous whose grim, gaunt visage
  lowers,
As if in league they were — like Titan
  powers
Victorious long o'er storms and earth-
  quake shocks —
To cast mute scorn on him whose doubt-
  ful path
Leads near the threatening shadows of
  their wrath.

XLVII.

From the charmed crowd then rose an
  easeful breath,
Lightening the dense air; but, 'midst
  doubt and bale,
Raves the wild Earl, reckless of life or
  death,
If so his tyrannous purpose could pre-
  vail;
For, almost mad, he smites his gloves of
  mail,
Goading with frenzied heel the steed
  beneath
His barbarous rule; in reason's fierce
  eclipse,
A blood-red foam burns on his writhing
  lips.

XLVIII.

Meanwhile, brief space for needful
  respite given,
With quickened pace, onward and
  upward still,
And fanned by freshening gales, as
  nearer heaven
He climbs o'er granite passways of the
  hill,
Oswald ascends, untamed of strength or
  will,

"The kingdom's princeliest youth besiege her ear.'

Striving, as ne'er before had mortal
    striven,
Boldly to win, and proudly wear as his,
The prize he bore of that bright, breath-
    ing bliss.

XLIX.

Two thirds, two thirds and more, of
    that last half
Of his fell journey had he stoutly won;
And now he pauses the cool breeze to
    quaff,
And feel the royal heartening of the sun
Nerving his soul for what must yet be
    done,
When with a gentle, quivering, flutelike
    laugh,
Holding a sob, the maiden rose and
    kissed
Her hero's lips, sought through a tremu-
    lous mist

L.

Of love and pride! The on-lookers,
    ranged afar,
Saw, and more boldly blessed them; all
    are moved
To trust that theirs may prove the for-
    tunate star
Fate brightly kindles for young lives
    beloved:
" His truth and valor hath he nobly
    proved;
How brave, how constant both these
    lovers are;
Sooth! the sweet heavens seem with
    them." Thus, full voiced,
Yet with some lingering doubts, the folk
    rejoiced.

LI.

Alas! for false forecasting, and surmise!
Though small the space betwixt him and
    his goal,
Oswald doth stagger now in feeblest
    wise,
And like some drunken carl, with heave
    and roll,
Blindly he staggers in his lost control

Of sense, or power; and so, with an-
    guished sighs,
Turned on his love — the goal in easy
    reach —
His yearning woe too deep for mortal
    speech.

LII.

Whereon the lady's arms are wildly
    raised,
Perchance in prayer, perchance with
    pitying aim
His strain to ease, when lo! (dear Christ
    be praised!)
It seemed new strength, fresh courage
    o'er him came,
And through his spirit rushed a glorious
    flame,
At which the crowd stood moveless,
    dumb, amazed,
For, like a god, with swift, resistless
    tread,
He strides to clasp the near goal o'er his
    head.

LIII.

A savage cliff of beetling brow it was,
Midmost the summit of the lowering
    height,
Rooted amongst low shrubs and sun-
    dried grass,
And reared in blackness, like a cloud of
    night,
On whose dull breast no beacon star is
    bright.
Thitherward, from cold terrors of the
    pass
Well nigh of death, the hero speeds
    amain,
Nor seems his matchless labor wrought
    in vain.

LIV.

Yea; for a single rood's length oversped
And victory crowns him! God! how
    still the crowd,
Once rife with voices! silent as the dead
Lodged in their earthly crypt and moul-
    dering shroud ;

But suddenly a great cry mounted loud
And shrill above them, as in ruthful
    dread,
They saw the lovers, linked in close
    embrace,
Fall headlong down by that wild trysting
    place.

LV.

Then comes a quick revulsion, when, the
    pain
Of fear and choking sympathy gone by;
Hope reappears — aye, joy and triumph
    reign —
For though supine on yonder height they
    lie,
Still, brow to brow, turned from the
    deepening sky,
'Tis but the faintness of the mighty
    strain —
Or so they dream — on o'erworked nerve
    and will,
Which leaves them moveless on the con-
    quered hill.

LVI.

Spurring his courser, in vexed doubt and
    haste,
The Earl charged on the dangerous
    height, as though
Firm-trenched, defiant, 'mid the rock-
    strewn waste
Glittered the spear-points of his mortal
    foe;
The horse's hoof struck fire, hurling
    below
Huge stones and turf his goaded limbs
    displaced,
Till checked midway, his reckless rider
    found
He needs must climb afoot the treacher-
    ous ground

LVII.

And next the throng had caught, and
    past him swept,
Clothed as he was in armor; a young
    knight

Headed the rout, whose feverish fingers
    crept
Oft to his sword hilt ; on the topmost
    height,
Pausing with veilèd eyes, his gaze he
    kept
Fixed on the prostrate pair, o'er whom
    the light
Of broadening sunrise now was mixed
    with shade,
And still the knight's hand wandered
    round his blade.

LVIII.

Impatient, spleenful, struggling with the
    tide
Of common folk, who seemed to heed
    no more
His sullen passion and revengeful
    pride,
Than if just then he were the veriest
    boor, —
The Earl at length with bent brows
    strode before
The mongrel horde, and unto Oswald
    cried:
"Rise, traitor, rise! by some foul, jug-
    .gling sleight,
Through the fiend's help, thou hast
    attained the height:

LIX.

Part them, I say!" To whom in meas-
    ured tone,
Measured and strange, the young knight
    answering said:
"Earl, well I know thou wear'st for
    heart a stone,
Yet dar'st thou part these twain whom
    death has wed,
No longer twain, but one ? Look! over-
    head
The burning sun mounts to his noonday
    throne;
But o'er the sun, as o'er this fateful
    sod,
Rules a great King, the King whose
    name is God!

LX.

"Deem'st thou for this day's work His
    wrath shall rest?"
Whereon, low murmuring like a hive of
    bees,
With stifled groans and tears, the people
    pressed
Round the fair corpses — women on their
    knees
Embraced them — and old men — but
    dusky lees
Of feeling left — did touch them, and
    caressed
The maid's soft hair, the woodsman's
    noble face,
Praying, under breath, that Christ would
    grant them grace.

.   .   .   .   .

LXI.

That mournful day had waned; by sun-
    set rose
A wailing wind from out the dim north-
    east;
Which, as the shadows waxed at twi-
    light's close
O'er moat and wood, to a shrill storm
    increased;
But in his castle hall, with song and
    feast,
Varied full oft by ribald gibes and blows
Twixt ruffian guests in rage or maudlin
    play,
The wild night raved its awful hours
    away.

LXII.

With not a pang at thought of her whose
    form
In pallid beauty lay unwatched and
    dead,
In a far turret chamber, where the storm,
Thundering each moment louder over-
    head,
Entered and shook the close-draped, som-
    bre bed,
The barbarous sire with wine and was-
    sail warm,

Lifting his cup 'mid brutal jest and
    jeer,
Banned his pale daughter, slumbering on
    her bier.

LXIII.

Just as those impious words had taken
    flight,
In the red dusk beyond the torch's
    glare,
Stole a vague shape that 'scaped the rev-
    ellers' sight,
Slowly toward Earl Godolf, unaware
Even as the rest, what fateful foe drew
    near.
Muffled the shape was, masked and black
    as night,
And now for one dread instant with
    raised sword
Stood hovering o'er the heedless banquet
    board.

LXIV.

And next with flashing motion fierce and
    fast,
Vengeance descended on that glittering
    blade;
The amazed spectators started, dumb,
    aghast,
While at their feet the caitiff lord was
    laid,
His heart's blood trickling o'er the pur-
    ple braid
(For through his heart the avenger's
    brand had passed),
And silver broidery of his gorgeous vest,
Drawn drop by drop from out his smitten
    breast.

LXV.

The muffled shape which as a cloud did
    rise
On the wild orgie, as a cloud departs;
Wan hands are swept across bewildered
    eyes,
And awe stilled now the throbbing at
    their hearts,
When suddenly one death-pale reveller
    starts

Up from the board and in shrill accent
    cries,
" Curst is this roof-tree, curst this meat
    and wine,
Fly, comrades; fly with me the wrath
    Divine!"

LXVI.

In haste, in horror, and great tumult,
    fled
The affrighted guests; then, on the va-
    cant room
No maddening voice thenceforth dis-
    quieted,
Fell the stern presence of a ghastly
    gloom.
A place 'twas deemed of hopeless, bale-
    ful doom;
Barred from all mortal view in darkness
    dread,
Only the spectral forms of woe and sin
Thro' the long years cold harborage
    found therein.

THE VENGEANCE OF THE GODDESS DIANA.*

WHAT time the Norman ruled in Sicily
At that mild season when the vernal sea,
O'erflitted by the zephyr's frolic wing,
Dances and dimples in the smile of
    spring
A goodly ship set sail upon her way
From Ceos unto Smyrna; through the
    play
Of wave and sunbeam touched with fra-
    grant calm,
She passed by beauteous island shores of
    palm,

Until so sweet the tender wooing breeze,
So fraught the hours with balms of slum-
    brous ease,
That those who manned her, in the ge-
    nial air
And dalliance of the time, forgot the
    care
Due to her courses; in the bland sun-
    shine
They lay enchanted, dreaming dreams
    divine,
While idly drifting on the halcyon
    water,
The bark obeyed whatever currents
    caught her.

Borne onward thus for many a cloudless
    day,
They reach at length a wide and wooded
    bay,
The haunt of birds whose purpling
    wings in flight
Make even the blushful morning seem
    more bright,
Flushed as with darting rainbows;
    through the tide,
By overripe pomegranate juices dyed,
And laving boughs of the wild fig and
    grape,
Great shoals of dazzling fishes madly
    ape
The play of silver lightnings in the deep
Translucent pools; the crew awoke from
    sleep,
Or rather that strange trance that on
    them pressed
Gently as sleep; yet still they loved to
    rest,
Fanned by voluptuous gales, by mor-
    phean languors blessed.

---

* Sixteen years ago, in a volume of com-
paratively youthful verses, the above poem
appeared under the title of " *Arolio ; a legend
of the island of Cos.*" The original narrative
has now been carefully rewritten and amend-
ed and upwards of a hundred and fifty lines
of entirely new matter have been added thereto.
So far as we know, the only poet who has cele-
brated this significant and beautiful tradition,
is William Morris, in the first section of whose
" Earthly Paradise " there is a story (called
" *The Lady of the Land* ") founded upon some
of its more obvious and popular incidents.
Since Morris's wonderful tales were not pub-
lished until 1868, we can, at least, assert the
humble claim of precedence in the poetical
treatment of *this* legend.

The shore sloped upward into foliaged
    hills,
Cleft by the channels of rock-fretted
    rills,
That flashed their wavelets, touched by
    iris lights,
O'er many a tiny cataract down the
    heights.

Green vales there were between, and
    pleasant lawns
Thick set with bloom, like sheen of
    tropic dawns,
Brightening the orient; further still the
    glades
Of whisperous forests, flecked with
    golden shades,
Stretched glimmering southward; on the
    wood's far rim,
Faintly discerned thro' veiling vapors,
    dim
As mists of Indian summer, the broad
    view
Was clasped by mountains flickering in
    the blue
And hazy distance; over all there hung
The morn's eternal beauty, calm and
    young.
Amid the throng, each with a marvel-
    ling face
Turned on that island Eden and its
    grace,
Was one — Avolio — a brave youth of
    Florence,
Self-exiled from his country, in abhor-
    rence
Of the base, blood-stained tyrants dom-
    inant there.

A gentleman he was, of gracious air,
And liberal as the summer, skilled in
    lore
Of arms, and chivalry, and many more
Deep sciences which others left un-
    learned.
He loved adventure; how his spirit
    burned
Within him, when, as now, a chance
    arose

To search untravelled forests, and
    strange foes
Vanquish by púissance of knightly
    blows,
Or rescue maidens from malignant
    spells,
Enforced by hordes of wizard sentinels.
So in the ardor of his martial glee,
He clapped his hands and shouted sud-
    denly:
"Ho! sirs, a challenge! let us pierce
    these woods
Down to the core: explore their sol-
    itudes,
And make the flowery empire all our
    own:
Who knows but we may conquer us a
    throne?
At least, bold feats await us, grand em-
    prise
To win us favor in our ladies' eyes;
By heaven! he is a coward who delays."

So saying, all his countenance ablaze
With passionate zeal, the youth sprang
    lightly up,
And with right lusty motion, filled a
    cup —
They brought him straightway — to the
    glistening brim
With Cyprus wine: "Now glory unto
    him,
The ardent knight, no mortal danger
    daunts,
Whose constant soul a fiery impulse
    haunts,
Which spurs him onward, onward, to
    the end;
Pledge we the brave! and may St. Ermo
    send
Success to crown our valiantest!"
               This said,
Avolio shoreward leaped, and with him
    led
The whole ship's company.

               A motley band
Were they who mustered round him on
    the strand,

Mixed knights and traders; the first fired
 for toil
Which promised glory; the last keen for
 spoil!
Thro' breezy paths and beds of blossom-
 ing thyme
Kept fresh by secret springs, the show-
 ery chime
Of whose clear falling waters in the dells
Played like an airy peal of elfin bells —
With eager minds, but aimless, idle
 feet
(The scene about them was so lone and
 sweet
It spelled their steps), 'mid labyrinths
 of flowers,
By mossy streams and in deep shadowed
 bowers,
They strayed from charm to charm
 thro' lengths of languid hours.
In thickets of wild fern and rustling
 broom,
The humble bee buzzed past them
 with a boom
Of insect thunder; and in glens afar
The golden firefly — a small animate
 star —
Shone from the twilight of the darkling
 leaves.
High noon it was, but dusk like mellow
 eve's
Reigned in the wood's deep places,
 whence it seemed
That flashing locks and quick arch
 glances gleamed
From eyes scarce human. Thus the
 fancy deemed
Of those most given to marvels; the rest
 laughed
A merry jeering laugh; and many a
 shaft
Launched from the Norman cross bow,
 pierced the nooks,
Or cleft the shallow channels of the
 brooks,
Whence, as the credulous swore, an Ore-
 ad shy,
Or a glad nymph, had peeped out cun-
 ningly.

Thus wandering, they reached a sombre
 mound
Rising abruptly from the level ground,
And planted thick with dim funereal
 trees,
Whose foliage waved and murmured,
 tho' the breeze
Had sunk to midnight quiet, and the sky
Just o'er the place seemed locked in
 apathy,
Like a fair face wan with the sudden
 stroke
Of death, or heart-break. Not a word
 they spoke,
But paused with wide, bewildered, gleam-
 ing eyes,
Standing at gaze; what spectral terrors
 rise
And coil about their hearts with serpent
 fold,
And oh! what loathly scene is this they
 hold,
Grasping with unwinking vision, as they
 creep,
Urged by their very horror, up the
 steep,
And the whole preternatural landscape
 dawns
Freezingly on them; a broad stretch of
 lawns,
Sown with rank poisonous grasses, where
 the dew
Of hovering exhalations flickered blue
And wavering on the dead-still atmos-
 phere —
Dead-still it was, and yet the grasses
 sere
Stirred as with horrid life amidst the
 sickening glare.
The affrighted crew, all save Avolio, fled
In wild disorder from this place of
 dread;
In him, albeit his terror whispered
 "fly!"
The spell of some uncouth necessity
Baffled retreat, and ruthless, scourged
 him on;
Meanwhile, the sun thro' darkening va-
 pors shone,

Nigh to his setting, and a sudden blast —
Sudden and chill — woke shrilly up, and
    passed
With ghostly din and tumult; airy
    sounds
Of sylvan horns, and sweep of circling
    hounds
Nearing the quarry.   Now the wizard
    chase
Swept faintly, faintly up the fields of
    space,
And now with backward rushing whirl
    roared by
Louder and fiercer, till a maddening
    cry —
A bitter shriek of human agony —
Leaped up, and died amid the stifling
    yell
Of brutes athirst for blood; a crowning
    swell
Of savage triumph followed, mixed with
    wails
Sad as the dying songs of nightingales,
Murmuring the name Actæon!
                  Even as one,
A wrapt sleep-walker, through the shad-
    ows dun
Of half oblivious sense, with soulless
    gaze,
Goes idly journeying through uncertain
    ways,
Thus did Avolio, sore perplexed in mind
(Excess of mystery made his spirit
    blind),
Grope through the gloom.   Anon he
    reached a fount
Whose watery columns had long ceased
    to mount
Above its prostrate Tritons.   Near at
    hand,
Dammed up in part by heaps of tawny
    sand,
All dull and lustreless, a streamlet
    wound
By trickling banks, with dark, dank
    foliage crowned,
That gloomed 'twixt sullen tides and
    lowering sky;
The melancholy waters seemed to sigh

In   wailful   murmurs   of   articulate
    woe,
Till at the last arose this strange dirge
    from below:

SONG OF THE IMPRISONED NAIAD.

"Woe! woe is me! the centuries pass
    away,
The mortal seasons run their ceaseless
    rounds,
While here I wither for the sunbright
    day,
Its genial sights and sounds.
        Woe! woe is me!

" One summer night, in ages long agone,
    I saw my woodland lover leave the
    brake;
I heard him plaining on the peaceful
    lawn
    A plaint ' for my sweet sake.'
        Woe! woe is me!

" My heart upsprang to answer that fond
    lay,
    But suddenly the star-girt planets
    paled,
And high into the welkin's glimmering
    gray
    Majestic Dian sailed!
        Woe! woe is me!

" She swept aloft, bold almost as the
    sun,
    And wrathful red as fiery-crested Mars;
Ah! then I knew some fearful deed was
    done
    On earth, or in the stars.
        Woe! woe is me!

" With ghastly face upraised, and shud-
    dering throat,
    I watched the omen with a prescient
    pain;
When, lightning-barbed, a beamy arrow
    smote,
    Or seemed to smite, my brain.
        Woe! woe is me!

" Oblivion clasped me, till I woke for-
          lorn,
Fettered and sorrowing on this lonely
          bed,
Shut from the mirthful kisses of the
          morn —
Earth's glories overhead.
          Woe! woe is me!

" The south wind stirs the sedges into
          song,
The blossoming myrtles scent the en-
          amored air;
But still, sore moaning for another's
          wrong,
I pine in sadness here.
          Woe! woe is me!

" Alas ! alas! the weary centuries
          flee,
The waning seasons perish, dark or
          bright;
My grief alone, like some charmed poi-
          son-tree,
Knows not an autumn blight.
          Woe! woe is me!"

The mournful sounds swooned off, but
          Echo rose,
And bore them up divinely to a close
Of rare mysterious sweetness ; never-
          more
Shall mortal winds to listening wood and
          shore
Waft such heart-melting music. "Where,
          oh! where,"
Avolio murmured — " to what haunted
          sphere —
Has fate at length my errant footsteps
          brought ? "

Launched on a baffling sea of mystic
          thought,
His reason in a whirling chaos, lost
Compass and chart and headway, vague-
          ly tossed
'Mid shifting shapes of wingèd fanta-
          sies.

Just then, uplifting his bewildered eyes,
He saw, half hid in shade, on either
          hand,
Twin pillars of a massive gateway grand
With gold and carvings; close behind it
          stood
A sombre mansion in a beech tree wood.

Long wreaths of ghostly ivy on its walls
Quivered like goblin tapestry, or palls,
Tattered and rusty, mildewed in the chill
Of dreadful vaults; across each window
          sill
Curtains of weird device and fiery hue
Hung moveless, — only when the sun
          glanced through
The gathering gloom, the hieroglyphs
          took form
And life and action, and the whole grew
          warm
With meanings baffling to Avolio's
          sense;
He stood expectant, trembling, with in-
          tense
Dread in his eyes, and yet a struggling
          faith,
Vital at heart.   A sudden passing
          breath —
Was it the wind ? — thrilled by his ting-
          ling ear,
Waving the curtains inward, and his
          fear
Uprose victorious, for a serpent shape,
Tall, supple, writhing, with malignant
          gape,
Which showed its cruel fangs — hissed
          in the gleam
Its own fell eyeballs kindled! Oh! su-
          preme
The horror of that vision! — as   he
          gazed,
Irresolute, all wordless, and amazed,
The monster disappeared — a moment
          sped!
The next it fawned before him on a bed
Of scarlet poppies. "Speak," Avolio
          said;
" What art thou ?   Speak! I charge
          thee in God's name!"

A death-cold shudder seized the serpent's
  frame,
Its huge throat writhed, whence bub-
  bling with a throe
Of hideous import, a voice thin and low
Broke like a muddied rill: "Bethink
  thee well,
This isle is Cos, of which old legends tell
Such marvels. Hast thou never heard
  of me,

The island's fated queen?" "Yea,
  verily,"
Avolio cried, "thou art that thing of
  dread ———"
Sharply the serpent raised its glittering
  head
And front tempestuous: "Hold! no
  tongue save mine
Must of these miseries tell thee! Then
  incline

"A monster meet for Tartarus, a thing
Whereon men gaze with awe and shuddering."

Thine ear to the dark story of my
  grief,
And with thine ear yield, yield me thy
  belief.
Foul as I am, there *was* a time,
  O youth,
When these fierce eyes were founts of
  love and truth;
There *was* a time when woman's
  blooming grace
Glowed through the flush of roses in
  my face;
When — but I sinned a deep and damn-
  ing sin,

The fruit of lustful pride nurtured
  within
By weird, forbidden knowledge — I
  defied
The night's immaculate goddess, purest
  eyed,
And holiest of immortals; I denied
The eternal Power that looks so cold and
  calm;
Therefore, O stranger, am I what I
  am,
A monster meet for Tartarus, a thing
Whereon men gaze with awe and shud-
  dering,

And stress of inward terror; through all
　　time,
Down to the last age, my abhorrèd
　　crime
Must hold me prisoner in this vile
　　abode,
Unless some man, large-hearted as a
　　God,
Bolder than Ajax, mercifully deign
To kiss me on the mouth!"

　　　　　　　　　　She towered amain,
With sparkling crest, and universal
　　thrill
Of frenzied eagerness, that seemed to
　　fill
Her cavernous eyes with jets of lurid
　　fire,
Pulsed from the burning core of unap-
　　peased desire.

Back stepped Avolio with a loathing
　　fear,
Sick to the inmost soul; then did he
　　hear
The awful creature vent a tortured
　　groan,
Her frantic neck and dragon's forehead
　　thrown
Madly to earth, whereon awhile she
　　lay,
Her glances veiled, her dark crest turned
　　away.

As thus she grovelled, quivering on the
　　ground,
Stole through the brooding silence a
　　faint sound
As 'twere of hopeless grief — it seemed
　　to be
A human voice weeping how piteously!
Yet its deep passion striving to sub-
　　due.
Just then the serpent writhed her folds
　　anew,
And while from earth her horrent crest
　　she rears,
The loathly creature's face is bathed in
　　tears!

"Lady!" the knight said, "if in sooth
　　thou art
A maid and human, wherefore thus de-
　　part
From truth's plain path to blind me?
　　well I know
This Dian, famed and worshipped long
　　ago
By heathen folk, was as the idle fume
Formed into shifting shapes of vaporous
　　bloom
O'er her vain altars. Ah!" (he shud-
　　dered now,
Growing death-pale from tremulous chin
　　to brow)
"Ah, God! I cannot kiss thee! Ne'er-
　　theless,
Fain am I in the true God's name to bless,
And even to mark thee with His sacred
　　cross!"

As one weighed down by anguish and
　　the loss
Of one last hope, in faltering tones and
　　sad
The serpent spake: "Deem'st thou that
　　Dian had
No life but that wherewith her votaries
　　vain
Invested a vague image of the brain?
Nay, she both *was* and *was not*, as on
　　earth,
Even to this day, full many a thing from
　　birth
To death lapses alike through bane and
　　bliss;
Full many a thing, which is not and
　　yet is,
Save to man's purblind vision; — in the
　　end
Some clearer spirits may rise to compre-
　　hend
This strange enigma! but meanwhile,
　　meanwhile
The sure heavens change not, star and
　　sunbeam smile
Fair as of yore; eternal nature keeps
Her strength and beauty, though the
　　mortal weeps

In desolation! Oh! wert *thou* but true
And brave enow this thing I ask to do,
Then human, happy, beauteous would I
    be,
Ye merciful Gods! once more!"

Then suddenly
She writhed her vast neck round, her
    glittering crest
Cast backward o'er the fierce, tumultu-
    ous breast,
Red as a stormy sunset — with a moan,
"Pass on, weak soul!" she said, "leave
    me alone;"
Then, wildly, "Go! I would not catch
    thine eye;
Go, and be safe! for swiftly, furiously,
Surges a cruel thought through all my
    blood,
And the brute instincts turn to hardi-
    hood
Of vengeful impulse all my gentler
    frame;
Go! for I would not harm thee; yet a
    flame
Of blasting torments have I power to
    raise
Through all thy being, and mine eyes
    could gaze,
Gloating on pain. Is this not horri-
    ble?"
And therewithal the wretched monster
    fell
To open weeping, with sad front, and
    bowed.

Something in such base cruelty avowed,
Blent with the softer will which disal-
    lowed
Its exercise, so on Avolio wrought,
That sore perplexed, revolving many a
    thought,
He lingered still, lost in a spiritual mist;
But when the mouth that waited to be
    kissed,
Fringed with a yellow foam, malignly
    rose
Before him, his first fear its terrible
    throes

Renewed. "And how, O baleful
    shape!" said he —
Striving to speak in passionless tones,
    and free —
"How can I tell, what certain gage have
    I,
That this strange kiss thine awful des-
    tiny
Hath not ordained — the least elaborate
    plan
Whereby to snare and slay me?" "O
    man! man!"
The serpent answered, with a loftier
    mien —
A voice grown clear, majestic and se-
    rene —
"Shall *matter* always triumph? the
    base mould
Mask the immortal essence, uncontrolled
Save by your grovelling fancies mean
    and cold?
O green and happy woods, breathing like
    sleep!
O quiet habitants of places deep
In leafy shades, that draw your peaceful
    breaths,
Passing fair lives to rest in tranquil
    deaths!
O earth! O sea! O heavens! forever
    dumb
To man, while ages go and ages come
Mysterious, have the dark Fates willed
    it so
That nevermore the sons of men shall
    know
The secret of your silence? the wide
    scope
Granted your basking pleasures, and
    sweet hope,
Revived in vernal warmth and spring-
    tide rains,
Your long, long pleasures, and your
    fleeting pains?
And must the lack of what is brave and
    true,
From other souls, callous or blind there-
    to,
From what themselves beauteous and
    truthful are,

Differ for aye as glow-worms from a
    star ?
Is such our life's decretal ? Shall the
    faith
Which even, perchance, the clearest
    spirit hath
In good within us, always prove less
    bold
Than keen suspicions, nursed by craven
    doubt,
Of treacherous ills, and evil from with-
    out ?"
Then, after pause, with passion: " O
    etern
And bland benignities, that breathe and
    burn
Throughout creation, are we but the
    motes
In some vague dream that idly sways
    and floats
To nothingness ? or are your glories
    pent
Within ourselves, to rise omnipotent
In bloom and music, when we bend
    above,
And wake them by the kisses of our
    love ?
I yearn to be made beautiful. Alas!
Beauty itself looks on, prepared to pass,
In hardened disbelief! *one* action kind
Would free and save me — why art thou
    so blind,
Avolio ? "   While she spoke, a timorous
    hare,
Scared by a threatening falcon from its
    lair,
Rushed to the serpent's side. With
    fondling tongue
She soothed it as a mother soothes her
    young.

Avolio mused : " Can innocent things
    like this
Take refuge by her ? then, perchance,
    some good,
Some tenderness, if rightly understood,
Lurks in her nature. *I will do the deed !*
Christ and the Virgin save me at my
    need."

He signed the monster nearer, closed
    his eyes,
And with some natural shuddering, some
    deep sighs!
Gave up his pallid lips to the foul kiss !
What followed then ? a traitorous ser-
    pent hiss,
Sharper for triumph ? Ah! not so — he
    felt
A warm, rich, yearning mouth approach
    and melt
In languid, loving sweetness on his own,
And two fond arms caressingly were
    thrown
About his neck, and on his bosom
    pressed
Twin lilies of a snow white virgin breast.

He raised his eyes, released from brief
    despair;
They rested on a maiden tall and fair —
Fair as the tropic morn, when morn is
    new —
And her sweet glances smote him through
    and through
With such keen thrilling rapture that he
    swore
His willing heart should evermore adore
Her loveliness, and woo her till he died.

" I am thine own," she whispered, "thy
    true bride,
If thou wilt take me!"
            Hand in hand they strayed
Adown the shadows through the wood-
    land glade,
Whence every evil influence shrank
    afraid,
And round them poured the golden even-
    tide.

Swiftly the tidings of this strange event
Abroad on all the garrulous winds were
    sent,
Rousing an eager world to wonderment!

Now 'mid the knightly companies that
    came
To visit Cos, was that brave chief, by
    fame

Exalted for bold deeds and faith divine,
So nobly shown erewhile in Palestine —
Tancred, Salerno's Prince — he came in
    state,
With fourscore gorgeous barges, small
    and great,
With pomp and music, like an ocean
    Fate;
His blazoned prows along the glimmer-
    ing sea
Spread like an eastern sunrise gloriously.

Him and his followers did Avolio feast
Right royally, but when the mirth in-
    creasèd,
And joyous-wingèd jests began to pass
Above the sparkling cups of Hippocras,
Tancred arose, and in his courtly phrase
Invoked delight and length of prosperous
    days
To crown that magic union; one vague
    doubt
The Prince did move, and this he dared
    speak out,
But with serene and tempered courtesy:
" It could not be that their sweet hostess
    still
Worshipped Diana and her heathen
    will ? "

" Ah sir! not so!" Avolio flushing
    cried,
" But Christ the Lord!"
            No single word replied
The beauteous lady, but with gentle pride
And a quick motion to Avolio's side
She drew more closely by a little space,
Gazing with modest passion in his face,
As one who yearned to whisper tenderly:
" O, brave kind heart! I worship only
    thee!"

------♦------

THE SOLITARY LAKE.

FROM garish light and life apart,
Shrined in the woodland's secret heart,
With delicate mists of morning furled
Fantastic o'er its shadowy world,

The lake, a vaporous vision, gleams
So vaguely bright, my fancy deems
'Tis but an airy lake of dreams.

Dreamlike, in curves of palest gold,
The wavering mist-wreaths manifold
Part in long rifts, through which I view
Gray islets throned in tides as blue
As if a piece of heaven withdrawn —
Whence hints of sunrise touch the
    dawn —
Had brought to earth its sapphire glow,
And smiled, a second heaven, below.

Dreamlike, in fitful, murmurous sighs,
I hear the distant west wind rise,
And, down the hollows wandering,
    break
In gurgling ripples on the lake,
Round which the vapors, still outspread,
Mount wanly widening overhead,
Till flushed by morning's primrose-red.

Dreamlike, each slow, soft-pulsing surge
Hath lapped the calm lake's emerald
    verge,
Sending, where'er its tremors pass
Low whisperings through the dew-wet
    grass;
Faint thrills of fairy sound that creep
To fall in neighboring nooks asleep,
Or melt in rich, low warblings made
By some winged Ariel of the glade.

With brightening morn the mockbird's
    lay
Grows stronger, mellower; far away
'Mid dusky reeds, which even the noon
Lights not, the lonely-hearted loon
Makes answer, her shrill music shorn
Of half its sadness; day, full-born,
Doth rout all sounds and sights forlorn.

Ah! still a something strange and rare
O'errules this tranquil earth and air,
Casting o'er both a glamour known
To *their* enchanted realm alone;
Whence shines, as 'twere a spirit's face,
The sweet coy genius of the place,

You lake beheld as if in trance,
The beauty of whose shy romance
I feel — whatever shores and skies
May charm henceforth my wondering
  eyes, —
Shall rest, undimmed by taint or stain,
'Mid lonely byways of the brain,
There, with its haunting grace, to seem
Set in the landscape of a dream.

---◇---

THE VOICE IN THE PINES.

THE morn is softly beautiful and still,
  Its light fair clouds in pencilled gold
    and gray
Pause motionless above the pine-grown
  hill,
Where the pines, tranced as by a wiz-
    ard's will,
  Uprise as mute and motionless as
    they!

Yea! mute and moveless; not one flick-
    ering spray
  Flashed into sunlight, nor a gaunt
    bough stirred;
Yet, if wooed hence beneath those pines
    to stray,
We catch a faint, thin murmur far away,
  A bodiless voice, by grosser ears un-
    heard.

What voice is this? what low and sol-
    emn tone,
  Which, though all wings of all the
    winds seem furled,
Nor even the zephyr's fairy flute is blown,
Makes thus forever its mysterious moan
  From out the whispering pine-tops'
    shadowy world?

Ah! can it be the antique tales are true?
  Doth some lone Dryad haunt the
    breezeless air,
Fronting yon bright immitigable blue,
And wildly breathing all her wild soul
    through
  That strange unearthly music of de-
    spair?

Or can it be that ages since, storm-
    tossed,
  And driven far inland from the roar-
    ing lea,
Some baffled ocean-spirit, worn and lost,
Here, through dry summer's dearth and
    winter's frost,
  Yearns for the sharp, sweet kisses of
    the sea?

Whate'er the spell, I hearken and am
    dumb,
  Dream-touched, and musing in the
    tranquil morn;
All woodland sounds — the pheasant's
    gusty drum,
The mock-bird's fugue, the droning in-
    sect's hum —
  Scarce heard for that strange, sorrow-
    ful voice forlorn!

Beneath the drowsèd sense, from deep to
    deep
  Of spiritual life its mournful minor
    flows,
Streamlike, with pensive tide, whose
    currents keep
Low murmuring 'twixt the bounds of
    grief and sleep,
  Yet locked for aye from sleep's divine
    repose.

---◆---

VISIT OF THE WRENS.

FLYING from out the gusty west,
To seek the place where last year's nest,
Ragged, and torn by many a rout
Of winter winds, still rocks about
The branches of the gnarled old tree
Which sweep my cottage library —
Here on the genial southern side,
In a late gleam of sunset's pride,
Came back my tiny, springtide friends,
The self-same pair of chattering wrens
That with arch eyes and restless bill
Used to frequent yon window sill,
Winged sprites, in April's showery
    glow.

'Tis now twelve weary months ago
Since first I saw them; here again
They drop outside the glittering pane,
Each bearing a dried twig or leaf,
To build with labor hard, yet brief,
This season's nest, where, blue and
    round,
Their fairy eggs will soon be found.
But sky and breeze and blithesome sun,
Until that little home is done,
Shall — wondering, maybe — hear and
    see
Such chatter, bustle, industry,
As well may stir to emulous strife
Slow currents of a languid life,
Whether in bird or man they run!

But when, in sooth, the nest complete
Swings gently in its green retreat,
And soft the mother birdling's breast
Doth in the cozy circlet rest,
How, back from jovial journeying,
Merry of heart, though worn of wing,
Her brown mate, proudly perched above
The limb that holds his brooding love,
His head upturned, his aspect sly,
Regards her with a cunning eye,
As one who saith, " How well you bear
The dullness of these duties, dear;
To dwell so long on nest or tree
Would be, I know, slow death to me;
But, then, you women folk were made
For patient waiting, in — the shade!"

So tame one little guest becomes —
'Tis the male bird — my scattered
    crumbs
He takes from window sill and lawn
Each morning in the early dawn;
And yesterday he dared to stand
Serenely on my outstretched hand,
While his wee wife, with puzzled
    glance,
Looked from her breezy seat askance!

My pretty pensioners! ye have flown
Twice from your winter nook unknown,
To build your humble homestead here,
In the first flush of springtide cheer;

But ah! I wonder if again,
Flitting outside the window pane,
When next the shrewd March winds
    shall blow,
Or in mild April's showers glow,
New come from out the shimmering
    west,
You'll seek the place of this year's
    nest,
Ragged and torn by then, no doubt,
And swinging in worn shreds about
The branches of the ancient tree.

Nay, who may tell? Yet, verily,
Methinks when, spring and summer
    passed,
Adown the long, low autumn blast,
In some dim gloaming, chill and drear,
You, with your fledglings, disappear,
That ne'er by porch or tree or pane
Mine eyes shall greet your forms again!

What then? At least the good ye
    brought,
The delicate charms for eye and thought
Survives; though death should be your
    doom
Before another spring flower's bloom,
Or fairer clime should tempt your wings
To bide 'mid fragrant blossomings
On some far Southland's golden lea,
Still may fresh spring morns light for
    me
Your tiny nest, their breezes bear
Your chirping, household joyance near
And all your quirks and tricksome ways
Bring back through many smiling days
Or future Aprils; not the less
Your simple drama shall impress
Fancy and heart, thus acted o'er
Toward each small issue, as of yore,
With sun and wind and skies of blue
To witness, wondering, all you do,
Because your happy toil and mirth
May be of fine, ideal birth;
Because each quick, impulsive note
May thrill a visionary throat,
Each flash of glancing wing and eye
Be gleams of vivid fantasy;

Since whatsoe'er of form and tone
A past reality hath known,
Most charming unto soul and sense,
But wins that subtle effluence,
That spiritual air which softly clings
About all sweet and vanished things,
Causing a bygone joy to be
Vital as actuality,
Yet with each earthlier tint or trace
Lost in a pure, ethereal grace!

FOREST PICTURES.

MORNING.

O GRACIOUS breath of sunrise! divine
  air!
  That brood'st serenely o'er the pur-
    pling hills;
O blissful valleys! nestling, cool and
  fair,
  In the fond arms of yonder murmur-
    ous rills,
Breathing their grateful measures to the
  sun;
O dew-besprinkled paths, that circling
  run
Through sylvan shades and solemn si-
  lences,
Once more ye bring my fevered spirit
  peace!

The fitful breezes, fraught with forest
  balm,
  Faint, in rare wafts of perfume, on my
    brow;
The woven lights and shadows, rife with
  calm,
  Creep slantwise 'twixt the foliage,
    bough on bough
Uplifted heavenward, like a verdant
  cloud
Whose rain is music, soft as love, or
  loud
With jubilant hope — for there, en-
  tranced, apart,.
The mock-bird sings, close, close to Na-
  ture's heart.

Shy forms about the greenery, out and
  in,
  Flit 'neath the broadening glories of
    the morn;
The squirrel — that quaint sylvan harle-
  quin —
  Mounts the tall trunks; while swift as
    lightning, born
Of summer mists, from tangled vine and
  tree
Dart the dove's pinions, pulsing vividly
Down the dense glades, till glimmering
  far and gray
The dusky vision softly melts away!

In transient, pleased bewilderment I
  mark
  The last dim shimmer of those lessen-
    ing wings,
When from lone copse and shadowy
  covert, hark!
  What mellow tongue through all the
    woodland rings!
The deer-hound's voice, sweet as the
  golden bell's,
Prolonged by flying echoes round the
  dells,
And up the loftiest summits wildly
  borne,
Blent with the blast of some keen hunts-
  man's horn.

And now the checkered vale is left be-
  hind;
  I climb the slope, and reach the hill-
    top bright;
Here, in bold freedom, swells a sover-
  eign wind,
  Whose gusty prowess sweeps the pine-
    clad height;
While the pines — dreamy Titans roused
  from sleep —
Answer with mighty voices, deep on
  deep
Of wakened foliage surging like a
  sea;
And o'er them smiles Heaven's calm
  infinity!

"The woven lights and shadows, rife with calm,
Creep slantwise 'twixt the foliage, bough on bough."

GOLDEN DELL.

BEYOND our moss-grown pathway lies
A dell so fair, to genial eyes
It dawns an ever-fresh surprise!

To touch its charms with gentler grace,
The softened heavens a loving face
Bend o'er that sweet, secluded place.

There first, despite the March wind's
  cold,
Above the pale-hued emerald mould
The earliest spring-tide buds unfold;

There first the ardent mock-bird, long
Winter's dumb thrall, from winter's
  wrong
Breaks into gleeful floods of song;

Till, from coy thrush to garrulous wren,
The humbler bards of copse and glen
Outpour their vernal notes again;

While such harmonious rapture rings,
With stir and flash of eager wings
Glimpsed fleetly, where the jasmine
  clings

To bosk and briar, we blithely say,
"Farewell! bleak nights and mornings
  gray,
Earth opes her festal court to-day!"

There, first, from out some balmy nest,
By half-grown woodbine flowers caressed,
Steal zephyrs of the mild southwest;

O'er purpling rows of wild-wood peas,*
So blandly borne, the droning bees
Still suck their honeyed cores at ease;

Or, trembling through yon verdurous
  mass,
Dew-starred, and dimpling as they pass
The wavelets of the billowy grass!

---

* In the Southern woods, often among sterile tracts of pine barren, a species of *wild pea* is found, or a plant which in all externals resembles the pea plant.

But, fairest of fair things that dwell
'Mid sylvan nurslings of the dell,
Is that clear stream whose murmurs swell

To music's airiest issues wrought,
As if a Naiad's tongue were fraught
With secrets of its whispered thought.

Yes, fairest of fair things, it flows
'Twixt banks of violet and of rose,
Touched always by a quaint repose.

How golden bright its currents glide!
While goldenly from side to side
Bird shadows flit athwart the tide.

So Golden Dell we name the place,
And aye may Heaven's serenest face
Dream o'er it with a smile of grace;

For next the moss-grown path it lies,
So pure, so fresh to genial eyes
It glows with hints of Paradise!

———◆———

ASPECTS OF THE PINES.

TALL, sombre, grim, against the morn-
    ing sky
  They rise, scarce touched by melan-
    choly airs,
Which stir the fadeless foliage dream-
    fully,
  As if from realms of mystical despairs.

Tall, sombre, grim, they stand with
    dusky gleams
  Brightening to gold within the wood-
    land's core,
Beneath the gracious noontide's tranquil
    beams —
  But the weird winds of morning sigh
    no more.

A stillness, strange, divine, ineffable,
  Broods round and o'er them in the
    wind's surcease,
And on each tinted copse and shimmer-
    ing dell
  Rests the mute rapture of deep heart-
    ed peace.

Last, sunset comes — the solemn joy and
  might
Borne from the West when cloudless
  day declines —
Low, flutelike breezes sweep the waves
  of light,
  And lifting dark green tresses of the
   pines,

Till every lock is luminous — gently float,
  Fraught with hale odors up the heav-
   ens afar
To faint when twilight on her virginal
  throat
  Wears for a gem the tremulous vesper
   star.

---◆---

MIDSUMMER IN THE SOUTH.

I LOVE Queen August's stately sway,
And all her fragrant south winds say,
With vague, mysterious meanings
  fraught,
Of unimaginable thought;
Those winds, 'mid change of gloom and
  gleam,
Seem wandering thro' a golden dream —
The rare midsummer dream that lies
In humid depths of nature's eyes,
Weighing her languid forehead down
Beneath a fair but fiery crown:
Its witchery broods o'er earth and skies,
Fills with divine amenities
The bland, blue spaces of the air,
And smiles with looks of drowsy cheer
'Mid hollows of the brown-hued hills;
And oft, in tongues of tinkling rills,
A softer, homelier utterance finds
Than that which haunts the lingering
  winds!

I love midsummer's azure deep,
Whereon the huge white clouds, asleep,
Scarce move through lengths of trancéd
  hours;
Some, raised in forms of giant towers —
Dumb Babels, with ethereal stairs
Scaling the vast height — unawares

What mocking spirit, æther-born,
Hath built those transient spires in
  scorn,
And reared towards the topmost sky
Their unsubstantial fantasy!
Some stretched in tenuous arcs of light
Athwart the airy infinite,
Far glittering up yon fervid dome,
And lapped by cloudland's misty foam,
Whose wreaths of fine sun-smitten spray
Melt in a burning haze away:
Some throned in heaven's serenest
  smiles,
Pure-hued, and calm as fairy isles,
Girt by the tides of soundless seas —
The heavens' benign Hesperides.

I love midsummer uplands, free
To the bold raids of breeze and bee,
Where, nested warm in yellowing
  grass,
I hear the swift-winged partridge pass,
With whirr and boom of gusty flight,
Across the broad heath's treeless height:
Or, just where, elbow-poised, I lift
Above the wild flower's careless drift
My half-closed eyes, I see and hear
The blithe field-sparrow twittering clear
Quick ditties to his tiny love;
While, from afar, the timid dove,
With faint, voluptuous murmur, wakes
The silence of the pastoral brakes.

I love midsummer sunsets, rolled
Down the rich west in waves of gold,
With blazing crests of billowy fire.
But when those crimson floods retire,
In noiseless ebb, slow-surging, grand,
By pensive twilight's flickering strand,
In gentler mood I love to mark
The slow gradations of the dark;
Till, lo! from Orient's mists withdrawn,
Hail! to the moon's resplendent dawn;
On dusky vale and haunted plain
Her effluence falls like balmy rain;
Gaunt gulfs of shadow own her might;
She bathes the rescued world in light,
So that, albeit my summer's day,
Erewhile did breathe its life away,

Methinks, whate'er its hours had won
Of beauty, born from shade and sun,
Hath not perchance so wholly died,
But o'er the moonlight's silvery tide
Comes back, sublimed and purified!

———◆———

CLOUD-PICTURES.

HERE in these mellow grasses, the whole
    morn,
I love to rest; yonder, the ripening corn
Rustles its greenery; and his blithesome
    horn

Windeth the frolic breeze o'er field and
    dell,
Now pealing a bold stave with lusty
    swell,
Now falling to low breaths ineffable

Of whispered joyance. At calm length
    I lie,
Fronting the broad blue spaces of the
    sky,
Covered with cloud-groups, softly jour-
    neying by:

An hundred shapes, fantastic, beau-
    teous, strange,
Are theirs, as o'er yon airy waves they
    range
At the wind's will, from marvellous
    change to change;

Castles, with guarded roof, and turret
    tall,
Great sloping archway, and majestic
    wall,
Sapped by the breezes to their noiseless
    fall!

Pagodas vague! above whose towers
    outstream
Banners that wave with motions of a
    dream—
Rising, or drooping in the noontide
    gleam;

Gray lines of Orient pilgrims: a gaunt
    band
On famished camels, o'er the desert
    sand
Plodding towards their prophet's Holy
    Land;

'Mid-ocean,—and a shoal of whales at
    play,
Lifting their monstrous frontlets to the
    day,
Thro' rainbow arches of sun-smitten
    spray;

Followed by splintered icebergs, vast
    and lone,
Set in swift currents of some arctic
    zone,
Like fragments of a Titan's world o'er-
    thrown;

Next, measureless breadths of barren,
    treeless moor,
Whose vaporous verge fades down a
    glimmering shore,
Round which the foam-capped billows
    toss and roar!

Calms of bright water—like a fairy's
    wiles,
Wooing with ripply cadence and soft
    smiles,
The golden shore-slopes of Hesperian
    Isles;

Their inland plains rife with a rare in-
    crease
Of plumèd grain! and many a snowy
    fleece
Shining athwart the dew-lit hills of
    peace;

Wrecks of gigantic cities — to the
    tune
Of some wise air-God built!—o'er
    which the noon
Seems shuddering; caverns, such as the
    wan Moon

Shows in her desolate bosom; then, a
crowd
Of awed and reverent faces, palely
bowed
O'er a dead queen, laid in her ashy
shroud —

A queen of eld — her pallid brow im-
pearled
By gems barbaric! her strange beauty
furled
In mystic cerements of the antique
world.

Weird pictures, fancy-gendered! — one
by one,
'Twixt blended beams and shadows, gold
and dun,
These transient visions vanish in the
sun.

———◆———

SONNET.

SUNSET, the god-like artist, paints on air
Pictures of loveliness and terror blent!
Lo! yonder clouds, like mountains tem-
pest-rent,
Through whose abysmal depths the
lightning's glare
Darts from wild gulfs and caverns of de-
spair:
O'er these a calm, majestic firmament,
Flushed with rich hues, with rainbow
isles besprent,
Like homes of peace in oceans heavenly
fair:

But *still*, beyond, one lone mysterious
cloud,
Steeped in the solemn sunset's fiery
mist,
Strange semblance takes of Him whose
visage bowed,
Divinely sweet, o'er all things, dark or
bright,
Yet draws the darkness ever toward
His light
The tender eyes and awful brow of
Christ!

IN THE PINE BARRENS.

SUNSET.

HARK! to the mournful wind; its burden
drear
Borne over leagues of desert wild and
dun,
Sinks to a weary cadence of despair,
Beyond the closing gateways of the
sun.

Yon clouds are big with flame, and not
with rain,
Massed on the marvellous heaven in
splendid pyres,
Whereon ethereal genii, half in pain
And half in triumph, light their fervid
fires:

Kindled in funeral majesty to rise
Above the perished day, whose latest
breath
Exhaled, a roseate effluence to the skies,
Still lingers o'er the pageantry of
death.

·　　　·　　　·　　　·　　　·

One stalwart hill his stern defiant crest
Boldly against the horizon line up-
rears,
His blasted pines, smit by the fiery West,
Uptowering rank on rank, like Titan
spears;

Fantastic, bodeful, o'er the rock-strewn
ground
Casting grim shades beyond the hill
slope riven,
Which mock the loftier shafts, keen,
lustre-crowned
And raised as if to storm the courts of
Heaven!

As sinks the wind, so wane those won-
drous lights;
Slowly they wane from hill and sky
and cloud,
While round the woodland waste and
glimmering heights
The mist of gloaming trails its silvery
shroud!

Through which, uncertain, vague as
   shifting ghosts,
The forms of all things touched by
   mystery seem,
I walk, methinks, on pale Plutonian
   coasts,
   And grope 'mid spectral shadows of a
     dream.

SONNET.

In the deep hollow of this sheltered dell
I hear the rude winds chant their giant
   staves
Far, far beyond me, where in darkening
   waves
The airy seas of cloudland sink or swell.

No faint breeze stirs the wild-flower's
   soundless bell,
Here in the quiet vale, whose rivulet
   laves
Banks silent almost as those desert
   graves,
Whereof the worn Zaharan wanderers
   tell.

Oh! thus from out still depths of tran-
   quil doom,
My soul beyond her views life's turmoil
   vast,
Hearkening the windy roar and rage of
   men,

Vain to *her* eyes as shades from cloud-
   land cast,
And to *her* ears like far-off winds that
   boom,
Heard, but scarce heard, in this Arca-
   dian glen!

THE WOODLAND PHASES.

Yon woodland, like a human mind,
   Hath many a phase of dark and
   bright;
Now dim with shadows, wandering blind,
   Now radiant with fair shapes of light.

They softly come, they softly go,
   Capricious as the vagrant wind,
Nature's vague thoughts in gloom or
   glow,
   That leave no airiest trace behind.

No trace, no trace! yet wherefore thus
   Do shade and beam our spirit's stir?
Ah! Nature may be cold to us,
   But we are strangely moved by her.

The wild bird's strain, the breezy spray,
   Each hour with sure earth-changes
   rife
Hint more than all the sages say,
   Or poets sing of death and life.

For truths half drawn from Nature's
   breast,
   Through subtlest types of form and
   tone,
Outweigh what man, at most, hath
   guessed
   While heeding his own heart alone.

And midway, betwixt heaven and us,
   Stands Nature in her fadeless grace,
Still pointing to our Father's house,
   His glory on her mystic face.

AFTER THE TORNADO.

Last eve the earth was calm, the heav-
   ens were clear;
A peaceful glory crowned the waning
   west,
And yonder distant mountain's hoary
   crest
The semblance of a silvery robe did
   wear,
Shot through with moon-wrought tis-
   sues; far and near
Wood, rivulet, field — all Nature's face
   — expressed
The haunting presence of enchanted rest.
One twilight star shone like a blissful
   tear,
Unshed. But now, what ravage in a
   night!

Yon mountain height fades in its cloud-
     girt pall;
The prostrate wood lies smirched with
     rain and mire;
Through the shorn fields the brook
     whirls, wild and white;
While o'er the turbulent waste and
     woodland fall,
Glares the red sunrise, blurred with
     mists of fire!

IN THE BOWER.

THE gusty and passionate March hath
     died;
And now in the golden April-tide
There sits in the shade of her jasmine
     bower
A maid more fair than an April flower.

The delicate curve of her perfect mouth,
Whose tints grow warm in the fervid
     South,
She stoops to press, as she murmurs
     low,
On a note upraised in her hand of snow.

What words are writ on the tiny scroll?
What thoughts lie deep in the maiden's
     soul?
Oh, is it with bliss of her love she sighs?
Is the light but love's in those shy
     brown eyes?

So thinks the mock-bird trilling his lay
On the tremulous top of the lilac spray;
He views the maid, on his perch apart,
And his song is meant for her secret
     heart.

So thinks the breeze, for its frolic free
With the rose's stem, and the wing o'
     the bee
It leaves, to sigh in the maiden's ear,
"He is coming, sweet! he is almost
     here!"

So thinks the sun, for his ardent beams
Grow mellow and soft as a virgin's
     dreams,

Through the vine-leaf shadows steal coy-
     ly down,
And she wears his light like a bridal
     crown.

Let the songster trill, and the breezes
     sigh,
And the sun weave crowns of his light i'
     the sky;
She heeds them not, for a step is heard,
And her soul leaps up like a startled
     bird —

Her soul leaps up, but it is not fear:
He is coming, sweet! he is here! is here!
And she flies to his bosom, (ah! panting
     dove),
And is folded home on the heart of love!

WHENCE?

EERILY the wind doth blow
     Through the woodland hollow;
Eërily forlorn and low,
     Tremulous echoes follow!

Whence the low wind's tortured plaint?
     Burden hopeless, dreary,
As the anguished tones that faint
     Down the *Miserere.*

Whence? From far-off seas its moan!
     Darksome waves and lonely,
Where the tempest, overblown,
     Leaves a death-calm only.

Thence it caught the awful cry
     Of some last pale swimmer,
O'er whose drowning brain and eye
     Life grows dim and dimmer—

Ere the billows claim their prey,
     Settling stern and lonely.
Where the storm-clouds, rolled away,
     Leave death-silence only!

So with pain the wind-heart sighs;
     Through its sad commotion
Weary sea-tides sob, and rise
     Wailing hints of Ocean!

Hist! oh hist! as spreads the mist,
   Wood and hill-slope doming,
By no grace of starlight kissed,
   'Mid the shadowy gloaming,

Drearier grows the wind, more drear
   Echoes shuddering follow,
Till a place of doom and fear
   Seems that haunted hollow!

"Uplift and bear me where the wild flowers grow,
By many a golden dell-side, sweet and low."

SONNET.

ENOUGH, this glimpse of splendor wed to
   shame;
Enough this gilded misery, this bright
   woe.
Pause, genial wind! that even here dost
   blow
Thy cheerful clarion; and from dust
   and flame
The noonday pest, the night-enshrouded
   blame,
Uplift and bear me where the wild flow-
   ers grow
By many a golden dell-side sweet and
   low,

Shrined in the sylvan Eden whence I
   came.
O woodland water! O fair-whispering
   pine!
Loved of the dryad none but I have
   viewed!
O dew-lit glen, and lone glade, breathing
   balm,
Receive and bless me, till this tumult
   rude
Merged in your verdant solitudes di-
   vine,
My soul once more hath found her an-
   cient calm!

VIOLETS.

"Rare wine of flowers." — FLETCHER.

A GUSTY wind o'ersweeps the garden
     close,
And, where the jonquil, with the white-
     rod glows,
     Riots like some rude hoyden uncon-
          trolled.
But here, where sunshine and coy
     shadows meet,
Out gleam the tender eyes of violets
     sweet,
     Touched by the vapory noontide's
          fleeting gold.

What subtlest perfume floats serenely up!
Ethereal wine that brims each delicate
     cup,
     Rifled by viewless Ariels of the air,
And lo! methinks from out these fairy
     flowers
Rise the strange shades of half forgotten
     hours,
     Pale, tearful, mute, and yet, O
          heaven, how fair!

Yea, fair and marvellous, gliding gently
     nigh,
Some with raised brows and eyes of con-
     stancy,
     Fixed with fond meanings on a goal
          above.
And some faint shades of weary, droop-
     ing grace,
Each with a nameless pathos on its face,
     Breathing of heart-break and sad
          death of love.

Slowly they vanish! while these odors
     steep
Spirit and sense, as if in waves of sleep,
     Mysterious and Lethean; languid
          streams
Flowing through realms of twilight
     thought apart,
Whereon the half-closed petals of the
     heart
     Pulse flower-like o'er a whispering
          tide of dreams: —

Nor wakes the soul to outward sound or
     sight,
Till, noonday beams declining, warm
     and light,
     A wood-breeze fans the dreamer's
          forehead calm;
Who feels as one long wrapped from
     pain and drouth,
By magic dreams dreamed in the fervid
     south,
     Beneath the golden shadows of the
          palm.

------◆------

BY THE GRAVE OF HENRY TIMROD.

WHEN last we parted — thy frail hand
     in mine —
     Above us smiled September's passion-
          less sky,
And touched by fragrant airs, the hill-
     side pine
     Thrilled in the mellow sunshine ten-
          derly;
          So rich the robe on nature's slow de-
               cay,
We scarce could deem the winter tide
     was near,
     Or lurking death, masked in imperial
          grace;
          Alas! that autumn day
Drew not more close to winter's empire
     drear
     Than thou, my heart! to meet grief
          face to face!

I clasped thy tremulous hand, nor
     marked how weak
     Its answering grasp; and if thine eyes
          did swim
In unshed tears, and on thy fading cheek
     Rested a nameless shadow, gaunt and
          dim, —
          My soul was blind; fear had not
               touched her sight
To awful vision; so, I bade thee go,
     Careless, and tranquil as that treach-
          erous morn;
          Nor dreamed how soon the blight

Of long-implanted seeds of care would
    throw
  Their nightshade flowers above the
    springing corn.

Since then, full many a year hath risen
    and set,
  With spring-tide showers, and au-
    tumn pomps unfurled
O'er gorgeous woods, and mountain walls
    of jet —
  While love and loss, alternate, ruled
    the world;
    Till now once more we meet — my
      friend and I —
Once more, once more — and thus, alas!
    we meet —
  Above, a rayless heaven; beneath, a
    grave;
    Oh, Christ! and dost thou lie
Neglected here, in thy worn burial-
    sheet ?
  Friend! were there none to shield
    thee, none to save ?

Ask of the winter winds — scarce colder
    they
  Than that strange land — thy birth-
    place and thy tomb:
Ask of the sombre cloud-wracks trooping
    gray,
  And grim as hooded ghosts at stroke
    of doom;
    At least, the winds, though chill,
      with gentler sweep
Seem circling round and o'er thy place
    of rest,
  While the sad clouds, as clothed in
    tenderer guise,
    Do lowly bend, and weep
O'er the dead poet, in whose living
    breast
  Dumb nature found a voice, how
    sweet and wise!

Once more we meet, once more — my
    friend and I —
  But ah! his hand is dust, his eyes
    are dark;

Thy merciless weight, thou dread mor-
    tality,
  From out his heart hath crushed the
    latest spark
    Of that warm life, benignly bright
      and strong;
Yet no; we have *not* met — my friend
    and I —
  Ashes to ashes in this earthly prison!
    Are these, O child of song,
Thy glorious self, heir of the stars and
    sky ?
Thou art not here, not *here*, for thou
    hast risen!

Death gave thee wings, and lo! thou
    hast soared above
  All human utterance and all finite
    thought;
Pain may not hound thee through that
    realm of love,
  Nor grief, wherewith thy mortal days
    were fraught,
    Load thee again — nor vulture want,
      that fed
Even on thy heart's blood, wound thee;
    idle, then,
  Our bitter sorrowing; what though
    bleak and wild
    Rests thine uncrownèd head ?
Known art thou now to angels and to
    men —
  Heaven's saint and earth's brave
    singer undefiled.

Even as I spake in broken under-breath
  The winds drooped lifeless; faintly
    struggling through
The heaven-bound pall, which seemed a
    pall of death,
  One cordial sunbeam cleft the opening
    blue;
  Swiftly it glanced, and settling, softly
    shone
O'er the grave's head; in that same in-
    stant came
  From the near copse a bird-song half
    divine;
    " Heart," said I, " hush thy moan,

List the bird's singing, mark the heaven-
　　born flame,
　God-given are these — an omen and a
　　sign!"

In the bird's song an omen *his* must
　live!
　In the warm glittering of that golden
　　beam,
A sign his soul's majestic hopes survive,
　Raised to fruition o'er life's weary
　　dream.
　　So now I leave him, low, yet, rest-
　　　ful here;
So now I leave him, high-exalted, far
　Beyond all memory of earth's guilt
　　or guile;
　Hark! tis his voice of cheer,
Dropping, methinks, from some mys-
　　terious star;
　His face I see, and on his face — a
　　smile!

———◆———

SONNET.

As one who strays from out some shad-
　　owy glade,
Fronting a lurid noontide, stern, yet
　　bright,
O'er mart and tower, and castellated
　　height,
Shrinks slowly backward, dazed and
　　half afraid —
So I, whose household gods their stand
　　have made
Far from the populous city's life and
　　light,
Its roar of traffic and its stormy might,
Shrink as I pass beyond my woodland
　　shade.
The wordy conflict, the tempestuous din
Of these vast capitals, on ear and brain
Beat with the loud, reiterated swell
Of one fierce strain of passion and of sin,
Strange as in nightmare dreams the
　　mad refrain
Of some wild chorus of the vaults of
　　Hell.

ARIEL.

"My dainty Ariel." —*Tempest.*

A VOICE like the murmur of doves,
　Soft lightning from eyes of blue;
On her cheek a flush like love's
　First delicate, rosebud hue;

Bright torrents of hazel hair,
　Which, glittering, flow and float
O'er the swell of her bosom fair,
　And the snows of her matchless
　　throat;

Lithe limbs of a life so fine,
　That their rhythmical motion seems
But a part of the grace divine
　Of the music of haunted dreams;

Low gurgling laughter, as sweet
　As the swallow's song i' the South,
And a ripple of dimples that, dancing,
　　meet
　By the curves of a perfect mouth;

O creature of light and air!
　O fairy sylph o' th' sun!
Hearts whelmed in the tidal gold of her
　　hair
　Rejoice to be *so* undone!

———◆———

SONNET.

THE glorious star of morning would we
　　blame
　Because it burns not on the front
　　of night?
　Or the calm evening planet, that her
　　light
Foretells not sunrise, with its herald-
　　flame?
All things that are should subtly own
　　the same
　Eternal law! the stars shine on aright,
　Each in his sphere; the souls of Love
　　and Might
Their separate bounds of grace or grand-
　　eur claim;

Not on the low or lofty, great or small,
  Should justice fix for judgment; the
    true soul,
  Which sways its own world in serene
    control,
Highest or humblest — such the Master's
    call
Shall summon upward, with its deep
    " well done,"
And the just Father crown his faith-
    ful son!

THE CLOUD-STAR.

A FABLE.

FAR up within the tranquil sky,
  Far up it shone;
Floating, how gently, silently,
  Floating alone!

A sunbeam touched its loftier side
  With deepening light:
Then to its inmost soul did glide,
  Divinely bright.

The cloud transfigured to a star,
  Thro' all its frame
Throbbed in the fervent heavens afar,
  One pulse of flame:

One pulse of flame, which inward turned,
  And slowly fed
On its own heart, that burned, and
    burned,
  'Till almost dead,

The cloud still imaged as a star,
  Waned up the sky;
Waned slowly, pallid, ghost-like, far,
  Wholly to die;

But die so grandly in the sun —
  The noonfire's breath —
Methinks the glorious death it won,
  Life! life! not death!

Meanwhile a million insect things
  Crawl on below,
And gaudy worms on fluttering wings
  Flit to and fro;

Blind to that cloud, which grown a star,
  Divinely bright,
Waned in the deepening heavens afar,
  Till — lost in light!

SWEETHEART, GOOD-BYE!

A SONG.

SWEETHEART, good-bye! Our varied day
Is closing into twilight gray,
And up from bare, bleak wastes of sea
The north-wind rises mournfully;
A solemn prescience, strangely drear,
Doth haunt the shuddering twilight air;
It fills the earth, it chills the sky —
    Sweetheart, good-bye!

Sweetheart, good-bye! Our joys are
    passed,
And night with silence comes at last;
All things must end, yea, — even love —
Nor know we, if reborn above,
The heart-blooms of our earthly prime
Shall flower beyond these bounds of time.
" Ah! death alone is sure!" we cry —
    Sweetheart, good-bye!

Sweetheart, good-bye! Through mists
    and tears
Pass the pale phantoms of our years,
Once bright with spring, or subtly strong
When summer's noontide thrilled with
    song;
Now wan, wild-eyed, forlornly bowed,
Each rayless as an autumn cloud
Fading on dull September's sky —
    Sweetheart, good-bye!

Sweetheart, good-bye! The vapors rolled
Athwart yon distant, darkening wold
Are types of what our world doth know
Of tenderest loves of long ago;
And thus, when all is done and said,
Our life lived out, *our* passion dead,
What can their wavering record be
But tinted mists of memory?
Oh! clasp and kiss me ere we die —
    Sweetheart, good-bye!

SONNET.

COMPOSED ON A MARCH MORNING IN
THE WOODS.

THE winds are loud and trumpet-clear
　　to-day;
　　They seem to sound an onset, half in
　　　　ire,
　　Half in the wildness of a vague desire
To force spring's fairy vanguard to de-
　　lay;
For here, methinks, worn winter stands
　　at bay,
　　Yet stands how vainly! spring-time's
　　　　subtlest fire
　　Melts his cold heart to nothingness,
　　　　while nigher
Draw April hosts, and rearward powers
　　of May —
All maiden verdures, concords of sweet
　　air,
　　Stealing as dawn steals gently on the
　　　　world;
　　Breezes, balm-laden, blown from dis-
　　　　tant seas,
　　With armies of blush-roses, dew-im-
　　　　pearled,
Till Earth reclaimed from winter's grim
　　despair
　　Blooms as once bloomed the fair Hes-
　　　　perides.

FRIDA AND HER POET.

A BRAVE young poet born in days of Eld,
Dwelt 'mid the frozen Northlands; he
　　beheld,
And wondering, sung the marvels of the
　　ice,
The swirl of snow-flakes, and the quaint
　　device
Wrought on the fir-trees by the glittering
　　sleet;
And loved on stormy heights, cloud-girt,
　　to greet
The gray ger-falcon towering o'er the
　　sea;
To watch the waves, and mark the cloud-
　　drifts flee,

Big with the wrath of tempests; yet his
　　heart,
Soft as the inner rose-leaves of the
　　spring,
Rich with young life, and love's sweet
　　blossoming,
Too soon, alas! from life and love did
　　part:
Veiled was the fate that smote him;
　　unaware
What sudden, blasting doom had drawn
　　so near,
A strange blight breathed upon him, and
　　he died!

On earth to die, in heaven be glorified,
Such was the Minstrel's portion; still he
　　went
Through all the heavenly courts in dis-
　　content
And sombre grief, the pathos of his
　　woe
Rising at times to such wild overflow
As forced its wailful utterance into
　　song.
That passionate rush of music, the
　　heart's wrong
Set to the sweetness of harmonious
　　chords,
The All-Father, Odin, o'er the clash of
　　swords,
And din of heroes feasting at the
　　boards
Of loud Valhalla, heard: thereon he
　　sought
This lonely soul, in highest heaven o'er-
　　fraught
With mortal memories.　"Wherefore
　　lift'st thou here,"
The All-Father asked, "these measures
　　of despair?"
"Because my mortal Love," the Poet
　　said,
"With time grows gray and wrinkled;
　　on her head,
So golden bright in youth's benignant
　　prime,
Chill frosts of age have left their hoary
　　rime;

Her eyes are dimmed, her soft cheeks'
    rosy red
Hath with the flowers of many a spring-
    time fled;
And so when Heaven shall claim her —
    ah! the pain! —
I shall not know mine earthly love
    again!''

To whom the God, ''But doth she love
    thee still?''
'' Her love, like mine, nor years, nor
    change can kill,''
The Minstrel answered: '' Faith, a cease-
    less shower,
Keeps fair and bright our love's immac-
    ulate flower.''
''I loose thy heavenly bonds, — I bid
    thee go!''
The All-Father cried, ''and seek thy
    Love below!''
To earth he came: drear waste and flow-
    ery lea
Beheld his search 'mid fettered folk and
    free;
Yet all his toils but brought the direful
    stress
Of lone heart-yearning, grief and weari-
    ness,
Till hope died out and all his soul was
    dark.

At last, when aimless as an autumn leaf
Borne on November's idle winds afar,
He roamed a sea-beach wild, by moon or
    star
Unlighted in its dreariest hour of grief
And desolate longing, on his eyes a
    spark
Of tiny radiance through the clouded
    night
Flashed from a cottage window on a
    height,
Next the dim billows of the moaning
    main.

There broke a sudden lightning on his
    brain
Of prescient expectation, — then, before

Its glow could fade, he trod the cottage
    floor,
And saw in tattered raiment, wan and
    dead.
An ancient withered woman on a
    bed,
Of whom a crone, as shrunk almost as
    she,
Said with drawn lips and blinking
    wearily
'' Lo! here thine old Love! Hast thou
    come so far
To find how cares may blight us, death
    may mar?''
As ebbs a flood-tide, so his eager breath
Sank slowly. '' Oh, the awful front of
    death!''
He moaned. '' Yet wherefore shudder?
    Thou, my love,
Art precious still; nor shalt thou move
    above,
An alien soul, albeit no longer fleet,
Nor fair, thou roam'st through Heaven
    with tottering feet,
Bent, aged form, and face bedimmed by
    tears;
I only ask to *know* thee, while the years
Eternal roll!''

               He bids a last farewell
To this world's life, again prepared to
    dwell
On heights celestial, in whose golden
    airs
The heart, at least, shall shed earth's
    wintry cares,
And blooming, breathe the vernal heats
    of Heaven.

Twice ransomed soul! thou spirit that
    hast striven
With countless ills, and conquered all
    thy foes,
Rise with the might of morning, the
    repose
Of moonlit night, and entering Heaven
    once more —
Behold! who first doth meet thee by the
    door,

With smiling brow, and gently parted lips,
And eyes wherein no vestige of eclipse
From pain, or death, or any evil thing,
Lies darkly, but whose passionate triumphing,
In peace attained, and true love crowned at last,
Hath such rare joy and sweetness round her cast,
She seems an angel on the heights of bliss.
And yet a mortal maid 'twere heaven to kiss!

To whom the singer, in a voice that seems
Vague, and half-muffled in the mist of dreams: —
" Art thou the little Frida that I knew
So long — ah! long ago ? Thine eyes are blue,
Deep blue like hers, and brimmed with tender dew,
Through which love's starlight smiles — art thou, in sooth,
The sweet, true-hearted Frida of my youth ? "

She drew more closely to the poet's side,
And nestling her small hand in his, replied,
As half in tremulous wonder, half delight : —
" I *am* thy little Frida, in thy sight
Fair once, and well beloved — Ah me! ah me!
Hast thou forgotten ? "   " Nay; but whose " (quoth he,)
" Yon withered corse, on which I gazed below,
With pale shrunk limbs, and furrowed face of woe ?
Thy corse, *thy* face, they told me! "
" Yea, but know,
O Love! that earth, and things of earth, are past:
That here, where, soul to soul, we meet at last,

The merciful gods have made this wise decree: —
Love, in heaven's tongue, means immortality
Of youth and joy ; then, wheresoe'er we go,
Loving and loved through these high courts divine,
Mine eyes eternal youth shall drink from thine;
And thou forevermore shalt find in me
The tender maid who walked the world with thee,
Thy little Frida, loved so long ago! ' "

———◆———

PREËXISTENCE.

WHILE sauntering through the crowded street,
Some half-remembered face I meet,

Albeit upon no mortal shore
That face, methinks, hath smiled before.

Lost in a gay and festal throng,
I tremble at some tender song —

Set to an air whose golden bars
I must have heard in other stars.

In sacred aisles I pause to share
The blessings of a priestly prayer —

When the whole scene which greets mine eyes
In some strange mode I recognize

As one whose every mystic part
I feel prefigured in my heart.

At sunset, as I calmly stand,
A stranger on an alien strand —

Familiar as my childhood's home
Seems the long stretch of wave and foam.

One sails toward me o'er the bay,
And what he comes to do and say

"While sauntering through the crowded street.
Some half-remembered face I meet."

I can foretell. A prescient lore
Springs from some life outlived of yore.

O swift, instinctive, startling gleams
Of deep soul-knowledge! not as *dreams*

For aye ye vaguely dawn and die,
But oft with lightning certainty

Pierce through the dark, oblivious brain,
To make old thoughts and memories
    plain —

Thoughts which perchance must travel
    back
Across the wild, bewildering track

Of countless æons; memories far,
High-reaching as yon pallid star,

Unknown, scarce seen, whose flickering
    grace
Faints on the outmost rings of space!

SONNET.

TO ——

FAIR Muse, beloved of all, thou art no
    high
Imperious goddess of the mount or
    main,
But a sweet maiden of the pastoral
    plain,
To whom the hum of bees, the west
    wind's sigh,
The lapse of waters murmuring tran-
    quilly,
Come, like soft music of a May-tide
    dream.
Yet, times there are when some imperial
    theme,
Born of a stormy sunset's marvellous
    sky,
And heralded by thunder and fierce
    flame,
Sweeps o'er thy vision with a mien sub-
    lime,

And mighty voices, calling on thy
    name:
Then dost thou rise, exultant, thrilled,
    inspired,
Thy song a clarion lay that stirs our
    time,
Hot from the soul some secret god hath
    fired!

A THOUSAND YEARS FROM NOW.

I SAT within my tranquil room;
    The twilight shadows sank and rose
With slowly flickering motions, waved
    Grotesquely through the dusk repose;
There came a sudden thought to me,
    Which thrilled the spirit, flushed the
      brow —
A dream of what our world would be
    A thousand years from now!

If science on her heavenward search,
    Rolling the stellar charts apart,
Or delving hour by hour to win
    The secrets of earth's inmost heart —
If that her future apes her past,
    To what new marvels men must bow,
Marvels of land, and air, and sea,
    A thousand years from now!

If empires hold their wonted course,
    And blind republics will not stay
To count the cost of laws which lead
    Unerring to the State's decay —
What changes vast of realm and rule,
    The low upraised, the proud laid low,
Shall greet the unborn ages still,
    A thousand years from now!

Our creeds may change with mellowed
    times
    Of nobler hope, and love increased,
And some new Advent flood the world
    In glory from the haunted East —
While souls on loftier heights of faith
    May mark the mystic pathway grow
Clearer between their stand and heaven's,
    A thousand years from now!

These things *may be!* but what, per-
    force,
  Must with the ruthless epochs pass ?
The millions' breath, the centuries'
    pomp,
  Sure as the wane of flowers or grass;
The earth so rich in tombs to-day,
  There scarce seems space for death to
    sow,
Who, who shall count her churchyard
    wealth
  A thousand years from now ?

And we — poor waifs! whose life-term
    seems,
  When matched with *after* and *before*,
Brief as a summer wind's, or wave's,
  Breaking its frail heart on the shore,
We — human toys — that Fate sets up
  To smite, or — spare I marvel how
These souls shall fare, in what strange
    sphere,
  A thousand years from now ?

Too vague, too faint for mortal ken
  That far, phantasmal future lies;
But sweet! one sacred truth I read,
  Just kindling in your tear-dimmed
    eyes,
That states may rise, and states may set,
  With age earth's tottering pillars bow,
But hearts like ours can ne'er forget,
  And though we know not *where*, nor
    how,
Our conscious love shall blossom yet,
  A thousand years from now!

SONNET.

I STOOD in twilight by the winter's sea;
The spectral tides with hollow, hungry
    roar,
Broke massed and mighty on the shrink-
    ing shore.
The sea-birds wailed; the foam flew wild
    and free.
Ruthless as fate, upborne victoriously,

A fierce wind clove the billows urged
    afar
With vengeful rhythm toward the west-
    ern star,
Just risen beyond a gaunt gray cypress
    tree.
Then twilight waned in cloud-descend-
    ing night,
The sole star died, as if some phantom
    hand
Wiped out its radiance; in the void pro-
    found
The wind and waters (blended in one
    sound,
Awful, mysterious), with invisible might
Thrilled the blank heavens, and smote
    the affrighted strand!

THUNDER AT MIDNIGHT.

AT midnight wakening, through my
    startled brain
The sudden thunder crashed a chord of
    pain ;

I rose, and, awe-struck, hearkened.
    Overhead
In one long, loud, reverberant peal of
    dread,

Ceaseless it rolled, till as a sea of fire,
The climax gained, must wave by wave
    retire ;

So, half-reluctant, up the heights of
    space
The refluent thunder softened into grace,

Its deep, harsh menace changed to mur-
    murs low
As the lost south wind's, muffled in the
    snow;

Waning through whisperous echoes less
    and less
Till the last echo sleeps in gentleness.

Thus 'minded am I of that law of old
Which down the slopes of awful Sinai
    rolled,

Smote men with judgment terrors; yet,
at last,
The lightning flame and mystic tumult
passed,

Lapsed down the ages, echoing less and
less
Jehovah's wrath, till, changed to tender-
ness,

The vengeful law, which once man's
faith sufficed,
Melts into mercy on the heart of Christ!

———◆———

ON THE DEATH OF CANON KINGSLEY.

MORTALS there are who seem, all over,
flame,
Vitalized radiance, keen, intense, and
high,
Whose souls, like planets in a dominant
sky,
Burn with full forces of eternity:

Such was his soul, and such the light
which came
From that pure heaven he lived in; ho-
liest worth
Of will and work was his, to brighten
earth,
Heal its foul wounds, and beautify its
dearth.

He dwelt in clear white purity apart,
Yet walked the world; through many a
sufferer's door
He shone like morning; comfort
streamed before
His footsteps; on the feeble and the poor

He lavished the rich spikenard of his
heart.
Christ's soldier! To his trumpet-call he
sprung,
Eager, elate; valiant of pen and tongue,
Grand were the words he spake, the
songs he sung.

Still, hero-priest! born out of thy due
time —
Thou should'st have lived when on thine
England's sod
Giants of faith and seers of freedom trod,
Daring all things to break the oppressor's
rod.

Great in thine own age, thou hadst been
sublime
In theirs — that age of fervent, fruitful
breath,
When, scorning treachery, and defying
death,
Her true knights girt their loved Eliza-
beth,

Seeing on her the centuries' hopes were
set;
Then hadst thou ranged with Raleigh
land and sea,
Bible and sword in hand, gone forth with
Leigh,
The tyrant smote, the heathen folk made
free!

Yea! but to God and grace thou hast
paid thy debt,
In measure scarce less glorious and com-
plete
Than theirs who bearded on his chosen
seat
The bloody Antichrist; or, fleet to fleet,

Thundered through storms of battle-
wrack and fire
At Britain's Salamis;* the heroic strain
Ran purpling all thy nature like a vein
Oped from God's heart to thine; the lof-
tiest plane

Of thought and action, purpose and desire
Thou trod'st on triumphing; thy Vi-
king's face
Showed granite-willed, yet softened into
grace
By effluence of good deeds, the angelic
race

———

* Alluding to the defeat of the "Invincible
Armada."

Of prayers to prompt, and aid them!
    Fare thee well,
Clear spirit and strong! thy life-work
    nobly done,
Shines beautiful as some unsetting sun
O'er arctic summers; chords of victory
    run
Even through the mournful boom of thy
    deep funeral knell!

WHEN ALL HAS BEEN SAID AND DONE.

TO RICHARD HENRY STODDARD.

(In reply to his poem called "Wishing and
Having.")

" Perhaps it will all come right at last ;
  It may be, when all is done,
We shall be together in some good world,
  Where to *wish* and to *have* are one."
        —STODDARD.

O FRIEND! be sure that a spirit came,
  In the gloom of your saddened hour,
To plant that hope in your hopeless heart,
  Like the seed of an Eden flower.
The seed may rest in your brooding
    breast,
  Half stifled in cold and night,
Or be only felt as a yearning dim
  Toward comforting peace and light;
But 'twill burst some day into perfect
    bloom,
  And fruition be brightly won;
For the earth-life fades like a dream o'
    the dark
When all has been said and done!

The earth-life fades in its sin and pain;
  But whatever of sweet and pure
Breathed over its pallor and flushed its
    gloom,
  Surviveth for evermore.
O, not as the ghost of a mortal joy,
  But as Joy herself from the dead
Upraised to the clear, calm courts of
    Heaven,
  With a halo around her head;

'Tis only the vile and the sad shall die
  With the wane of an earthly sun,
And pass like a vision as man awakes
  When all has been said and done!

Do you think you have lost your days
    for aye
  In the heart of the woods of spring,
By that seaside town that is glimpsed
    through mist,
  Like the white of a petrel's wing ?
Do you think that the patter of tiny feet
  Shall never come back again,
And that those whom the rage of Death
    had killed
  Are in sooth forever slain ?
Look up! look up! as the hope com-
    mands,
  From the ruth of the angels won;
The earth-woe fades like a dream o' the
    night,
  When all has been said and done!

O God, we wander in devious ways,
  Till the end comes, stern and stark;
We lift our voices of useless wail
  From the depths of the hollow dark;
Yet the Christ is there, though we see
    him not.
  But only when sorrow lowers
Wildest, we feel through the hollow
    dark
  A strange, warm hand in ours;
And a voice is heard in the music of
    heaven,
  Saying: " Courage and hope, O,
    son!"
The earth-woe fades like a dream o' the
    night,
  When all has been said and done!

THE VISION IN THE VALLEY.

AMID the loveliest of all lonely vales,
  Couched in soft silences of mountain
    calm,
  And broadly shadowed both by pine
    and palm,

O'er which a tremulous golden vapor sails
Forever, though unbreathed on by a
    breeze
Or any wind of heaven, serenely sleeps
A lucid fountain, from whose fathom-
    less deeps
Come murmurs stranger than the twi-
    light sea's.

That golden vapor, buoyed without a
    breath,
    Tints to its own fair bloom the limpid
    tide,
Through which erewhile the solemn
    vision rose
Of a calm face, benignly glorified
By all we dream or yearn for of pure
    rest,
Profound, Lethéan, passionless repose.
    Still through the silence mystic mur-
    murs sighed,
Fraught with far meanings, vague and
    unexpressed,
    Till at the last, upbreathing, weird
    and near,
The voice of that pale phantom thrilled
    mine ear —
" *Behold the face, the marvellous face,*
    of Death! "

THE ARCTIC VISITATION.

SOME air-born genius, with malignant
    mouth,
Breathed on the cold clouds of an Arctic
    zone—
Which o'er long wastes of shore and
    ocean blown
Swept threatening, vast, toward the
    amazèd South:

Over the land's fair form at first there
    stole
A vanward host of vapors, wild and
    white;
Then loomed the main cloud cohorts,
    massed in might,
Till earth lay corpse-like, reft of life and
    soul;

Death-wan she lay, 'neath heavens as
    cold and pale;
All nature drooped toward darkness and
    despair;
The dreary woodlands, and the ominous
    air
Were strangely haunted by a voice of
    wail.

The woeful sky slow passionless tears did
    weep,
Each shivering rain-drop frozen ere it fell;
The woodman's axe rang like a muffled
    knell;
Faintly the echoes answered, fraught
    with sleep.

The dawn seemed eve; noon, dawn
    eclipsed of grace;
The evening, night; and tender night be-
    came
A formless void, through which no starry
    flame
Touched the veiled splendor of her sor-
    rowful face;

Like mourning nuns, sad-robed, fune-
    real, bowed,
Day followed day; the birds their qua-
    vering notes
Piped here and there from feeble, quer-
    ulous throats.
Fierce cold beneath — above, one riftless
    cloud

Wrapped the mute world — for now all
    winds had died —
And, locked in ice, the fettered forests
    gave
No sign of life; as silent as the grave
Gloomed the dim, desolate landscape far
    and wide.

Gazing on these, from out the mist one
    day
I saw, a shadow on the shadowy sky,
What seemed a phantom bird, that fal-
    tering nigh,
Perched by the roof-tree on a withered
    spray;

With drooping breast he stood, and
    drooping head;
This fateful time had wrought the min-
    strel wrong;
Even as I gazed, our southland lord of
    song
Dropped through the blasted branches,
    breathless, dead!

Yet chillier grew the gray, world-haunt-
    ing shade,
Through which, methought, quick,
    tremulous wings were heard;
Was it the ghost of that heartbroken bird
Bound for a land where sunlight cannot
    fade?

THE WIND OF ONSET.

WITH potent north winds rushing
    swiftly down,
Blended in glorious chant, on yester-
    night
Old Winter came with locks and beard
    of white,
    The hoarfrost glittering on his ancient
        crown:

He sent his icy breathings through the
    pane,
He raved and rattled at the close-shut
    doors,
Then waned with hollow murmur down
    the moors,
    To rise, revive and sweep the world
        again.

The chorus of great winds which gird
    him round
Hold many voices — the deep trumpet's
    swell,
The air harp's mournful burden of fare-
    well,
    The fife's shrill tones, the clarion's
        silvery sound:

But o'er the roof-tree, 'round the gable
    rings
Loudest his wind of onset, hour by hour,

Till a new sense of almost rapturous
    power
    Comes on the mighty waftage of his
        wings;

Sense of fresh hope and faith's re-
    kindled glow,
The awakened aim, the brain drawn
    tense and high,
To shoot its fiery thoughts against the
    sky,
    Like arrows launched from some deft
        archer's bow!

All latent forces of our being start
To marshalled order, ranged in battle
    line,
While the roused life-blood with a thrill
    divine
    Runs tingling thro' the chambers of
        the heart.

Summer is rich with dreams of languid
    tone;
October sunsets feed the soul with
    light;
But give *me* winter's war wind in his
    might,
    O'er the scourged lands and turbulent
        oceans blown.

THE VISIT OF MAHMOUD BEN SU-
LEIM TO PARADISE.

BENEATH the shadow of a breezeless
    palm
Mahmoud Ben Suleim, in the evening
    calm,
Sat, with his gravely meditative eyes
Turned on the waning wonder of the
    skies;
What time beside him paused a brother
    sage,
Whose flowing locks, like his, were white
    with age:
His gaze a half-veiled fire, seemed sadly
    cast
Inward, to scan the records of his past —

"On yesternight

Old Winter came with locks and beard of white."

Perchance the past of man — and thence
   to draw
From far experience, sanctified by awe
Of God's mysterious ways, some hint to
   tell
Who of the dead in heaven and who in
   hell
Dwelt now in endless bliss or endless
   bale.

Thus, while he mused, the old man's
   face grew pale
With stringent memories; on his labor-
   ing thought
Vague speculations, dim and doubtful,
   wrought
From out the fragments of the vanished
   years.
At length he said : " Ben Suleim, lend
   thine ears
To that I fain would ask thee. Thou
   art wise
In sacred lore, in pure philosophies;
So tell me now thine inmost thought of
   heaven
And heaven's fair habitants."

         " Whoe'er hath striven,"
Ben Suleim answered, " to the extremest
   verge
Of spiritual power, across death's dreary
   surge
Hath passed to find the fathomless peace
   of God!"

" Yea," quoth the other, smiting on the
   sod
His staff impatiently. " I know! I
   know!
But who of all *we* have seen or loved
   below
Think'st thou in Aidenn?"

         Slowly from his lips,
Wrapped by the smoke-wreaths in a
   half-eclipse,
Ben Suleim's pipe was lowered: " My
   friend," said he,
" Hark to this vision of eternity,

Which in the long-gone time of youth
   did seem
To rise before me in a twilight dream.
Methought the life on earth had passed
   away,
That near me spread the new, immortal
   day
Of Paradise; but yet mine eyes looked
   back
On this our clouded world, and marked
   the track
My waning life-course still left glimmer-
   ing there.
Behold! all dues of funeral dole and
   prayer
Mine heirs had paid me; through the
   cypress gloom
I saw the glitter of my new-made
   tomb,
Whereon so many a blazoned virtue
   shone,
A blush seemed gathering o'er the har-
   dened stone,
And I, albeit a spirit, flushed with
   shame.
Nathless, just then to Eden gates I
   came,
And, at the outmost wicket thundering
   loud,
Summoned full soon an angel from the
   cloud
Which girds those heavenly portals, blent
   with mist
Of shifting rainbow arcs of amethyst,
Who, somewhat harshly for an angel,
   said
I knocked as if an hundred thousand
   dead,
Not *one* poor soul, besieged the heavenly
   door.
He raised his luminous hands, which
   hovered o'er
For a brief moment, like a flash of stars,
The sapphire brilliance of the circling
   bars,
Then one by one unclosed them. En-
   tered in
The realm celestial, safe from pain and
   sin,

I stretched at ease, with shadows cool
    and dim
Floating about me, thus did question
    him:
' Fair Seraph, speak. Is not this land
    divine,
Rife with pure souls, once faithful
    friends of mine ? '
' Nay! be content if wandering here and
    there,
Thou meet'st a *few*—none in the loftiest
    sphere.'
' Where, then,' I cried, ' is holy Ibn
    Becár ?
If not the highest he, surely not far
Beneath the highest that clear spirit
    beams ? '
' Ah! thou art muffled still in earthly
    dreams,'
The angel answered. ' If on *him* thou'dst
    call,
Pass downward, for he's not in Heaven
    at all ! '
' Dread Allah ! can it be ? So just a man
Walked not, methought, the streets of
    Ispahan.
Morn after morn, year after year his
    feet,
Alike in summer's bloom and winter's
    sleet,
Bore him to worship in the sacred place;
What righteous zeal burned hotly in his
    face !
And when inspired his heavenly vows
    he made,
Or 'neath the innermost mosque devoutly
    prayed,
Why, even the roaring Dervish, robed
    and cowled,
Shrank from those pious lungs, which
    almost howled
Creation deaf. A saint we deemed him—
    one
Pure as the snow, yet ardent as the
    sun,
Who, not content with turning toward
    the light
His own blest feet, must set on paths of
    right

All erring brethren !' ' True,' the an-
    gel cried;
' But Ibn Becár, down to the day he
    died,
Kept on his neighbor's ways so keen an
    eye
He lost at length his own straight course
    thereby ;
And though the purblind world hath
    guessed it not,
He bides in Eblis' kingdom; fierce and
    hot
The waves of Hades roll above him
    now.'
Amazed, I bowed my head, just whisper-
    ing low
An ' *Allah Kebur.*' Next: ' How fares
    it, then,'
I asked, ' with Hafiz, the wise scribe,
    whose pen
Signed many a deed of gift, and scored
    his name
High on the roll of charitable hearts ? '
Clear came the answer: ' 'Mid thy
    public marts
No soul more sordid strove with heaven
    to drive
Its wicked bargains. Largely would he
    give
To general charities; but, sooth to say,
Whene'er he 'scaped the broad, bright
    gaze of day,
He stamped with cruel heel the writhing
    poor,
Would turn the perishing beggar **from**
    his door,
And wring from friendless widows the
    last crust
Saved for their half-starved children.
    God is just;
So Hafiz dwells not here.'

                    In faltering tone,
As dropped from one who deals with
    things unknown,
I questioned next: 'Abdallah, *he* is
    saved ? '
' Nay; for, albeit with seeming truth he
    braved

Temptation, and each wise and sacred
saw
Wrought from the precepts of our
prophet's law,
Fell soft as Hybla's honey from his
mouth,
Yet his whole nature withered in the
drouth
Of drear hypocrisy. By stealth he
bought
Strong waters of the Giaour, and nightly
sought
Oblivion from sweet opiates of the
South.
Sickness he feigned, to gain in these his
cure;
And once, that he might tipple more
and more,
Moved to a province rife with serpents
dread,
Because, by such as knew his wiles,
'twas said
He drank the poison of each treacher-
ous throat,
To seek in fiery wine an antidote.
Nathless, a serpent slew him, and his
home
Is far from ours.'
My thoughts began to roam
Vaguely, in loose disorder. Yet again:
'What of Kalkarri, he whose songs of
pain
And joy alike forever struck the key,
The under-note of golden purity,
Virtue his theme and heavenly love his
muse?'
'Thou fool and blind! Kalkarri could
not choose
But sing mellifluous verses; yet in him
The light of truth was always blurred
and dim.
A tireless trick of tinkling rhymes he
had,
And naught he cared what spirit, good
or bad,
O'erruled his lay. The good, perchance,
paid best;
Therefore he sang of heavenly joy and
rest,

But sang of that whereof he shall not
taste.'
'Just Allah!' sighed I, 'see what barren
waste
Drinks up my hopes. Since none of all
I named
Here for the sacred roll hath Allah
claimed,
I pray thee tell me *whom* his will hath
blessed.'
'Dost thou remember Saädi?' 'What,
that wretch
Who shod the Bactrian camels — who
would fetch
Strange oaths from far to sow our whole-
some air
With moral poison?' 'True, the man
did swear,'
Confessed the Bright One, sadly. 'Yet
so strong
His penitent sorrow o'er the hateful
wrong
Done his own soul and Allah, and so
rife
With tireless effort his whole earnest
life
To smite the giant tempters in his soul,
To kill them outright, or with firm con-
trol
Hold them in native darkness chained
and cowed —
At last he conquered and our Lord al-
lowed
His weary soul to quaff the founts of
balm!'

Amazement held me dumb. Within
the palm
Waving above, just then a whispering
breeze
Rose, and passed up the long-ranked,
radiant trees
Which lined the hills of heaven. It
seemed a sigh
Born of soft Mercy's immortality
Wafted toward the throne! The Bright
One then,
Lifting his voice harmonious, spake
again:

'Ferdusi, the small merchant by the
  quays
Too poor to give, but with a heart as
  broad
As the broad sky, reverent of faith and
  God;
Islal-ed-Din, who, though he could not
  make
The commonest prayer, would yet ex-
  claim Amen!
To those who did, so warmly, for the
  sake
Of truth and fervent worship, all might
  see
His generous spirit's large sincerity —
Both *these* are with us,'
                    'But Wassaf,' said I,
The blameless teacher, who methinks
  came nigh
Virtue as pure as frail humanity
On earth may compass?' 'Yea; his
  soul *is* here,
But his soul wanders in the humblest
  sphere.
For, mark thee, though no damning sin
  did stain
This Wassaf's record, still in blood and
  brain
So weak was he, his pale life-currents
  flowed
So like dull streamlets through a wan
  abode
Of windless deserts, that he lived and
  died
Ne'er by a sharp temptation terrified;
And if his course the Prophet's law ful-
  filled
And near his path all passionate gusts
  were stilled,
What credit to him? His to coldly live,
Act, fade — a creature tamely negative.
But lo! in flaming contrast the hot stir
Of Agha's fate — Agha, the flute player,
Glutton on earth, wine-bibber, and the
  rest,
He still is held in heaven a nobler guest
Than all your Wassafs — proper, crime-
  less, cool,
And soulless, almost, as a stagnant pool,

For Agha's blood a furious torrent ran;
Half brutal he, half tiger and half
  man,
In health and power, the body's lustful
  force,
Whose strength to fetter in its turbulent
  course
Had taxed an angel's will. His nature
  sore
Tormented him; yet o'er and o'er and
  o'er
From some vast fall he lifted prayerful
  eyes,
And like a Titan strove to *storm* the
  skies,
Which, through unequalled strife and
  travails passed,
His hero-soul hath grandly won at last!

No more! no more! the glorious pres-
  ence said.
'In light to come thy knowledge per-
  fected
Shall bloom in flower and fruit; but, Su-
  leim, say,
Hast thou beheld the swift sky-rocket's
  ray
Burn up the heavens? How beautiful
  at first
Its splendors gleamed, too soon, alas! to
  burst
And die in outer darkness! Thus it is
With many a soul, soaring, men dream,
  to bliss.
Awhile they mount, clear, dazzling,
  drunk with light,
To sink in ruin and the desolate night.
Would'st know the true believer? *He*
  is one
Whose faith in deeds shines perfect as
  the sun.
*His soul, a shaft feathered by works of
  grace,*
*Death, the grim archer, launches forth
  in space ;*
*It cleaves the clouds, o'ershoots the va-
  porous wall*
*That waves 'twixt earth and heaven its
  mystic pall,*

To light, at last, unerring, strong and
*   fleet,*
In the deep calm which lies at Allah's
*   feet!' "*

MY DAUGHTER.

THOU hast thy mother's eyes, my child —
Her deep dark eyes: the undefiled
Sweetness which breathes around her
    mouth,
A perfect rosebud of the south,
And the broad brow, as smooth to-day
As when on life's auspicious May
I clasped her to an ardent breast
With yearnings of divine unrest.

Thou hast thy mother's voice, as low
And soft as happy winds that blow
At springtime o'er the wild-bloom beds,
When the blue harebells lift their heads
To hearken to those strains of peace,
And through the lustrous day's decease
Drink in the sunset-beams that float
Downward from glittering airs remote.

Thou hast thy mother's heart, no less
Than all her body's loveliness —
A heart as firmly brave and true,
O'er-brimming now with morning dew
Of hopeful light as doth a flower;
Yet strong to meet misfortune's hour,
And for the sake of loving ruth
Lie down and perish in its youth.

Child! child! so fair, so good thou art,
Sometimes an awful pang my heart
Pierces as thus I gaze on thee.
Too rare a thing thou seem'st to be
Long in this barren world to smile;
Methinks, with many a heavenly wile,
Unseen, but felt, the angels stray
Near thee, to tempt thy soul away.

Oh! heed them not. Why should they
    cull
My one sweet blossom? Heaven is full

Of just such spirits. Leave her here,
Kind seraphs! our poor joys to share,
Our griefs to brighten by her love;
Pass on to your calm homes above,
And thus in mercy spare to earth
The angel of my heart and hearth.

'Tis strange, but yet so fresh and whole,
So radiant in my brain and soul
Doth this enchanting image dwell,
This pure, unrivalled miracle
Of maidenhood and modest grace,
I vow that I behold her face,
Hear her low tones, and mark her mien
So gentle, virginal, serene,

Clearly, as if her voice and brow,
In softest sooth, beguiled me now;
As if, incarnate and benign,
She placed her little hand in mine,
And her long midnight tresses rare
Were mingling with my snow-touched
    hair.
And yet she only lives for me
In golden realms of fantasie,
A creature born of air and beam,
The delicate darling of a dream.

OUR "HUMMING-BIRD."

AH, well I know the reason why
They called her by that graceful name:
She seems a creature born with wings,
O'er which a rainbow spirit flings
Fair hues of softly shifting flame;
Light is she as the changeful air,
Borne on gay humors everywhere,
        Bewitchingly.

Her soul hath seldom breathed a sigh;
No hint of care hath ever stirred
Her being; sunshine and the breeze
Have been the fairy witnesses
Of all those joys our happy bird
Hath from the golden fountains drawn
Of youth unsullied as the dawn,
        So lavishly.

Full many a flower, just hovering nigh,
In life's broad garden, rife with sweets,
She deftly drains of nectar dew;
Then, sylph-like, sweeps o'er pathways
          new
To taste some balmier bliss she meets;
Now flashing fast through myrtle
          bowers,
Now clinging to red lips of flowers,
                    Capriciously.

Forbear, rash heart! forbear to try
Our bird to capture with your wiles,
For, lo! she glimmers like a beam

Of fancy, on from dream to dream:
Vain are a lover's tears or smiles
To check her flight bewildering,
To tame her soul, or chain her wing
                    Submissively.

Nay! let the dazzling fairy fly
From flower to flower, so gladly whirled;
Cruel it were her matchless light
By one rude touch to dim or blight,
To see her luminous pinions furled
In grosser airs than those which stray
Round the fresh rosebuds of the May,
                    Deliciously.

LATER POEMS.

LATER POEMS

OF IMAGINATION, SENTIMENT, AND DESCRIPTION.

UNVEILED.

I CANNOT tell when first I saw her face;
  Was it athwart a sunset on the sea,
When the huge billows heaved tumul-
    tuously,
Or in the quiet of some woodland place,
  Wrapped by the shadowy boon
Of breezeless verdures from the summer
    noon?
  Or likelier still, in a rock-girdled dell
  Between vast mountains, while the
    midnight hour
  Blossomed above me like a shining
    flower,
Whose star-wrought petals turned the
    fields of space
To one great garden of mysterious light?

    Vain! vain! I cannot tell
When first the beauty and majestic
    might
Of her calm presence, bore my soul apart
  From all low issues of the grovelling
    world; —
    About me their own peace and gran-
      deur furled, —
    Filling the conscious heart
With vague, sweet wisdom drawn from
    earth or sky, —
    Secrets that glance towards eternity,
Visions divine, and thoughts ineffable!

But ever since that immemorial day,
A steadfast flame hath burned in brain
    and blood,
  Urging me onward in the perilous
    search

For sacred haunts our queenly mother
    loves;
    By field and flood,
Thro' neighboring realms, and regions
    far away,
Have I not followed, followed where she
    led,
  Tracking wild rivers to their fountain
    head,
And wilder desert spaces, mournful,
    vast,
Where Nature, fronting her inscrutable
    past,
  Holds bleak communion only with the
    dead;
  Yearning meanwhile, for pinions like
    a dove's,
    To waft me further still,
Beyond the compass of the unwinged
    will;
Yea; waft me northward, southward,
    east, or west,
  By fabled isles, and undiscovered
    lands,
  To where enthroned upon his moun-
    tain-perch,
  The sovereign eagle stands,
Guarding the unfledged eaglets in their
    nest,
  Above the thunders of the sea and
    storm?

    Oh! sometimes by the fire
Of holy passion, in me, all subdued,
And melted to a mortal woman's mood,
    Tender and warm, —
She, from her goddess height,
In gracious answer to my soul's desire,

Descending softly, lifts her Isis veil,
To bend on me the untranslated light
Of fathomless eyes, and brow divinely
     pale:
She lays on mine her firm, immortal
     hand;
And I, encompassed by a magical mist,
Feel that her lips have kissed
Mine eyes and forehead; — how the in-
     fluence fine
Of her deep life runs like Arcadian
     wine
Through all my being! How a moment
     pressed
To the large fountains of her opulent
     breast,
A rapture smites me, half akin to pain;
A sun-flash quivering through white
     chords of rain!

Thenceforth, I walked
The earth all-seeing; — not her stateliest
     forms
Alone engrossed me, nor her sounds of
     power;
Mountains and oceans, and the rage of
     storms;
Fierce cataracts hurled from awful steep
     to steep,
Or, the gray water-spouts, that whirling
     tower
Along the darkened bosom of the deep;
But all fair, fairy forms; all vital things,
That breathe or blossom 'midst our
     bounteous springs;
In sylvan nooks rejoicingly I met
The wild rose and the violet;
On dewy hill-slopes pausing, fondly
     talked
With the coy wind-flower, and the
     grasses brown,
That in a subtle language of their own
(Caught from the spirits of the wan-
     dering breeze),
Quaintly responded; while the heavens
     looked down
     As graciously on these
Titania growths, as on sublimer
     shapes

Of century-moulded continents, that
     bemock
Alike the earthquake's and the
     billows' shock
By Orient inlands and cold ocean
     capes!

The giant constellations rose and set:
I knew them all, and worshipped all I
     knew;
Yet, from their empire in the pregnant
     blue,
Sweeping from planet-orbits to faint
     bars
Of nebulous cloud, beyond the range
     of stars,
I turned to worship with a heart as
     true,
Long mosses drooping from the cypress-
     tree;
The virginal vines that stretched re-
     motely dim,
     From forest limb to limb;
Network of golden ferns, whose
     tracery weaves
In lingering twilights of warm August
     eves,
Ethereal frescoes, pictures fugitive,
Drawn on the flickering and fair-
     foliaged wall
Of the dense forest, ere the night
     shades fall:
Rushes rock-tangled, whose mixed colors
     live
In the pure moisture by a fountain's
     brim;
The sylph-like reeds, wave-born, that
     to and fro
Move ever to the waters' rhythmic
     flow,
Blent with the humming of the wild-
     wood bee,
And the winds' under thrills of mystery;
The twinkling " ground-stars," full of
     modest cheer,
     Each her cerulean cup
     In humble supplication lifting up,
To catch whate'er the kindly heavens
     may give

Of flooded sunshine, or celestial dew;
And even when, self-poised in airy
    grace,
  Their phantom lightness stirs
Through glistening shadows of a secret
    place
  The silvery-tinted gossamers;
For thus hath Nature taught amid her
    All, —
The complex miracles of land and sea,
And infinite marvels of the infinite air,
No life is trivial, no creation small!

Ever I walk the earth,
  As one whose spiritual ear
Is strangely purged and purified to
    hear
Its multitudinous voices; from the
    shore
Whereon the savage Arctic surges roar,
And the stupendous bass of choral
    waves
Thunders o'er "wandering graves,"
From warrior-winds whose viewless co-
    horts charge

"Have I not followed, followed where she led,
Tracking wild rivers to their fountain head."

The banded mists through Cloudland's
    vaporous dearth,
Pealing their battle bugles round the
    marge
Of dreary fen and desolated moor;
Down to the ripple of shy woodland rills
Chanting their delicate treble 'mid the
    hills,
And ancient hollows of the enchanted
    ground, —
I pass with reverent thought,
Attuned to every tiniest trill of sound,
  Whether by brook or bird
  The perfumed air be stirred.
But most, because the unwearied strains
    are fraught

With Nature's freedom in her happiest
    moods,
I love the mock-bird's, and brown
    thrush's lay,
  The melted soul of May.
Beneath those matchless notes,
From jocund hearts upwelled to fervid
    throats,
  In gushes of clear harmony,
  I seem, oft-times I seem
To find remoter meanings; the far tone
Of ante-natal music faintly blown
From out the misted realms of mem-
    ory;
The pathos and the passion of a dream;
Or, broken fugues of a diviner tongue

That e'er hath chanted, since our earth
was young,
And o'er her peace-enamored solitudes
The stars of morning sung!

———◆———

MUSCADINES.

SOBER September, robed in gray and
dun,
Smiled from the forest in half-pensive
wise;
A misty sweetness shone in her mild
eyes,
And on her cheek a shy flush went and
came,
As flashing warm between
The autumnal leaves of slowly dying
green,
The sovereign sun
Tenderly kissed her; then (in ruthful
mood
For the vague fears of modest maiden-
hood)
Behold him gently, lovingly retire;
Beneath the foliaged screen,
Veiling his swift desire —
Even as a king, wed to some virgin
queen,
Might doom his sight to blissful, brief
eclipse,
After his tender lips
Had touched the maiden's trembling
soul to flame.

Through shine and shade,
Thoughtful I trod the tranquil forest
glade,
Up-glancing oft
To watch the rainless cloudlets, white
and soft,
Sail o'er the placid ocean of the sky.
The breeze was like a sleeping infant's
sigh,
Measured and low, or, in quick, palpi-
tant thrills
An instant swept the sylvan depths
apart

To pass and die
Far off, far off, within the shrouded
heart
Of immemorial hills,

Through shade and shine
I wandered, as one wanders in a dream,
Till, near the borders of a beauteous
stream
O'erhung by flower and vine,
I pushed the dense, perplexing boughs
aside,
To mark the temperate tide
Purpled by shadows of the Muscadine.

Reclining there at languid length I sank,
One idle hand outstretched beyond the
bank,
With careless grasp
The sumptuous globes of these rare
grapes to clasp.
Ah! how the ripened wild fruit of the
South
Melted upon my mouth!
Its magic juices through each captured
vein
Rose to the yielding brain,
Till, like the hero of an old romance,
Caught by the fays, my spirit lapsed
away,
Lost to the sights and sounds of mortal
day.

Lost to all earthly sights and sounds
was I,
But blithesomely,
As stirred by some new being's won-
drous dawn,
I heard about me, swift though gently
drawn,
The footsteps of light creatures on the
grass.
Mine eyelids seemed to open, and I saw,
With joyance checked by awe,
A multitudinous company
Of such strange forms and faces, quaint,
or bright
With true Elysian light,
As once in fairy fantasies of eld

"Sober September, robed in gray and dun,
Smiled from the forest in half-pensive wise."

High-hearted poets through the wilds
    beheld
Of shadowy dales and lone sea beaches
    pass,
At spring-tide morn or holy hush of
    night.

    Then to an airy measure,
Low as the sea winds when the night at
    noon
Clasps the frail beauty of an April
    moon,
Through woven paces at soft-circling
    leisure,
They glided with elusive grace adown
The forest coverts — all live woodland
    things,
    Black-eyed or brown,
Firm-footed or up-poised on changeful
    wings,
Glinting about them 'mid the indolent
    motion
    Of billowy verdures rippling slow
    As the long, languid underflow
Of some star-tranced, voluptuous South-
    ern ocean.

The circle widened, and as flower-
    wrought bands,
    Stretched by incautious hands,
Break in the midst with noiseless wrench
    asunder,
So brake the dancers now to form in
    line
Down the deep glade — above the shift-
    ing lights,
Through massive tree-boles, on majestic
    heights;
    The blossoming turf thereunder,
Whence, fair and fine,
Twinkling like stars that hasten to be
    drawn
    Close to the breast of dawn,
Shone, with their blue veins pulsing
    fleet,
    Innumerable feet,
White as the splendors of the milky
    way,
Yet rosy warm as opening tropic day,

With lithe, free limbs of curvature di-
    vine,
And dazzling bosoms of unveilèd glow,
Save where the long, ethereal tresses
    stray
Across their unimaginable snow.

    One after one,
By sun-rays kissed or fugitive shades
    o'errun,
All vision-like they passed me.   First
    there came
A Dryad coy, her sweet head bowed in
    shame,
And o'er her neck and half-averted face
    The faintest delicate trace
Of the charmed life-blood pulsing softly
    pure.
Next, with bold footsteps, sure,
And proudly set, from her untrammelled
    hills,
Fair-haired, blue-eyed, upon her lofty
    head
A fragrant crown of leaves, purple and
    red,
Chanting a lay clear as the mountain rills,
A frank-faced Oread turned on me
Her cloudless glances, laughter-lit and
    free
As the large gestures and the liberal air
    With which I viewed her fare
    Down the lone valley land, —
Pausing betimes to wave her happy
    hand
As in farewell; but ere her presence died
    Wholly away,
    Her voice of golden swell
    Breathed also a farewell.
Farewell, farewell, the sylvan echoes
    sighed,
From rock-bound summit to rich blos-
    soming bay —
    Farewell, farewell!

Fauns, satyrs flitted past me — the whole
    race
    Of woodland births uncouth —
    Until I seemed, in sooth,
Far from the garish track

Of these loud days to have wandered,
    joyful, back
Along the paths, beneath the crystal sky
Of long, long-perished Arcady.
But last of all, filling the haunted space
With odors of the flower-enamored tide,
Whose wavelets love through many a
    secret place
Of the deep dell and breezeless bosk to
    glide,
    Stole by, lightsome and slim
As Dian's self in each swift, sinuous
    limb,
Her arms outstretched, as if in act to
    swim
The air, as erst the waters of her home,
A naiad, sparkling as the fleckless foam
Of the cool fountain-head whereby she
    dwells.

O'er her sloped shoulders and the pure
    pink bud
Of either virginal breast is richly rolled
    (O rare, miraculous flood!)
The torrent of her freed locks' shim-
    mering gold,
Through which the gleams of rainbow-
    colored shells,
And pearls of moon-like radiance flash
    and float
    Round her immaculate throat.

Clothed in her beauty only wandered she,
'Mid the moist herbage to the streamlet's
    edge,
Where, girt by silvery rushes and brown
    sedge,
She faded slowly, slowly, as a star
Fades in the gloaming, on the bosom
    bowed
    Of some half-luminous cloud,
Above the wan, waste waters of the sea.

Then, sense and spirit fading inward too,
I slept oblivious; through the dim, dumb
    hours,
Safely encouched on autumn leaves and
    flowers,
I slept as sleep the unperturbèd dead.

At length the wind of evening, keenly
    chill,
Swept round the darkening hill;
Then throbbed the rush of hurried wings
    o'erhead,
Blent with aerial murmurs of the pine,
Just whispering twilight. On my brow
    the dew
Dropped softly, and I woke to all the low,
Strange sounds of twilight woods that
    come and go
So fitfully; and o'er the sun's decline,
Through the green foliage flickering high,
    Beheld, with dreamy eye,
Sweet Venus glittering in the stainless
    blue.

.   .   .   .   .

Thus the day closed whereon I drank the
    wine —
The liquid magic of the Muscadine.

IN A SPRING GARDEN.

When Heaven was stormy, Earth was
    cold,
    And sunlight shunned the wold and
    wave, —
Thought burrowed in the churchyard
    mould,
    And fed on dreams that haunt the
    grave: —

But now that Heaven is freed from strife,
    And Earth's full heart with rapture
    swells,
Thought soars the realms of endless life
    Above the shining asphodels!

What flower that drinks the south wind's
    breath,
    What sparkling leaf, what Hebe-Morn,
But flouts the sullen graybeard, Death,
    And laughs our Arctic doubts to scorn?

Pale scientist! scant of healthful blood,
    Your ghostly tomes, one moment,
    close;
Pluck freshness with a spring-time bud,
    Find wisdom in the opening rose:

From toil which, blindly delving, gropes
  When time but plays a juggler's part,
Ah go! and breathe the dew-lit hopes
  That cluster round a violet's heart:

Mark the white lily whose sweet core
  Hath many a wild-bee swarm enticed,
And draw therefrom a honeyed lore
  Pure as the tender creed of Christ:

Yea! even the weed which upward holds
  Its tiny ear, past bower and lawn,
A lovelier faith than yours enfolds,
  Caught from the whispering lips of
      dawn!

IN DEGREE.

THY life is full of motion, perfume,
    grace;
Mine, a low blossom in a shaded place,
Whereto the zephyrs whisper, only they,
Through the long lapses of the lone-
    some day.

Thy lordly genius blooms for all to see
On the clear heights of calm supremacy;
My humbler dower they only find who
    pass
With eyes that seek for violets mid the
    grass.

THE SKELETON WITNESS.

ROOTED in soil dull as a dead man's eye,
  Dank with decay, yon ghastly oak as-
    pires,
As if in mockery, to the alien sky,
  Frowning afar through clouded sunset
    fires.

No garb of summer greenery girds it now:
  Stripped as some naked soul at
    Judgment-morn,
It rears its blasted arms, its sullen brow,
  Defiant still, though wasted, scarred,
    forlorn!

Not all its ruin came through storm or
    time;
  Ages ago, 'mid winter's dreariest
    blight,
It saw and strove to shroud an awful
    crime,
  But slowly withered from that fateful
    night!

An evil charm its many-centuried rings
  Robbed of their pith; no more with
    healthful start
Its lusty life-sap, nursed by countless
    springs,
  Coursed through great veins, and
    warmed its giant heart.

Now all men shun the gaunt accursèd
    thing—
  Only the raven with monotonous
    croak,
Tortures the silence, staining with black
    wing
  The leprous whiteness of the rotting
    oak!

STORM-FRAGMENTS.

THE storm had raved its furious soul
    away;
O'er its wild ruins Twilight, spectral,
    gray,

Stole like a nun, 'midst wounded men
    and slain,
Walking the bounds of some fierce battle-
    plain.

The ghost of thunder muttered faintly
    by;
While down the uttermost spaces of the
    sky,

Just where the sunset's glimmering verge
    grew pale,
The baffled winds outbreathed their dy-
    ing wail!

The sombre clouds that thronged a shad-
    owy west
Writhed, as if tortured monsters of un-
    rest,

Whose depths the keen sheet-lightnings
    rent apart,
To show what fiery torment throbbed at
    heart!

Where raged of late the war of elements
    dread,
Brooded a solemn silence overhead,

Through which, beyond the cloud-strewn,
    heavenly field,
The moon shone gory as a warrior's
    shield,

Dipped in the veins of many a van-
    quished foe;
Blood-red, I marked the wandering va-
    pors flow

Vaguely about her, while her lurid
    light
Scared the vague vanguard of the shades
    of night;

Their banded hosts retreating, wild and
    dim,
In shattered cohorts o'er the horizon's
    rim:

Yet, the broad empire of those baleful
    beams
Heaved with strange shapes and hues of
    nightmare dreams!

Here, as from cloud-born Himalayas
    rolled,
I saw what seemed a cataract's rush of
    gold,

Hurled between shores of darkness, dense
    and dire,
Down to a seething mountain-lake of fire;

There, dismal catacombs, whose nether
    glooms
Yawned, to reveal their loathsome place
    of tombs:

Caverns of mystic depth, whence bub-
    bling came
The blue-tinged horror of sulphureous
    flame;

Fragments of castles, with fresh blood
    besprent,
Gaunt, ruined tower, and blasted battle-
    ment —

On which, flame-clad, and tottering to
    their fall,
Dark eyes of frenzy flashed o'er cope and
    wall!

With awful ocean-spaces, limitless, grand,
Where spectral billows lashed a viewless
    land;

Their mountainous floods a frowning
    zenith kissed,
But glimpsed, at times, 'twixt folds of
    phantom-mist,

I viewed, as faintly touched by muffled
    stars,
The semblance of dead forms, on ship-
    wrecked spars

Whirled upward, and dead faces, a white
    spume
Smote to false life against that turbulent
    gloom,

Where mournful birds, on pinions gray
    or dun,
Circled, methought, o'er some half-per-
    ished sun,

Whose feeble lustre, faltering upward,
    flings
A sad-hued radiance round their pallid
    wings;

Yea! all fantastic shapes of terror,
    wrought
'Twixt errant fancy and dream-haunted
    thought,

Until I seemed with Dante's soul to fly,
Through new Infernos, shifted to — the
    sky!

ABOVE THE STORM.

THE winds of the winter have breathed
 their dirges
 Far over the wood and the leaf-strown
 plain;
They have passed, forlorn, by the moun-
 tain verges
 Down to the shores of the moaning
 main;
And the breast of the smitten sea divides,
Till the voice of winds and the voice of
 tides
Seem blent with the roar of the central
 surges,
 Whose fruitless furrows are sown with
 rain.

The pines look down, and their branches
 shiver
 On the misty slopes of the mountain
 wall,
And I hear the shout of a mountain river
 Through the gloom of the ghostly
 gorges call;
While from drifting depths of the troub-
 led sky
Outringeth the eagle's wild reply,
So shrill that the startled echoes quiver;
 And the veil of the tempest is over all.

O groaning forest! O wind that rushes
 Unfettered and fierce as a doom malign!
How the pulses leap, how the heart-tide
 flushes
 The temples and brow like the flush
 of wine,
As I pause, as I hearken the vast com-
 motion
Of the air, of the earth, of the wakened
 ocean;
And my soul goes forth with the storm
 that crushes,
 With the battling foam and the blind-
 ing brine.

Yea, my soul is rent by a tempest stronger
 Than ever was Nature's, with ruin
 rife,

And the flame of its lightnings can bide
 no longer,
 Ensheathed at the core of a clouded
 life;
And its pent-up thunders, unloosed at
 last,
Keep time to the rhythmic rage of the
 blast,
For my spirit, half-maddened by Fates
 that wrong her,
 Is shaken by passion, and hot with
 strife!

Ah, God! for the wings of the eagle
 above me,
 With their steadfast vigor and royal
 might;
Ah, God! for an impulse like theirs to
 move me
 In endless courses of upward flight;
The clouds may billow, the vapors
 heave,
But still his pinions the darkness cleave;
And proudly serene, in those realms
 above me
 He is soaring from conquered height to
 height:

Till at length, his great, broad vans at
 even
 And stately poise on the airy stream,
I mark, through the rifts of the turbid
 heaven
 His form outflashed like a wingèd
 beam;
And I ask, " Shall *my* spirit soar like his?
Shall it ever soar in the peace and bliss
Of the shining heights and the glory
 given
 To the will unvanquished, the faith
 supreme?"

UNDERGROUND — A FANTASY.

MAJESTIC dreams of heavenly calms,
Bright visions of unfading palms,
 Wherewith the brows of saints are
 crowned, —

Awhile my soul resigns them all,
Content to rest death's dreamless thrall,
    Safe underground!

Rest! rest! oblivious rest I crave,
Though narrowed to a pine-clad grave,
    With sylvan shadows shimmering
        round;
The peace of Heaven, if fair and deep,
Scarce wooes me like Earth's ebon sleep,
    Far underground.

By infinite weariness oppressed
Of soul and senses, blood and breast,
    Where can such Gilead balm be
        found
As that which breathes from out the sod
Baptized by rain and dews of God,
    Deep underground?

A century's space I yearn to be
Untroubled, slumbering tranquilly,
    There, by the haunted woodlands
        bound;
What suns shall set, what planets rise
O'er pulseless brain and curtained eyes,
    Dark underground!

A century's sleep might bring redress
To these dull wounds of weariness,
    Till the soothed spirit, hale and
        sound,
Grow conscious of the sacred trust
Which holds immortal bloom in dust,
    Safe underground.

Yea! conscious grow of rustling wings,
And keen, mysterious whisperings,
    Blown flame-like o'er the burial-
        mound:
My soul would feel thy Orient kiss,
Angel of Palingenesis,
    Thrilled underground!

---◇---

THE DRYAD OF THE PINE.

AH, forest sweetheart! over land and
    sea
I come once more, once more to stand
    by thee;

My sylvan darling! set 'twixt shade and
    sheen,
Soft as a maid, yet stately as a queen!

Thy loyal head, crowned by one lonely
    star,
Flickers thro' twilight, coldly fine, and
    far;
But thy earth-yearning branches bend
    to greet
The lowliest wood-grass tangled round
    my feet.

Leaning on thee, I feel the subtlest thrill
Stir thy dusk limbs, tho' all the heavens
    are still;
And 'neath thy rings of rugged fretwork,
    mark
What seems a heart-throb muffled in the
    dark!

Here lingering long, amid the shadowy
    gleams,
Faintly I catch (yet scarce as one that
    dreams)
Low words of alien music, softly sung,
And rhythmic sighs in some sweet un-
    known tongue.

And something rare, I cannot clasp or
    see,
Flits vaguely out from this mysterious
    tree —
A viewless glory, an ethereal grace,
Which make Elysian all the haunted
    place!

Ethereal! viewless! yet divinely dear!
Ah me! what strange enchantment hov-
    ers near.
What breaths of love the old, old dreams
    renew!
What kisses fall, like charmed Thessa-
    lian dew!

My Dryad-Love hath slipped the impris-
    oning bark,
Her heart on mine, unmuffled by the
    dark.

WELCOME TO FROST.

O SPIRIT! at whose wafts of chilling
  breath
Autumn unbinds her zone, to rest in
  death;
Touched by whose blight the light of
  cordial days
Is lost in sombre browns and sullen
  grays;
Thou seemest of all sad things a mourn-
  ful part:
Yet now we greet thee with exultant
  heart.

Not as a thief, at night-time bearing
  doom,
But a brave messenger of grace and
  bloom;
Thy flickering robe and footsteps soft we
  mark
Down the dim borders of the tremulous
  Dark;
And though before thee flowers and fo-
  liage wane,
Thou layest a magic hand on human
  pain.

Red Fever, soothed by thy cool finger-tips,
Ebbs from hot cheek and wildly-mutter-
  ing lips;
Delirious dreams and frenzied fancies
  fade
Into fine landscapes of enchanted shade,
With low of kine and lapse of lyric
  rills
Through the cleft channel of Arcadian
  hills;
Till the worn patient feels his languid
  eyes
Flushed with what seems an earthly
  Paradise,
And life's old blissful tide, with lustier
  strain,
Revels in music through each ransomed
  vein.

Therefore, O monarch of all cold device,
Wrought in strange temples of Siberian
  ice!

Lord of fair realms and watery worlds
  grotesque!
Majestic afreet of weird Arabesque!
We hail thee sovereign in these fevered
  lands.
No more with alien hearts and folded
  hands,
But as an angel from the fadeless
  palms,
And the great River of God's central
  calms,
Whose silent charm must work benign
  release,
Whose touch is healing, and whose breath
  is — peace!

———◆———

THE PINE'S MYSTERY.

I.

LISTEN! the sombre foliage of the
  Pine,
  A swart Gitana of the woodland
    trees,
Is answering what we may but half di-
  vine,
  To those soft whispers of the twilight
    breeze!

II.

Passion and mystery murmur through
  the leaves,
  Passion and mystery, touched by death-
    less pain.
Whose monotone of long, low anguish
  grieves
  For something lost that shall not live
    again!

———◆———

TO A BEE.

SMALL epicurean, would to heaven that I
  Could borrow your lithe body and
    swift wing
To speed, a lightning atom through the
  sky,
  The blithest courier on the winds of
    spring!

O blissful mite! native of light and air!
  In eager zeal you haste your spoils to
    win;
From half-blown bud to flower all ma-
    tron-fair,
  Sucking the nectared sweetness
    shrined within!

The jonquil wooes you with her golden
    blush,
  And blossoming quince (each flower a
    fairy Mars,
That tints its heaven of green with crim-
    soned flush),
  While the pure "white-rod" blooms
    in silvery stars,

Open to yield their delicate richness up.
  But most you love on vernal noons, to
    dart
'Mid jasmine bowers, and drain each
    petalled cup
  With fervid lip and warm voluptuous
    heart.

There, safely couched, you hum a low
    refrain,
  Of such supreme and rare contentment
    born,
Its happy monotone mocks our human
    pain,
  And subtly stings us with unconscious
    scorn.

Thence, honey-freighted, you steal lazily
    out,
  Pausing a moment on some leafy brink,
As if enmeshed by viewless webs of
    doubt
  From what next fount of luscious life
    to drink —

A moment only. Soon your matchless
    flight
  Cleaves the far blue; your elfin thun-
    der booms
In elfin echoes from yon glimmering
    height,
  To fall and die amid these ravished
    blooms.

Gone, like a vision! Yet, be sure that he
  Hath only flown through lovelier
    flowers to stray,
Anacreon's soul, thus prisoned in a bee,
  Still sips and sings the springtide
    hours away!

THE FIRST MOCKING - BIRD IN SPRING.

WINGED poet of vernal ethers!
  Ah! where hast thou lingered long?
I have missed thy passionate, skyward
    flights
  And the trills of thy changeful song.
Hast thou been in the hearts of wood-
    lands old,
Half dreaming, and, drowsed by the
    winter's cold,
Just crooning the ghost of thy springtide
    lay
To the listless shadows, benumbed and
    gray?
Or hast thou strayed by a tropic shore,
And lavished, O sylvan troubadour!
The boundless wealth of thy music free
On the dimpling waves of the Southland
    sea?
What matter? Thou comest with magic
    strain,
To the morning haunts of thy life again,
And thy melodies fall in a rhythmic rain.

The wren and the field-lark listen
  To the gush from their laureate's
    throat;
And the blue-bird stops on the oak to
    catch
  Each rounded and perfect note.
The sparrow, his pert head reared aloft,
Has ceased to chirp in the grassy croft,
And is bending the curves of his tiny ear
In the *pose* of a critic wise, to hear.
A blackbird, perched on a glistening
    gum,
Seems lost in a rapture, deep and dumb;
And as eagerly still in his tranced hush,

'Mid the copse beneath, is a clear-eyed
thrush.
No longer the dove by the thorn-tree
root
Moans sad and soft as a far-off flute.
All Nature is hearkening, charmed and
mute.

We scarce can deem it a marvel,
For the songs *our* nightingale sings
Throb warm and sweet with the
rhythmic beat
Of the fervors of countless springs.
All beautiful measures of sky and earth
Outpour in a second and rarer birth
From that mellow throat. When the
winds are whist,
And he follows his mate to their sunset
tryst,
Where the wedded myrtles and jasmine
twine,
Oh! the swell of his music is half di-
vine!
And I vaguely wonder, O bird! can it be
That a human spirit hath part in thee?
Some Lesbian singer's, who died per-
chance
Too soon in the summer of Greek ro-
mance,
But the rich reserves of whose broken
lay,
In some mystical, wild, undreamed-of
way,
Find voice in thy bountiful strains to-
day!

THE RED AND THE WHITE ROSE.

THE Red Rose bowed one golden sum-
mer's night,
The Red Rose bent, low whispering to
the White,

"Thou pallid shadow of a beauteous
flower,
Unchanged from purpling dawn to sun-
set hour;

Whose calm, cold heart beneath all lights
that beam,
Seems centred always in an Arctic
dream;

Prim, puritanic, passionless, austere,
What would'st thou give my opulent
life to share?

To every breeze — the daintiest breeze
that blows,
Each petalled curve of mine more richly
glows; —

And all the countless tints of heaven-
born grace
But touch to make more bright my Hebe
face!"

"Ah! well, fulfil thy fate!" the White
Rose said;
"List to the wooing winds! uplift thy
head

In sovereign pride through every radiant
phase
Of star-illumined nights and cloudless
days;

Let wingèd lovers thy warm leaves dis-
part,
To find voluptuous shelter next thy
heart.

Fulfil thy fate, O Queen! but leave to me
My stainless calm and cloistral sanctity;

Those passionate airs that trembling
round thee meet,
Sink in soft worship at my veilèd feet;

The reverent sun-rays shimmering gently
down,
Weave o'er my brows a halo for a crown;

And while I muse in star, or moonshine
faint,
The flowers seem murmuring, 'Lo! our
garden saint!'"

The Red Rose heard, but ere she spoke,
  her mouth
Thralled by the light, quick kisses of the
  South,

Passed from arch wonder, blent with gay
  disdain,
Back to its dimpled mirthfulness again;

And she,—the garden's empress—proud
  yet fond, —
Of summer flowers, the matchless Rosa-
  mond,—

Looked at her pale-hued sister, dew-
  impearled,
As that fair marvel of the island world,

Might, in her ruddier nature's Tropic
  glow,
Have viewed a calm St. Agnes' brow of
  snow,

With some dim sense of mystic space
  between
The heaven-bound votaress and the
  earthly queen!

---◆---

BEFORE THE MIRROR.

WHERE in her chamber by the Southern
  sea,
Her taper's light shone soft and silvery,
Fair as a planet mirrored in the main,
Fresh as a blossom bathed by April
  rain,
A maiden robed for restful sleep aright,
Stood in her musing sweetness, pure and
  white
As some shy spirit in a haunted place:
Her dew-bright eyes and faintly flushing
  face
Viewed in the glass their delicate beauty
  beam,
Strange as a shadowy "dream within a
  dream"
With fingers hovering like a white dove's
  wings,

'Mid little, tender sighs and murmur-
  ings
(Joy's scarce articulate speech), her
  eager hands
Loosed the light coif, the ringlet's golden
  bands,
Till, by their luminous loveliness em-
  braced,
From lily-head to lithe and lissome waist,
Poured the free tresses like a cascade's
  fall.
Her image answered from the shimmer-
  ing wall,
Answered and deepened, while the
  gracious charms
Of brow and cheek, bared breast and
  dimpling arms,
To innocent worship stirred her happy
  heart:
Her lips — twin rosebud petals blown
  apart —
Quivered, half breathless; then, subdued
  but warm,
Around her perfect face, her pliant
  form
A subtler air seemed gathering, touched
  with fire
By many a fervid thought and swift de-
  sire,
With dreams of love, that, bee-like, came
  and went,
To feed the honeyed core of life's con-
  tent!
Closer toward her mirrored self she
  pressed,
With large child-eyes, and gently pant-
  ing breast,
Bowed as a flower when May-time
  breezes pass,
And kissed her own dear Image in the
  glass!

---◆---

TWO EPOCHS.

LOVERS by a dim sea strand
Looking wave-ward, hand in hand;
Silent, trembling with the bliss
Of their first betrothal kiss:

Lovers still, tho' wedded long!
(Time true love can never wrong!
Gazing — faithful hand in hand,
O'er a darker sea and strand:

Ah! one lover's face is wan
As a wave the moon shines on;
But those strange tides stretched afar
Know not sun, nor moon, nor star!

"O masterful wind and cruel! at thy sweep,
From the bold hill-top to the valley deep,
Surprise and fear through all the woodlands run."

WIND FROM THE EAST.*

THE Spring, so fair in her young incompleteness,
Of late the very type of tender sweetness;
Now, through frail leaves and misty branches brown,
Looks forth, the dreary shadow of a frown
Chasing the frank smile from her innocent face;
What marvel this? for the East Wind's disgrace
Smites, like a buffet, April's tingling cheek,
Whence the swift, outraged blood doth ebb to seek
The affrighted heart!
    The Earth, herself so gay,
Buoyant, and happy, at the dawn of day,

Thrills, shivering low with every flaw increased,
And fraught with salt-sea coldness from the East!

O masterful wind and cruel! at thy sweep,
From the bold hill-top to the valley-deep,
Surprise and fear through all the woodlands run,
Till the coy nestling-places of the sun
Are ruffled up, from shine to shade, as when
At the first note of storm the moorland hen
Ruffles her wings ere yet their warmth be spread
About each tremulous nestling's dusky head.

On the tall trees the foremost buds, half bare,
Stared, as wild-eyed, on the keen, rasping air;

* This piece is (for the most part) a rhymed version of an exceedingly graphic description of the East wind, which occurs in Mr. Blackmore's admirable novel, "Cripps, the Carrier." Mr. Blackmore is a poet, although he writes in prose.

Then shook — but not with softly-palpi-
tant thrills,
As when, o'erlooking the freed moun-
tain-rills,
They felt their life by loving arms ca-
ressed —
Warm, viewless arms of zephyrs of the
West —
But with the sense, the cold and shivery
stress
Of utter and forlornest nakedness.
The twigs that bore them flattened up-
ward, lost
To all but rigid consciousness of frost;
And their full-foliaged branches which
so blindly
Bowed in meek homage when the winds
were kindly
Strained upward, too, in stiff, rebellious
fashion,
With throes of anguish and deep moans
of passion,
Wrung from them by wild beatings of
the gale!

Then many a tiny leaf, though waxing
pale,
Cloud-shadowed; all unfrayed, yet quiv-
ering, shrunk
Behind the mosses of some giant
trunk,
To wait till the shrewd tempest hurtling
by
Left Spring once more empress of earth
and sky —
While many a large leaf, almost riven
apart,
Piped a sad dirge from out its fluted
heart,
And knowing what sombre selvage must
be seen —
Alas, too soon! — to film its glow of
green,
Bewailed the hour whose treacherous
brightness came
To warm its life-blood into genial flame
Only to send the blissful-flowing tide
Back through the baffled veins unsatis-
fied,

Its nascent joy nipped by the arctic
breath
And merciless waftage of this Wind of
Death!

———◆———

PEACH BLOOMS.

O! tenderly beautiful, beyond compare,
Flushed from pale pink to deepest
rosebud hue —
Nurslings of tranquil sunshine and mild
air,
Of shadowless dawn, and silvery twi-
light dew —
Ye blush and burn, as if your flickering
grace
Were love's own tint on Spring's en-
amored face!

And day by day — yea, golden hour by
hour
Your subtle fragrance and rich beauty
tell
(Each fairy blossom rounded into flower),
How matchless once that lost Arcadian
spell,
Which dwelt in leafy bowers and vernal
dyes
Whence coyly peeped the Dryad's fawn-
like eyes!

And yet, while all so fair and bounteous
seems,
While the birds carol — each his dain-
tiest part,
Veiled in soft brightness, and like mu-
sical dreams
In some blithe soul — the bee-swarms
haunt your heart.
Lo! severed slowly from yon roseate
crown,
A scarlet snowdrift, silent, falters down.

The reign of these rich blooms is almost
done;
Soon to the languid Zephyr's feeblest
breath,
Their loosened petals, yielding one by
one,

Must find the Lethe of unwakening
    death.
Ah me! of all the bourgeoned buds that
    shoot
Even to full flower, how few shall bear
    us fruit!

Their little day is closing fast in gloom;
    Nor will they reck — poor wilted waifs,
        and blind!
What germs of richness wax from faded
    bloom,
    To charm the pampered taste of hu-
        man kind;
Forever dropped from off their parent
    stem,
What have man's thoughts or tastes to
    do with them ?

So let them rest, I pray you, let them rest,
    Small, perishing sweethearts of the
        sun and rain:
O! mother-earth, thou hast a ruthful
    breast,
    Which yearns to fold thy humblest
        child from pain.
Men fall like flowers; both claim the
    self-same balm,
The equal peace of thy majestic calm!

THE AWAKENING.

FROM day to day the dreary heaven
    Outpoured its hopeless heart in rain;
The conscious pines, half shuddering,
    heard
    The secret of the East wind's pain.

Mist veiled the sun — the sombre land,
    In floating cloud-wracks densely furled,
Seemed shut forever from the bloom
    And gladness of the living world.

From week to week the changeless
    heaven
    Wept on — and still its secret pain
To the bent pine-trees sobbed the wind,
    In hollow truces of the rain.

Till in a sunset hour, whose light
    Pale hints of radiance pulsed o'erhead,
Afar the moaning East wind died,
    And the mild West wind breathed in-
        stead.

Then the clouds broke, and ceased the
    rain;
    The sunset many a kindling shaft
Shot to the wood's heart; nature rose,
    And through her soft-lipped verdures
        laughed.

Low to the breeze; as some fair maid,
    Love wakes from troublous dreams,
        might rise,
Half dazed, yet happy — mists of sleep
    Still hovering in her haunted eyes.

LOVE'S AUTUMN.
[To My Wife.].

I WOULD not lose a single silvery ray
Of those white locks which like a milky
    way
Streak the dusk midnight of thy raven
    hair;

I would not lose, O sweet! the misty
    shine
Of those half-saddened, thoughtful eyes
    of thine,
Whence Love looks forth, touched by
    the shadow of care;

I would not miss the droop of **thy** dear
    mouth,
The lips less dewy-red than when the
    South, —
The young South wind of passion sighed
    o'er them;

I would not miss each delicate flower that
    blows
On thy wan cheeks, soft as September's
    rose
Blushing but faintly on its **faltering**
    stem;

I would not miss the air of chastened
    grace
Which breathed divinely from thy patient
    face,
Tells of love's watchful anguish, merged
    in rest;

Naught would I miss of all thou hast, or
    art,
O! friend supreme, whose constant,
    stainless heart,
Doth house unknowing, many an angel
    guest;

Their presence keeps thy spiritual
    chambers pure;
While the flesh fails, strong love grows
    more and more
Divinely beautiful with perished years;

Thus, at each slow, but surely deepening
    sign
Of life's decay, we will not, Sweet! re-
    pine,
Nor greet its mellowing close with thank-
    less tears;

Love's spring was fair, love's summer
    brave and bland,
But through love's autumn mist I view
    the land,
The land of deathless summers yet to be;

There, I behold thee, young again and
    bright,
In a great flood of rare transfiguring
    light,
But there as here, thou smilest, Love! on
    me!

—————

THE SPIREA.

[This exquisite plant blooms in the Southern
States as early as the middle of February.]

OF all the subtle fires of earth
    Which rise in form of spring-time
        flowers,
Oh, say if aught of purer birth
    Is nursed by suns and showers

Than this fair plant, whose stems are
        bowed
    In such lithe curves of maiden grace,
Veiled in white blossoms like a cloud
    Of daintiest bridal lace?

So rare, so soft, its blossoms seem
    Half woven of moonshine's misty bars,
And tremulous as the tender gleam
    Of the far Southland stars.

Perchance — who knows? — some virgin
        bright,
    Some loveliest of the Dryad race,
Pours through these flowers the kindling
        light
    Of her Arcadian face.

Nor would I marvel overmuch
    If from yon pines a wood-god came,
And with a bridegroom's lips should
        touch
    Her conscious heart to flame;

While she, revealed at that strange tryst,
    In all her mystic beauty glows,
Lifting the cheek her Love had kissed,
    Paled like a bridal rose.

—————

COQUETTE.

[Among the family portraits.]

I.

YES! there from out the gallery gloom,
Retaining still a flush of bloom,
I mark our bright ancestress glow —
The maiden Rose of long ago.
She lived in times of sumptuous dress,
And rich colonial stateliness;
But through the strong restraints of art
I seem to view her heaving heart,
As if a protest warm it made
'Gainst that stiff bodice of brocade,
While in her fair cheeks' deepening dyes,
Her lifted brows and roguish eyes,
Her swan-like neck and dimpled chin—
Cleft for small Loves to ambush in —

"Ah! many a gallant loved her well
In those old days."

I can not fail (who could ?) to see
All potent charms of coquetry —
The wiles whose glamour, swift and
    sure,
Smote hapless victims by the score;
And even now (although they be
Discerned in pictured phantasy)
Not all innocuous, but possessed
Of power to pierce the manly breast,
If frosted to its shivering core
By forty arctic years or more.

II.

Ah! many a gallant loved her well
In those old days! Her features tell
The world-wide story o'er again,
Of *others'* passion, *her* disdain;
Of hearts that spent their best to make
Her own more tender for love's sake,
Only in time to find, perchance,
Dull ending to a life's romance,
Since trivial natures are not stirred
Save by the lightly trivial word;
And much I fear, despite the fine
Rare beauty of each faultless line —
Her face, of gay *insouciance,* shows
No golden gulfs of pure repose
Deep in her inmost being shrined —
But shallow thoughts and purpose blind.
And yet who knows ? My erring sight
May not have read its meanings right,
And something of ethereal grace
May lurk beneath that careless face,
Which masks with inconsiderate mirth
A soul not wholly wed to earth!

III.

Therefore, sweet flesh and blood, I trust
That, ere ye passed to senseless dust,
Your beauty played a worthier part —
The love-*rôle* of the loyal heart.

. . . . .

No answer comes; for time doth mar
Our records. Only, like a star
Scarce touched by vapors vague and chill,
Your gracious image haunts us still.
But none, alas! may truly guess
What fate befell your loveliness.

SKATING.

I CHASED the maid with rapid feet,
    Where ice and sunbeam quiver;
But still beyond me, shyly fleet,
    She flashed far down the river.

Sometimes, blown backward in the chase,
    With balmy, soft caresses,
I felt across my glowing face
    The waft of perfumed tresses.

Sometimes a glance she shot behind,
    O'er graceful shoulders turning
A cheek whose tints the eager wind
    Had set like sunrise burning.

Then, in a sudden onward glide,
    She rushed with even motion,
As a long wave the restless tide
    Drives shoreward fast from ocean;

And swift as some winged creature sped
    Far down the crystal river,
Until the shining form that fled
    I dreamed might fly forever.

———◆———

THE WORLD WITHIN US.

A FANTASY.

PERCHANCE our *inward* world may
    partly be
But *outward* Nature's fine epitome;

Now, o'er it floats some cloud of tender
    pain
Too frail to hold the sad reserves of rain;

And now behold some breezy impulse
    run
O'er Thought's bright surface, glittering
    in the sun;

Whereon, like birds, the flocks of fancy
    throng,
And all is peace and sweetness, light and
    song:

Anon, dim moods like shadowy wood-
        lands rise
As 'twere between the spirit's earth and
        skies:

All fair suggestions, hints of twilight
        grace,
Safe harborage seek within the spell-
        bound space;

Music is there, low laughter, and the
        sound
Of fairy voices, echoing gently round

The cool recesses of the veilèd mind:
While on the surge of memory's phan-
        tom wind,

Ghosts of dead loves, swathed in a
        silvery mist
Pass by us; and the lips our lips had
        kissed,

In youth's glad prime, unutterable things
Whisper, through wafts of visionary
        wings.

Ah, yes! our *inward* world but mirrors
        true,
This *outward* world of sense; — it hath
        its dew,

Its sunshine, and fresh roses, white and
        red;
It holds a tender moonlight over head;

The dews of yearning, mild, or fiery-
        bright,
The flowers of peace, or passion; the
        calm light

Of reasoning thought, and retrospection
        fine,
All merged in subtlest beauty — half
        divine!

It hath its mounts of vision, and its vales
Of contemplation, where fond nightin-
        gales,

Born of the brain, and 'gainst some
        thorns of woe,
Setting their breasts — but sing more
        sweetly so:

Fountains it owns of shyest fantasie;
Glad streams of inspiration, swift and
        free,

Rolling toward Thought's central ocean
        vast
Wherein all lesser forms of thought, at
        last

Sink, as the rivulets perish in a sea; —
Thus, rounded, whole, our spirit-land-
        scapes be,

Our spirit-world thus perfect; over all,
No clouds of doubt hang, stifling as a
        pall;

But if the soul be healthful, noble,
        high,
God's promise lights it, like a sleepless
        eye!

———◆———

FOREST QUIET.
[In the South.]

So deep this sylvan silence, strange and
        sweet,
Its dryad-guardian, virginal Peace, can
        hear
The pulses of her own pure bosom beat;

And her low voice echoed by elfin rills,
And far-off forest fountains, sparkling
        clear
'Mid haunted hollows of the hoary
        hills;

No breeze, nor wraith of any breeze that
        blows,
Stirs the charmed calm; not even yon
        gossamer-chain,
Dew-born, and swung 'twixt violet and
        wild rose,

Thrills to the airy elements' subtlest
   breath;
Such marvellous stillness almost broods
   like pain
O'er the hushed sense, holding dim hints
   of death!

What shadows of sound survive, the
   waves' far sigh,
Drowsed cricket's chirp, or mock-bird's
   croon in sleep,
But touch this sacred, soft tranquillity

To yet diviner quiet: the fair land
Breathes like an infant lulled from deep
   to deep
Of dreamless rest, on some wave-whis-
   pering strand!

THE MOCKING-BIRD.

[At night.]

A GOLDEN pallor of voluptuous light
Filled the warm southern night:
The moon, clear orbed, above the sylvan
   scene
Moved like a stately queen,
So rife with conscious beauty all the
   while,
What could she do but smile
At her own perfect loveliness below,
Glassed in the tranquil flow
Of crystal fountains and unruffled
   streams ?
Half lost in waking dreams,
As down the loneliest forest dell I
   strayed,
Lo! from a neigboring glade,
Flashed through the drifts of moonshine,
   swiftly came
A fairy shape of flame.
It rose in dazzling spirals overhead,
Whence to wild sweetness wed,
Poured marvellous melodies, silvery trill
   on trill;
The very leaves grew still
On the charmed trees to hearken; while
   for me,
Heart-trilled to ecstasy,

I followed — followed the bright shape
   that flew,
Still circling up the blue,
Till as a fountain that has reached its
   height,
Falls back in sprays of light
Slowly dissolved, so that enrapturing
   lay,
Divinely melts away
Through tremulous spaces to a music-
   mist,
Soon by the fitful breeze
   How gently kissed
Into remote and tender silences.

A STORM IN THE DISTANCE.

[Among the Georgian Hills.]

I SEE the cloud-born squadrons of the
   gale,
   Their lines of rain like glittering
     spears deprest
(While all the affrighted land grows
   darkly pale),
   In flashing charge on earth's half-
     shielded breast;

Sounds like the rush of trampling
   columns float
   From that fierce conflict; volleyed
     thunders peal,
Blent with the maddened wind's wild
   bugle-note;
   The lightnings flash, the solid wood-
     lands reel!

Ha! many a foliaged guardian of the
   height,
   Majestic pine or chestnut, riven and
     bare,
Falls in the rage of that aerial fight,
   Led by the Prince of all the powers of
     air!

Vast boughs, like shattered banners
   hurtling fly
   Down the thick tumult : while, like
     emerald snow,

Millions of orphaned leaves make wild
the sky,
Or drift in shuddering helplessness
below.

Still, still, the levelled lances of the rain
At earth's half-shielded breast take
glittering aim;
All space is rife with fury, racked with
pain,
Earth bathed in vapor, and heaven
rent by flame!

At last the cloud-battalions through long
rifts
Of luminous mists retire; . . . the
strife is done;
And earth once more her wounded
beauty lifts,
To meet the healing kisses of the sun.

THE VISION BY THE SEA.

" A thing of beauty is a joy forever."

I.

A HAUNTING face! with strange, ethereal
eyes,
Deep as unfathomed gulfs of tranquil
skies
When o'er their brightness a vague mist
is drawn,
Breathed from the half-veiled lips of
melting dawn;
A mouth whose passionate love and
sweetness seem
But just released from kisses in a dream;
A brow like Psyche's, pensive, broad,
and low
And white as winter's whitest wreath of
snow;
While round that gracious forehead,
calmly fair,
Ripples an April rain of golden hair.

II.

For some rapt moments, on the ocean
strand,
Unconscious, beautiful, I saw her stand,
As tremulous wave on wave, with
freightage sweet
Of murmured music, fawned about her
feet,
Then died in one divine, harmonious
sigh;
The breeze bewitched, could only falter
nigh,
And in shy delicate wafts of homage
play
With her rare tresses; like incarnate
May,
She seemed the earth, the tides, the
heaven, to bless:
For once I gazed on Beauty's perfectness.

III.

I gazed for some rapt moments, but no
more;
Then lowered mine eyes and slowly left
the shore
Made marvellous by that vision of de-
light;
Yet evermore its beauty, day and night,
Standing between the blue sky and the
sea,
Shines like a star of immortality
Through all my being; it becomes a part
Of the deep life that quickens soul and
heart
To sense of things ideal and supreme —
A palpable bliss, yet wedded to a dream.

THE VISIONARY FACE.

I AM happy with her I love,
In a circle of charmed repose;
My soul leaps up to follow her feet
Wherever my darling goes;
Whether to roam through the garden
walks,
Or pace the sands by the sea; —
There's never a shadow of doubt or fear
Brooding 'twixt her and me: —
But through memory's twilight mists,
Sometimes, I own, in sooth,
Falters the face of one I loved
In the fervent years of youth; —

The soft pathetic brow is there,
  With its glimmer and glance of golden
    hair,
And scarcely shadowed by death's eclipse
The delicate curve of the faultless lips,
The tremulous, tender lips I kissed,
So coyly raised at the sunset tryst,
As we stood from the restless world
    apart,
'Mid the whispering foliage, heart to
    heart,
  In the fair, far years of youth.
Yet, the vision is pure as heaven,
  Untouched by a hint of strife.
From the passion that moved itself to
    sleep,
  On the morning strand of life;
And I know that my living Love would
    feel
  The tremor of ruthful tears,
If I told of the sweetness and hope that
    drooped,
  So soon in the vanished years:
She would not banish the phantom
    sad
Of a beauty discrowned and low; —
Can jealousy rest in the rose's breast
Of a lily under the snow ?
Can the passion so warm and strong
    to-day
  Envy a ghost from the cypress shades
  For an hour astray ?
Or, the love that waned like a blighted
    May,
  In the dead days, long ago,
    Ah! long, how long ago!

THE ROSE AND THORN.

SHE's loveliest of the festal throng
  In delicate form and Grecian face;'
A beautiful, incarnate song;
  A marvel of harmonious grace;
And yet I know the truth I speak:
  From those gay groups she stands
    apart,
A rose upon her tender cheek,
  A thorn within her heart.

Though bright her eyes' bewildering
    gleams,
  Fair tremulous lips and shining hair,
A something born of mournful dreams,
  Breathes round her sad enchanted
    air;
No blithesome thoughts at hide and seek
  From out her dimples smiling start;
If still the rose be on her cheek,
  A thorn is in her heart.

Young lover, tossed 'twixt hope and fear,
  Your whispered vow and yearning
    eyes
Yon marble Clytie pillared near
  Could move as soon to soft replies;
Or, if she thrill at words you speak,
  Love's memory prompts the sudden
    start;
The rose has paled upon her cheek,
  The thorn has pierced her heart.

THE RED LILY.

I CALL her the Red Lily. Lo! she stands
  From all her milder sister flowers
    apart;
A conscious grace in those fair-folded
    hands,
  Pressed on the guileful throbbings of
    her heart!

I call her the Red Lily. As all airs
  Of North or South, the Lily's leaves
    that stir,
Seem lost in languorous sweetness that
    despairs
  Of blissful life or hope, except through
    her;

So this Red Lily of maids, this human
    flower,
  Yielding no love, all sweets of love
    doth take,
Twining such spells of passion's secret
    power
  As, woven once, what lordliest will
    can break ?

LAKE WINNIPISEOGEE.

ONE day the River of Life flowed o'er
The verge of heaven's enchanted shore,
And falling without lapse or break.
Its waters formed this wondrous lake.

Hence the far sheen of Eden palms
Is mirrored in its silvery calms,
And all its rich cerulean dyes
Are deep as Raphael's splendid eyes.

And hence the unimagined grace
Which sanctifies this lonely place,—
A subtle, soft, ethereal spell
Of light and sound ineffable.

Surely such tempered glory paints
The mystic City of the Saints;
Such music breathes its dying falls
Above the heavenly palace walls.

O lake of peace! whose still expanse
Gleams through a golden-misted trance,
Earth holds thee sacred and apart,
The cloistered darling of her heart.

LAKE MISTS.

[Composed near Lake Winnipiseogee.]

As I gazed on the prospect enchanted,
On waves the sun-glory had kissed,
There slowly swept down from the dis-
tance,
The phantom-like bands of the mist.

On their feet that were spectrally sound-
less,
They glided fantastic and chill,
While a prescient pallor crept over
The beauty of lake-side and hill!

All nature grew cold at their advent!
Like Thugs of the air, demon-born,
With their coils of blue vapor they
strangled
The virgin effulgence of morn.

By that ambush of darkness was girdled
Each bright beam in dreary embrace,

Till the fairest young dawn of September
Lay wan on her death-shadowed face.

When wildly and weirdly from sea-ward,
A low wind how mournfully stole!
Like an anthem outbreathed for the
morning,
Thus sternly divorced from her soul!

THE INEVITABLE CALM.

THE sombre wings of the tempest,
In fetterless force unfurled,
Buffet the face of beauty,
And scar the grace of the world;

But they fade at length with the dark-
ness,
And softly·from sky to sod
Peace falls like the dew of Eden,
From the opened palm of God!

Earthquake, the angered Titan,
A continent cleaves apart;
Yet soon the' glamour of quiet heals
Earth's smitten and tortured heart.

And soon o'er the ruin of cities
The sun-bright virginal grass
Courtesies and curves into dimples,
At the kiss of the winds that pass.

One lesson all nature teaches,
As balm to the troubled breast,
That after the turmoil of passion
There cometh a time of rest.

For the anguish of life wanes downward
Like fire unfanned by a breath;
And deep is the ashen stillness
On the hearthstone cold of death!

THE DEAD LOOK.

Lo! in its still, soft-shrouded place,
The pathos of a death-pale face!

I view the marks of mortal care
Time's hopeless sorrows branded there.

Waning beneath the noiseless glide
Of Lethe's dim, ethereal tide,

As furrows on some twilight lea
Fade in calm wave-sweeps of the sea!

Across that bare, unbended brow
The chrism of peace has fallen now,

And, lightening life's austere eclipse,
A star-soft smile hath touched the
    lips:

Though his sealed sight the death-mists
    mar,
He hath a strange look, fixed afar:—

As if wan folds of curtained eyes
Trembled almost in act to rise,

And show where each cold-lidded sheath
Now veils the wide, weird orbs beneath,

The mirrored glow, the blest surprise
Of some first glimpse of Paradise!

"While grimly down the moonlit bay,
The wrecked hull gleamed from far."

JETSAM.

BESIDE the coast for many a rood
    Were fragments of a shipwreck
        strewn;
And there in sad and sombre mood
    I walked the sands alone.

Torn bales and broken boxes lay,
    Heaped high 'mid shattered sails and
        spar,
While grimly down the moonlit bay
    The wrecked hull gleamed from far.

Well had the storm its mission wrought,
    With thunder crash and billowy roar;
For not one precious waif was brought
    Safe to the rugged shore.

Yet stay! what tiny sparkling thing
    Shines faintly in the moonbeams
        cold?
I stooped, and wondering, grasped a
    ring,
    A fairy ring of gold.

Of great and small, of rich and rare,
    Of all yon stranded vessel bore,
Only this gem the waves would spare
    To cast unharmed ashore.

With what a deep and tender thrill
    I put the modest gem away,
And while the silvery vapors chill
    Crept ghost-like up the bay,

I dreamed of shivering human lives
 Wrecked on Fate's cold and cruel
  lee,
Trusting that some small hope survives,
 Spared to them from the sea!

---♦---

FAMELESS GRAVES.

I WALKED the ancient graveyard's am-
 ple round,
 Yet found therein not one illustrious
  name
 Wedded by Death to Fame.

The sea-winds moaned by each deserted
 mound,
 Where mouldering marbles shed their
  pungent must
 O'er that worn human dust.

Thin cloudlets passed, with purpled
 skirts of rain
 Grazing the sentinel pine-trees, gaunt
  and tall;
 Some trembling to their fall.

From out the misty marsh-lands next
 the main,
 Long lines of curlews in the sunset
  flame,
 With dissonant noises came;

O'erswept the tombs in slow, high-
 wheeling flight,
 And while the sunset verged on eve-
  ning's gray,
 Faded, ghostlike, away.

Yet down the dusky, shimmering, weird
 twilight
 (Though lost their forms beyond the
  outmost hill),
 Their strange cries sounded still; —

Prolonged by elfin echoes, 'mid the
 rocks,
 Or lapsing in sad, plaintive wails to
  die
 'Twixt darkling wave and sky.

The garrulous sparrows, in home-wend-
 ing flocks,
 Sought their rude nests among those
  shattered tombs,
 Veiled now in vesper glooms;

Till o'er the scene a mystic influence
 stole;
 The wave-enamored winds their pin-
  ions furled;
 Pale Silence clasped the world.

Beside a grave, the lowliest of the whole
 Obscure republic of the fameless dead,
 Pausing, I mused, and said: —

All graves are equal! His, the laurelled,
 great,
 Miraculous Shakspeare's, some far day
  shall rest
 As level on Earth's breast, —

And all unknown — through stern be-
 hests of Fate —
 As this, round which the rustling
  dock-leaves meet
 Here, tangled at my feet. —

All graves are equal to all-conquering
 Time;
 Scornful, he laughs at monumental
  stones, —
 Wasting a great man's bones,

A great man's sepulchre, though reared
 sublime
 Toward heaven, until both stone and
  record pass,
 Mocked by the flippant grass;

The feeblest weeds in Nature flaunting
 high
 Above a Shakespeare's or a Dante's
  dust: —
 Just then a gentle gust

Breathed from beyond the gloaming:
 Night's first sigh
 Of conscious life touched the awakened
  trees,
 And blended with the sea's

Monotonous murmur, seemed to whisper low:
"I rise, and sink, am born, and lose my breath,
Yet am not held by Death.

"For since the world began — when sunset's glow
Melts in the western tides — my air of balm
Rises, if earth be calm.*

"My spell is sacred, wheresoe'er it falls;
The dreariest graves grow brighter at my voice,
And human hearts rejoice,

"Because that I, winged from these twilight halls,
In this, my life renewed, would subtly seem
A sweet, half-uttered dream

"Of immortality, made bright by love:
That love which binds the humblest human clod
Fast to the throne of God."

I left the graves; but now my gaze above
Ranged through the heavenly spaces, clear and far;
I marked the vesper star

Silver the edges of the wavering mist,
And centred in an air-wrought, luminous isle
Of lambent glory, smile; —

Smile like an angel whom the Lord hath kissed,
And freed from arms divine, in soft release,
To bless our earth with peace.

---

* What dweller by the ocean can have failed to remark the almost invariable rising, just after sunset on quiet evenings, of this gentle air, a very sigh of tranquillity, a breath, as it were, from God?

WINTER ROSE.

God's benison upon each happy day
Dead now and gone!—its gentle ghost our feet
Doth follow, singing faintly; and how sweet—
Tenderly sweet, as through a luminous mist—
Its shadowy lips draw near us, to be kissed!
And though they melt upon the yearning mouth
Like fairy balm from some phantasmal south,
Their touch is magic; and we feel the start
As of an unsealed fountain, close at heart—
Till, warmed, restored, breathing a fine repose,
Our innermost nature, wakening, glows anew;
While, gemmed by sunset memory's radiant dew,
Lo! the heart blossoms, like a Winter Rose!

——◆——

TRISTRAM OF THE WOOD.

Once, when the autumn fields were dim and wet,
The trumpets rang; the tide of battle set
Toward gray Broceliande, by the western sea.

In the fore-front of conflict grimly stood,
Clothed in dark armor, Tristram of the Wood,
And round him ranged his knights of Brittany.

Of lordlier frame than even the lordliest there,
Firm as a tower, upon his vast *destrere*,
He looked as one whose soul was steeped in trance.

Ne'er spake nor stirred he, though the
trumpet's sound
Echoed abroad, and all the glittering
ground
Shook to the steel-clad warriors' swift
advance;

Ne'er spake nor stirred he, for the mys-
tic hour
Closed o'er him then; the glamour of its
power
Dream-wrought, and sadly beautiful
with love —

Love of the lost Iseult. In marvellous
stead
Of thronging faces, with looks stern and
dread,
Through the dense dust, the hostile
plumes above,

He saw his fair, lost Iseult's passionate
eyes,
And o'er the crash of lances heard her
cries,
Shrill with despair, when last they
twain did part.

While others thrilled to strife, he, thrilled
with woe,
Felt his life-currents shuddering cold and
low
Round the worn bastions of his broken
heart.

Then rolled his way the battle's furious
flood;
Squadrons charged on him blindly;
blows and blood
Showered down like hail and water;
vainly drew

The whole war round him; still his
broadsword's gleam
Flashed in death's front, and still, as
wrapped in dream,
He fought and slew, witting not whom
he slew,

Nor knew whose arm had smitten him
deep and sore —
So deep that Tristram never, never
more
Shone in the van of conflict; but the
smart

Of his fierce wound tortured him night
and day,
Till, through God's grace, his life-blood
ebbed away,
And death's sweet quiet healed his
broken heart.

———◆———

HINTS OF SPRING.

[COMPOSED IN SICKNESS.]

"When the hill-side breaks into green, every
hollow of blue shade, every curve of tuft, and
plume and tendril, every broken sunbeam on
spray of young leaves is *new! No spring
is a representation of any former spring!*" —
GOETHE.

A SOFTENING of the misty heaven,
A subtle murmur in the air;
The electric flash through coverts old
Of many a shy wing, touched with gold;
The stream's unmuffled voice, that calls,
Now shrill and clear, now silvery low,
As if a fairy flute did blow
Above the sylvan waterfalls;
Each mellowed sound, each quivering
wing
Heralds the happy-hearted Spring:
Earth's best beloved is drawing near.

Amid the deepest woodland dells,
So late forlornly cold and drear,
Wafts of mild fervor, procreant breaths
Of gentle heat, unclose the sheaths
Of fresh-formed buds on bower and tree;
A spirit of soft revival looks
Coyly from out the young-leaved nooks,
Just dimpling into greenery;
Through flashes of faint primrose bloom,
Through delicate gleam and golden
gloom,
The wonder of the world draws near.

On some dew-sprinkled, cloudless morn,
She, in her full-blown joyance rare,
Will pass beyond her Orient gate,
Smiling, serene, calmly elate,
All garmented in light and grace:
Her footsteps on the hills shall shine
In beauty, and her matchless face
Make the fair vales of earth divine.
O goddess of the azure eyes,
The deep, deep charm that never dies,
Delay not long, delay not long!
Come clad in perfume, glad with song,
Breathe on me from thy perfect lips,
Lest mine be closed, and death's eclipse
Rise dark between
Me and thine advent, tender queen,
Albeit thou art so near, so near!

THE HAWK.

AMBUSHED in yonder cloud of white,
Far-glittering from its azure height,
He shrouds his swiftness and his might!

But oft across the echoing sky,
Long-drawn, though uttered suddenly,
We hear his strange, shrill, bodeful cry.

Winged robber! in his vaporous tower
Secure in craft, as strong in power,
Coolly he bides the fated hour,

When thro' cloud-rifts of shadowy rise,
Earthward are bent his ruthless eyes,
Where, blind to doom, the quarry lies!

And from dense cloud to noontide glow,
(His fiery gaze still fixed below),
He sails on pinions proud and slow!

Till, like a fierce, embodied ray,
He hurtles down the dazzling day, —
A death-flash on his startled prey;

And where but now a nest was found,
Voiceful, beside its grassy mound,
A few brown feathers strew the ground!

OVER THE WATERS.

I.

OVER the crystal waters
She leans in careless grace,
Smiling to view within them
Her own fair happy face.

II.

The waves that glass her beauty
No tiniest ripple stirs:
What human heart thus coldly
Could mirror grace like hers?

THE TRUE HEAVEN.

THE bliss for which our spirits pine,
That bliss we feel shall yet be given,
Somehow, in some far realm divine,
Some marvellous state we call a
heaven.

Is not the bliss of languorous hours
A glory of calm, measured range,
But life which feeds our noblest powers
On wonders of eternal change?

A heaven of action, freed from strife,
With ampler ether for the scope
Of an immeasurable life
And an unbaffled, boundless hope.

A heaven wherein all discords cease,
Self-torment, doubt, distress, turmoil,
The core of whose majestic peace
Is godlike power of tireless toil.

Toil, without tumult, strain or jar,
With grandest reach of range endued,
Unchecked by even the farthest star
That trembles thro' infinitude;

In which to soar to higher heights
Through widening ethers stretched
abroad,
Till in our onward, upward flights
We touch at last the feet of God.

Time swallowed in eternity!
  No future evermore; no past,
But one unending NOW, to be
  A boundless circle round us cast!

THE BREEZES OF JUNE.

OH! sweet and soft,
  Returning oft,
    As oft they pass benignly,
The warm June breezes come and go,
Through golden rounds of murmurous
      flow,
    At length to sigh,
    Wax faint and die,
Far down the panting primrose sky,
      Divinely!

Though soft and low
  These breezes blow,
    Their voice is passion's wholly;
And ah! our hearts go forth to meet
The burden of their music sweet,
    Ere yet it sighs,
    Faints, falters, dies,
Down the rich path of sunset skies —
    Half glad, half melancholy!

Bend, bend thine ear!
  Oh! hark and hear
What vows each blithe new-comer,
Each warm June breeze that comes and
      goes,
Is whispering to the royal rose,
    And star-pale lily, trembling nigh,
    Ere yet in subtlest harmony
    Its murmurs die,
    Wax faint and die,
On thy flushed bosom, passionate sky,
    Of youthful summer!

A MOUNTAIN FANCY.

[Respectfully inscribed to Mrs. R. S. Storrs.]

CLOSE to each mountain's towering peak
A white cloud leans its tearful cheek,
Till all its soul of mystic pain
Dissolves in slow, soft, vaporous rain.

Thus, when our heart-griefs seek aright
Some heavenly Thought's majestic
      height,
Their passion, touched by loftier air,
Dissolves in tender mists of prayer!

Jefferson Hill House, White Mountains, N.H.,
      September, 1879.

ABSENCE AND LOVE.

WE need the clasp of hand in hand,
  The light flashed warm from neighbor-
      ing eyes:
Or else as weary seasons pass —
    Alas! alas!
  Our tenderest love grows wan and
      dies.

The fatal years like seas expand
  'Twixt souls that long have dwelt
      apart,
Till, broadening o'er our being's verge,
  The ruthless surge
  Love's memory sweeps from out the
      heart.

O Absence! thou unreverenced Death!
  Thy dense, unconsecrated clay
Inurns affection past regret;
    No hint is set
  Thereon of Resurrection Day.

THE FALLEN PINE-CONE.

I LIFT thee, thus, thou brown and rug-
      ged cone,
    Well poised and high,
Between the flowering grasses and the
      sky;
  And, as sea-voices dwell
In the fine chambers of the ocean-shell,
    So fancy's ear
Within thy numberless, dim complexities
  Hath seemed ofttimes to hear
The imprisoned spirits of all winds that
      blow;
Winds of late autumn that lamenting
      moan

Across the wild sea-surges' ebb and flow;
Storm-winds of winter mellowed to a
    sigh,
Long-drawn and plaintive; or — how
    lingeringly! —
Soft echoes of the spring-tide's jocund
    breeze,
Blent with the summer south wind, mur-
    muring low!

What wonder, fairy cone, that thou
    should'st hold
The semblance of these voices? day and
    night,
Proudly enthroned upon the wavering
    height
Of yon monarchal pine, thou did'st
    absorb
The elemental virtues of all airs,
    Timid or bold.
Measures of gentle joys and wild despairs,
Breathed from all quarters of our change-
    ful orb;
Whether with mildness freighted or with
    might,
Into thy form they entered, to remain
Each the strange phantom of a perished
    tone,
    An eerie, marvellous strain
Pent in this tiny Hades made to fold
Ghosts of the heavenly couriers long ago,
Sunk as men dreamed by ocean and by
    shore,
Into the void of silence evermore!

STERN TRUTHS TRANSFIGURED.

THOSE mountain forms of giant girth
Are rooted deep in moveless earth;
But lo! their yearning heights with-
    drawn,
Are melting in soft seas of dawn.

What golden lights and shadows kiss
Brown ledge and Titan precipice!
Till all the rock-bound, sullen space
Glows like a visionary face:

Thus frowning truths whose roots are
    furled
Round bases of some granite world,
May lift their mellowed light afar,
Transfigured by love's morning-star.

DISTANCE.

WHY is it that yon far-off, mellowed
    horn
Sounds like an antique story, half-for-
    lorn,
Half-sweet, with iterance of rare echoes
    sent
Up the serenely listening firmament?

I thrill, soul-smitten by each melting
    tone
About the golden distant spaces blown,
As if soft pathos came on rhythmic sighs
From out the heart of vanished centu-
    ries.

Distance is magic! in its fairy hold
Are alchemies that change even dross to
    gold, —
While beauty's nymph, too closely seen
    or pressed,
Melts to mere shadow from the enamored
    quest!

HORIZONS.

I LOVE to gaze along the horizon's
    verge —
    To strain my sight where steeped in
        golden-gray
The sun-illumined vapors gently surge,
    To melt in measureless distances away.

I gaze and gaze, till tears bedim my eyes,
    And tongueless fancies haunt me,
        vague and fond;
Ethereal boundary! blending earth and
    skies,
    Ah! dost thou veil some marvellous
        realm beyond?

Deep spirit of mine! thou, too, art
  strangely bound
  By far horizons, vaporous, dim, and
    vast;
Beyond the range of whose enchanted
    round,
  Not even the genii of weird dreams
    have passed!

IN THE GRAY OF THE EVENING.

AUTUMN.

WHEN o'er yon forest solitudes
The sky of autumn evening broods —
A heaven whose warp, but palely bright,
Shot through with woofs of crimson
    light,
So slowly wanes with waning day —
Whatever thoughts, pathetic, sweet
Are wont to fawn round Memory's feet,
Pleading with soft and sacred stress
To be upcaught in tenderness;
Whatever thoughts like these there are,
Choose the weird hour 'twixt sun and
    star,
Of failing breeze, and whisperous sea,
And that still heaven o'er leaf and lea,
To come — each thought a temperate
    bliss —
Embracing the calmed soul, to kiss
The pallor of old cares away.

O twilight sky of mellow gray,
Flushed with faint hues! O voiceful
    trees,
Lilting low ballads to the breeze!
O all ye mild amenities
Wherewith the solemn eve is rife,
At this strange hour 'twixt death and
    life;
The death of beauteous day, whose last
Dim tints are almost overpast,
Who lives alone in odors blent
Of every subtlest element,
Borne on a fairy rain-like dew,
Exhaled, not dropped from out the blue;
The life of stars that one by one
Are mustering o'er the sunken sun,

And wafts of vague earth-perfume blown
Up to the pine-tree's quivering cone,
From heath-flowers hidden in cool
    grass, —
Like spells of delicate balm, ye pass
Into my wearied heart and brain.

What room for any sordid pain
Within me now? Ah! Nature seems
Through something sweeter than all
    dreams,
To woo me; yea, she seems to speak
How closely, kindly, her fond cheek
Rested on mine, her mystic blood
Pulsing in tender neighborhood,
And soft as any mortal maid,
Half veilèd in the twilight shade,
Who leans above her love to tell
Secrets almost ineffable!

THE VISION AT TWILIGHT.

[To E. R., October, 1879.]

WITHOUT the squares of misted pane,
I saw the wan autumnal rain,
And heard, o'er tufts of churchyard
    grass,
The wind's low *miserere* pass.

Within, more bright for outward gloom,
I saw her wild-rose cheeks abloom,
And, deep as stars in uppermost skies,
The lustre of dark Syrian eyes!

Without, still drearier grew the sigh
Of the chill east wind shuddering by,
Wilder the sad, strange moaning made
Beneath the elm-trees' rayless shade.

Within, as if the embodied south
Had opened her enchanted mouth,
I caught, through twilight's gray eclipse,
The music from her gracious lips.

It breathed such sweetness, purely deep,
On my dull pain it dropped like sleep.
"How vain," I thought, "this gathering
    gloom;
Some heavenly presence fills the room!"

"O twilight sky of mellow grey,
    Flushed with faint hues."

And when her warm hand, pulsing
youth,
On mine she pressed in guileless ruth,
One moment, charmed through blood
and brain,
I felt my own lost youth again!

With quickened heart and lifted head
I viewed the vision near my bed,
But lovelier for that envious gloom,
Her heavenly presence blessed the room!

AN HOUR TOO LATE.

I HAVE loved you, oh, how madly!
I have wooed you softly, sadly,
As the changeful years went by;
Yet you kept your haughty distance,
Yet you scorned my brave persistence,
While the long, long years went by.

Now that colder lovers leave you,
Now that Fate and Time bereave you
(For the cruel years *will* fly),
In your beauty's pale declension
You would grace with condescension
The love that touched you never
When your bloom and hopes were high.

Ah! but what if I discover
That too long in antique fashion
I have nursed a fruitless passion,
Whose rage and reign (thank Heaven!)
Are passed at length and over —
That fate hath locked forever love's
golden Eden gate ?
There's a wrong beyond redressing,
There's a prize not worth possessing,
And a lady's condescension
May come an hour *too late!*

"TOO LOW AND YET TOO HIGH!"

HE came in velvet and in gold;
He wooed her with a careless grace;
A confidence too rashly bold
Breathed in his language and his face.

While she — a simple maid — replied:
"No more of love 'twixt thee and me!
These tricks of passion I deride,
Nor trust thy boasted verity.
Thy suit, with artful smile and sigh,
Resign, resign:
*No mate am I for thee or thine,
Being too low, and yet too high!*"

His spirit changed; his heart grew warm
With genuine passion; morn by morn
More perfect seemed the virgin charm
That crowned her 'mid the ripening
corn.
And now he wooed with fervent mien,
With soul intense, and words of fire,
But reverence-fraught, as if a queen
Were hearkening to his heart's desire.
She brightly blushed, she gently sighed,
Yet still the village maid replied
(Though in sad accents, wearily):
"Thy suit resign,
Resign, resign!
*Lord Hugh, I never can be thine.
Too low am I, and yet too high!*"

THE LORDSHIP OF CORFU.
A LEGEND OF 1516.

WHAT time o'er gory lands and threat-
ening seas
Fair fortune, wearied, fled the Genoese —
What time from many a realm the
waters woo
Iu the warm south, "*Who now shall
rule Corfu?*"
Rose with the eager passion and fierce
greed
Of those who preyed on every empire's
need, —
There fell upon that isle's disheartened
brave
A wild despair, such as in one dark
grave
Might well have whelmed the prostrate
nation's pride,
Her honor, strength, traditions — all
beside

Which crowns a race with sovereignty.
        Sublime
Above the reckless purpose of his time
Their Patriarch stood, and such wise
        words he spake
The basest souls are thrilled, the feeblest
        wake
To some high aim, some passion grand
        and free,
Some cordial grace of magnanimity:
By such unwonted power they yield their
        all
To him that came, as if at Godhead's
        call,
To save the state, whose stricken pillars
        reel.

How works the Patriarch for his people's
        weal?
Calmly he bids them launch their stanch-
        est keel —
A gorgeous galley: on her decks they
        raise
Great golden altars, girt by lights that
        blaze
Divinely, and by music's mystic rain,
Blent of soft spells, half sweetness and
        half pain,
Fallen from out the highest heaven of
        song.

And there, to purify all souls of wrong
And latent sin, he calls from far and
        near
Nobles and priests and people. Every
        where
The paths are full, which, sloping
        steeply down
From the green pasture and the wallèd
        town,
Lead oceanward, where, anchored near
        the quay,
That sacred galley heaved along the
        sea —
Her captain no rude mariner, with soul
Tough as the cordage his brown hands
        control,
But the gray Patriarch, lifting eyes of
        prayer,

While o'er the reverent thousands, calm
        in air,
The sacred host shone like an awful
        star.

" Children! " the Patriarch cried, " If
        strong ye are
To trust in heaven — albeit heaven's
        message sent
This day through me, seem strange, and
        strangely blent
With chance-fed issues — swear, what-
        e'er betide,
When once our unmoored bark doth
        fleetly glide
O'er the blue spaces of the midland
        sea —
What flag soe'er first greets our eager
        view,
Our own to veil, and humbly yield there-
        to
The faith and sovereign claims of fair
        Corfu."

They vowed a vow methinks ne'er vowed
        before,
The while their galley, strangely laden,
        bore
Down the south wind, which freshly
        blew from shore.

Past Vido and San Salvador they
        sped,
Past stormy heights and capes whose
        rock-strewn head
Baffled the surges; still no ship they
        met,
Till, sailing far beyond the rush and
        fret
Of shifting sand-locked bars, at last they
        gain
The open and illimitable main.

There in one line two gallant vessels
        rode;
From this the lurid Crescent banner
        glowed,
From that the rampant Lion of St.
        Mark's!

Much, much they wondered when
    athwart them drew,
With glittering decks, the galley from
    Corfu,
Lighted by tapers tall of myriad dyes,
And echoing chants of holy litanies.

Soon unto both the self-same message
    came;
For loud o'er antique hymn and altar
    flame
Thrilled the chief's voice, " Hearken, ye
    rival powers!
Whichever first may touch our armèd
    towers*
Thenceforth shall be the lords of fair
    Corfu!"

Changed was the wind, and landward
    now it blew;
Smiting the waves to foam-flakes wild
    and white.
All sails were braced, the rowers rowed
    with might,
But soon the island men turned pale to
    see
The Turk's prow surging vanward stead-
    ily,
Till five full lengths ahead, careering
    fast,
With flaunting flag and backward-swoop-
    ing mast,
And scores of laboring rowers bent as one
Toward oars which made cool lightnings
    in the sun,
The Paynim craft — unless some mar-
    vellous thing
Should hap to crush her crew or clip her
    wing —
Seemed sure as that black Fate which
    urged her on
Victor to prove, and that proud island
    race
To load with sickening burdens of dis-
    grace!

---

* These " Towers," we must remember, were
built in with the substance of the city walls,
which rose abruptly out of the waters of the
sea.

And now on crowded decks and crowd-
    ed shore
Naught but the freshening sea wind's
    hollow roar
Was heard, with flap of rope and clang
    of sail,
Veering a point to catch the changing
    gale,
Or furious lashes of the buffeting oar!

Just then the tall Venetian strangely
    changed
Her steadfast course, with open port-
    holes ranged
'Gainst the far town. Across the sea-
    waste came,
First, a sharp flash and lurid cloud of
    flame,
Then the dull boom of the on-speeding
    ball,
Followed by sounds which to the isles-
    men seem
Sweet as the wakening from some night-
    mare dream —
The sounds of splintered tower and
    crashing wall!
Then rose a shrill cry to the shivering
    heaven —
" *Thus, thus to us your island realm is*
    given! "
Burst as one voice from out the conquer-
    ing crew:
" *Thus Venice claims the lordship of*
    Corfu! "

TALLULAH FALLS.

ALONE with nature, where her passion-
    ate mood
Deepens and deepens, till from shadowy
    wood,
And sombre shore the blended voices
    sound
Of five infuriate torrents, wanly crowned
With such pale-misted foam as that
    which starts
To whitening lips from frenzied human
    hearts!

Echo repeats the thunderous roll and
　　boom
Of these vexed waters through the foli-
　　aged gloom
So wildly, in their grand reverberant
　　swell
Borne from dim hillside to rock-bounded
　　dell,
That oft the tumult seems
The vast fantastic dissonance of dreams;
A roar of adverse elements, torn and
　　riven
In dark recesses of some billowy hell,
But sending ever through the tremulous
　　air,
Defiance laden with august despair
Up to the calm and pitiful face of
　　heaven!

From ledge to ledge the impetuous cur-
　　rent sweeps
Forever tortured, tameless, unsubdued,
Amid the darkly humid solitude,
Through waste and turbulent deeps
It cleaves a terrible pathway, over-
　　run
Only by doubtful flickerings of the
　　sun,
To meet with swift cross-eddies, whirl-
　　pools set
On verges of some measureless abyss,
　　Above the stir and fret,
　　The lion's hollow roar, or serpent
　　　hiss
Of whose unceasing conflict waged be-
　　low
　The gorges of the giant precipice,
Shines the mild splendor of a heavenly
　　bow.

But blinded to the rainbow's glory
　　shed
Fair as the aureole 'round an angel's
　　head
Still with dark vapors all about it furled
The demon spirit of this watery world,
Through many a maddened curve, and
　　stormy throe,
Speeds to its last tumultuous overflow,

When downward hurled, from 'wilder-
　　ing shock to shock,
Its wild heart breaks upon the outmost
　　rock
That guards the empire of this rule of
　　wrath!
Henceforth, beyond the shattered cata-
　　ract's path,
The tempered spirit of a gentler guide
Enters, methinks the unperturbèd
　　tide;
Its current sparkling in the blest re-
　　lease
From wasting passion, glides through
　　shores of peace, —
O'er brightened spaces and clear con-
　　fluent calms,
Float the hale breathings of near mead-
　　ow balms,
And still by silent cove and silvery
　　reach,
The murmurous wavelets pass;
Lip the green tendrils of the delicate
　　grass,
And tranquil hour by hour,
Uplift a crystal glass,
Wherein each lithe Narcissus-flower,
May mark its slender frame and beau-
　　teous face
Mirrored in softly visionary grace,
And still, by fairy-bight and shelving
　　beach,
The fair waves whisper low as leaves in
　　June
(Small gossips lisping in their woodland
　　bower),
And still, the ever-lessening tide
Lapses, as glides some once imperious
　　life
From haughty summits of demoniac
　　pride,
Hatred and vengeful strife,
Down through time's twilight-valleys
　　purified;
Yearning, alone, to keep
A long-predestined tryst with night and
　　sleep,
Beneath the dew-soft kisses of the
　　moon!

DIVIDED.

As not a bud that burgeons 'mid the
  bowers;
  As not a leaf on any tree that grows,
  But to its neighbor some unlikeness
  shows,
Made clearer still through all the blos-
  soming hours.

Thus hath it chanced that, since the
  world began,
  No soul hath found its fellow; fates
  may blend
  In the close ties of lover, husband,
  friend,
Yet through some subtle difference, man
  from man

Severed, sees not his brother's innermost
  life;
  The lover his sweet mistress knows
  in part,
  And each to other half revealed in
  heart,
Pass deathward, the true husband and
  true wife.

Shall heaven make all things plain?
  Nay, who can tell?
  Only, sick heart! like the sore-
  wounded dove
  Seeking her distant nest, *hold fast to
  love,*
Till death's ·deep curfew tolls its vesper
  bell.

"Gurgle, gurgle, gurgle,
Over ledge and stone."

THE MEADOW BROOK.

Gurgle, gurgle, gurgle,
  Over ledge and stone;
How I'm going, flowing,
  Westward, all alone;
All alone, but happy,
  Happy and hale am I,
Clasped by the emerald meadows,
  Flushed by the golden sky!

No kindred brook is calling,
  To woo these tides in glee;
I hear no neighboring voices
  Of inland rill, or sea;

But the sedges thrill above me,
  And where I blithely pass,
Coy winds, like nymphs in ambush,
  Seem whispering through the grass.

Tinkle, tinkle, tinkle;
  Hark! the tiny swell
Of wavelets softly, silverly
  Toned like a fairy bell,
Whose every note, dropped sweetly
  In mellowed glamour round,
Echo hath caught and harvested
  In airy sheaves of sound!

THE VALLEY OF ANOSTAN.

[In Ælian's "Various History," book iii., chapter xviii., the following legend, or parable, will be found. How vividly it recalls to us the words of the Master: "Unless ye be converted, and *become as little children*, ye cannot enter into the kingdom of heaven!"]

An Orient legend, which hath all the light
And fragrance of the asphodels of heaven,
Smiles on us from old Ælian's mellowed page;
And thus it runs, smooth as the stream of joy
Whereof it tells, yet with some discord blent,
Which, hearkened rightly, makes the music true
To man's mysterious instincts and his fate:

In the strange valley of Anostan dwelt
The far Meropes, through whose murmurous realm
Two mighty rivers — one a stream of joy,
Divine and perfect; one a stream of bale —
Flowed side by side, 'twixt forest shades and flowers
(Bright shades and sombre, poison flowers and pure),
Down to a distant and an unknown sea.

On either bank were fruit-trees and ripe fruit,
Whereof men plucked and ate; but whoso ate
Of the wan fruitage of the stream of bale
Went ever after weeping gall for tears,
Till death should find him; but whoe'er partook
Of the rare fruitage of the stream of joy
Straightway was lapped in such ecstatic peace,
Such fond oblivion of all base desires,

His soul grew fresh, dew-like, and sweet again,
And through his past, his golden yesterdays,
He wandered back and back, till youth, regained,
Shone in the candid radiance of his eyes,
That still waxed larger, holier, crystal-clear,
With resurrection of life's tenderest dawn
Of childlike faith; by which illumed and warmed,
He walks, himself a dream within a dream,
Yearning for infancy. This found at last,
Gently he passes upward unto God,
Not through death's portal, wrapped in storms and wrath,
But the fair archway of the gates of birth!

———◆———

TWO SONGS.

FIRST SONG.

Let me die by the sea!
When his billows are haughty and high,
And the storm-wind's abroad, —
When his dark passion grasps at the sky
With the power of a god, —
When all his fierce forces are free —
Let me die by the sea.

Let me die by the sea!
To his rhythms of tempest and rain.
I would pass from the earth,
Through death that is travail and pain,
Through death that is birth;
'Mid the thunders of waves and of lea,
Let me die by the sea.

Let me die by the sea!
When the great deeps are sundered and stirred,
And the night cometh fast,
Let my spirit mount up like a bird,
On the wings of the blast.

O'er the tumults of wave and of lea,
  O'er their ravage and roar,
    She would soar, she would soar,
    Where peace waits her at last:
Oh! Fate, let me die by the sea.

SECOND SONG.

Ah, no! Ah, no! I would not go
  While earth and heaven are black:—
When all is wildly drear and dark,
  Guard, guard, O God! this vital
    spark!

But I would go when winds are low,
  And distant, dreamy rills
Are heard to lapse with lingering flow,
  Between the twilight hills:
With earth, and wave, and heaven at
    peace,
Then let these outworn pulses cease.

SONNETS.

ON VARIOUS THEMES.

I.

FRESHNESS OF POETIC PERCEPTION.

DAY followed day; years perish; still
    mine eyes
Are opened on the self-same round of
    space;
Yon fadeless forests in their Titan grace,
And the large splendors of those opulent
    skies.
I watch, unwearied, the miraculous dyes
Of dawn or sunset; the soft boughs
    which lace
Round some coy dryad in a lonely place,
Thrilled with low whispering and strange
    sylvan sighs:
Weary? the poet's mind is fresh as dew,
And oft re-filled as fountains of the
    light.
His clear child's soul finds something
    sweet and new
Even in a weed's heart, the carved
    leaves of corn,

The spear-like grass, the silvery rim of
    morn,
A cloud rose-edged, and fleeting stars at
    night!

II.

LAOCOON.

A GNARLED and massive oak log, shape-
    less, old,
Hewed down of late from yonder hill-
    side gray,
Grotesquely curved, across our hearth-
    stone lay;
About it, serpent-wise, the red flames
    rolled
In writhing convolutions; fold on fold
They crept and clung with slow portent-
    ous sway
Of deadly coils; or in malignant play,
Keen tongues outflashed, 'twixt vapor-
    ous gloom and gold.
Lo! as I gazed, from out that flaming
    gyre
There loomed a wild, weird image, all
    astrain
With strangled limbs, hot brow, and
    eyeballs dire,
Big with the anguish of the bursting
    brain:
Laocoon's form, Laocoon's fateful pain.
A frescoed dream on flickering walls of
    fire!

III.

AT LAST.

IN youth, when blood was warm and
    fancy high,
I mocked at death. How many a quaint
    conceit
I wove about his veilèd head and feet.
Vaunting aloud. *Why need we dread
    to die?*
But now, enthralled by deep solemnity.
Death's pale phantasmal shade I darkly
    greet:
Ghostlike it haunts the hearth, it haunts
    the street,
Or drearier makes drear midnight's
    mystery.

Ah, soul-perplexing vision! oft I deem
That antique myth is true which pic-
    tured death
A masked and hideous form all shrank
    to see;
But at the last slow ebb of mortal
    breath,
Death, his mask melting like a night-
    mare dream,
Smiled, — heaven's high-priest of Im-
    mortality!

IV.

A PHANTOM IN THE CLOUDS.

ALL day the blast, with furious ramp
    and roar,
Sweeps the gaunt hill-tops, piles the
    vapors high,
Thro' infinite distance, up the tortured
    sky —
Till to one nurtured on the ocean-
    shore,
It seems — with eyes half-shut to hill
    and moor —
The anguished sea waves' multitudinous
    cry —
It changes! deepening . . Christ! what
    agony
Doth some doomed spirit on these
    wild winds outpour!
At last a lull! stirred by slow wafts of
    air!
When lo! o'er dismal wastes of stormy
    wreck,
Cloud-wrought, an awful form and face
    abhorred!
Thine, thine, Iscariot! smitten by mad
    despair,
With lurid eyeballs strained, and writh-
    ing neck,
Round which is coiled a blood-red
    phantom cord!

V.

JAPONICAS.

BENEATH the sullen slope of shadowy
    skies,
Midmost this flowerless, wind-bewil-
    dered space

(Once a fair garden, now a desert-
    place)
Ah! what voluptuous hues are these
    that rise
In sudden lustre, on my startled eyes ?
They glow like roses on an orient face,
Glimpsed in swift flashes of enchant-
    ing grace,
'Twixt the shy harem's gold-wrought
    tapestries!
Ye bright Japonicas! your glorious
    gleam
Tints with strange light the enamored
    waves of air,
And wafts of such coy fragrance round
    you float
Fancy transcends these boundaries
    blanched and bare,
For beauty lures her in a ravishing
    dream
Of roseate lips, dark locks, and swan-
    white throat!

VI.

THE USURPER.

FOR weeks the languid southern wind
    had blown,
Fraught with Floridian balm; thro'
    winter skies
We seemed to catch the smile of April's
    eyes;
A queenly waif, from her far temperate
    zone
Wayfaring — half bewildered and alone,
Yet, by the delicate fervor of her grace,
And the arch beauty of her changeful
    face,
Making an alien empire all her own.
So day by day that sweet usurper's reign
Gladdened the world. One eve the
    south wind sighed
Her soft soul out; the north wind raved
    instead;
All night he raved; when morning
    dawned again,
Winter, rethroned, looked down with
    scornful pride
Where April, dying, bowed her golden
    head!

VII.
DECEMBER SONNET.

ROUND the December heights the clouds
  are gray —
Gray, and wind-driven toward the
  stormy west,
They fly, like phantoms of malign un-
  rest,
To fade in sombre distances away.
A flickering brightness o'er the wreck
  of day,
Twilight, like some sad maiden, grief-
  oppressed,
Broods wanly on the farthest mountain
  crest;
All nature breathes of darkness and
  decay
Now from low meadow land and drowsy
  stream.
From deep recesses of the silent vale,
Night-wandering vapors rise formless
  and chill,
When, lo! o'er shrouded wood and
  shadowy hill,
I mark the eve's victorious planet
  beam,
Fair as an angel clad in silver mail!

VIII.
A COMPARISON.

I THINK, ofttimes, that lives of men may
  be
Likened to wandering winds that come
  and go,
Not knowing whence they rise, whither
  they blow
O'er the vast globe, voiceful of grief or
  glee.
Some lives are buoyant zephyrs sporting
  free
In tropic sunshine; some long winds
  of woe
That shun the day, wailing with mur-
  murs low,
Through haunted twilights, by the un-
  resting sea;
Others are ruthless, stormful, drunk
  with might,

Born of deep passion or malign desire:
They rave 'mid thunder-peals and clouds
  of fire.
Wild, reckless all, save that some power
  unknown
Guides each blind force till life be
  overblown,
Lost in vague hollows of the fathomless
  night.

IX.
FATE, OR GOD ?

BEYOND the record of all eldest things,
Beyond the rule and regions of past
  time,
From out Antiquity's hoary-headed
  rime,
Looms the dread phantom of a King of
  kings:
Round His vast brows the glittering
  circlet clings
Of a thrice royal crown; behind Him
  climb,
O'er Atlantean limbs and breast sublime
The sombre splendors of mysterious
  wings;
Deep calms of measureless power, in
  awful state,
Gird and uphold Him; a miraculous rod,
To heal or smite, arms His infallible
  hands:
Known in all ages, worshipped in all
  lands,
Doubt names this half-embodied mys-
  tery — Fate,
While Faith, with lowliest reverence,
  whispers — God!

X.
SONNET.

Written on a fly-leaf of "The Rubaiyat"
of Omar Kháyyám, the astronomer-poet
of Persia.

WHO deems the soul to endless death is
  thrall,
That no life breathes beyond that mo-
  ment dire,
When every sense *seems* lost as out-
  blown fire; —

Must walk, clothed round with darkness
    like a pall,
Or on false gods of sensual rapture call;
*Pluck the rich rose-leaves! lift the wine
    cup higher!*
Wed delicate Instinct to malign Desire,
(*Like some Greek girl clasped by a bar-*
    barous Gaul!)
Thus Omar preached, thus practised,
    centuries since;
Wine, beauty, idlesse, orgies crowned
    by lust;
All these he chanted in voluptuous song;
Yet who shall vow, deep Thinker!
    poet Prince!
Thy rhythmic creed the unnatural voice
    of wrong,
If man, dust-born, shall still return to
    dust ?

XI.
EARTH ODORS — AFTER RAIN.

LIFE-YIELDING fragrance of our mother
    earth!
Benignant breath exhaled from summer
    showers! —
All Nature dimples into smiles of flowers,
From unclosed woodland, to trim gar-
    den girth; —
These perfumes softening the harsh
    soul of dearth,
Are older than old Shinar's arrogant tow-
    ers, —
And touched with visions of rain-fresh-
    ened hours,
On Syrian hill-slopes 'ere the patriarch's
    birth!
Nay! the charmed fancy plays a subtler
    part! —
Lo! banished Adam, his large, wonder-
    ing eyes
Fixed on the trouble of the first dark
    cloud!
Lo! tremulous Eve, — a pace behind,
    how bowed, —
Not dreaming, 'midst her painful pants
    of heart,
What balm shall fall from yonder omi-
    nous cloud!

XII.
SONNET.

I LAY in dusky solitude reclined,
The shadow of sleep just hovering
    o'er mine eyes,
When from the cloudland in the west-
    ern skies
Rose the strange breathings of a tremu-
    lous wind.
As sound upborne o'er water, through
    some blind,
Mysterious forest, so this wind did rise,
Laden, methought, with half-articu-
    late sighs,
Wafted like spirit-memories o'er the
    mind.
Then the night deepened; through my
    window-bars
I saw the gray clouds billowing fast and
    free,
Smit by the splendor of the solemn
    stars.
Then the night deepened; wind and
    cloud became
A blended tumult, crossed by spears of
    flame,
While the great pines moaned like a
    moaning sea.

XIII.
POVERTY.

ONCE I beheld thee, a lithe mountain
    maid,
Embrowned by wholesome toils in lusty
    air;
Whose clear blood, nurtured by strong,
    primitive cheer,
Through Amazonian veins, flowed una-
    fraid.
Broad-breasted, pearly-teethed, thy pure
    breath strayed,
Sweet as deep-uddered kine's curled in
    the rare
Bright spaces of thy lofty atmosphere,
O'er some rude cottage in a fir-grown
    glade.
Now, of each brave ideal virtue stripped,
O Poverty! I behold thee as thou art,

A ruthless hag, the image of woeful
dearth
Or brute despair, gnawing its own
starved heart.
Thou ravening wretch! fierce-eyed and
monster-lipped,
Why scourge forevermore God's beaute-
ous earth ?

XIV.
WASTE.

How many a budding plant is born to
fade!
How many a May bloom wilt with quick
decay!
Ofttimes the ruddiest rose holds briefest
sway,
While heart and sense are evermore be-
trayed
Alike in nature's shine and nature's
shade.
Vainly earth-tendered seeds have sought
the day,
And countless threads of rivulets wind
astray,
For one that joins the vast main unem-
bayed.
O prodigal nature, why this spendthrift
waste
Of light, strength, beauty given to earth
or man ?
Thy richest realm may lie in trackless
seas,
Thy tenderest loves, perchance, die un-
embraced ;
While faith and reason watch thy 'wil-
dering plan,
The baffled soul's cloud-compassed Hy-
ades!

XV.
A MORNING AFTER STORM.

ALL night the north wind blew; the
harsh north rain
Lashed like a spiteful whip at roof and
sill.
Now the pale morning lowers, bewil-
dered, chill,

Leaning her cheek against the misted
pane,
Like some worn outcast, sick in heart
and brain.
The wind that raved all night, though
muttering still,
Moans fitfully, with faint, irresolute
will,
Through dreary interludes, its low re-
frain.
In desolate mood I turn to rest once
more,
Closing my senses to this hopeless
morn,
This dismal wind. Still must the
morning gloom,
Still the low sighing pass sleep's muffled
door,
Till her veiled life is filled with dreams
forlorn,
With hollow sounds and bodeful shapes
of doom.

XVI.
DEAD LOVES.

WHENE'ER I think of old loves wan and
dead,
Of passion's wine outpoured in senseless
dust,
Of doomed affection's and long-buried
trust,
Through all my soul an arctic gloom is
shed ;
And ah! I walk the world disquieted.
Thou, my own love! white lily of April!
must
Thy beauty, perfume, radiance, all be
thrust
Earthward, to crumble in a grass-grown
bed ?
Yea, sweet, 'tis even so! How long, how
long
The dust of her who once was tender
Ruth,
Hath mouldered dumbly! And how oft
the clod,
Which binds, like hers, all perished love
and truth,

Strives with pale weeds to veil death's
  hopeless wrong,
Or through chill lips of flowers appeals
  to God!

XVII.
NATURE AT EASE.

I FEEL the kisses of this lingering
  breeze,
Warm, close, and ardҙֺ as the lips of
  love,
I quaff the sunshine streaming from
  above,
Like mellow wine of antique vintages;
Now, serene nature, at luxurious ease,
Her deep toils perfected, and richly
  rife
With subtlest meanings — all her opu-
  lent life
Reveals in tremulous brakes and whis-
  pering seas.
If, then, the reverent soul doth lean
  aright,
Close to those voices of wood, wind, and
  wave,
What wondrous secrets bless the spir-
  itual ear,
Born, as it were, of music winged with
  light,
Sweeter than those strange songs which
  Orpheus gave
To earth and heaven, while both grew
  dumb to hear!

XVIII.
THE CNYDIAN ORACLE.

" What though the Isthmus lacks an
  ocean-gate,
Delve not the soil ! If Jove had willed
  it so,
His watchful power had opened long ago
The channelled pathways of a billowy
  strait."
Thus spake the Cnydian Oracle but too
  late;
For men are blinder than blind winds
  that blow
Round midnight waves, yet idly dream
  they know

Some Hermes' trick to steal the goods of
  fate.
Fools! trench your Isthmus, delving fast
  and deep;
And as ye toil uplift your boastful
  breath
O'er swift inrushings of the turbulent
  sea —
Too swift, by heaven! for, lo! its
  treacherous sweep
O'erwhelms the graded dykes, the oppos-
  ing lea,
While ye that mocked at fate, fate
  whirls to death!

XIX.
THE HYACINTH.

HERE in this wrecked storm-wasted gar-
  den-close
The grave of infinite generations fled
Of flowers that now lay lustreless and
  dead,
As the gray dust of Eden's earliest rose.
What bloom is this, whose classical
  beauty glows
Radiantly chaste, with the mild splen-
  dor shed
Round a Greek virgin's poised and per-
  fect head,
By Phidias wrought 'twixt rapture and
  repose ?
Mark the sweet lines whose matchless
  ovals curl
Above the fragile stem's half shrink-
  ing grace,
And say if this pure hyacinth doth not
  seem
(Touched by enchantments of an an-
  tique dream)
A flower no more, but the low droop-
  ing face
Of some love-laden, fair Athenian girl ?

XX.
THE WOOD FAR INLAND.

I CLOSE mine eyes in this lone inland
  place,
This wood, far inland, thronged with
  sombrous trees —

"Now, serene nature, at luxurious ease,
 . . . all her opulent life
Reveals in tremulous brakes and whispering seas."

Our southland pines — in whose dark
    boughs the breeze
Mourns like a spirit shorn of joy and
    grace;
The same wild genius whose half-
    veilèd face
Dawns on the barren brink of wave-
    washed leas,
Fraught with the ancient mystery of the
    seas,
Whose hoary brow bears many a
    storm-bolt's trace;
I close mine eyes; but lo! a spiritual
    light
Steals round me: I behold through foam
    and mist
A dreary reach of wan, slow-shifting
    sand,
By transient glints of flickering star-
    beams kissed,
And hear upborne athwart the desolate
    strand
Voices of ghostly billows of the night.

XXI.

[Composed just after midnight on the 31st of
December, 1878.]

A MOMENT since his breath dissolved in
    air!
And now divorced from life's last hectic
    glow,
He joins the old ghostly years of long
    ago,
In some cloud-folded realm of vague de-
    spair;
Ah me! the unsceptred years that wan-
    der there!
With cold, wan hands, and faces white
    as snow,
And echoes of dead voices quavering low
The phantom-burden of long-perished
    care!
Perchance all unsubstantialized and
    gray,
Time's earliest year now greets his last,
    deceased;
Or he that dumbly gazed on Adam's
    fall,
Palely emerging from the shadowy east,

With flickering semblance of cold crown
    and pall,
Clothes the dim ghost of him just passed
    away!

XXII.

MAGNOLIA GARDENS.

YES, found at last, — the earthly para-
    dise!
Here by slow currents of the silvery
    stream
It smiles, a shining wonder, a fair dream,
A matchless miracle to mortal eyes:
What whorls of dazzling color flash and
    rise
From rich azalean flowers, whose pet-
    als teem
With such harmonious tints as bright-
    ly gleam
In sunset rainbows arched o'er perfect
    skies!
But see! beyond those blended blooms
    of fire,
Vast tier on tier the lordly foliage tower
Which crowns the centuried oaks' broad
    crested calm:
Thus on bold beauty falls the shade of
    power;
Yet beauty still unquelled, fulfils desire,
Unfolds her blossoms, and outbreathes
    her balm!

XXIII.

ENGLAND.

CLOUD-GIRDED land, brave land beyond
    the sea!
Land of my father's love! how oft I
    yearn
Toward thy famed ancestral shores to
    turn,
Roaming thy glorious realm in liberty;
All English growths would sacred seem
    to me,
From opulent oak to flickering wayside
    fern;
Much from her delicate daisies could I
    learn,
And all her home-bred flowers by lake
    or lea.

But most I dream of Shropshire's mead-
　　ow grass,
Its grazing herds, and sweet hay-scented
　　air;
An ancient hall near a slow rivulet's
　　mouth;
A church vine-clad; a graveyard gloom-
　　ing south;
These are the scenes through which I
　　fain would pass;
There lived my sires, whose sacred dust
　　is there.

XXIV.
DISAPPOINTMENT.

AH! phantom pale, why hast thou come
　　with pace
Thus slow, and such sad deprecating
　　eyes?
What! dost thou dream *thy* presence
　　could surprise
One the born vassal of thy realm and
　　race?
I looked in boyhood on thy clouded face;
In youth dissevered from all cordial
　　ties,
Heard the deep echoes of thy murmured
　　sighs
In many a shadowy, grief-enshrouded
　　place;
Therefore, O sombre Genius, be not
　　coy!
When have we dwelt so alien and apart
I could not faintly feel thy muffled
　　heart?
Till even should hope's fruition softly
　　shine,
I well might deem beneath the mask
　　of joy
Lurked that sad brow, those twilight
　　eyes of thine!

XXV.
THE LAST OF THE ROSES.

A ROYAL rose! A rose how darkly red!
A proud, voluptuous, full blown flower,
　　that sways
Her sceptre o'er the wind-swept gar-
　　den-ways,

With mantling cheek and bold, imperious
　　head!
Alone she lifts above yon desolate bed
A beauty past all terms of raptured
　　praise,
The statelier that she rules in autumn
　　days,
When every rival flower is dimmed or
　　dead!
A haughty Cleopatra! there she smiles,
Unwitting that her sovereign love is
　　lost —
Her Antony! a gorgeous sunflower
　　bloom!
Ah! vain henceforth her beauty and
　　sweet wiles!
Queen! art thou blind? Thy lord hath
　　met his doom;
His Actium came with winter's van-
　　guard — Frost!

XXVI.
THE AXE AND PINE.

ALL day, on bole and limb the axes ring,
And every stroke upon my startled
　　brain
Falls with the power of sympathetic
　　pain;
I shrink to view each glorious forest-
　　king
Descend to earth, a wan, discrownèd
　　thing.
Ah, Heaven! beside these foliaged giants
　　slain,
How small the human dwarfs, whose
　　lust for gain
Hath edged their brutal steel to smite and
　　sting!
Hark! to those long-drawn murmurings,
　　strange and drear!
The wail of Dryads in their last distress;
O'er ruined haunts and ravished loveli-
　　ness
Still tower those brawny arms; tones
　　coarsely loud
Rise still beyond the greenery's waning
　　cloud,
While falls the insatiate steel, sharp,
　　cold and sheer!

XXVII.
BETROTHAL NIGHT.

THROUGH golden languors of low glim-
    mering light,
Deep eyes, o'erbrimmed with passion's
    sacred wine,
Heart-perfumed tears—yearning towards
    me, shine
Like stars made lovelier by faint mists
    at night;
Her cheeks, sweet lilies change to roses
    bright,
Blown in love's realm, fed by his breath
    divine;
And even those virginal tremors seem
    the sign
Of perfect joy through love's unchal-
    lenged right:
O happy breast, that heavest soft and
    fair
Through silvery clouds of luminous silk
    and lace!
O, gracious hands, O flower-enwoven
    head,
O'er which hope's charm its delicate
    warmth has shed!
While smiles and blushes wreathe her
    dimpling face,
Set in the splendor of dark Orient hair!

XXVIII.
"THE OLD MAN OF THE SEA."

GRIEVOUS, in sooth, was luckless Sind-
    bad's plight,
Saddled with that foul monster of the
    sea;
But who of some soul-harrowing weight
    is free?
And though we veil our woe from public
    sight,
Full many a weary day and dismal
    night,
It chafes our spirits sorely! Yet, for
    thee,
Whate'er, O friend, thy special grief
    may be,
Range thou against it all thy manhood's
    might.

Thus, though thou may'st not smite on
    brow or breast
That irksome incubus, be sure some
    day
The load that blights shall droop and fall
    away,
And thou, because of torture borne so
    well,
Shall pass from out thy long, malign
    unrest
And walk thy future paths invincible!

XXIX.
TWO PICTURES.

SHE stood beneath the vine-leaves flushed
    and fair;
The dimpling smiles around her tender
    mouth,
Seemed born of mellow sunshine of
    the South;
A light breeze trembled in her unbound
    hair;
No young Greek goddess, in the violet
    air
Of vales immortal, shone with purer
    grace;
A delicate glory touched her form and
    face,
Whence the sweet soul looked on us,
    nobly bare, —
As Heaven itself, unclouded: — thus she
    stood,
But when I saw her next (O God! the
    woe!)
Love, mirth, and life had fled forever
    more;
Prostrate she lay, about her a dark wood,
And many a helpless mourner, wailing
    low;
The cruel waves which drowned her
    lapped the shore.

XXX.
THE MIGHT HAVE BEEN.

ONCE in the twilight hour there stole on
    me
A strange, sweet spirit! In her tender
    eyes

Shone a far beauty, like the morning
  skies,
And tranquil was she as a summer sea;
An air of large, divine benignity
Breathed, like a living garb of spiritual
  dyes
About her — with the gentle fall and
  rise
Of her heart pulses tuned to mystery —
But, as I gazed, a sadness deep as death
Crept o'er the beauty of her brow serene
And a faint tremor stirred her shadowy
  lips;
"Thou know'st me not, "she sighed,
  with mournful breath;
"How can'st thou know me? Lo,
  through Fate's eclipse,
Thou seest, too late, too late, thy MIGHT
  HAVE BEEN!"

XXXI.
NIGHT-WINDS IN WINTER.

WINDS! *are* they winds? — or myriad
  ghosts, that shriek?
Ghosts of poor mariners, drowned in
  Northern seas,
Beside the surf-tormented Hebrides,
Whose voices now of tide-born terror
  speak
In tones to blanch the boldest listener's
  cheek?
Hark! how they thunder down the far-off
  leas,
Sweep the scourged hills, and smite the
  woodland trees,
To die where towers yon glittering moun-
  tain-peak!
A moment's stillness! Then with lus-
  tier might
Of wing and voice, these marvellous
  wraiths of air
Fill with dread sound the ominous
  heights of night.
Athwart their stormful breath the star-
  throngs fade:
How dimmed is Cassiopæia's radiant
  chair,
While Perseus droops, touched by trans-
  figuring shade!

XXXII.
TO THE QUERULOUS POETS.

THROW by the trappings of your tinsel
  rhyme!
Hush the crude voice, whose never-
  ending wail
Blights the sweet song of thrush, or
  nightingale, —
Set to the treble of our querulous time;
Is earth grown dim? Hath heaven
  her grace sublime,
Her pomp of clouds, and winds, and
  sunset showers
Merged in the twilight of funereal hours,
And Time's death-signal struck its iron
  chime?
O! false, frail dreamer! not one tiniest
  note
From yonder green-girt copse, but whis-
  pers "shame!" —
Love, beauty, rapture, swell the war-
  bler's throat, —
The self-same joy, the passion blithe
  and young,
Thrilled by the force of whose immacu-
  late flame,
The first glad stars, the stars of morn-
  ing, sung!

XXXIII.
IN THE PORCH.

IN this old porch, fast mouldering to de-
  cay,
But wreathed in vines and girt by shad-
  owy trees,
All day I hear the dreamful hum of
  bees,
Soft-rustling foliage, and the fragrant
  sway
Of breezes borne from some far ocean
  bay;
And oft with half-closed eyelids,
  stretched at ease —
The pines above me voiced like distant
  seas —
I seem to mark a coy young Dryad stray
Out from the tangled greenery over-
  head,

"Winds! *are* they winds? — or myriad ghosts, that shriek? . . .
Hark! how they thunder down the far-off leas."

Her brow leaf-crowned, her eyes of twi-
light fire
Deep with Arcadian mysteries softly
shed;
And near her, wafted from the ambro-
sial South,
A white-limbed Nereid, round whose
balmy mouth
Breathe the wave's freshness and the
wind's desire.

XXXIV.

THE PHANTOM—SONG.

IN museful hours, when thoughts of
grace divine
Roll wave-like up the stormless strand
of dreams;—
When that which *is* grows vague as that
which *seems*,—
I mark, far-off, a radiant shade incline
From heaven to earth,—whose face of
marvellous shine,
(Half veiled in mystic beauty), softly
beams
With delicate lustres, and elusive
gleams,
Caught from some viewless Eden—hy-
aline:—
Ethereal, as the wavering hues that start
From chorded rainbows;—lingering
scarce so long
As the last sun-ray flashed in twilight's
eye,
I hail this phantom of a perfect song;—
And I, some day, shall pass the phantom
by,—
To feel the embodied music next my
heart!

XXXV.

SMALL GRIEFS AND GREAT.

How oft by trivial griefs our spirits
tossed
Drift vague and restless round this
changeful world!
Yet when great sorrows on our lives are
hurled,
And fate on us has wreaked his utter-
most,

O'er wounded breasts our steadfast arms
are crossed;
We front the blast, silent, with un-
bowed head
And stoic mien; for fear with hope is
dead;
And calm the voice which whispers:
"All is lost!"
Thence to the end, our being, stripped
and bare
Of love, and peace, and gracious joys of
of earth,
Like some storm-shattered tree, its with-
ered might
May lift defiant, dauntless in its dearth,
Seeming Death's bolt, that final stroke,
to dare,
A dreary watcher on a blasted height!

XXXVI.

THE SHALLOW HEART!

"PITY her," say'st thou, "pity her!"
nay, not I!
Her heart is shallow as yon garrulous
rill
That froths o'er pebbles: grief, *true*
grief is still,
Deathfully solemn as eternity
Thro' whose dread realm its silent fan-
cies fly
Seeking the lost and loved; sorrows that
kill
Life's hope, are like those poisons which
distil
Their noiseless dews beneath the mid-
night sky:—
Their venom works in secret! gnaws the
heart,
And withers the worn spirit, albeit no
sign
Shows the sad inward havoc, till some
day,
(Pledging our calm friend o'er the pur-
pling wine),
Sudden, he falls amongst us, and we
start
At a low whisper, "He has passed
away!"

XXXVII.

THE STORMY NIGHT.

[Written on a stormy Christmas night (1873).]

How roars this wintry tempest, fierce
and loud,
Borne from far passes of the ice-locked
hills!
How raves this desolate rain, whose tu-
mult fills
The whole dark heaven up-piled with
cloud on cloud;
While yonder quivering pine-trees,
drenched and bowed,
Blend their strange moaning with the
noise of rills,
And one swift stream, whose angry
clarion shrills,
Piercing the mists which o'er it cling and
crowd!
Roar, mighty wind! rave on, thou mer-
ciless rain!
Uproot, and madly ravage — whilst ye
may;
Your furious voices smite mine ears in
vain,
For, housed and warmed by this bright
fireside cheer, —
Safe as on some calm springtide's calm-
est day,
I mock your ire, nor heed your wild de-
spair.

PERSONAL SONNETS.

I.

TO HENRY W. LONGFELLOW.

I THINK earth's noblest, most pathetic
sight
Is some old poet, round whose laurel-
crown
The long gray locks are streaming softly
down; —
Whose evening, touched by prescient
shades of night,
Grows tranquillized, in calm, ethereal
light: —

Such, such art *thou*, O master! worthier
grown
In the fair sunset of thy full renown, —
Poising, perchance, thy spiritual wings
for flight!
Ah, heaven! why shouldst thou from thy
place depart ?
God's court is thronged with minstrels,
rich with song;
Even now, a new note swells the immac-
ulate choir, —
But thou, whose strains have filled our
lives so long,
Still from the altar of thy reverent
heart
Let golden dreams ascend, and thoughts
of fire!

II.

TO GEORGE H. BOKER.

Addressed to George H. Boker, of Philadel-
phia — after the perusal of Sonnets contained
in his " Plays and Poems."

IT hath been thine to prove what use
and power,
What sweetness, and what glorious
strength belong
To the brief compass of that slandered
song
We term the Sonnet. Thine hath been
the dower
Whereby its richly fruitful, fairy shower
Of poesy hath flooded o'er our hearts;
And thine the dominant magic which
imparts
Life to its thrilling music. Hour by
hour,
My soul from this small fountain, in
whose deep
The sunshine of thy passionate genius
plays,
Doth drink delight, till fancy melts in
sleep,
Charmed by the witchery of thy perfect
lays, —
Not dreamless, but flushed through with
joys that keep
Some fervent gleam of youth's volup-
tuous days.

III.

TO ALGERNON CHARLES SWINBURNE.

NOT since proud Marlowe poured his
  potent song
Through fadeless meadows to a marvel-
  lous main,
Has England hearkened to so sweet a
  strain —
So sweet as thine, and ah! so subtly
  strong!
Whether sad love it mourns, or wreaks
  on wrong
The rhythmic rage of measureless dis-
  dain,
Dallies with joy, or swells in fiery pain,
What ravished souls the entrancing
  notes prolong!
At thy charmed breath pale histories
  blush once more:
See! Rosamond's smile! drink love from
  Mary's eyes;
Quail at the foul Medici's midnight
  frown.
Or hark to black Bartholomew's an-
  guished cries!
Blent with far horns of Calydon widely
  blown
O'er the grim death-growl of the ensan-
  guined boar!

But crowned by hope, winged with
  august desire,
Thy muse soars loftiest, when her breath
  is drawn
In stainless liberty's ethereal dawn,
And "songs of sunrise" her warm lips
  suspire:
High in auroral radiance, high and
  higher,
She buoys thee up, till, earth's gross
  vapors gone,
Thy proud, flame-girdled spirit gazes on
The unveiled fount of freedom's crystal
  fire.
When thou hast drained deep draughts
  divinely nurst
'Mid lucid lustres, and hale haunts of
  morn,

On lightning thoughts thy choral thun-
  ders burst
Of rapturous song! Apollo's self, new-
  born,
Might thus have sung from his Olympian
  sphere;
All hearts are thrilled; all nations
  hushed to hear!

IV.

TO EDGAR FAWCETT.

ART thou some reckless poet, fiercely
  free,
Singing vague songs an errant brain
  inspires ?
Mad with the ravening force of inward
  fires,
Whose floods o'erwhelm him like a
  masterless sea ?
No! art and nature wisely blend in
  thee!
Thy soul has learned from lays of loftiest
  lyres
What laws should bind weird fancy's
  wild desires,
Rounded to rhythmic immortality!
Thus golden thoughts in golden har-
  monies meet:
Thy fairy conceptions reel not with false
  glow,
Through frenzied realms by metrical
  motley swayed;
But passion-curbed, with voices strong
  and sweet,
Born of regret or rapture, love or woe,
Pass from rich sunshine to dew-haunted
  shade!

V.

CARLYLE.

O GRANITE nature; like a mountain
  height
Which pierces heaven! yet with found-
  ations deep,
Rooted where earth's majestic forces
  sleep,
In quiet breathing on the breast of
  night : —

Proud thoughts were his that scaled the
　　infinite
Of loftiest grasp, and calm Elysian
　　sweep;
Fierce thoughts were his that burnt the
　　donjon keep
Of ancient wrong, to flood its crypts
　　with light:
Yet o'er his genius, firm as Ailsa's
　　rock,
Large, Atlantean, with grim grandeur
　　dowered, —
Love bloomed, and buds of tender
　　beauty flowered: —
Yet down his rugged massiveness of
　　will
Unscarred by alien passion's fiery shock,
Mercy flowed melting like an Alpine
　　rill!

VI.

TO JEAN INGELOW.

BRAVE lyrist! like the sky-lark, heaven-
　　possessed,
Thy glance is sunward; and thy soul
　　grown wise,
Fronts the full splendor of Apollo's
　　eyes,
While following still thy muse's high
　　behest:
Strength, sweetness, subtlety, are all
　　expressed
In thy clear lays, — whether they dare
　　the skies,
O'ertopping radiant dawns, or rill-like
　　rise,
To thread with rhythmic pulse earth's
　　pastoral breast!
Proud inspiration, hand in hand with
　　act

Hath made thy winged feet beautiful
　　along
The haloed heights of thine eternal song:
So near our human love, though born
　　afar,
Its mellow concord on the listener's
　　heart
Melts with the softness of a falling star!

VII.

TO M. I. P.

YOUR gracious words steal o'er like the
　　breeze
That blows from far-off southland isles
　　benign, —
All steeped in perfume, sweet as fairy
　　wine,
Yet touched with salt keen breathings
　　of the seas!
What smiling thoughts of tender min-
　　istries
Passionless service, and strong faith
　　divine,
Rest with this pictured sister's face of
　　thine,
And sister's love: — (blent fire and
　　balms of ease!)
O love! a two-faced shield of light thou
　　art,
Whose golden-sided glamour long hath
　　shone,
In wedded bliss and affluence on my
　　life;
A sister's love — the fair shield's silvery
　　zone,
Turns on me now! — thy deathless
　　fervor, wife,
Blends with the sweetness of this new
　　found heart!

MACDONALD'S RAID. — A.D. 1780.

[The hero of the following ballad, though a Scotchman by birth, was a determined, enthusiastic Whig. Marion's men, among whom he served during the whole of the war for Independence, regarded him with an admiration bordering sometimes upon awe. His gigantic size and strength, and a species of "Berserker rage" which came over him in battle, were the means by which he performed many a feat of " derring-do," characteristic rather of the Middle Ages than the times of practical "Farmer George." Of all his desperate escapades, the raid through Georgetown, South Carolina, with a force of only four troopers (Georgetown being a fortified post, defended by a garrison of three hundred English regulars), proved, naturally enough, the most notorious. Authorities differ as to the origin and details of this remarkable affair. Some inform us that Sergeant Macdonald had been commanded by Marion to take a small party of his men and merely reconnoitre the enemy's lines, and that he chose to exceed his orders ; while others affirm that Macdonald himself, acting independently, as he often did, proposed the mad scheme of " bearding the British lion in his den," as a charming relief to the *ennui* of camp life. The latter authorities have furnished the groundwork of our ballad. "Nothing," observes Horry, in his Life of General Marion, " ever so mortified the British as did this mad frolic. ' That half a dozen d——d young rebels,' they exclaimed, ' should thus dash in among us, in open daylight, and fall to cutting and slashing the *king's troops* at this rate ! And after all, to gallop away without the least harm in hair and hide ! 'Tis high time to turn our bayonets into pitchforks, and go to foddering the cows.' "]

I REMEMBER it well; 'twas a morn dull and gray,
And the legion lay idle and listless that day,
A thin drizzle of rain piercing chill to the soul,
And with not a spare bumper to brighten the bowl,
When Macdonald arose, and unsheathing his blade,
Cried, " Who'll back me, brave comrades ?   I'm hot for a raid.
Let the carbines be loaded, the war harness ring,
Then swift death to the Redcoats, and down with the King!"

We leaped up at his summons, all eager and bright,
To our finger-tips thrilling to join him in fight;
Yet he chose from our numbers *four* men and no more.
" Stalwart brothers," quoth he, " you'll be strong as fourscore,
If you follow me fast wheresoever I lead,
With keen sword and true pistol, stanch heart and bold steed.
Let the weapons be loaded, the bridle-bits ring,
Then swift death to the Redcoats, and down with the King!"

In a trice we were mounted; Macdonald's tall form
Seated firm in the saddle, his face like a storm
When the clouds on Ben Lomond hang heavy and stark,
And the red veins of lightning pulse hot through the dark;
His left hand on his sword-belt, his right lifted free,
With a prick from the spurred heel, a touch from the knee,
His lithe Arab * was off like an eagle on wing —
Ha! death, death to the Redcoats, and down with the King!

* Macdonald owned a magnificent horse, named Selim, of pure Arabian blood, which he obtained possession of through a cunning trick played at the expense of a certain wealthy Carolina Tory.

'Twas three leagues to the town, where, in insolent pride,
Of their disciplined numbers, their works strong and wide,
The big Britons, oblivious of warfare and arms,
A soft *dolce* were wrapped in, not dreaming of harms,
When fierce yells, as if borne on some fiend-ridden rout,
With strange cheer after cheer, are heard echoing without,
Over which, like the blast of ten trumpeters, ring,
" Death, death to the Redcoats, and down with the King!"

Such a tumult we raised with steel, hoof-stroke, and shout,
That the foemen made straight for their inmost redoubt,
And therein, with pale lips and cowed spirits, quoth they,
" Lord, the whole rebel army assaults us to-day.
Are the works, think you, strong ?   God of heaven, what a din!
'Tis the front wall besieged — have the rebels rushed in ?
It must be; for, hark! hark to that jubilant ring
Of ' death to the Redcoats, and down with the King!' "

Meanwhile, through the town like a whirlwind we sped,
And ere long be assured that our broadswords were red;
And the ground here and there by an ominous stain
Showed how the stark soldier beside it was slain:
A fat sergeant-major, who yawed like a goose,
With his waddling bow-legs, and his trappings all loose,
By one back-handed blow the Macdonald cuts down,
To the shoulder-blade cleaving him sheer through the crown,
And the last words that greet his dim consciousness ring
With " Death, death to the Redcoats, and down with the King!"

Having cleared all the streets, not an enemy left
Whose heart was unpierced, or whose headpiece uncleft,
What should we do next, but — as careless and calm
As if we were scenting a summer morn's balm
'Mid a land of pure peace — just serenely drop down
On the few constant friends who still stopped in the town.
What a welcome they gave us!   One dear little thing,
As I kissed her sweet lips, did I dream of the King ? —

Of the King or his minions ?   No; war and its scars
Seemed as distant just then as the fierce front of Mars
From a love-girdled earth; but, alack! on our bliss,
On the close clasp of arms and kiss showering on kiss,
Broke the rude bruit of battle, the rush thick and fast
Of the Britons made 'ware of our rash *ruse* at last;
So we haste to our coursers, yet flying, we fling
The old watch-words abroad, " Down with Redcoats and King!"

As we scampered pell-mell o'er the hard-beaten track
We had traversed that morn, we glanced momently back,
And beheld their long earth-works all compassed in flame:
With a vile plunge and hiss the huge musket-balls came,
And the soil was ploughed up, and the space 'twixt the trees
Seemed to hum with the war-song of Brobdingnag bees;
Yet above them, beyond them, victoriously ring
The shouts, "Death to the Redcoats, and down with the King!

Ah! *that* was a feat, lads, to boast of! What men
Like you weaklings to-day had durst cope with *us* then?
Though I say it who should not, I am ready to vow
I'd o'ermatch a half score of your fops even now —

"I remember it well; 'twas a morn cold and gray, . . .
A thin drizzle of rain piercing chill to the soul."

The poor puny prigs, mincing up, mincing down,
Through the whole wasted day the thronged streets of the town:
Why, their dainty white necks 'twere but pastime to wring —
Ay! *my* muscles are firm still; *I* fought 'gainst the King!

Dare you doubt it? well, give me the weightiest of all
The sheathed sabres that hang there, uplooped on the wall;
Hurl the scabbard aside; yield the blade to my clasp;
Do you see, with one hand how I poise it and grasp
The rough iron-bound hilt? With this long hissing sweep
I have smitten full many a foeman with sleep —
That forlorn, final sleep! God! what memories cling
To those gallant old times when we fought 'gainst the King.

THE BATTLE OF KING'S MOUNTAIN.

Supposed to have been narrated by an aged volunteer, who had taken part in the fight, to certain of his friends and neighbors, upon the fiftieth anniversary of the conflict, viz. Oct. 7. 1830.

[Written for the Centennial Celebration of the battle on Oct. 7, 1880.]

OFTTIMES an old man's yesterdays o'er his frail vision pass,
Dim as the twilight tints that touch a dusk-enshrouded glass;
But, ah! youth's time and manhood's prime but grow more brave, more bright,
As still the lengthening shadows steal toward the rayless night.

So deem it not a marvel, friends, if, gathering fair and fast,
I now behold the gallant forms that graced our glorious past,
And down the winds of memory hear those battle bugles blow,
Of strifeful breath, or wails of death, just fifty years ago.

Yes, fifty years this self-same morn, and yet to me it seems
As if time's interval were spanned by a vague bridge of dreams,
Whose cloud-like arches form and fade, then form and fade again,
Until a beardless youth once more, 'mid stern, thick-bearded men,

I ride on Rhoderic's bounding back, all thrilled at heart to feel
My trusty "smooth-bore's" deadly round, and touch of stainless steel —
And quivering with heroic rage — that rush of patriot ire
Which makes our lives from head to heel, one seething flood of fire.

There are some wrongs so blackly base, the tiger strain that runs,
And sometimes maddens thro' the veins, of Adam's fallen sons,
Must mount and mount to furious height, which only blood can quell,
Who smite with hellish hate must look for hate as hot from hell!

And hide it as we may with words, its awful need confessed,
War is a death's-head thinly veiled, even warfare at its best;
But *we* — heaven help us! — strove with those by lust and greed accurst,
And learned what untold horrors wait on warfare at its worst.

You well may deem my soul in youth dwelt not on thoughts like these;
Timed to strong Rhoderic's tramp my pulse grew tuneful as the breeze,
The hale October breeze, whose voice, borne from far ocean's marge,
Pealed with the trumpet's resonance, which sounds "To horse, and charge!"

A mist from recent rains was spread about the glimmering hills;
Far off, far off, we heard the lapse of streams and swollen rills,
While mingling with them, or beyond, from depths of changeful sky,
Rose savage, sullen, dissonant, the eagle's famished cry.

We marched in four firm columns, nine hundred men and more,
Men of the mountain fortresses, men of the sea-girt shore;

Rough as their centuried oaks were these, those fierce as ocean's shocks,
When mad September breaks her heart across the Hatteras rocks.

We marched in four firm columns, till now the evening light
Glinted through rifting cloud and fog athwart the embattled height,
Whereon, deep-lined, in dense array of scarlet, buff or dun,
The haughtiest British "regulars" outflashed the doubtful sun.

Horsemen and footmen centred there, unflinching rank on rank,
And the base Tories circled near, to guard each threatened flank;
But, pale, determined, sternly calm, our men, dismounting, stood,
And at their leader's cautious sign, crouched in the sheltering wood.

What scenes come back of ruin and wrack, before those ranks abhorred!
The cottage floor all fouled with gore, the axe, the brand, the cord;
A hundred craven deeds revived, of insult, injury, shame—
Deeds earth nor wave nor fire could hide, and crimes without a name.

Such thoughts but hardened soul and hand. Ha! "dour as death" were we,
Waiting to catch the voice which set our unleashed passion free.
At last it came deep, ominous, when all the mountain ways
Burst from awed silence into sound, and every bush ablaze,

Sent forth long jets of wavering blue, wherefrom, with fatal dart,
The red-hot Deckhard bullets flew, each hungering for a heart;
And swift as if our fingers held strange magic at their tips,
Our guns, reloaded, spake again from their death-dealing lips,

Again, again, and yet again, till in a moment's hush,
We heard the order, "Bay'nets charge!" when, with o'ermastering rush,
Their "regulars" against us stormed, so strong, so swift of pace,
They hurled us backward bodily for full three furlongs' space.

But, bless you, lads, we scattered, dodged, and when the charge was o'er,
Felt fiercer, pluckier, madder far, than e'er we had felt before;
From guardian tree to tree we crept, while upward, with proud tramp,
The British lines had slowly wheeled to gain their 'leaguered camp.

Too late; for ere they topped the height, Hambright and Williams strode
With all their armèd foresters, across the foeman's road,
What time from right to left there rang the Indian war-whoop wild,
Where Sevier's tall Waturga boys through the dim dells defiled.

"Now, by God's grace," cried Cleaveland (my noble colonel he),
Resting (to pick a Tory off) quite coolly on his knee—
"Now, by God's grace, we have them! the snare is subtly set;
The game is bagged; we hold them safe as pheasants in a net."

And thus it proved; for galled and pressed more closely hour by hour,
Their army shrank and withered fast, like a storm-smitten flower;
Blank-eyed, wan-browed, their bravest lay along the ensanguined land,
While of the living, few had 'scaped the bite of ball or brand.

Yet sturdier knave than Ferguson ne'er ruled a desperate fray:
By heaven! you should have seen him ride, rally, and rave that day,
His fleet horse scoured the stormy ground from rock-bound wall to wall,
And o'er the rout shrilled wildly out his silvery signal call.

"That man must die before they fly, or yield to us the field."
Thus spake I to three comrades true beneath our oak-tree shield;
And when in furious haste again the scarlet soldiers came
Beside our fastness like a fiend, hurtling through dust and flame,

Their sharp demurrers on the wind our steadfast rifles hurled,
And one bold life was stricken then from out the living world.
But, almost sped, he reared his head, grasping his silver call,
And one long blast, the faintest, last, wailed round the mountain wall.

Ah, then the white flags fluttered high; then shrieks and curses poured
From the hot throats of Tory hounds beneath the avenger's sword —
Those lawless brutes who long had lost all claims of Christian men,
Whereof by sunset we had hanged the worst and vilest ten.

We slept upon the field that night, 'midmost our captured store,
That seemed in gloating eyes to spread and heighten more and more.
Truly the viands ravished us; our clamorous stomachs turned
Eager toward the provender for which they sorely yearned.

Apicius! what a feast was there blended of strong and sweet,
Cured venison hams, Falstaffian pies, and fat pigs' pickled feet:
While here and there, with cunning leer, and sly Silenus wink,
A stoutish demijohn peered out, and seemed to gurgle, "Drink!"

Be sure we revelled merrily, till eyes and faces shone;
Our lowliest felt more lifted up than any king on throne;
Our singers trolled; our jesters' tongues were neither stiff nor dumb;
And, by Lord Bacchus! how we quaffed that old Jamaica rum!

Perchance (oh, still, through good and ill, his honest name I bless!) —
Perchance my brother marked in me some symptoms of excess;
For gently on my head he laid his stalwart hand and true,
And gently led me forth below the eternal tent of blue;

He led me to a dewy nook, a soft, sweet, tranquil place,
And there I saw, upturned and pale, how many a pulseless face!

"That man must die before they fly, or yield to us the field."

Our comrades dead — they scarce seemed fled, despite their ghastly scars,
But wrapped in deep, pure folds of sleep beneath the undying stars.

My blood was calmed; all being grew exalted as the night,
Whence solemn thoughts sailed weirdly down, like heavenly swans of white,
With herald strains ineffable, whose billowy organ-roll —
Thrilled to the loftiest mountain peaks and summits of my soul.

Then voices rose (or seemed to rise) close to the raptured ear,
Yet fraught with music marvellous of some transcendent sphere,
While fancy whispered: These are tones of heroes, saved and shriven,
Who long have swept the harps of God by stormless seas in heaven!

Heroes who fought for right and law, but, purged from selfish dross,
Above whose conquering banners waved a shadowy Christian cross:
Whose mightiest deed no ruthless greed had smirched with sad mistrust,
And whose majestic honors scorn all taint of earthly dust.

Doubt, doubt who may! but, as I live, on the calm mountain height
Those voices soared, and sank, and soared up to the mystic night.
A dream! perhaps; but, ah! such dreams in ardent years of youth
Transcend, as heaven transcends the earth, your sordid daylight truth.

The voices soared, and sank, and soared, till, past the cloud-built bars,
They fainted on the utmost strand and silvery surge of stars.
Then *something* spoke: Your friends who strove the battle tide to stem,
Who died in striving, have passed up beyond the stars with them.

. . . . .

What, lads! you think the old man crazed to talk in this high strain,
Or deem the punch of years gone by still buzzes in his brain?
Down with such carnal fantasy! nor let your folly send
Its blunted shafts to smite the truth you may not comprehend.

Would ye be worthy of your sires who on King's Mountain side
Welcomed dark death for freedom's sake as bridegrooms clasp a bride?
Then must your faith be winged above the world, the worm, the clod,
To own the veiled infinitudes and plumbless depths of God!

The roughest rider of my day shrank from the atheist's sneer,
As if Iscariot's self were crouched and whispering at his ear;
The stormiest souls that ever led our mountain forays wild
Would ofttimes show the simple trust, the credence, of a child.

True faith goes hand in hand with power — faith in a holier charm
Than fires the subtlest mortal brain, the mightiest mortal arm;
And though 'tis right in stress of fight " to keep one's powder dry,"
What strength to feel, beyond our steel, burns the great Captain's eye!

THE HANGING OF BLACK CUDJO.

(1780.)

A DIALECT BALLAD.

The incidents of this Ballad are literally true. Our readers will find them circumstantially recorded in Horry's "Life of Marion." Captain Snipes (Phoebus! *what* a name) was a notable patriot during the Revolutionary war, but is likely to be known to the future, rather as the master of Cudjo, than as an active member of a Partisan Band.

He resided in the low country of South Carolina; and Cudjo's quaint *patois* is an *exact* representation of the broken English spoken by the slaves of that section in the *ante bellum* times:

" WELL, Maussa! if you wants to heer, I'll tell you 'bout um 'true.
   Doh de berry taut ob dat bad time is fit to tun me blue;
   A sort ob brimstone blue on black, wid jist a stare o' wite,
   As when dem cussed Tory come fur wuck deir hate dat nite!

" Mass Tom and me was born, I tink, 'bout de same year and day,
   And we was boys togedder, Boss! in ebbery sport and play —
   Ole missis gib me to Mass Tom wid her las' failin bret:
   Aud so I boun' — in conscience boun', fur stick to him till det.

" At las' ole Maussa, *he* teck sick wid chill and feber high,
   And de good Dokter shake 'e head, and say he sur fur die,
   And so true 'nuff de sickness bun' and freeze out all he life,
   And soon ole Maussa sleep in peace long side e' fateful wife.

" Den ebbery ting de lan' could show, de crap, de hoss, de cows.
   Wid all dem nigger in de fiel', and all dem in de house,
   Dey b'long to my Mass Tom fur true, and so dat berry year,
   He pick *me* out from all de folks to meck me Obersheer!

" I done my bes', but niggers, sir — dey seems a lazy pack,
   One buckra man will do mo' wuck dan five and twenty black,
   I jeered dem and I wolloped dem, and cussed dem too — but law!
   De Debble self could nebber keep dem rascal up to tau!

" But still we done as good as mose, wid cotton, rice and corn,
   Till in de year dat '*Nuttin' tall*' * (my oldest chile) was born,
   De Tory war, de bloody war, 'bout which you've heerd dem tell,
   Come down on all de country yeh, as black and hot as hell!

" Mass Tom he jine de Whig, you know; in course I follow him,
   And Gor' a mighty! how he slash dem Tory limb from limb,
   When fust I heer the war-cry shout and see de flow ob blood'—
   I long fur hide this woolly head like cootah in de mud!

---

* The negro is a humorous creature. We have credibly heard of a negro father whose son being *abnormally small*, at birth, coolly had the ebony youngster christened, " *Nuttin' Tall (Nothing at all)*. We have borrowed so characteristic a name, and bestowed it upon Cudjo's supposititious " son and heir."
This is the single touch of fancy in the whole ballad.

" But Lawd! I soon git n'used to blood, de broadswed and de strife,
And nebber care a pig tail eend fur 'tudder folks's life;
Only, I heerd my Maussa yell thro' all dem battle-call,
And sneaked dis big fat karkiss up betwixt him and de ball!

" Well, sir! one day Mass Tom come home, 'e close and hoss blood red,
And say sense all dem Tory kill, he gwine dat once to bed;
' I needs a long fine snooze,' sez he, ' so don't you wake me soon,
' But Cudjo! let me snore oncalled till late to-morrow noon!';

" Somehow, my mine misgib me dem; so by de kitchin light,
I sot and smoked, with open ears, a listenen' true de nite:
And when de fus cock crow, I heer a fur soun, down de road,
And knowed 'um fur de hosses' trot, and de clash ob spur and sword:

" Quick I run outside in de yad, and quick outside de gate —,
And there I see de Tory come as fas' and sho' as fate;
I run back to my Maussa room, and den wid pull and push
I shub 'um by de side way out, and hide 'um in de bush!

" He only hab he nite shut on, and how he rabe and cuss!
' But Maussa! hush,' sez I, ' before you meck dis matter wuss;'
I tun to fin' some hidin' too, but de moon shine bright as sun,
And de d—d Tory ride so swif', dey ketch me on de run.

" Den, dey all screech togedder, loud, ' Boy, is your Boss widin?
' Say where he hide, or by de Lawd! your life not wut a pin!'
I trembled at dese horrid tret, but sweer my Boss was fled,
Yet when, or where, poor Cudjo knowed no better dan de dead.

" One Tory debble teck my head, another teck my foot
To drag me like a Chrismass hog to de ole oak tree root;
Dey fling a tick rope roun' my neck, dey drawed me quick and high,
I seed a tousan' million star a-flashin' from de sky.

" And dèn I choke, and all de blood keep rushin' to my head
I tried to yell, but only groaned, and guggled low enstead;
Till ebbery ting growed black as nite, and my last taut was, sho,
Dis nigger is a gone coon now, he'll see de wuld no mo'!

" But, Boss! I was a hale man den, and tough as tough could be;
Dey loose de rope and let me down quite safely from de tree;
But when I seed and heered agen, come de same furious cry,
' Say where your Maussa hide, you dog, quick, quick, or else you die!'

" I gib dem de same answer still, and so, dey hang me higher;
I feel de same hot chokin' sob; see de same starry fire;
Dey heng me twice, tree time dey heng; but de good Lawd was dere,·
And Jesus self, *he* bring me safe from all de pain and fear.

"Mose dead dey lef' me, stiff and cole, stretched on de swashy groun'
While all de house, big house and small, was blazin', fallin' roun'.
When pore Mass Tom from out de briar creep in he half-torn shut,
To bless and ring me by bote han' dere in de damp and dut!

"And when de war was ober, Boss, Mass Tom, he come to me,
And say, I sabe he life dat time, and so he meck me free;
'I'll gib you house and lan' (sez he,) 'and wid dem plough and mule,'
I tenk him kind, 'but Boss,' (says I,) 'wha' meck you tink me fool?'

"'If you, Mass Tom, was like," (sez I,) *some* buckra dat I know,
Cudjo bin run and hug de swamp — Lawd bless you! — long ago,
But I got all ting dat I want, wid not one tax to pay;
Now go long, Maussa! why you wish for dribe ole Cuj away?

"'I nebber see free nigger yet, but what he lie and steal,
Lie to 'e boss, 'e wife, 'e chile, in de cabin, and de fiel' —
And as for tieffin', dem free cuss is all like 'lightfoot Jack,'
Who carry de lass blanket off from he sick mudder back!

"'I stays wid you, (sez I again,) I meck de nigger wuck,
I wuck myself, and may be, Boss, we'll bring back de ole luck;
But don't you pizen me no more wid talk ob "freedom sweet,"
But sabe dat gab to stuff de years of de next fool you meet!'"

CHARLESTON RETAKEN.

DEC. 14, 1782.

As some half-vanquished lion,
  Who long hath kept at bay
A band of sturdy foresters
  Barring his blood-stained way —
Sore-smitten, weak and wounded —
  Glares forth on either hand;
Then, cowed with fear, his cavernous lair
  Seeks in the mountain land:

So when their stern Cornwallis,
  On Yorktown heights resigned,
His sword to our great leader,
  Of the stalwart arm and mind —
So when both fleet and army
  At one grand stroke went down
And Freedom's heart beat high once more
  In hamlet, camp and town; —

Through wasted Carolina,
  Where'er from plain to hill
The Briton's guarded fortresses
  Uprose defiant still,
Passed a keen shock of terror,
  And the breasts of war-steeled men
Quailed in the sudden blast of doom
  That smote their spirits then.

"Our cause is lost!" they muttered,
  Pale browed, with trembling lips;
"Our strength is sapped, our hope o'er-
      whelmed,
  In final, fierce eclipse;
And what to us remaineth
  But to blow our earthworks high,
And hurl our useless batteries
  In wild fire to the sky?"

'Twas done! each deadly fastness
  In flaming fragments driven
Farther than e'er *their* souls could
    climb
  Along the path to heaven —
Coastward the Britons hurried,
  In reckless throngs that flee
Wild as December's scattered clouds
  Storm-whirled toward the sea.

In Charleston streets they gathered,
  Each dazed wiseacre's head
Wagging, perchance in prophecy,
  Or more perchance in dread.
Horsemen and footmen mingled,
  They talked with bated breath
Of the shameful fate that stormed the
    gate,
  Of wrack, and strife, and death!

"Three hundred noble vessels
Rose on the rising flood,
Wherein with sullen apathy
Embarked those men of blood."

Meanwhile our squadrons hastened,
  Keen as a sleuth-hound pack
That near their destined quarry
  By some drear wild-wood track,
Ah, Christ! what desolation
  Before us grimly frowned!
The roadways trenched and furrowed,
  The gore-ensanguined ground,
With many a mark (oh! deep and dark!)
  Made ghastlier by the star-white frost,
'Twixt broken close and thorn-hedge-
    row,
Of desperate charge and mortal blow
  In conflicts won or lost!

Proud manors once the centre
  Of jubilant life and mirth,
Now silent as the sepulchre,
  Begirt by ruin and dearth;

Their broad domains all blackened
  With taint of fire and smoke,
And corpses vile with a death's-head
    smile,
  Swung high on the gnarlèd oak.

No sportive flocks in the pasture,
  No aftermath on the lea;
No laugh of the slaves at labors
  No chant of birds on the tree;
But all things bodeful, dreary,
  As a realm by the Stygian flood,
With odors of death on the uplands,
  And a taste in the air of blood!

On, on our squadrons hastened,
  Sick with the noisome fumes
From man and beast unburied,
  Through the dull funeral gloom

Till in unsullied sunshine
  One glorious morn we came
Where far aloof, o'er tower and roof,
  We viewed our brave St. Michael's
    spire
Flushed in the noontide flame!

Without their ruined ramparts,
  Beyond their shattered lines,
Just where the soil, bent seaward,
  In one long slope declines,
The foe had sent their messengers,
  Who vowed the vanquished host
Would leave unscathed our city,
  Would leave unscathed our coast!

Only due time they prayed for
  (Meek, meek our lords had grown)
To range their broken legions,
  And rear ranks overthrown —
So that, though smirched and tainted
  Their martial fame might be,
In order meet their stately fleet
  Should bear them safe to sea.

Who win, may well be gracious;
  We did not stint their boon,
Though the white 'kerchiefs of our
    wives
  Were fluttered in the noon,
On house-top and on parapet
  Each token fair and far
Shone through the golden atmosphere
  Like some enchanted star!

Next morn their signal-cannon
  Roared from the vanward wall,
And to the ranks right gleefully
  We gathered, one and all,
Our banners scarred in many a fight,
  Could still flash back the winter light,
And proud as knights of old renown,
  With sunburnt hands and faces
    brown,

Borne through the joyous, deepening
    hum,
'Mid ring of fife and beat of drum,
'Mid purpling silk and flowery arch,
Our long, unwavering columns march;

And yet (good sooth!) we almost seem
Like weird battalions of a dream;
Our souls bewildered scarce can deem
  We tread once more,
  Released, secure,
With fetterless footsteps as of yore,
The pathways of the ancient town!

And still, as borne through dreamland,
  We glanced from side to side,
While mothers, wives and daughters
    rushed
  To greet us, tender-eyed;
Each hoary patriot proudly
  Lifted his brave, gray head,
And the forms of careworn captives
    rose
  Like spectres from the dead —

Like spectres whom the trumpets
  Of freedom's cohorts call
To burst their grave-like dungeon,
  And spurn their despot's thrall;
To take once more the image
  Of manhood's loftier grace,
And, chainless now, the universe
  Look boldly in the face!

And the young girls scattered flowers,
  And the lovely dames were bright
With something more than beauty,
  In their faithful hearts' delight;
The very babes were crowing
  Shrill welcome to our bands,
And, perched on matron shoulders,
    clapped
  Blithely their dimpled hands:

And naught but benedictions
  Lightened that sacred air,
Freed from the awful burden
  Of two long years' * despair —
Two years so thronged with anguish,
  So fraught with bitter wrong,
They seemed in mournful retrospect
  Well nigh a century long.

---

* The precise period of the British occupa-
tion of Charleston was two years, seven
months and two days.

But if years of mortal being
  Trebled threescore and ten,
At the last, our souls exultant,
  Would recall that scene again,
With its soft "God bless you, gentle-
      men?"
  Its greetings warm and true,
And the tears of bliss our lips did
      kiss
  From dear eyes black or blue.

Nathless, despite our rapture,
  Down to the harbor-mouth
We dogged the Britons doomed to
      fly
  Forever from our South!
They left as some foul vulture
  Might leave his mangled prey,
And pass with clotted beak and wing
  Reluctantly away.

Three hundred noble vessels
  Rose on the rising flood,
Wherein with sullen apathy
  Embarked those men of blood;
Then streamed their admiral's pen-
      nant —
  The northwest breeze blew free;
With sloping mast, and current fast,
  Out swept their fleet to sea.

We strained our vision waveward,
  Watching the white-winged ships,
Till the vague clouds of distance
  Wrapped them in half eclipse:
And still we strained our vision
  Till, dimmer and more dim,
The rearmost sail, a phantom pale,
  Died down the horizon's rim.

Thus, o'er the soul's horizon,
  Did thoughts of blood and war,
Through time's enchanted distances
  Receding, fade afar,
Thus o'er the soul's horizon,
  Our strife's last ghastly fear,
Like all the rest, down memory's west
  Did slowly disappear.

*TO THE AUTHOR OF "THE VICTO-
      RIAN POETS."*

So keen, so clear thy genius, that no mist
  Of subtlest phrase can baffle or delay
  The lance-like, swift illuminating ray,
Wherewith, O art-enamored annalist,
Thy lightning logic cleaves the elusive
      gist
  Of thoughts Protean; or, in lowlier
      play,
  Smites tinselled weakness to a red dis-
      may—
As swordsmen smite by one deft turn of
      wrist.
Yet oft that glittering and remorseless
      blade
  Thy logic wields is dropped that thou
      may'st take
Some gracious lyre, and sing with liquid
      breath
  By many a haunted dell and shadowy
      lake,
Where faun and naiad wander undis-
      mayed,
  Lays of Arcadian love, or painless
      death.

HERA.
(IN THE HERAEUM.)

ONCE between Argos and Mycaenæ shone
  Half-veiled in myrtle and mysterious
      pine,
  The ivory splendors of that holy shrine,
Wherein embowered, majestic, and alone
Her sculptured brow with wavering locks
      o'erblown,
  As if by airs ethereal and divine,
  Smiled the calm goddess of Olympian
      line,
Girt by awed silence, like a sacred zone:

Save that mild murmurings sounding
      vague and far,
  From suppliant women—through frail-
      hearted dread
Touched the shy pulses of that strange
      repose,
  Till the last petal dropped from sun-
      set's rose,

And gleamed through twilight, like a
    flawless star,
The chastened glory of proud Hera's
    head!

BELOW AND ABOVE.

I SEE in the forest coverts
    The sheen of shimmering lights;
They gleam from the dusky shadows,
    They flash from the ghostly heights:

No lights of the tranquil homestead
    Or the hostel warm are they;
But warring flames of the Titan fire
    Which stormed through the woods to-
      day.

Each darts with an aimless passion,
    Or sinks into lurid rest
Like the crest of a wounded serpent
      drooped
    On the scales of its treacherous breast.

Let them idly dart and quiver,
    Or sink into lurid rest —
Above, like a child-saint's face in heav-
      en,
    There's a sole, sweet star in the west.

Ah! slowly the earth-lights wither;
    But the star, like a saintly face,
Shines on, with the steadfast strength of
      peace,
    In its God-appointed place.

THE WOODLAND GRAVE.

WE roam, my love and I,
    'Mid the rich woodland grasses,
Where, through dense clouds of green-
      ery,
    The softened sunshine passes;
But near a rivulet's lonely wave
We come half startled, on — a grave!

We pause, my love and I,
    Each thinking, " *Who* reposes
Here, in the forest tranquilly,
    Beneath these sylvan roses ? "
When, 'twixt the wild flowers' tangled
      flame,
Wind-parted, we beheld — a name.

We mark, my love and I,
    With thoughts that swiftly vary,
Of doubt, surprise, solemnity,
    The flickering name of " Mary;"
My love's own name! — but flickering
      there,
Each letter burns a hint of fear.

We shrink, my love and I,
    Pierced by prescient sorrow,
" To think, my sweet! that *thou* may'st
      die
To-night or else to-morrow!"
Each murmurs sadly, under breath:
" O love, malignly watched by death!"

We turn, my love and I,
    From that strange grave together,
And o'er our spirits' darkened sky
    Roll mists of mournful weather;
With boding grief our hearts are rife —
Death's shadow steals 'twixt love and
      life!

A CHARACTER.

" The most impenetrable mask for a ma-
licious design is — well-acted candor." — *From
the French of De Larrimère.*

YES, madame, I know you better, far
    better than those can know
Whose plummet of judgment never is
    dropped to the depths below;

Whose test is a surface-seeming, the
    glitter of lights that gleam
With a moment's rainbow lustre on the
    shifting face of the stream.

"We turn, my love and I,
From that strange grave together."

Because you have bold, blunt manners,
  because you can broadly smile,
With the devil's own art in veiling your
  infinite gulfs of guile,

There are some who bring you homage,
  who vow your nature is free
And frank as the life of summer, when
  fullest on land and sea:

And yet your soul is a charnel where
  many a ruined name
Rots, festering vile and loathsome in
  burial-shrouds of shame;

A sepulchre dark, that's crowded with
  ashes of old and young,
Dead fames you have foully poisoned
  with your pitiless serpent's tongue!

Beware! by the God above us, who part-
  eth the false from true,
There's a curse in the future, *some-
  where* — an ambushed curse for you.

It will burst from the wayside fiercely,
  when least you dream of a blow.
A tigerish fate in its fury, to rend, and
  to lay you low!

But ere it has sucked your heart's blood,
  and stifled your latest breath,
The thought of *your* victims, woman!
  will sharpen the sting of death!

LYRIC OF ACTION.

'Tis the part of a coward to brood
  O'er the past that is withered and
    dead:
What though the heart's roses are ashes
  and dust ?
  What though the heart's music be
    fled ?
  Still shine the grand heavens o'er-
    head,

Whence the voice of an angel thrills
    clear on the soul,
" Gird about thee thine armor, press on
    to the goal!' "

If the faults or the crimes of thy youth
  Are a burden too heavy to bear,
What hope can rebloom on the desolate
    waste
  Of a jealous and craven despair
  Down, down with the fetters of fear!
In the strength of thy valor and man-
    hood arise,
With the faith that illumes and the will
    that defies.

" *Too late !* " through God's infinite
    world,
  From his throne to life's nethermost
    fires,
" *Too late !* " is a phantom that flies at
    the dawn
  Of the soul that repents and aspires.
  If pure thou hast made thy desires.
There's no height the strong wings of
    immortals may gain
Which in striving to reach thou shalt
    strive for in vain.

Then, up to the contest with fate,
  Unbound by the past, which is dead!
What though the heart's roses are ashes
    and dust ?
  What though the heart's music be
    fled ?
  Still shine the fair heavens o'erhead ;
And sublime as the seraph who rules in
    the sun
Beams the promise of joy when the con-
    flict is won!

BY A GRAVE.

IN SPRING.

Ah, mother! canst thou feel her ? . . .
    spring has come!
Birds sing, brooks murmur, woods no
    more are dumb;

And for each grief that vexed thine
earthly hour,
Nature has kissed thy grave! and lo! . .
a flower.

Here wails no nightingale against her
thorn,
But like the incarnate soul of May-
flushed morn,
The mocking-bird above thy splendor
sings,
With rapturous throat, and upraised
quivering wings;

Half drowsed between brief glooms and
mellowed gleams,
The sun smiles gently, like a god in
dreams;
His sacred light across thy place of
rest,
Steals with the softness of a hand that
blessed!

Thro' magic ministers of spring-tide
grace,
Thy grave transfigured lifts a radiant
face,
O'er which elusive golden shadows
run,
A waft of wind-wrought dimples in the
sun:

Ah! if thy soul, that loved all beauty
here,
May yet look earthward from her holier
sphere,
'Twill joy to mark, from even those
heights august,
In what a mantle Nature wraps thy
dust.

And still the brown bird rears his poet-
head,
And pours his matchless music o'er the
dead,
'Till touched and wakened by the mar-
vellous flow,
I seem to hear a thrilled heart throb be-
low!

SEVERANCE.

Ah! who can tell how strong the tie
Which subtly binds us, heart to heart,
Till the dark master, Death, comes
nigh,
To wrench our kindred lives apart ?

Then, pondering on the sombre bed,
Where one we cherished dumbly
lies,
With pulseless hands, low-smitten head,
And the wan droop of curtained eyes,

The torpor of the death-sleep cold,
The mystic quiet's awful spell,
Whose fathomless silence seems to hold
Such pathos of supreme farewell,

Our clouded spirits throb and reel,
As if some viewless power in air
Had driven a keen ethereal steel
Through quivering heart-depths of
despair!

Paled is the dream of heavenly grace,
The jasper sea, the unwaning calms;
We can but mark that breathless face,
Those sightless orbs and folded palms!

A moment since, she softly spake,
Her soul looked forth still hale and
clear;
Now, who her wondrous sleep can
break ?
And she! where hath she vanished, —
where ?

Ah, Christ! yon shape of ice-locked
clay,
Yon fading image, frail and thin,
Touched, as we gaze, by swift decay,
Shrivelled without, and wan within,

What is it but an empty husk,
O'er which (at Death's mysterious
kiss)
Freed Psyche soars from doubt and dusk
Beyond earth's crumbling chrysalis ?

Ay! "dust to dust!" — the soil she trod
  Claims soon her outworn fleshly dress;
But her true life puts forth, with God,
  Fresh blooms of everlastingness!

---◇---

TWO GRAVES.

I.

It glooms forlornly 'mid wan ocean
    dunes,
  A desolate grave-mound on a dreary
    lea,
Touched by sad splendors of gray-misted
    moons,
  Or veiled by shivering spray-drifts
    from the sea.

There, all unmarked, the dim days come
    and go;
  No tender hand renews its crumbling
    turf,
On which the o'erwearied sea-winds
    faintly blow,
  Blent with far murmurings of the
    mournful surf.

Vaguely the uncompanioned hours flit
    by,
  Wrapped in pale clouds that some-
    times mutely weep
Some ghost of Lethe haunts that hollow
    sky,
  Where even the doubtful noontides
    seem asleep,

Save when autumnal tempests fiercely
    rise,
  Baring the harbor-mouth's black teeth
    of rocks,
And like a Maenad, with wild hair and
    eyes,
  Raves from the North the infuriate
    Equinox.

II.

Here, peace divine, o'er glimmering
    grove and grass,
  Hallows the sunshine in the noon's
    warm lull;

Ethereal shadows gently pause, or
    pass,
  Flecking with gold the hill-slope beau-
    tiful.

This grave, all wreathed with flowers
    and glad with spring
  Looks skyward like a half-veiled,
    museful eye,
Which answers subtly while the wood-
    birds sing
  Heaven's smile of forecast immortal-
    ity.

Can deathly dust pervade a spot so
    sweet?
  Or hath the form it guarded stolen
    away,
And ere its hour of ransom, gone to
    meet
  The unborn soul of Resurrection Day?

---◆---

THE WORLD.

QUATRAINS.

The world is older than our earliest
    dates;
  All thoughts, all feelings, all desires, all
    fates,
Were known and tested, long ere
    Adam's crime
  Set the keen sword of flame at Eden-
    gates!

Billions of years on billions more have
    fled,
  Since first love's kiss a maiden cheek
    turned red;
Since the first mother nursed her inno-
    cent babe —
  The first wild mourner wept above his
    dead.

These ancient clods our vagrant feet dis-
    place,
  May once have held the loftiest soul of
    grace;

This dateless dust that dims our garden
    flowers,
May once have smiled — a beauteous
    woman's face!

Older than all man's wisdom and his
    dreams,
Older than all which is, than all which
    seems,
Our world rolls on, where wrapped in
    cloud-like fire,
Phantasmal, pale, her awful death-morn
    gleams!

THE MAY SKY.

O sky! O lucid sky of May!
    O'er which the fleecy clouds have
      stolen,
In bands snow-white, and glimmering-
      gray,
    Or heart-steeped in a lustre golden.

O sky! that tak'st a thousand moods,
    Enshadowed now, and now out-beam-
      ing,
Swept by low winds like interludes
    Of music 'twixt soft spells of dreaming,

Type of the poet's soul thou art
    In spring-time of his teeming fancies,
When heavenly glamours brim his heart,
    And heavenly glory lights his glances;

As morning's dubious vapors form
    In wavering lines and circlets tender,
Pure as an infant's brow, or warm
    With tintings of a primrose splendor;

Thus o'er the poet's soul his thought
    Pale first as mist-wreaths scarce cre-
      ated,
With fire-keen breaths of ardor fraught,
    From radiance born, to beauty mated,

Takes shape like yonder cloud out-
      spanned
    Above the murmurous woodland
      spaces,

Whose brightening rifts, methinks, are
    grand
    With mystic lights and marvellous
      faces;

Or, merges in some fancy vain,
    Yet rare beyond the worldling's
      measure;
Some delicate cloudlet of the brain
    That melts far up its quivering azure!

A LYRICAL PICTURE.

COMPOSED NEAR THE SEA-COAST.

    SEE! see!
How the shadows steal along,
Blending in a golden throng,
    Softly, lovingly;
From each mossed and quaint tree-col-
    umn,
Stretched toward the dimpling river,
    How they quiver!
While in low, pathetic tone
Twilight's herald-breeze is blown
    Down the sunset solemn!

    Hear! hear!
Dropped from gray mists, circling high,
The sea-wending curlew's cry,
    Strangely wild and drear;
Echoed by a voice that thrills us,
From the murmurous verge of ocean —
    Voice that fills us
With a sense of mystery old,
And vague memories which enfold
    Many a weird emotion.

    Turn! turn!
From yon loftier cloud-land dun;
Mark what splendors of the sun
    Westward throb and burn —
Burn as if some glorious angel
Blessed the air and land and river
    With his mute evangel:
All things own so rich a grace
That in Heaven's divine embrace
    Earth seems clasped forever!

LAMIA UNVEILED.

HER step is soft as a fay's footfall,
  And her eyes are wonderful founts of
    blue;
But I've seen that small foot spurning
    hearts,
  And the soul that burns so strangely
    through
      Those orbs of blue,
O! is't a *human* soul at all?

I never have gazed on their cloudless
    light,
  But there came a chill to my blood and
    brain,
And their ominous beauty hath struck
    me dumb
  With a secret and nameless pain:
      Ay, blood and brain
Grew cold as with spells of a witch's
    blight.

Is't true? Can it be that a mortal
    frame
  Of the tenderest mould, of the fairest
    grace,
May hold but a serpent's soul in sooth?
  That the white and red of the daintiest
    face
      May mask the trace
Of subtle guile, that shall wake to
    flame

And smite with the sting of a poisoned
    jest,
  Or the sudden flashing of deadly
    scorn,
If it be, I know that your Charmian
    there,
  In her fragile grace, is a Lamia, born
      To blight the morn
Of the passion that clings to her faithless
    breast!

Why, look! As we speak, she has turned
    her wiles
  On the gilded wooer her eyes had
    sought,

While *you* were steeped in the roseate
    gulf
  Of a sweet, voluptuous thought:
      Some loves are bought,
And you'll yearn in vain for her 'wilder-
    ing smiles.

From this night forth, until placid and
    meek,
  (Oh! meek as a saint, as an angel bland!)
With a faint rose flushing her brow and
    cheek,
  She whispers, "*Adieu! I must give my
    hand,
      At the heart's command.
Win a worthier love; you have only to
    seek!*"

————◇————

RACHEL.

INSCRIBED TO MRS. M. D., OF GEORGIA.

"A more desolate Rachel than she of old,
because, although her children 'are not,' yet
the fountain of her tears is sealed."

THE wan September moonbeams, strug-
    gling down
  Through the gray clouds upon her des-
    olate head,
  The coldness of their muffled radiance
    shed
Faintly above her like a spectral crown:

So, glimmering ghostlike in the dreary
    light,
  Recounting her strange sorrows o'er
    and o'er,
  Her words rang hollow as far waves
    ashore
Rolled through the sombre void of wind-
    less night.

Nor in her mortal weakness could she win
  Even brief redemption from the soul's
    eclipse.
  She looked like suffering Patience, on
    whose lips
Cold fingers press to keep the wild grief
    in.

Suddenly on the pathos and the woe
  Of that sad vision broke the gleeful
    noise
  From the near playground of blithe
    girls and boys,
Through shine and shadow hurrying to
    and fro.

A wearier shade the pallid face o'er
    crossed;
  She shivered, drooping; but through
    flowery bars
  Of the rude trellis sought the distant
    stars,
Saying, low: " *Where dwell in heaven
    my loved and lost?*

Dear Christ, I thought, if soft and ruth-
    ful, thou
  Still reign'st beyond us,— ah! assuage
    the pain
  Of this worn soul, more laden than
    hers of Nain;
Ope thy deep heavens for one swift mo-
    ment now;

And, while her very heart-throbs seem
    to cease
  For rapture, let those hungering eyes
    behold
  Her lost beloved transfigured in thy
    fold,
Crowned with the palm, walking the
    fields of peace!

THE SNOW-MESSENGERS.

Dedicated to John Greenleaf Whittier and
Henry Wadsworth Longfellow, with pen por-
traits of both.

THE pine-trees lift their dark bewildered
    eyes —
Or so I deem — up to the clouded skies;
No breeze, no faintest breeze, is heard
    to blow:
In wizard silence falls the windless
    snow.

It falls in breezeless quiet, strangely
    still;
'Scapes the dulled pane, but loads the
    sheltering sill.
With curious hand the fleecy flakes I
    mould,
And draw them inward, rounded, from
    the cold.

The glittering ball that chills my finger-
    tips
I hold a moment's space to loving lips;
For from the northward these pure
    snow-flakes came,
And to *my* touch their coldness thrills
    like flame.

Outbreathed from luminous memories
    nursed apart,
Deep in the veiled *adytum* of the heart,
The type of Norland dearth such snows
    may be:
They bring the soul of summer's warmth
    to me.

Beholding them, in magical light ex-
    pands
The changeful charm that crowns the
    northern lands,
And a fair past I deemed a glory fled
Comes back, with happy sunshine
    round its head.

For Ariel fancy takes her airiest flights
To pass once more o'er Hampshire's
    mountain heights,
To view the flower-bright pastures
    bloom in grace
By many a lowering hill-side's swarthy
    base;

The fruitful farms, the enchanted vales,
    to view,
And the coy mountain lakes' transcen-
    dent blue,
Or flash of sea-waves up the thunderous
    dune,
With wan sails whitening in the mid-
    night moon;

The cataract front of storm, malignly
    rife
With deathless instincts of demoniac
    strife,
Or, in shy contrast, down a shaded dell,
The rivulet tinkling like an Alpine
    bell;

And many a cool, calm stretch of cul-
    tured lawn,
Touched by the freshness of the crystal
    dawn,
Sloped to the sea, whose laughing waters
    meet
About the unrobed virgin's rosy feet.

"To pass once more o'er Hampshire's mountain heights, . . .
The fruitful farms, the enchanted vales, to view,
And the coy mountain lakes' transcendent blue."

But, tireless fancy, stay the wing that
    roams,
And fold it last near northern hearts
    and homes.

These tropic veins still own their kin-
    dred heat,
And thoughts of thee, my cherished
    South, are sweet —
Mournfully sweet — and wed to memories
    vast,
High-hovering still o'er thy majestic
    past.

But a new epoch greets us; with it blends
The voice of ancient foes now changed
    to friends.
Ah! who would friendship's outstretched
    hand despise,
Or mock the kindling light in generous
    eyes ?

So, 'neath the Quaker-poet's tranquil
    roof,
From all dull discords of the world aloof,
I sit once more, and measured converse
    hold
With him whose nobler thoughts are
    rhythmic gold;

See his deep brows half puckered in a
    knot
O'er some hard problem of our mortal
    lot,
Or a dream soft as May winds of the
    south
Waft a girl's sweetness round his firm-set
    mouth.

Or should he deem wrong threats the
    public weal,
Lo! the whole man seems girt with
    flashing steel;

His glance a sword thrust, and his words
of ire
Like thunder-tones from some old proph-
et's lyre.

Or by the hearth-stone when the day is
done,
Mark, swiftly launched, a sudden shaft
of fun;
The short quick laugh, the smartly smit-
ten knees,
And all sure tokens of a mind at ease.

Discerning which, by some mysterious
law,
Near to his seat two household favor-
ites draw,
Till on her master's shoulders, sly and
sleek,
Grimalkin, mounting, rubs his furrowed
cheek;

While terrier Dick, denied all words to
rail,
Snarls as he shakes a short protesting tail,
But with shrewd eyes says, plain as plain
can be,
" *Drop that sly cat. I'm worthier far
than she.*"

And he who loves all lowliest lives to
please,
Conciliates soon his dumb Diogenes,
Who in return his garment nips with
care,
And drags the poet out, to take the air.

God's innocent pensioners in the wood-
lands dim,
The fields and pastures, know and trust
in him;
And in *their* love his lonely heart is
blessed,
Our pure, hale-minded Cowper of the
West!

.　　.　　.　　.　　.

The scene is changed; and now I stand
again
By one, the cordial prince of kindly men,

Courtly yet natural, comrade meet for
kings,
But fond of homeliest thoughts and
homeliest things.

A poet too, in whose warm brain and
breast
What birds of song have filled a golden
nest,
Till in song's summer prime their wings
unfurled,
Have made Arcadian half the listening
world,

Around whose eve some radiant grace of
morn
Smiles like the dew-light on a mountain
thorn.
Blithely he bears Time's envious load to-
day:
Ah! the green heart o'ertops the head of
gray.

Alert as youth, with vivid, various
talk
He wiles the way through grove and gar-
den walk,
Fair flowers untrained, trees fraught
with wedded doves,
Past the cool copse and willowy glade he
loves.

Here gleams innocuous of a mirthful
mood
Pulse like mild fire-flies down a dusky
wood,
Or keener speech (his leonine head un-
bowed)
Speeds lightning-clear from thought's
o'ershadowing cloud.

O deep blue eyes! O voice as woman's
low!
O firm white hand, with kindliest
warmth aglow!
O manly form, and frank, sweet, courte-
ous mien,
Reflex of museful days and nights se-
rene!

Still are ye near me, vivid, actual still,
Here in my lonely fastness on the hill;
Nor can ye wane till cold my life-blood
flows,
And fancy fades in feeling's last repose.

What! snowing yet ? The landscape
waxes pale;
Round the mute heaven there hangs a
quivering veil,
Through whose frail woof like silent
shuttles go
The glancing glamours of the glittering
snow.

Yes, falling still, while fond remem-
brance stirs
In these wan-faced, unwonted messen-
gers.
Dumb storm! outpour your arctic heart's
desire!
Your flakes to me seem flushed with
fairy fire!

TO ALEXANDER H. STEPHENS.

LAST of a stalwart time and race gone
by,
That simple, stately, God-appointed
band,
Who wrought alone to glorify their
land,
With lives built high on truth's eternity,
While placemen plot, while flatterers
fawn or lie,
And foul corruptions, wave on wave,
expand,
I see thee rise, stainless of heart as
hand,
O man of Roman thought and radiant
eye!

Through thy frail form, there burn
divinely strong
The antique virtues of a worthier day;
Thy soul is golden, if thy head be gray,
No years can work that lofty nature
wrong;

They set to concords of ethereal song
A life grown holier on its heavenward
way.

THE ENCHANTED MIRROR.

FROM THE PERSIAN.

WHAT time o'er Persia ruled that up-
right Khan
Khosru the Good, in Shiraz lived a
man,
A beggar-carle, to whose rough hands
were given —
I know not how — a mirror clear as
heaven
On beauteous, vernal mornings, and
more bright
Than streamlets sparkling in midsum-
mer's light;
And, strange to say, whoso should look
therein,
Though uglier than a nightmare dream
of sin,
Grew comely as the loveliest shapes we
know;
The while — oh, wonder! a fair form and
face
Caught straightway somewhat of celes-
tial grace.

Where'er in twilight dusk, or noontide
glow
With swift, firm pace or footstep sad
and slow,
Where'er he walked through the broad
land of palms,
Or yet his lips unclosed to plead for
alms,
The beggar held his mystic treasure
high
To glass the forms of those who passed
him by;
And all who came within that marvel's
range,
Paused spell-bound by the strangely-daz-
zling change;

Lords, ladies, gazed! the prospect
pleased them well;
"Ah, heavens!" they sighed, "how
irresistible!"
E'en the coarse hag, foul, wrinkled, and
unclean,
Beamed like a blushing virgin of six-
teen.

Hearts are transformed with faces; out-
ward beauty
Seems to make quick the inward sense
of duty;
For none, of all the charmèd throng that
pass
Revivified within the fairy glass,
But pours upon the beggar pence with
praise,
Invoking on his head long, golden days,
And every joy that lights our mortal
ways.

In vain!—the beggar sickened. While
he lay
In death's cold shadow, prostrate and
forlorn,
He bade his wife call to him, on a morn,
His only son: "Guard well when I am
dead,"
Feebly, with fluttering breath, the old
man said;
"This mystic glass, whereby great
things are won—
Be shrewd, be watchful; do as I have
done,
And thou shalt prosper likewise, O my
son!"

He took the precious gift—that brain-
less wight—
But, scorning to employ its powers
aright,
Returned all pale and penniless at night.

"Fool!" cried the angry father, "well
I guess
Why thus thou seek'st me, pale and
penniless:
O stupid dolt! vain peacock! arrant ass!

Thou hast watched all day thine own
face in the glass;
Go to! this foolish fruit of idle pride
No human heart hath ever satisfied,
Far less an empty pocket lined with
gold;
Thy coxcomb pate to base self-love is
sold!
Yet hearken once again: *he's only wise*
Who dupes the world through flattery's
mirrored lies;
But past all terms of scorn the insensate
elf
Who holds its glass therein to view—
himself!"

———◆———

THE IMPRISONED SEA-WINDS.

VOICES of strange sea breezes caught,
Half tangled in the pine-tree tall,
With ocean's tenderest music fraught,
Serenely rise, and sweetly fall.

They charm the lids of wearied eyes,
And all the dreamy senses bless
With breath of wave-born symphonies,
And balms of mild forgetfulness,

'Till o'er the fragrant calms of peace,
My soul, scarce moved, benignly
glides,
Or in all sorrows' soft surcease,
Rocks trancèd on the phantom tides:

But still those faint sea voices speak,
Those prisoned sea winds rise and fall,
The ghost of sea foam sweeps my cheek,
And the sea's mystery sighs through
all.

———◆———

BLANCHE AND NELL.

A BALLAD.

OH, Blanche is a city lady,
Bedecked in her silks and lace:
She walks with the mien of a stately
queen,
And a queen's imperious grace.

But Nell is a country maiaen,
  Her dress from the farmstead loom:
Her step is free as a breeze at sea,
  And her face is a rose in bloom.

The house of Blanche is a marvel
  Of marble from base to dome;
It hath all things fair, and costly and
    rare,
  But alas! it is not — home!

Nell lives in a lonely cottage
  On the shores of a wave-washed isle;
And the life she leads with its loving
    deeds
  The angels behold and smile.

Blanche finds her palace a prison,
  And oft, through the dreary years,
In her burdened breast there is sad un-
    rest,
  And her eyes are dimmed with tears.

But to Nell her toils are pastime,
  (Though never till night they cease);
And her soul's afloat like a buoyant
    boat
  On the crystal tides of peace.

Ah! Blanche hath many a lover,
  But she broodeth o'er old regret;
The shy, sweet red from her cheek is
    fled
  For the star of her heart has set.

Fair Nell! but a single lover
  Hath she in the wide, wide world;
Yet warmly apart in her glowing heart
  Love bides, with his pinions furled.

To Blanche all life seems shadowed,
  And she but a ghost therein;
Thro' the misty gray of her autumn
    day
  Steal voices of grief and sin.

To Nell all life is sunshine,
  All earth like a fairy sod,
Where the roses grow, and the violets
    blow,
  In the softest breath of God.

What meaneth this mighty contrast
  Of lives that we meet and mark ?
One bright as the flowers from May-tide
    showers,
  One rayless, sombre, and dark ?

O, folly of mortal wisdom,
  That neither will break nor bow,
That riddle hath vexed the thought per-
    plexed
  Of millions of souls ere now!

O, folly of mortal wisdom!
  From your guesses what good can
    come ?
We can learn no more than the wise of
    yore;
  'Tis better to trust, and — be dumb!

THE DARK.

A FANTASY.

THE passionless twilight slowly fades
Beyond the gray, grim woodland glades,
Till now, with mournful eyes, I mark
    The approaching dark:

A clouded spirit, borne from far,
Whose sombre front no delicate star
Brightens, — to tint with silvery light
    Her realms of night:

An *awful* spirit! her pale lips
Low whispering down the drear eclipse,
Send thro' those rayless spaces chill
    An ominous thrill:

Her tongue's strange language none
    may know;
We only feel it ebb and flow
In murmurs of half-muffled sighs,
    And vague replies:

All hail! akin to me thou art,
Dim angel of the veilèd heart —
Ah! wrap me close, ah! fold me deep!
    I fain would sleep!

IN THE STUDIO.

You walk my studio's modest round,
With slowly supercilious air;
While in each lifted eyebrow lurks,
The keenness of an ambushed sneer.

You lift your glass, and scan the walls,
Between the pictures — with a glance
Which takes the curtained drapery in,
But views the art-work all askance:

A sigh! a shrug! and then you turn
Homeward — your judgment fixed as
fate —
The labors of a life-time gauged,
Serenely in your shallow pate!

WASHINGTON!
Feb. 22, 1732.

Bright natal morn! what face appears
Beyond the rolling mist of years? —
A face whose loftiest traits combine
All virtues of a stainless line
Passed from leal sire to loyal son;
The face of him whose steadfast zeal
Drew harmonies of law and right
From chaos and anarchic night:
Who with a power serene as Fate's
Wrought from rude hordes of turbu-
lent States
The grandeur of our commonweal: —
All hail! all hail! to Washington!

Freedom he wooed in such brave guise,
Men gazing in her luminous eyes
Beheld all heaven reflected shine
Far down those sapphire orbs divine:
And, worshipped her so chastely won;
If still she panted, fresh from strife,
And blood-stains flecked her gar-
ment's rim,
They could not make its whiteness
dim;
For, shed by hearts sublimely true,
Such drops are changed to sacred dew.
The chrism of patriot light and life, —
Baptizing first our Washington.

For cloudless years, benignant still.
This Freedom worked her bounteous
will; —
Mingling with homespun man and maid,
Her pale cheek caught a browner shade
In fields where harvest toils were done;
To theirs she tuned her rhythmic
tongue
Veiling in part her goddess-mien:
The woman smiled above the queen;
While stationed always by her side,
Men saw — as bridegroom near his bride,
(O bride, forever fair and young!) —
Her chosen hero — Washington!

She wove for him a civic crown;
She made so pure his hale renown,
All glories of the antique days,
Waned in the clear, immaculate blaze
Poured from his nature's noontide
sun;
No slave of folly's catchword school,
His instincts proud of blood and race
She tempered with sweet, human
grace,
Till his broad being's rounded flow
Sea-like, embraced the high and low,
Swayed by the golden-sceptred rule,
The equal will of Washington.

His influence spread so wide and deep,
Earth's fettered millions stirred in sleep;
And murmurs born of wakening flame
On the wild winds of twilight came
From lands by despot-swarms o'errun;
They too would win the priceless boon
Of Freedom's dower; — they too
would see,
And clasp the robes of Liberty;
But, throned within the virgin west,
She heard them not; — she loved to rest
In dew-lit dawn and tranquil noon,
Next the strong heart of Washington!

Through shower and sun the seasons
rolled,
November's gray and April's gold;
They only raised (more calmly grand)
His genius of supreme command,

"You walk my studio's modest round, . . .
While in each eyebrow lurks
The keenness of an ambushed sneer."

Whose course, in blood and wrath be-
gun,
Grew gentler, as the mellowing lights
Of peace made beauteous sky and sod;
His evening came;— he walked with
God;
And down life's gradual sunset-slope,
He hearkened to a heavenly hope;—
" Look up! behold the fadeless heights
Which rise to greet thee,— Washing-
ton!"

He dies! the nations hold their breath!
He dies! but is he thrall to Death?—
Thousands who quaff earth's sunshine
free,
Are less alive on earth than he;
Lacking that power which thrills
through none
But God's elect, that wingèd spell
Which like miraculous lightning darts
Electric to all noble hearts;—
Flashed from his soul's sublimer
sphere,
'Tis still a matchless influence here!
Majestic spirit! all is well,
Where'er thou rulest,— Washington!

———◆———

IN AMBUSH.

THE crescent moon, with pallid glow,
Swept backward like a bended bow:
Across, a shaft of phantom light
Thrilled, like an arrow winged for
flight.

Just when that flickering shaft was
aimed
Venus in mellow radiance flamed,
Unmindful of the treacherous dart
Which seemed upreared to pierce her
heart;

For, fain to smite her through and
through,
Dian lay ambushed in the blue:
Half veiled from sight, still, still below,
She aimed her shaft, she clasped her
bow.

For ever thus, since time was born,
Cold virtue points *her* shaft of scorn
At passionate love, in whose warm
beam
Her own but seems a crescent dream.

———◆———

SOUTH CAROLINA TO THE STATES OF THE NORTH.*

ESPECIALLY TO THOSE THAT FORMED A
PART OF THE ORIGINAL THIRTEEN.

Dedicated to His Excellency, Wade Hampton.

I LIFT these hands with iron fetters
banded:
Beneath the scornful sunlight and cold
stars
I rear my once imperial forehead
branded
By alien shame's immedicable scars;
Like some pale captive, shunned by all
the nations,
I crouch unpitied, quivering and
apart—
Laden with countless woes and desola-
tions,
The life-blood freezing round a broken
heart!

About my feet, splashed red with blood
of slaughters,
My children gathering in wild, mourn-
ful throngs;
Despairing sons, frail infants, stricken
daughters,
Rehearse the awful burden of their
wrongs;
Vain is their cry, and worse than vain
their pleading:

---

* This Poem was composed at a period when
it seemed as if all the horrors of misgovern-
ment, so graphically depicted by Pike in his
"*Prostrate State*," would be perpetuated in
South Carolina.

It was a significant and terrible epoch; a
time American statesmen would do well to
remember occasionally as a warning against
patchwork political re-constructions.

I turn from stormy breasts, from
 yearning eyes,
To mark where Freedom's outraged form
 receding,
Wanes in chill shadow down the mid-
 night skies!

I wooed her once in wild tempestuous
 places,
The purple vintage of my soul out-
 poured,
To win and keep her unrestrained em-
 braces,
What time the olive-crown o'ertopped
 the sword;
O! northmen, with your gallant heroes
 blending,
Mine, in old years, for this sweet god-
 dess died;
But now — ah! shame, all other shame
 transcending!
Your pitiless hands have torn her
 from my side.

*What! 'tis a tyrant-party's treacherous
 action —
Your hand is clean, your conscience
 clear, ye sigh ;*
Ay! but ere now your sires had throt-
 tled faction,
Or, pealed o'er half the world their
 battle-cry;
Its voice outrung from solemn mountain-
 passes
Swept by wild storm-winds of the At-
 lantic strand,
To where the swart Sierras' sullen
 grasses,
Droop in low languors of the sunset-
 land!

Never, since earthly States began their
 story,
Hath any suffered, bided, borne like
 me:
At last, recalling all mine ancient glory,
I vowed my fettered commonwealth to
 free:

Even at the thought, beside the pros-
 trate column
Of chartered rights, which blasted lay
 and dim —
Uprose my noblest son with purpose sol-
 emn,
While, host on host, his brethren fol-
 lowed *him*:

Wrong, grasped by *truth,* arraigned by
 law, (whose sober
Majestic mandates rule o'er change
 and time) —
Smit by the *ballot,* like some flushed Oc-
 tober,
Reeled in the autumn rankness of his
 crime;
Struck, tortured, pierced — but not a
 blow returning.
The steadfast phalanx of my honored
 braves
Planted their bloodless flag where sun-
 rise burning,
Flashed a new splendor o'er our mar-
 tyrs' graves!

What then? O, sister States! what wel-
 come omen
Of love and concord crossed our
 brightening blue,
The foes we vanquished, are they not
 your foemen,
Our laws upheld, your sacred safe-
 guards, too?
Yet scarce had victory crowned our
 grand endeavor,
And peace crept out from shadowy
 glooms remote —
Than — as if bared to blast all hope for-
 ever,
Your tyrant's sword shone glittering
 at my throat!

Once more my bursting chains were re-
 united,
Once more barbarian plaudits wildly
 rung
O'er the last promise of deliverance
 blighted,

The prostrate purpose, and the palsied
  tongue:
Ah! faithless sisters, 'neath my swift
  undoing,
Peers the black presage of your wrath
  to come;
Above your heads are signal clouds of
  ruin,
  Whose lightnings flash, whose thun-
  ders are not dumb!

There towers a judgment-seat beyond
  our seeing;
  There lives a Judge, whom none can
  bribe or blind;
Before whose dread decree, your spirit
  fleeing,
  May reap the whirlwind, having sown
  the wind:
I, in that day of justice, fierce and torrid,
  When blood — *your* blood — outpours
  like poisoned wine,
*Pointing to these chained limbs, this
  blasted forehead,*
  *May mock your ruin, as ye mocked at
  mine!*

----◆----

THE STRICKEN SOUTH TO THE
NORTH.

[Dedicated to Oliver Wendell Holmes.]

"We are thinking a great deal about the
poor fever-stricken cities of the South, and all
contributing according to our means for their
relief. Every morning as the paper comes,
the first question is 'What is the last ac-
count from Memphis, Grenada, and New
Orleans.'" — *Extract from a private letter of
Dr. Holmes.*

WHEN ruthful time the South's memor-
  ial places —
  Her heroes' graves — had wreathed in
  grass and flowers;
When Peace ethereal, crowned by all her
  graces,
  Returned to make more bright the
  summer hours;
When doubtful hearts revived, and
  hopes grew stronger;

When old sore-cankering wounds that
  pierced and stung,
Throbbed with their first, mad, feverous
  pain no longer,
  While the fair future spake with flat-
  tering tongue;
When once, once more she felt her pulses
  beating
  To rhythms of healthful joy and brave
  desire;
Lo! round her doomed horizon darkly
  meeting,
  A pall of blood-red vapors veined with
  fire!

O! ghastly portent of fast-coming sor-
  rows!
  Of doom that blasts the blood and
  blights the breath,
Robs youth and manhood of all golden
  morrows —
  And life's clear goblet brims with
  wine of death! —
O! swift fulfilment of this portent dreary!
  O! nightmare rule of ruin, racked by
  fears,
Heartbroken wail, and solemn *miserere*,
  Imperious anguish, and soul-melting
  tears!
O! faith, thrust downward from celestial
  splendors,
  O! love grief-bound, with palely-mur-
  murous mouth!
O! agonized by life's supreme surren-
  ders —
  Behold her now — the scourged and
  suffering South!

No balm in Gilead? nay, but while her
  forehead
Pallid and drooping, lies in foulest dust,
There steals across the desolate spaces
  torrid,
  A voice of manful cheer and heavenly
  trust,
A hand redeeming breaks the frozen
  starkness
  Of palsied nerve, and dull, despondent
  brain:

Rolls back the curtain of malignant
    darkness,
And shows the eternal blue of heaven
    again —
Revealing there, o'er worlds convulsed
    and shaken,
    That face whose mystic tenderness
        enticed
To hope new-born earth's lost bereaved,
    forsaken!
Ah! still beyond the tempest smiles the
    Christ!

Whose voice? Whose hand? Oh, thanks,
    divinest Master,
    Thanks for those grand emotions
        which impart
Grace to the North to feel the South's
    disaster,
    The South to bow with touched and
        cordial heart!
Now, now at last the links which war
    had broken
    Are welded fast, at mercy's charmed
        commands;
Now, now at last the magic words are
    spoken
    Which blend in one two long-divided
        lands!
O North! you came with warrior strife
    and clangor;
    You left our South one gory burial
        ground;
But love, more potent than your haughti-
    est anger,
    Subdues the souls which hate could
        only wound!

———◆———

THE RETURN OF PEACE.

[Written by request of the committee of
arrangements, for the opening ceremonies of
the International Cotton Exposition, in At-
lanta, Georgia, Oct. 5, 1881.

I HAD a vision at that mystic hour,
    When in the ebon garden of the Night,
Blooms the Cimmerian flower
    Of doubt and darkness, cowering from
        the light.

I seemed to stand on a vast lonely
    height,
    Above a city ravished and o'erthrown,
The air about me one long lingering
    moan
Of lamentation like a dreary sea
Scourged by the storm to murmurous
    weariness;
    Then, from dim levels of mist-folded
        ground
    Borne upward suddenly.
Burst the deep-rolling stress
    Of jubilant drums, blent with the sil-
        very sound
Of long-drawn bugle notes — the clash of
    swords
    (Outflashed by alien lords) —
And warrior-voices wild with victory.

They could not quell the grieved and
    shuddering air,
That breathed about me its forlorn de-
    spair:
It almost seemed as if stern Triumph
    sped
To one whose hopes were dead,
And flaunting there his fortune's ruddier
    grace,
Smote — with a taunt — wan Misery in
    the face!

    Lo! far away,
(For now my dream grows clear as lu-
    minous day,)
The victor's camp-fires gird the city
    round;
But she, unrobed, discrowned —
A new Andromeda, beside the main
    Of her own passionate pain;
    Bowed, naked, shivering low —
Veils the soft gleam of melancholy eyes,
    Yet lovelier in their woe, —
Alike from hopeless earth and hopeless
    skies.
No Perseus, for her sake, serenely fleet,
Shall cleave the heavens with winged
    and shining feet: —
    Ah me! the maid is lost —
    For sorrow, like keen frost

Shall eat into her being's anguished
core —
Atlanta (not Andromeda in this),
What outside helper can bring back her
bliss ?
Can re-illume, beyond its storm-built
bar,
Her youth's auroral star,
Or wake the aspiring heart that sleeps
forever more.

O! lying prophet of a sombre mood,
This city of our love
Is no poor, timorous dove,
To crouch and die unstruggling in the
mire;
If, for a time, she yields to force and fire,
Blinded by battle-smoke, and drenched
with blood,
Still must that dauntless hardihood
Drawn to her veins from out the iron
hills,
(Nerving the brain that toils, the soul
that wills,)
Shake off the lotus-languishment of
grief!
I see her rise and clasp her old belief,
In God and goodness — with imperial
glance,
Face the dark front of frowning Circum-
stance, —
While trusting only to her strong right
arm
To wrench from deadly harm,
All civic blessings and fair fruits of
peace!
High-souled to gain (despite her
ravished years),
And dragon-forms of monstrous doubts
and fears,
The matchless splendor of Toil's " golden
fleece!"

I see her rise, and strive with strenuous
hands firmly to lay
The fresh foundations of a nobler
sway —
War-wasted lands
Laden with ashes, gray and desolate —

Touched by the charm of some regener-
ate fate —
Flush into golden harvests prodigal;
Set by the steam-god's fiery passion free,
I hear the rise and fall
Of ponderous iron-clamped machinery,
Shake, as with earthquake thrill, the
factory halls;
While round the massive walls
Slow vapor, like a sinuous serpent
steals —
Through which revolve in circles,
great or small,
The deafening thunders of the tireless
wheels!

Far down each busy mart
That throbs and heaves as with a human
heart
Quick merchants pass, some debonair
and gay,
With undimmed, youthful locks —
Some wrinkled, sombre, gray —
But all with one accord
Dreaming of him — their lord —
The mighty monarch of the realm of
stocks!
And year by year her face more frankly
bright,
Glows with the ardor of the bloodless
fight
For bounteous empire o'er her
cherished South.
More sweet the smile upon her maiden
mouth,
Just rounding to rare curves of woman-
hood:
Because all unwithstood
The magic of her power and stately pride
Hath called from many a clime
Of tropic sunshine and of winter rime,
The world's skilled art and science to
her side;
Hence from her transient tomb,
Three lustra since, a hideous spot to
see —
Grows the majestic tree
Of heightened and green-leaved pros-
perity.

Hence, her broad gardens bloom
With rose and lily, and all flowers of
    balm.
    And hence above the lines
Of her vast railways, droop the laden
    vines —
A luscious largess thro' the summer
    calm!

.   .   .   .   .

Feeling her veins sc full of lusty blood,
    That pulsed within them like a rhyth-
        mic flood,
And eager for sweet sisterhood, — the
    bond
        Blissful and fond,
That yet may hold all nations in its
    thrall,
    Atlanta — from a night of splendid
        dreams,
Roused by soft kisses of the morning
    beams,
        Decreed a glorious festival
        Of art and commerce in her brave
            domain;
She sent her summons on the courier
    breeze;
        Or thro' the lightning wingèd wire
        Flashed forth her soul's desire: —
            Swiftly it passed,
O'er native hills and streams and prairies
    vast, —
    And o'er waste barriers of dividing
        seas
'Till from all quarters, like quick tongues
    of flame,
That warm, but burn not, — cordial an-
    swers came,
    And waftage of benignant messages.

Thus, thus it is a mighty concourse
    meets
O'erflowing squares and streets —
Borne at flood-tide toward the guarded
    ground,
Where treasures of two hemispheres are
    found,
To tax the inquiring mind, the curious
    eye!
Grain of the upland and damp river-bed,

In yellow stalks, or sifted meal for
    bread;
Unnumbered births of Ceres clustered
    nigh;
    Beholding which — as touched by
        tropic heat, —
(The old-world picture never *can* grow
    old,
    Nor the deep love that thrills it dumb
        and cold) —
Clear fancy looks on Boaz in the wheat,
    And in her simple truth,
    The tender eyes of Ruth
Holding the garnered fragments at his
    feet!

But piled o'er all, thro' many an un-
    bound bale
Peering to show its snow-white softness
    pale,
— Snow-white, yet warm, and destined
    to be furled
    In some auspicious day,
    For which we yearn and pray,
Round half the naked misery of the
    world,
A fleece more rich than Jason's, glances
    down.
Ah! well we know no monarch's jewelled
    crown,
    No marvellous koh-i-noor,
Won, first perchance, from gulfs of
    human gore,
Or life-toil of swart millions, gaunt and
    poor,
        Hath e'er outshone its peerless sover-
            eignty.

.   .   .   .   .

The wings of song unfold
Towards thy noontide-gold;
The eyes of song are clear,
(Turned on thy broadening sphere)
To mark, oh! city of the midland-weald,
And follow thy fair fortunes far afield —
    The years unborn,
    Doubtless must bring to thee
Trials to test thy spirit's constancy;
(While unthrift aliens wear the mask of
    scorn)

Financial shocks without thee and within:
Wrought by shrewd moneyed Shylocks hot to win
Their brazen game of monstrous usury;
Ravage of bandit "rings" whose boundless maw
Can swallow all things glibly, save — the law!
    And many a subtler ill
    Sudden and subtle as the ambush laid,

By black-browed "stranglers" 'mid an Orient glade;
    But thou, with keenest will,
Shalt cut the bonds of stealthy fraud apart,
And if force fronts thee with a murderous blade,
Pierce the rash son of Anak to the heart!

    Oh! queen! thy brilliant horoscope
    Was cast by Helios in the halls of hope;

"War-wasted lands . . .
Touched by the charm of some regenerate fate —
Flush into golden harvests prodigal."

And hope becomes fulfilment, as thy tread —
Firm, placed between the living and the dead —
    Wins the high grade which owns a heavenward slope;
    For force and fraud undone,
    And stormless summits won.
In thee I view heaven's purpose perfected:
    Thou shalt be empress of all peaceful ties,
    All potent industries,

All world-embracing magnanimities;
A warrior-queen no more, but mailed in love,
    Thy spear a fulgent shaft of sunsteeped grain;
Thy shield a buckler, the field-fairies wove
    Of strong green grasses, in the silvery noon
    Of some full harvest-moon,
Thy stainless crown, red roses, blent with white!
Now, throned above the half-forgotten pain

Of dreadful war, and war's remorseless
blight,
Thy heart-throbs glad and great,
Sending through all thy Titan-statured
state,
Fresh life and gathering tides of grander
power
From glorious hour to hour,
Thousands thy deeds shall bless
With strenuous pride, toned down to
tenderness:
Shall bless thy deeds, exalt thy name;
Till every breeze that sweeps from hill
to lea,
And every wind that furrows the deep
sea,
Shall waft the fragrance of thy soul
abroad
The sweetness and the splendor of thy
fame: —
For thou, midmost a large and opulent
store,
Of all things wrought to meet a nation's
need,
Thou, nobly pure,
Of any darkening taint of selfish greed,—
Wert pre-ordained to be
Purveyor of divinest charity, —
The love-commissioned almoner of God.

---◆---

YORKTOWN CENTENNIAL LYRIC.

[Written at the request of the Yorktown Cen-
tennial Commission, appointed by Congress,
to conduct the celebration of the surrender of
Lord Cornwallis, to the combined forces of
France and America, upon the 19th of Oct. 1781,
at Yorktown, Va.]

HARK, hark! down the century's long
reaching slope
To those transports of triumph, those
raptures of hope,
The voices of main and of mountain
combined
In glad resonance borne on the wings of
the wind,

The bass of the drum and the trumpet
that thrills
Through the multiplied echoes of jubi-
lant hills.
And mark how the years melting up-
ward like mist
Which the breath of some splendid en-
chantment has kissed,
Reveal on the ocean, reveal on the shore
The proud pageant of conquest that
graced them of yore,
When blended forever in love as in
fame
See, the standard which stole from the
starlight its flame,
And type of all chivalry, glory, romance,
The lilies, the luminous lilies of France.

Oh, stubborn the strife ere the conflict
was won!
And the wild whirling war wrack half
stifled the sun.
The thunders of cannon that boomed
on the lea,
But re-echoed far thunders pealed up
from the sea,
Where guarding his sea lists, a knight
on the waves,
Bold De Grasse kept at bay the bluff
bull-dogs of Graves.
The day turned to darkness, the night
changed to fire,
Still more fierce waxed the combat,
more deadly the ire,
Undimmed by the gloom, in majestic
advance,
Oh, behold where they ride o'er the red
battle tide,
Those banners united in love as in
fame,
The brave standard which drew from
the star-beams their flame,
And type of all chivalry, glory, romance,
The lilies, the luminous lilies of France.

No respite, no pause; by the York's
tortured flood,
The grim Lion of England is writhing
in blood.

Cornwallis may chafe and coarse Tarleton aver,
As he sharpens his broadsword and buckles his spur,
" *This blade, which so oft has reaped rebels like grain,*
Shall now harvest for death the rude yeomen again. "
Vain boast! for ere sunset he's flying in fear,
With the rebels he scouted close, close in his rear,
While the French on his flank hurl such volleys of shot
That e'en Gloucester's redoubt must be growing too hot.
Thus wedded in love as united in fame,
Lo! the standard which stole from the starlight its flame,
And type of all chivalry, glory, romance,
The lilies, the luminous lilies of France.

O morning superb! when the siege reached its close;
See! the sundawn outbloom, like the alchemist's rose!
The last wreaths of smoke from dim trenches upcurled,
Are transformed to a glory that smiles on the world.
Joy, joy! Save the wan, wasted front of the foe,
With his battle-flags furled and his arms trailing low; —
Respect for the brave! In stern silence they yield,
And in silence they pass with bowed heads from the field.
Then triumph transcendent! so Titan of tone
That some vowed it must startle King George on his throne.

When Peace to her own, timed the pulse of the land,
And the war weapon sank from the war-wearied hand,
Young Freedom upborne to the height of the goal

She had yearned for so long with deep travail of soul,
A song of her future raised, thrilling and clear,
Till the woods leaned to hearken, the hill slopes to hear: —
Yet fraught with all magical grandeurs that gleam
On the hero's high hope, or the patriot's dream,
What future, tho' bright, in cold shadow shall cast
The proud beauty that haloes the brow of the past.
Oh! wedded in love, as united in fame,
See the standard which stole from the starlight its flame,
And type of all chivalry, glory, romance,
The lilies, the luminous lilies of France.

ON THE PERSECUTION OF THE JEWS IN RUSSIA.

" Be advised! Do not trample upon my people. *Nations and men that oppress us do not thrive.*" — *From Charles Reade's " Never Too Late to Mend.*"

WHAT murmurs are these that so wofully rise
  Into heart-storms of agony borne from afar ?
A tempest of passion, a tumult of sighs ?
There is dread on the earth, and stern grief in the skies,
  While the nations, appalled, watch the realm of the Czar!

Can humanity's sun have gone down in an hour,
  Or a fiend have struck mercy's soft key-note ajar,
That upwhirled on the fierce winds of madness and power,
This cloud — with its hail of harsh hatreds — should lower
  O'er those who still call on their " father," the Czar ?

Can hell have burst upward, and
  spawned from its womb
The worst of all demons that menace
  and mar?
O God! see an empire recking in
  gloom —
Hark! the death-shock, the shriek, the
  wild volleys of doom —
Ay! the riot of hell shakes the land of
  the Czar!

The fields are flame-girdled, the rivers
  roll red
Through the sulphurous fumes and
  swift ravage of war,
A war on the helpless, unhelmeted head,
Which tortures the living and spares not
  the dead;
Is he sleeping, or dumb, their "good
  father" the Czar?

Ah, no! — through the corridors stately
  and vast
Of his palace that gleams like a pale
  polar star,
On a gale from the south these black
  tidings have passed:
He hears! and the lightnings of justice
  at last
Quiver hissing and hot in the hand of
  the Czar!

The world holds its breathing to mark
  them in flame
On their limitless course that no bul-
  wark can bar;
But instead, through his wily state par-
  asite came
A rescript so false, its unspeakable
  shame
Should haunt to his death the dark
  dreams of the Czar!

No word for the victims, all butchered
  and bare,
By the hearth-stone defiled, and the
  blood-tainted lar;
For the poor ravished maid, whose sole
  shroud is her hair;

For the mother's lament, or the father's
  despair:
No pity for such thrills the thought of
  the Czar;

But his spirit leans, tender and yearn-
  ing, above
The mad helots who riot, rage, murder
  afar;
To them he is soft as a nest-brooding
  dove;
But the *murdered!* alas! *they* are
  stinted of love,
Right, justice, or ruth, in the creed of
  the Czar!

Shall grim carnage goad onward, em-
  bruted and base,
The black coursers that strain at her
  iron-wrought car,
While those of high purpose and fetter-
  less race
Idly gaze on the foul mediæval disgrace
Which poisons all earth from yon
  realm of the Czar?

Wake, England, your thunders! America,
  fling
To the wind the shrewd statecrafts
  that hamper, or mar!
Blend your voices of wrath! your deep
  warnings outring,
To smite the dulled ears, and blind soul
  of the king —
Who rules — Heaven help them!
  those realms of the Czar!

———◆———

ASSASSINATION.

O BLINDED readers of the scroll of
  time,
Think ye that freedom yields her hand
  to crime?

Or the fair whiteness of her virginal
  bud
Of heavenly hope, would desecrate with
  blood?

Her eyes are chastened lightnings, and
  the fire
Of her divinely purified desire

Burns not in ambush by assassins
  trod,
But on the holiest mountain heights of
  God!

So, ye that fain would meet her fond
  embrace,
Purge the base soul, unmask the
  treacherous face,

Drop bowl or dagger while ye bring her
  naught
But the grand worship of a selfless
  thought!

ENGLAND.

LAND of my father's love, my father's
  race,
  How long must I in weary exile
    sigh
To meet thee, O my empress, face to
  face,
  And kiss thy radiant robes before I
    die?

O England! in my creed, the humblest
  dust
  Beside thy haunted shores and shadowy
    streams,
Is touched by memories and by thoughts
  august,
  By golden histories and majestic
    dreams.

O England! to my mood thy lowliest
  flower
  Feeds on the smiles of some transcen-
    dent sky;
Thy frailest fern-leaf shrines a spell of
  power!
  Ah! shall I walk thy woodlands ere I
    die?

Thy sacred places, where dead heroes
  rest
  By temples set in ivy-twilight deep;
Thy fragrant fields topped by the sky-
  lark's crest;
  Thy hidden waters breathing balms of
    sleep:

Thy castled homes, and granges veiled
  afar
  In antique dells; thy ruins hoar and
    high;
Thy mountain tarns, each like a glitter-
  ing star,
  Shall I behold their marvels ere I die?

Thine opulent towns, throned o'er the
  subject-main,
  Girt by brave fleets, their weary canvas
    furled,
Deep-laden argosies through storm and
  strain,
  Borne from the utmost boundaries of
    the world

O'er all, thy London! every stone with
  breath
  Indued to question, counsel, or reply;
City of mightiest life and mightiest
  death,
  Shall I behold thy splendors ere I die?

But most I yearn, in body as heart, to
  bow
  Before our England's poets, strong and
    wise,
Watch some grand thought uplift the
  laureate's brow,
  And flash or fade in Swinburne's fiery
    eyes.

And other glorious minstrels would I
  greet
  Bound to my life by many a rhythmic
    tie,
When shall I hear their welcomes frankly
  sweet,
  And clasp those cordial hands, before
    I die?

Fair blow the breezes; high are sail and
    steam;
  Soon must I mark brave England's
    brightening lea;
Fulfilled at length, the large and lustrous
    dream
  Which lured me long across the sum-
    mer sea!

Alas! a moment's triumph! — false as
    vain!
O'er dreary hills the gaunt pines moan
    and sigh;
Pale grows my dream, pierced through
    by bodeful pain;
  England! I shall not see thee ere I
    die!

---◆---

TO LONGFELLOW.

(ON HEARING HE WAS ILL.)

O THOU, whose potent genius (like the
    sun
  Tenderly mellowed by a rippling
    haze)
  Hast gained thee all men's homage,
    love and praise,
Surely thy web of life is not outspun,
Thy glory rounded, thy last guerdon
    won!
  Nay, poet, nay! — from thought's calm
    sunset ways
May new-born notes of undegenerate
    lays
Charm back the twilight gloom ere day
    be done!

But past the poet crowned I see the
    friend —
  Frank, courteous, true — about whose
    locks of gray,
Like golden bees, some glints of summer
    stray;
  Clear-eyed, with lips half poised
    'twixt smile and sigh;
A brow in whose soul-mirroring man-
    hood blend
  Grace, sweetness, power and mag-
    nanimity!

"PHILIP MY KING." *

"PHILIP, my king," ay, still thou art a
    king,
  Though storms of sorrow on thy suf-
    fering head
  Have flashed and thundered through
    the midnight's dread;
Ah, lofty soul! fraught with the sky-
    lark's wing
To capture heaven, the sky-lark's voice
    to sing
Such notes ethereal through veiled
    brightness shed
  Their gracious power to liquid pathos
    wed,
Thrills like the soft rain-pulses of the
    spring:

Banned from earth's day — thine *inward*
    sight expands
  Above the night-bound senses' birth or
    bars;
Lord of a larger realm, of subtler scope,
Where thou at last shalt press the lips of
    Hope,
And feel God's angel lift in radiant
    hands
  Thy life from darkness to a place of
    stars!

Meanwhile, alas! despite these inward
    spells
  Of voice and vision, and fond hope
    to be,
  Perchance,—though vaguely shadowed
    forth to thee,—
Oft-times thy thought but echoes the
    deep knells
Of buried joy; oft-times thy spirit swells
  With moaning memories, like a smitten
    sea,
  When the worn tempest wandering up
    the lea,
Leaves a low wind to breathe its wild
    farewells.

---

* "*Philip my King*," Miss Mulock's exquisite
song, all lovers of poetry must recall. The
little hero of that lyric was Philip Marston,
the author's god-son.

O brother! — pondering dreary and apart
O'er the dead blossoms of deciduous years:
O poet! fed too long on bitter tears!

I waft, o'er seas, a white-winged courier-dove,
Bearing to thee this balmy spray of love,
Warm from the nested fragrance of my heart.

"Old passions may be purged of blood,
Old memories cannot die."

A PLEA FOR THE GRAY.

[A discussion has recently been inaugurated in the city of Mobile, Ala., among the military companies, as to the propriety of changing the *Gray* for the *Blue* or some other uniform.]

WHEN the land's martyr, mid her tears,
Outbreathed his latest breath,
The discord of long, festering years,
Lay also dumb in death:
Our souls a new-born friendship drew
With spells of kindliest sway;
At last, at last, the conquering Blue
Blent with the vanquished Gray!

Yet, *who* thro' this south-land of ours,
While faith and love are free,
But still must cast memorial flowers
Across the grave of Lee?
And oft their ancient grief renew
O'er "Stonewall's" cherished clay?
The heart that's pledged to guard the Blue
Must honor still the Gray!

O veterans of Potomac's flood,
  Or Vicksburg's lurid sky,
Old passions may be purged of blood,
  Old memories cannot die!
They fill your eyes with fiery dew,
  Revive your manhood's May,
And past the bright victorious Blue,
  Bring back the stainless Gray!

O martyrs of the desperate fight,
  All weak and broken now,
With shattered nerves, or blasted sight,
  Frail arms and furrowed brow!
What think ye of the *patriot* view
  Flashed on your minds to-day?
Too old to don the prosperous Blue,
  Ye clasp your tattered Gray!

From many a worn and wasted mound,
  And dust-encumbered clod,
The voices of dead heroes sound,
  Rising from earth to God!
"Our doom was dark, our lives were
    true,
  Ah! cast not quite away,
What time ye hail the favored Blue —
  Old dreams that crowned the Gray!"

Can honor in his sacred grave
  Less fair and glorious be?
Can faith on fortune's fickle wave,
  Change with the changeful sea?
Beware lest what ye rashly do
  Should end in shamed dismay,
And all pure champions of the Blue,
  Scorn traitors to the Gray!

UNION OF BLUE AND GRAY.

[Suggested by the recent visit of Governor
Bigelow and the Connecticut companies to
Charleston, South Carolina.]

THE Blue is marching south once more,
  With serried steel and stately tread;
Their martial music pealed before,
  Their flag of stars flashed overhead.

Ah! not through storm and stress they
    come,
The thunders of old hate are dumb,
And frank as clear October's ray
This meeting of the Blue and Gray.

A Phœnix from her outworn fires,
  Her gory ashes, rising free,
Fair Charleston with her stainless spires
  Gleams by the silver-stranded sea.
No hurtling hail nor hostile ball
Breaks through the treacherous battle-
    pall;
True voices speak from hearts as true,
For strife lies dead 'twixt Gray and Blue.

Grim Sumter, like a Titan maimed,
  Still glooms beyond his shattered keep;
But where his bolts of lightning flamed
  There broods a quiet, mild as sleep;
His granite base, long cleansed of blood,
Is circled by a golden flood.
Type of that peace whose sacred sway
Enfolds the Blue, exalts the Gray.

The sea-tides faintly rise afar,
  And — wings of all the breezes furled,
Seem slowly borne o'er beach and bar,
  Dream-murmurings from a spirit
    world,
Through throbbing drum and bugle-trill
The distant calm seems deeper still —
Deep as that faith whose cordial dew
Hath soothed the Gray and charmed the
    Blue.

O'er Ashley's breast the autumn smiles,
  All mellowed in her hazy fold,
While the white arms of languid isles
  Are girdled by ethereal gold.
All Nature whispers: war is o'er,
Fierce feuds have fled our sea and shore;
Old wrongs forget, old ties renew,
O heroes of the Gray and Blue!

The southern Palm and northern Pine
  No longer clash through leaf and
    bough;
Tranquillities of depth benign
  Have bound their blending foliage now,

Or, tranced by cloudless star and moon,
Serene they shine in sun-lit noon.
Their equal shadows softly play
Above the Blue, across the Gray.

THE KING OF THE PLOW.

THE sword is re-sheathed in its scab-
    bard,
    The rifle hangs safe on the wall;
No longer we quail at the hungry
    Hot rush of the ravenous ball,
The war-cloud has hurled its last light-
    ning,
    Its last awful thunders are still,
While the demon of conflict in Hades
    Lies fettered in force as in will:
Above the broad fields that he ravaged,
    What monarch rules blissfully now?
Oh! crown him with bays that are
    bloodless,
    The king, the brave king of the
        plow!

A king! ay! what ruler more potent
    Has ever swayed earth by his nod?
A monarch! aye, *more* than a monarch,
    A homely, but bountiful God!
He stands where in earth's sure protec-
    tion
    The seed-grains are scattered and
        sown,
To uprise in serene resurrection
    When spring her soft trumpet hath
        blown!
A monarch! yea, *more* than a monarch,
    Though toil-drops *are* thick on his
        brow;
O! crown him with corn-leaf and wheat-
    leaf,
    The king, the strong king of the
        plow!

Through the shadow and shine of past
    ages,
    (While tyrants were blinded with
        blood)

He reared the pure ensign of Ceres
    By meadow, and mountain, and
        flood,
And the long, leafy gold of his harvests
    The earth-sprites and air-sprites had
        spun,
Grew rhythmic when swept by the
        breezes,
    Grew royal, when kissed by the
        sun;
Before the stern charm of his patience
    What rock-rooted forces must bow!
Come! crown him with corn-leaf and
    wheat-leaf,
    The king, the bold king of the plow!

Through valleys of balm-drooping
        myrtles,
    By banks of Arcadian streams,
Where the wind-songs are set to the
        mystic
    Mild murmur of passionless dreams;
On the storm-haunted uplands of Thule,
    By ice-girdled fiords and floes,
Alike speeds the spell of his god-
        hood,
    The bloom of his heritage glows;
A monarch! yea, *more* than a monarch,
    All climes to his prowess must bow;
Come crown him with bays that are
        stainless,
    The king, the brave king of the
        plow.

Far, far in earth's uttermost future,
    As boundless of splendor as scope,
I see the fair angel!—fruition,
    Outspeed his high heralds of hope;
The roses of joy rain around him,
    The lilies of sweetness and calm,
For the sword has been changed to the
        plowshare,
    The lion lies down with the lamb!
O! angel-majestic! We know thee,
    Though raised and transfigured art
        thou,
This lord of life's grand consumma-
        tion
    Was once the swart king of the plow!

IN MEMORIAM.

I.

LONGFELLOW DEAD.

Ay, it is well! Crush back your selfish
        tears;
For from the half-veiled face of earthly
        spring
Hath he not risen on heaven-aspiring
        wing
To reach the spring-tide of the eternal
        years ?

With life full-orbed, he stands amid his
        peers,
The grand immortals! a fair, mild-eyed
        king,
Flushing to hear their potent welcomes
        ring
Round the far circle of those luminous
        spheres.

Mock not his heavenly cheer with mor-
        tal wail,
Unless some human-hearted nightin-
        gale,
Pierced by grief's thorn, shall give such
        music birth
That he, the new-winged soul, the
        crowned and shriven,
May lean beyond the effulgent verge of
        heaven,
To catch his own sweet requiem, borne
        from earth!

Such marvellous requiem were a pæan
        too —
(Woe touched and quivering with
        triumphant fire);
For him whose course flashed always
        high and higher,
Is lost beyond the strange, mysterious
        blue:
Ah! yet, we murmur, *can* this thing be
        true ?
Forever silent here, that tender lyre,
Tuned to all gracious themes, all pure
        desire,
Whose notes dropped sweet as honey,
        soft as dew ?

No tears! you say — since rounded,
        brave, complete,
The poet's work lies radiant at God's
        feet.
Nay! nay! our hearts with grief *must*
        hold their tryst:
How dim grows all about us and above!
Vainly we grope through death's bewil-
        dering mist,
To feel once more his clasp of *human*
        love!

II.

ON THE DEATH OF PRESIDENT GARFIELD.

I see the Nation, as in antique ages,
        Crouched with rent robes, and ashes
        on her head:
Her mournful eyes are deep with dark
        presages,
        Her soul is haunted by a formless
        dread!

"O God!" she cries, "why hast Thou
        left me bleeding,
        Wounded and quivering to the heart's
        hot core ?
Can fervid faith, winged prayer, and
        anguished pleading
        Win balm and pity from thy heavens
        no more ?

"I knelt, I yearned, in agonizing pas-
        sion,
        Breathless to catch thy 'still small
        voice' from far;
Now thou *hast* answered, but in awful
        fashion,
        And stripped our midnight of its last
        pale star.

"What tears are given me in o'ermas-
        tering measure,
        From fathomless floods of Marah,
        darkly free,
While that pure life I held my noblest
        treasure
        Is plunged forever in death's tideless
        sea!

"Hark to those hollow sounds of lam-
    entation,
  The muffled music, the funereal bell;
From far and wide on wings of desola-
    tion
  Float wild and wailful voices of fare-
    well.

"The North-land mourns her grief in
    full libation,
  Outpoured for him who died at vic-
    tory's goal;
And the great West, in solemn ministra-
    tion,
  May not recall her hero's shining
    soul.

"Yea, the North mourns; the West; a
    stricken mother,
  Droops as in sackcloth with veiled
    brow and mouth;
And what old strifes, what waning hates,
    can smother
  The generous heart-throbs of the pity-
    ing South?

"Did doubt remain? — *She* crushed its
    latest ember
  At that stern moment when the vic-
    tim's fall
Changed loveliest summer to a grim De-
    cember,
  Paled by the hiss of Guiteau's murder-
    ous ball.

"Thus by the spell of one vast grief
    united
  (Where cypress boughs their death-
    cold shadows wave),
My sons, I trust, a holier faith have
    plighted,
  And sealed the compact by *his* sacred
    grave."

.   .   .   .   .

'Twas thus she spoke; but still in pros-
    trate sorrow,
  While lowlier earthward drooped her
    brow august.

To-day is dark; vague darkness clouds
    to-morrow.
  Ah! in God's hand the nations are
    but — dust!

III.

DEAN STANLEY.

DEAD! dead! in sooth his marbled brow
    is cold,
  And prostrate lies that brave, majestic
    head;
True! his stilled features own death's
    arctic mould,
  Yet, by Christ's blood, I know he is
    not dead!

Here fades the cast-off vestment that he
    wore,
  The robe of flesh, whence his true self
    hath fled;
Whate'er be false, one faith holds fast
    and sure,
  Great souls like his abide not with the
    dead:

Eyried with God, beyond all mortal pain,
  Breathing the effluence of ethereal
    birth,
Through deeds divine, his spirit walks
    again,
  On rhythmic feet the mournful paths
    of earth!

In heaven immortal, yet on earth su-
    preme,
  The glamour of his goodness still sur-
    vives,
Not in vain glimpses of a flattering
    dream,
  But flower and fruit of ransomed hu-
    man lives.

His hopes were ocean-wide, and clasped
    mankind;
  No Levite plea his mercy turned apart,
But wounded souls — to whom all else
    were blind —
  He soothed with wine and balsam of
    the heart.

With stainless hands he reared his Mas-
ter's cross;
His Master's watchword pealed o'er
land and sea;
And still through days of gain, and days
of loss,
Proclaimed the golden truce of char-
ity.

All men were brethren to his larger creed,
But given the thought sincere — the
earnest aim;
God's garden will not spurn the humblest
weed
That yearns for purer air and loftier
flame.

This sweet evangel of the unborn years,
Seer-like he spake, as one that viewed
his goal,
While the world felt through darkness
and through tears,
Mysterious music thrill its raptured
soul.

Dead! nay, not dead! while eagle
thoughts aspire,
Clothed in winged deeds across the
empyreal height,
And all the expanding space is flushed
with fire,
And deep on deep, heaven opens to
our sight,—

He *cannot* die! yet o'er his dust we shed
Our rain of human sorrow; on his
breast
Cross the pale palms; and pulseless heart
and head
Leave to the quiet of his cloistered
rest.

Sleep, knightly scholar! warrior-saint,
repose!
Thy life-force folded like an unfurled
sail!
Spent is time's rage —its foam of crested
woes —
And thou hast found, at last, the Holy
Grail!

IV.

HIRAM H. BENNER.

[Dedicated to the Wife of this Hero and
Martyr.]

WHEN the war-drums beat and the trum-
pets blare,
When banners flaunt in the stormy
air,
When at thought of the deeds that must
soon be done,
The hearts of a thousand leap up as
one,
Who could not rush through the din and
smoke,
The cannon's crash and the sabre stroke,
Scarce conscious of ebbing blood or
breath,
With a laugh for wounds and a scoff at
death?

But when on the sullen breeze there
comes
No thrill of trumpets nor throb of drums,
But only the wail of the sick laid low
By the treacherous blight of a viewless
foe —
Who, then, will upgird his loins for fight
With the loathsome pest in the poisoned
night,
No martial music his pulse to start,
But the still, small voice of the ruthful
heart?
Who then? Behold him, the calm, the
brave,
On his billowy path to an alien grave!
Serene in the charm of his God-like
will,
This soldier is armored to save, not kill.
Ah! swiftly he speeds on the mist-bound
stream
This pilgrim wrapped in his tender
dream,
His vision of help for the sick laid low
By the evil spell of an ambushed foe.

Ah! swiftly he speeds 'mid the hollow
boom
Of bells that are tolling to death and
doom.

Till even the sounds of the bells grow
    still;
For the hands of their ringers are lax
    and chill.
And the hum of the mourners is heard
    no more
On the misty slope and the vacant shore,
And the few frail creatures that greet
    him seem
But the ghosts of men by a phantom
    stream.

Still the hero his own great soul enticed
To suffer and toil in the name of Christ,
He follows wherever his Lord had led,
To the famished hut or the dying bed.
He medicines softly the fevered pain;
To the starving he bringeth his golden
    grain;
And ever before him and ever above
Is the sheen of the unfurled wings of
    love.

Meanwhile, in his distant home are those
That his going has robbed of their sweet
    repose.
The days pass by them like leaden years;
The nights are bitter with tears and
    fears —
Till at last, by the lightning glamour
    sped,
Comes a name and date, with the one
    word, " Dead!"
And the arms of the smitten are lifted
    high,
And the heavens are rent by an anguished
    cry!

Dead! dead! Vain word for the wise to
    hear!
How false its echo on heart and ear!
To the earth and earth's he may close
    his eyes,
But who dares tell us a martyr dies?
And of him just gone it were best to say
That in some charmed hour of night or
    day —
Having given us all that his soul could
    give —
Brave Hiram Benner began to live.

V.

W. GILMORE SIMMS.

A POEM

Delivered on the night of the 13th of December, 1877 "at the Charlestown Academy of Music," as prologue to the "Dramatic Entertainment" in aid of the "Simms Memorial fund."

THE swift mysterious seasons rise and
    set;
The omnipotent years pass o'er us,
    bright or dun; —
Dawns blush, and mid-days burn, 'till
    scarce aware
Of what deep meaning haunts our
    twilight air,
We pause bewildered, yearning for the
    sun;
Only to find in that strange evening-
    tide,
By the last sunset pathos sanctified,
Pale memory near us, and divine re-
    gret!

Then memory gently takes us by the
    hand;
And doubtful boundaries of a faded
    time,
Half veiled in mist and rime,
Emerge, grow bright, expand;
The past becomes the present to our
    eyes;
Poor slaves of dust and death,
(As if some trump of resurrection
    clear
Somewhere outpealed, *our* senses could
    not hear)
Rise, freed from churchyard taint and
    mortal stain;
Old friends! dear comrades! *have* we
    met again ?
God! how these dismal years
Of anguished desolation, and veiled
    tears,
Of fettered feeling, and despondent
    sighs,
Wither and shrivel like a parchment
    scroll

Seized by the fury of consuming fire,
Before the rapture of the illumined
    soul,
Lifted and lightened by our love's
    desire!

Old friends! dear comrades! _have_ we
    met once more?
Come! let us fondly mark
In this weird truce, whose moments
    soon must flee,
'Twixt the charmed heart and dread
    reality,
Those well-belovéd features that ye wore
Once on this earthly shore,
Now rescued from the void and treach-
    erous dark!
O! faces soft or strong,
Familiar faces! how ye press and throng
Closely about us, while the enchanted
    light
Changes to noonday our long spiritual
    night!
The faithful eyes that beamed in ours of
    yore,
Shine on us in their ancient guileless
    way,
Undimmed, unshorn of _one_ beneficent
    ray,
And vital seeming as our own, to-day;
Lips smile, as once they smiled with
    innocent zest,
    When round the social board
The impetuous flood-tide poured
Of curbless mirth, and keen sparkling
    jest
Vanished like wine-foam on its golden
    crest!
    We feel the loyal grasp
Of many a warm hand, yielding clasp
    for clasp;
But may not stay, alas! we may not
    stay
    To greet ye one by one,
Comrades! returned from realms beyond
    the sun;
For lo! in rightful precedence of power,
"A Saul amongst his brethren," than
    the rest

Loftier, if ruder in his natural might,
The man who toiled through fortune's
    bitterest hour,
As calmly steadfast and supremely
    brave,
As if above a fair life's tranquil wave.
Brooded the halcyon with unruffled
    breast;
The man whose sturdy frame upheld
    aright,
We meet, (O friends), to consecrate to-
    night!

All pregnant powers that wait
On intellectual state.
Favored and loved him; earliest, dear-
    est came
Imagination, robed in mystical flame;
Her clear eyes searching all created
    things
Heavenly and earthly; with vast breadth
    of wings
Engirdled by the magic of a spell ineffa-
    ble;
And like the sportive nymph of wood-
    land bowers.
Fancy stole on him coyly, pranked with
    flowers,
Whereof the fairest her white fingers
    shed,
To crown his bended head.
Bluff humor true, if broad,
Placed in his hand a mirth-evoking rod,
While satire, from the heights of reason
    proud,
Flashed a keen gleam, like lightning from
    a cloud
The levin-bolt so sheerly cuts in two,
The cloud disparts, to leave — a lumi-
    nous blue!

All that he was, all that he owned, we
    know
Was lavished freely on _one_ sacred
    shrine,
The shrine of home and country! from
    the first
Fresh blush of youth, when merged in
    sanguine glow,

His life-path seemed a shadowless steep
  to shine,
Leading forever upward to the stars;
Through many a desperate and embit-
  tered strife
  That raging, rose and burst
Above the storm-wracked waste of mid-
  dle-life.

Down to the day, a few sad years ago,
When a grave veteran with his age's
  scars,
He moved among us, like a Titan
  maimed;
  Only *one* glorious goal,
Through fate, grief, change, the pure al-
  legiance claimed

" Pale memory near us."

Of his unconquered and majestic soul;
The goal of honor; not that *he* might
  rise
Alone and dominant; *but that all men's
  eyes*
*Might view, perchance through much
  brave toil of his,*
His country stripped of every filthy weed
*Of crime imputed ; in thought, word and
  deed,*
A noble people, none would dare despise
  In their unsullied *Palingenesis,*
  (Which he with blissful awe,

And all a poet's prescient faith foresaw;)
A *noble people,* o'er their subject-lands
Ruling with constant hearts and stain-
  less hands;
Their feet firm planted as McGregor's
  were,
Deep in the herbage of their native sod,
And every honest forehead free to rear
  A front unquelled by fear,
Untouched by shame, unfurrowed by
  despair, —
High in man's sight, or bowed alone to
  God!

So, let us rear the shaft, and poise the
　　bust
Above the mouldering, but ah! priceless
　　dust
Of vanished genius! Let our homage be
Large as that splendid prodigality
Of force and love, wherewith he
　　stanchly wrought
Out from the quarries of his own deep
　　thought,
Unnumbered shapes; whether of good or
　　ill,
No puny puppets whose false action
　　frets
On a false stage, like feeble *Marion-
　　ettes;*
　　But life-like, human still;
Types of a by-gone age of crime and
　　lust;
Or, grand historic forms, in whom we
　　view
Re-vivified, and re-created stand,
The braves who strove through cloud-
　　encompassed ways,
Infinite travail, and malign dispraise,
To guard, to save, to wrench from tyrant
　　hordes,
By the pen's virtue, or the lordlier
　　sword's
Unravished Liberty,
The virgin huntress on a virgin strand!

I, through whose song your hearts have
　　spoken to-night,
Soul-present with you, yet am far away;
Outside my exile's home, I watch the
　　sway
Of the bowed pine-tops in the gloaming
　　gray,
Casting across the melancholy lea,
　　A tint of browner blight;
Outside my exile's home, borne to and
　　fro,
I hear the inarticulate murmurs flow
Of the faint wind-tides breathing like a
　　sea;
When, in clear vision, softly dawns on
　　me,
(As if in contrast with yon slow decay),

The loveliest land that smiles beneath
　　the sky,
The coast-land of our Western Italy;
I view the waters quivering; quaff the
　　breeze,
Whose briny raciness keeps an *under*
　　taste
Of flavorous tropic sweets (perchance
　　swept home,
　　Across the flickering waste
Of summer waves, capped by the Ariel
　　foam),
From Cuba's perfumed groves, and gar-
　　den spiceries!

Along the horizon-line a vapor swims,
Pale rose and amethyst, melting into
　　gold;
Up to our feet the fawning ripples rolled,
Glimmer an instant, tremble, lapse,
　　and die;
The whole rare scene, its every element
Etherealized, transmuted subtly, blent
　　By viewless alchemy,
Into the glory of a golden mood,
Brings potent exaltations, while I walk.
　　(A joyful youth again),
The snow-white beaches by the Atlant.c
　　Main!
Ah! *not* alone! the carking curse of
　　Time
Far from him yet; his bold hopes unsub-
　　dued
By the long anguish of the woes to be,
Midmost his years, in mellow-hearted
　　prime,
Beside me stands our stalwart-statured
　　Simms!

See! what a Viking's mien!
Half tawny locks in careless masses
　　curled
Over his ample forehead's massive dome!
Eyes of bold outlook, that sometimes
　　beneath
Their level-fronted brows, shine lam-
　　bent, deep,
With inspirations scarce aroused from
　　sleep;

And sometimes rife with ire,
Sent forth as sword-blades from an un-
    bared sheath,
    Flashes of sudden fire!
His whole air breathes of combat, unse-
    rene
Profounds of feeling, by a scornful world
Too early stirred to impotent disdains;
Generous withal; bound by all liberal ties
Of lordly-natured magnanimities;
    Whereof we mark the sign
In the curved fullness of a mobile
    mouth,
Almost voluptuous; hinting of the
    south,
Whose suns high summer shed through
    all his veins:
Blending the mildness of a cordial grace
With sterner traits of his Berserker face,
    Firm-set as granite, haughty, leo-
    nine.

No prim Precisian he! his fluent talk
Roved thro' all topics, vivifying all;
Now deftly ranging level plains of
    thought,
To sink, anon in metaphysical deeps;
Whence, by caprice of strange transition
    brought
Outward and upward, the free current
    sought
Ideal summits, gathering in its course,
Splendid momentum and imperious
    force,
Till, down it rushed as mighty cataracts
    fall,
    Hurled from gaunt mountain steeps!

Sportive he could be as a gamesome boy!
By heaven! as 'twere but yesterday, I
    see
His tall frame quake with throes of jolli-
    ty;
Hear his rich voice that owned a jovial
    tone,
    Jocund as Falstaff's own;
And catch moist glints of steel-blue eyes
    o'errun
Sideways, by tiny rivulets of fun!

Alas! this vivid vision slowly fades!
Its serious beauty, and its flush of joy
Pass into nothingness! . . . Stern
    Death resumes
His sombre empire in the dusk of
    tombs;
And the deep umbrage of the cypress
    glades
    Is wanly, coldly cast
In lengthening gloom o'er the reburied
    past!
What then? the spirit of him
We mourn and fain would honor, grows
    not dim;
On earth will live with consummated
    toil
Worthily wrought, despite the hot tur-
    moil
Of open enmity, the secret guile,
That mole-like burrowed 'neath the
    fruitful soil
Of his broad mental acres, but to show
Marks of its crawling littleness between,
    Each far-extended row
Of those hale harvests, glittering gold or
    green!

And somewhere, *somewhere* in the infi-
    nite space,
Like all true souls by our Soul-Father
    prized,
It dwells *forever individualized;*
No ghost bewildered 'midst a "No
    Man's Land;"
    Outlawed and banned
Of fair identity's redeeming grace,
Shivering before its wretched phantom
    self,
Marred by Lethean moonshine — a pale
    elf,
A passionless shadow, but in mind and
    heart,
The mortal creature's marvellous coun-
    terpart;
Only exalted, nobler; down on us
Gazing thro' fathomless ethers lumi-
    nous;
Watching the earth and earth-ways
    from afar,

Perhaps with somewhat of a scornful
　　smile;
Yet tempered by the tolerance which be-
　　seems
One long translated from *our* sphere of
　　dreams,
　　Hollow illusions, vacant vanities,
To that vast actual, which beyond us
　　lies,
Where who may guess? midst yonder
　　opulent skies;
Clear "coigns of vantage," in some
　　deathless star!

VI.

DICKENS.

METHINKS the air
Throbs with the tolling of harmonious
　　bells,
　　Rung by the hands of spirits; every-
　　where
　　We feel the presence of a soft despair
And thrill to voices of divine farewells.

Sweet Fancy lost,
Wandering in darkness, now makes sil-
　　very moan;
　　While Pathos, pale, and shadowy, like
　　a ghost,
　　Sobs upon Humor's breast, that
　　mourns him most,
The wizard king who leaves them all —
　　alone.

Wan genii throng,
From earth's four quarters hurrying,
　　mount and mart,
　　Pure woodland peace, the city's din
　　and wrong.
　　Each breathing low a fond funereal
　　song,
Each sadly bowed o'er that grand, silent
　　heart.

The children's tears
Mingle with manhood's woe, that falls
　　like rain;
　　Low lieth one who towered above his
　　peers,

And nevermore, through all the fruit-
　　ful years,
Our eyes shall greet the master's like
　　again.

Creations fine,
His prodigal offspring, crowd so thickly
　　round
　　That Wit falls foul of Sorrow, Cupids
　　twine
　　Warm arms with Avarice, and Love's
　　strength divine
Hath vanquished Hate on Hate's own
　　chosen ground.

Though gone, his art
Triumphant spans the threatening clouds
　　of death;
　　Its rainbow hues forever pulse and
　　start,
　　Steeped in the life-blood of the human
　　heart,
And woven on heavens beyond Time's
　　stormy breath.

VII.

TO BAYARD TAYLOR BEYOND US.

A VISION OF CHRISTMAS EVE, 1878.

As here within I watch the fervid coals,
　　While the chill heavens without shine
　　wanly white,
I wonder, friend! in what rare realm of
　　souls,
　　You hail the uprising Christmas-tide
　　to-night!

I leave the fire-place, lift the curtain's
　　fold,
　　And peering past these shadowy win-
　　dow-bars,
See through broad rifts of ghostly clouds
　　unrolled,
　　The pulsing pallor of phantasmal
　　stars.

Phantoms they seem, glimpsed through
　　the clouded deep,
　　Till the winds cease, and cloudland's
　　ghastly glow

Gives place above to luminous calms of
  sleep,
  Beneath, to glittering amplitudes of
  snow!

Some stars like steely bosks on blazoned
  shields,
  Stud constellations measureless in
  might;
Some lily-pale, make fair the ethereal
  fields,
  In which, O friend, art thou ensphered
  to-night?

Where'er mid yonder infinite worlds it be,
  Its souls, I know, are clothed with
  wings of fire;
How wouldst *thou* scorn even Immor-
  tality,
  In whose dull rest thou couldst not
  still aspire!

There, Homer raised where genius can-
  not nod,
  Hears the orbed thunders of celestial
  seas;
And Shakespeare, lofty almost as a God,
  Smiles his large smile at Aristophanes;

With earth's supremest souls, still
  grouped apart,
  Great souls made perfect in the eternal
  noon,
There thy loved Goethe holds thee to his
  heart,
  Re-born to youth and all life's chords
  in tune.

While in the liberal air of that wide
  heaven,
  He whispers: "Come! we share the
  self-same height;
To me on earth thy noblest toils were
  given,
  Brothers, henceforth, we walk these
  paths of light."

Clear and more clear the radiant vision
  gleams!
  More bright grand shapes and glorious
  faces grow;

While like deep fugues of victory, heard
  in dreams,
  A thousand heavenly clarions seem to
  blow!

VIII.

BAYARD TAYLOR (UPON DEATH).

" More than once I have met death, but
without fear! Nor do I fear now! Without
being able to demonstrate it, I KNOW that my
soul cannot die. . . Indeed, to me the infinite
is more comprehensible than the finite ! "
  These words occur in a letter of Bayard
Taylor's to me, written not many weeks before
his death. They have suggested the following
sonnet : —

" OFT have I fronted Death, nor feared
  his might!
To me immortal, this dim Finite seems
Like some waste low-land, crossed by
  wandering streams
Whose clouded waves scarce catch our
  yearning sight:
Clearer by far, the imperial Infinite!
Though its ethereal radiance only gleams
In exaltations of majestic dreams,
Such dreams portray God's heaven of
  heavens aright!"
Thou blissful Faith! that on death's
  imminent brink
Thus much of heaven's mysterious truth
  hast told!
Soul-life aspires, though all the stars
  should sink;
Not vain our loftiest instinct's upward
  stress,
Nor hath the immortal hope shone clear
  and bold,
To quench at death, his torch in noth-
  ingness!

IX.

RICHARD H. DANA, SEN.

O DEEP grave eyes! that long have
  seemed to gaze
  On our low level from far loftier days,
O grand gray head! an aureole seemed to
  gird,
  Drawn from the spirit's pure, immacu-
  late rays!

At length death's signal sounds! From
    weary eyes
  Pass the pale phantoms of our earth
    and skies;
The gray head droops; the museful lips
    are closed
  On life's vain questionings and more
    vain replies!

Like some gaunt oak wert thou, that
    lonely stands
  'Mid fallen trunks in outworn desert
    lands;
Still sound at core, with rhythmic leaves
    that stir
  To soft swift touches of aerial hands.

Ah! long we viewed thee thus, forlornly
    free,
  In that dead grove the sole unravished
    tree;
Lo! the dark axe man smites! the oak
    lies low
  That towered in lonely calm o'er land
    and sea!

X.

BRYANT DEAD!

Lo! there he lies, our Patriarch Poet,
    dead!
  The solemn angel of eternal peace
Has waved a wand of mystery o'er his
    head,
  Touched his strong heart, and bade
    his pulses cease.

Behold in marble quietude he lies!
  Pallid and cold, divorced from earthly
    breath,
With tranquil brow, lax hands, and
    dreamless eyes,
  Yet the closed lips would seem to smile
    at death.

Well may they smile; for death, to such
    as he,
  Brings purer freedom, loftier thought
    and aim;

And, in grand truce with immortality,
  Lifts to song's fadeless heaven his
    star-like fame!

XI.

THE POLE OF DEATH.

IN MEMORY OF SIDNEY LANIER.

How solemnly on mournful eyes
  The mystic warning rose,
While o'er the Singer's forehead lies
  A twilight of repose.

The twilight deepens into night, —
  That night of frozen breath,
The rigor of whose Arctic blight,
  We recognize as — death!

But since beyond the polar ice
  May shine bright baths of balm;
Past its grim barriers' last device,
  A crystal-hearted calm, —

Thus, ice-bound Death that guards so
    well
  His far-off, secret goal,
May clasp a peace ineffable,
  For some who reach his pole!

My poet — is it thus with thee,
  Beyond this twilight gray, —
This frozen blight, this sombre sea, —
  Ah! hast thou found the Day?

XII.

THE DEATH OF HOOD.*

THE maimed and broken warrior lay,
By his last foeman brought to bay.

No sounds of battlefield were there —
The drum's deep bass, the trumpet's
    blare.

---

* During the terrible yellow fever season of
1878, General Hood and his wife died at very
nearly the same time. They left a large
family of children unprovided for, under cir-
cumstances which aroused the sympathy of
the public, north and south. At the South, a
considerable fund was subsequently raised for
their support; while northern philanthropists,
we understand, adopted two of the children.

No lines of swart battalions broke
Infuriate, thro' the sulphurous smoke.

But silence held the tainted room
An ominous hush, an awful gloom,

Save when, with feverish moan, he
    stirred,
And dropped some faint, half-muttered
    word,

Or outlined in vague, shadowy phrase,
The changeful scenes of perished days!

What thoughts on his bewildered brain,
Must then have flashed their blinding
    pain!

The past and future, blent in one, —
Wild chaos round life's setting sun.

But most his spirit's yearning gaze
Was fain to pierce the future's haze,

And haply view what fate should find
The tender loves he left behind.

" O God! outworn, despondent, poor,
I tarry at death's opening door,

While subtlest ties of sacred birth
Still bind me to the lives of earth.

How *can* I in calm courage die,
Thrilled by the anguish of a cry

I know from orphaned lips shall start
Above a father's pulseless heart ? "

His eyes, by lingering languors kissed,
Shone like sad stars thro' autumn mist;

And all his being felt the stress
Of helpless passion's bitterness.

When, from the fever-haunted room,
The prescient hush, the dreary gloom,

A blissful hope divinely stole
O'er the vexed waters of his soul,

That sank as sank that stormy sea,
Subdued by Christ in Galilee.

It whispered low, with smiling mouth,
" She is not dead, — thy queenly South.

And since for her each liberal vein
Lavished thy life, like vintage rain,

When round the bursting wine-press
    meet
The Ionian harvesters' crimsoned feet;

And since for her no galling curb
Could bind thy patriot will superb.

Yea! since for her thine all was spent,
Unmeasured, with a grand content, —

Soldier, thine orphaned ones shall rest,
Serene, on her imperial breast.

Her faithful arms shall be their fold,
In summer's heat, in winter's cold;

And her proud beauty melt above
Their weakness in majestic love!"

Ah! then the expiring hero's face,
Like Stephen's, glowed with rapturous
    grace.

Mad missiles of a morbid mood,
Hurled at his heart in solitude,

No longer wounding, round it fell;
Peace sweetened his supreme farewell!

For sure the harmonious hope was true,
O South! he leaned his faith on you!

And in clear vision, ere he died,
Saw its pure promise justified.

———◆———

MEDITATIVE AND RELIGIOUS.

I.

CHRIST ON EARTH.

HAD we but lived in those mysterious
    days,
    When, a veiled God 'mid unregenerate
      men,
Christ calmly walked our devious mortal
    ways,

Crowned with grief's bitter rue in place
    of bays, —
    Ah! had we lived but then:

Lived to drink in with every wondering
    breath,
    A consciousness beyond all human
    ken,
That clothed in flesh, as long conceived
    in faith,
We viewed the Lord of life and Lord of
    death, —
    Ah! had we lived but then:

To mark all Nature quickening where
    He trod,
    Whether thro' golden field, or shadowy
    glen,
While a strange sweetness breathed from
    leaf and clod,
As thro' man's image they divined their
    God; —
    Ah! had we lived but then!

Wild birds above him passed on reverent
    wing,
    And savage sovereigns of dark dune
    or den,
Out stole to greet Him with mild mur-
    muring,
Soft as a nested dove's song in the
    spring —
    Ah! had we lived but then!

At "peace: be still!" the storm-wind
    ceased to roar,
    And the lulled waters seemed to sigh
    "amen!"
Fear — the soul's mightier tempest —
    surged no more,
But a strange stillness fell on sea and
    shore; —
    Ah! had we lived but then!

With our own ears to hear the words He
    said,
    (Their music pondering o'er and o'er
    again!)
The wine of wisdom quaff from wisdom's
    head,

View the lame leap, and watch the up-
    rising dead:
    Ah! had we lived but then!

The world grows old.   Faith, once a
    mountain stream,
    Now crawls polluted down a poisonous
    fen;
The Bethlehem star hath lost its morning
    beam;
Thy face, dear Christ, wanes like a
    wasted dream, —
    How changed, how cold since then.

Ah! 'tis our sordid lives whose promise
    fails:
    These languorous lives of low, lost,
    aimless men;
Thro' mockery's mist our Lord's pure
    aureole pales,
Yet tenderer than the Syrian nightin-
    gales,
    His voice sounds *now* as *then*.

II.

HARVEST–HOME.

O'er all the fragrant land this harvest
    day,
    What bounteous sheaves are garnered,
    ear and blade!
Whether the heavens be golden-glad, or
    gray, —
    And the swart laborers toil in sun or
    shade: —

Like some fair mother in time's morning
    beams,
    When mortal beauty lured immortal
    eyes,
Here, Earth lies smiling in ethereal
    dreams,
    While her deep-bosomed breathings
    fall and rise!

Through half-closed lids she views o'er
    lawn and lea,
    Rich-fruited trees, vast piles of glim-
    mering grain, —

"O'er all the fragrant land this harvest day,
What bounteous sheaves are garnered, ear and blade."

And from the mountain boundaries to
the sea,
Hears the low rumbling of the loaded
wain.

A magical murmur born of ocean-deeps,
Blent with the pine-tree's lingering
music thrills
Up the brown pastures to the trackless
steeps,
And ancient caverns of the lonely
hills.

Far-flashing insects flicker thro' the
grass;
The humble-bee with burly bass drones
by;
Afar the plover pipes; the curlews pass
In long lithe lines across the violet sky:

A mellowed radiance rings creation
round;
Plenty and peace the auspicious season
bless;
The full year pauses proudly, clothed
and crowned
In consummation of high queenliness:

All nature seems to throb with rhythmic
fires;
Dawns rise harmonious; splendid sun-
sets roll
Down to the chorus of invisible choirs—
Strange winds in tune with Earth's
victorious soul!—

Thus, on the verge of winter's dreary
rest,
Nature rejoices in rare pomps of
power;
To breeze and sunbeam bares her prodi-
gal breast,
And robes in purple her last shadowless
hour.

Ah, when Life's autumn nears the eter-
nal main,
May the heart's granary its rich depths
unfold, —

Brimmed with immaculate sheaves of
heavenly grain,
And flushed with fruitage of unfading
gold!

III.
RECONCILIATION.

[From the South to the North. Written in
view of the new year.]

LAND of the North! I waft to thee
The South's warm *benedicite!*
Thou camest when all was grief and pain,
The feverish blood, the tortured brain,
When through hot veins delirium ran,
Thou cam'st, the true Samaritan!

The charm of ruthful grace divine,
The golden oil and perfumed wine,
Have soothed far deeper wounds than
those
Which harmed the body's hale repose;
On anguished souls dropped purely calm,
And sweet as Mary's "spikenard"
balm!

Lo! now o'er all the world are drawn
Clear splendors of the New-year's dawn!
O North! O South! let warfare cease!
Hark! to *that* prince whose name is
peace!
And ere time's new-born child departs,
Be joined in hands and joined in
hearts!

Once wedded thus, O North! O South!
Should discord ope her Marah mouth,
Smite the foul lips so basely fain
To outpour hate's salt tides again:
Long raged the storm, long lowered the
night, —
O faction, fly our morning light!

IV.
A VERNAL HYMN.

THE fresh spring burgeons into bloom—
And Earth with all her vernal charms
Lies like a queenly bride enclasped
Within her heavenly bridegroom's
arms;

The storms that raved have sunk to
　　peace;
　　Freed rivulets weave a blithesome lay,
And blissful Nature softly sings
　　Preludings of her perfect day!

Meanwhile there's not a breeze that
　　thrills
　　Leaf, bud, and flower with genial
　　　　kiss, —
Which does not breathe *thy* mystic hope,
　　Oh, soul of Palingenesis: —

Glance where we may, the symbols rise
　　Of loftier loves and lives to be: —
This marvellous spring-time seems to
　　grasp
　　The skirts of immortality!

V.
CHRISTIAN EXALTATION.

O CHRISTIAN soldier! shouldst thou rue
Life and its toils, as others do —
Wear a sad frown from day to day,
And garb thy soul in hodden-gray?
O rather shouldst thou smile elate,
Unquelled by sin, unawed by hate, —
Thy lofty-statured spirit dress
In moods of royal stateliness; —
For say, what service so divine
As that, ah! warrior heart, of thine,
High pledged alike through gain or loss,
To thy brave banner of the cross?

Yea! what hast *thou* to do with gloom,
Whose footsteps spurn the conquered
　　tomb?
Thou that through dreariest dark can
　　see
A smiling immortality?

Leave to the mournful doubting slave,
Who deems the whole wan earth a grave,
Across whose dusky mounds forlorn
Can rise no resurrection morn,
The sombre mien, the funeral weed,
That darkly match so dark a creed;
But be *thy* brow turned bright on all,
Thy voice like some clear clarion call,

Pealing o'er life's tumultuous van
The keynote of the hopes of man,
While o'er thee flames through gain,
　　through loss, —
That fadeless symbol of the cross.

VI.
SOLITUDE; IN YOUTH AND AGE.

IN youth we shrink from solitude!
　　Its quiet ways we shun,
Because our hearts are fain to dance
　　With others' in the sun; —
Life's nectar bubbling brightly up,
O'erfloweth toward our brother's cup.

In age we shrink from solitude,
　　Because our God is there;
And something in his " still, small voice"
　　Doth bid our souls " beware!"
Who flies from God and conscience, can
But seek his fellow-sinner — man!

VII.
DENIAL.

WE look with scorn on Peter's thrice-
　　told lie;
Boldly we say, " Good brother! you
　　nor I,
　　So near the sacred Lord, the Christ,
　　　　indeed,
Had dared His name and marvellous
　　grace deny."

Oh, futile boast! Oh, haughty lips, be
　　dumb!
Unheralded by boisterous trump or
　　drum,
　　How oft 'mid silent eves and midnight
　　　　chimes,
Vainly to us our pleading Lord hath
　　come —

Knocked at our hearts, and striven to
　　enter there;
But we poor slaves of mortal sin and care,
　　Sunk in deep sloth, or bound by
　　　　spiritual sleep,
Heard not the voice divine, the tender
　　prayer!

Ah! well for us if some late spring-tide
    hour
Faith still may bring, with blended shine
    and shower;
If through warm tears a late remorse
    may shed,
Our wakened souls put forth *one*
    heavenly flower!

VIII.
LESSON OF SUBMISSION.

BEN YOUSSUF, bound to Mecca, day by
    day
Toiled bravely o'er the desert's fiery
    way,
Till its hot sands and flint-sown courses
    sore
Pressed on the broidered sandals which
    he wore,
Scorching and cutting! at the last they
    fell
Loosely abroad ; — he seemed to fare
    through hell,
So blistering now, the flame-hued rocks
    and dust : —
"O mighty Allah!" cried he, "art thou
    just,
To let thy faithful pilgrim, serving thee,
Pass onward, thus, in nameless agony?"
With bitter thoughts and half-rebellious
    mind
He left, at length, the desert sands
    behind,
And still in that dark temper — far
    from grace —
Went where his brethren midst the
    holy place
Kneeled, by the *Caäba's* sanctity en-
    thralled ; —
Lo! there he marked a smitten wretch
    who crawled
Nearer the shrine, on bleeding hands
    and knees,
Yet his deep eyes were stars of prayer
    and peace ; —
And ah, how Youssuf's heart remorse-
    ful beat,
To find *he* lacked not only shoes, but —
    feet!

IX.
THE SUPREME HOUR.

THERE comes an hour when all life's
    joys and pains
  To our raised vision seem
But as the flickering phantom that
    remains
  Of some dead midnight dream!

There comes an hour when earth recedes
    so far,
  Its wasted wavering ray
Wanes to the ghostly pallor of a star
  Merged in the milky way.

Set on the sharp, sheer summit that
    divides
  Immortal truth from mortal fantasie ;
We hear the moaning of time's muffled
    tides
  In measureless distance die!

Past passions — loves, ambitions and
    despairs,
  Across the expiring swell
Send thro' void space, like wafts of
    Lethean airs,
  Vague voices of farewell.

Ah, then! from life's long-haunted
    dream we part,
  Roused as a child new-born,
We feel the pulses of the eternal heart
  Throb thro' the eternal morn.

X.
A CHRISTMAS LYRIC.

THO' the Earth with age seems whitened,
  And her tresses hoary and old
No longer are flushed and brightened
  By glintings of brown or gold,
A voice from the Syrian highlands,
  O'er waters that flash and stir,
By the belts of their tropic islands,
  Still singeth of joy to her!

A song which the centuries hallow!
  Though softer than April rain
That soweth on field and fallow,
  A spell that shall rise in grain —

Yet deep as the sea-strain chanted
　　On the fluctuant ocean-lyre,
By the magical west-wind haunted,
　　With the pulse of his soul on fire!

A promise to lift the lowly, —
　　To weed the soul of its tares,
And change into harmonies holy
　　The discord of fierce despairs:
A glory of high Evangels,
　　Of rhythmical storms and calms;
All hail to the voices of angels,
　　Heard over the starlit palms!

A hymn of hope to the ages,
　　The music of deathless trust,
No frenzy of mortal rages
　　Can darken with doubt or dust;
A rapture of high evangels,
　　But centred in sacred calms!
Ah! still the chorus of angels
　　Thrills over the Bethlehem palms!

Still heralds the day-spring tender,
　　That never can melt or close,
Till the noon of its deepening splendor
　　Out-blooms, like a mystic rose,
Whose petals are rays supernal
　　Of love that hath all sufficed, —
And whose heart is the grace eternal,
　　Of the fathomless peace of Christ!

XI.
THE PILGRIM.

THROUGH deepening dust and dreary
　　dearth
I walk the darkened wastes of earth,
A weary pilgrim sore beset,
By hopeless griefs and stern regret.

With broken staff and tattered shoon
I wander slow from dawn to noon —
From arid noon till dew-impearled,
Pale twilight steals across the world.

Yet sometimes through dim evening
　　calms
I catch the gleam of distant palms;
And hear, far off, a mystic sea
Divine as waves on Galilee.

Perchance through paths unknown,
　　forlorn,
I still may reach an orient morn;
To rest when Easter breezes stir,
Around the sacred sepulchre.

XII.
PENUEL.

NEAR Jabbok Ford, endued with sacred
　　might,
The patriarch strove with *one* that silent
　　came,
Obscurely limned against the twilight
　　flame —
Strove thro' slow watches of the marvel-
　　lous night!

" *Ungird thine arms, for lo! 'tis morning
　　light,*"
Spake the weird stranger! — "*nay, but
　　grant the claim,
Made good thro' strife divine, and bless
　　my name,
'Ere yet thou goest from doubtful clasp
　　and sight!*"

Thus Jacob, in the slowly ebbing swell
Of power and passion, — yearning still
　　to mark
That wrestler's face between the dawn
　　and dark:

Again, "*wilt thou not bless me?*" . . .
　　yea! and yea!"
Dropped a still voice, what time the
　　new-born dáy
Haloed an angel's head at Penuel!

XIII.
PATIENCE.

SHE hath no beauty in her face,
　　Unless the chastened sweetness there
And meek long-suffering yield a grace
　　To make her mournful features fair.

Shunned by the gay, the proud, the
　　young,
　　She roams through dim unsheltered
　　　ways;

Nor lover's vow, nor flatterer's tongue,
Brings music to her sober days.

At best, her skies are clouded o'er,
And oft she fronts the stinging sleet,
Or feels on some tempestuous shore
The storm-waves lash her naked feet!

Where'er she strays, or musing stands
By lonesome beach, by turbulent
mart, —
We see her pale, half-tremulous hands
Crossed humbly o'er her aching heart.

Within, a secret pain she bears,
A pain too deep to feel the balm
An April spirit finds in tears, —
Alas! all cureless griefs are calm!

Yet in her passionless strength supreme,
Despair beyond her pathway flies,
Awed by the softly steadfast beam
Of sad, but heaven-enamored eyes!

Who pause to greet her, vaguely seem
Touched by fine wafts of holier air,
As those who in some mystic dream
Talk with the angels unaware!

XIV.
THE LATTER PEACE.

WE have passed the noonday summit,
We have left the noonday heat,
And down the hillside slowly
Descend our weary feet.
Yet the evening airs are balmy,
And the evening shadows sweet.

Our summer's latest roses
Lay withered long ago;
And even the flowers of autumn
Scarce keep their mellowed glow.
Yet a peaceful season woos us
Ere the time of storms and snow.

Like the tender twilight weather
When the toil of day is done,
And we feel the bliss of quiet
Our constant hearts have won —
When the vesper planet blushes,
Kissed by the dying sun.

So falls that tranquil season,
Dew-like, on soul and sight,
Faith's silvery star rise blended
With memory's sunset light,
Wherein life pauses softly
Along the verge of night.

XV.
GAUTAMA.

SEVEN weary centuries ere our star-like
Christ
Rose on the clouded heavens of mortal
faith
Gautama came, the stern high priest
of death,
Oblivion's sombre, dark evangelist.
Millions of souls hath this dread creed
enticed
To wander lost through realms of bale-
ful breath,
Ghoul-haunted, rife with shapes of sin
and scath,
Monstrous, yet dim, as births of mid-
night mist:

All life, he taught, hath been, all life
must be
Accursed! the gift of demons! All
delight
Lies at the far-off goal of pulseless peace.

NOTE. — We yield to none in our cordial
admiration of Mr. Edwin Arnold's "Light
of Asia;" but we regard that most eloquent,
pathetic, and beautiful poem, chiefly as a
poem — and by no means as an absolutely
authoritative presentation of Gautama's creed,
or its tendencies. It even seems to us that
Mr. Arnold is himself somewhat in the dark as
to these matters. The "prodigious contro-
versy among the erudite in regard to Gautama's
doctrines," Mr. Arnold confronts chiefly by his
own firm conviction that "a third of mankind
would never have been brought to believe in
blank abstractions, or in nothingness, as the
crown of Being!" *Au contraire,* we cannot
fairly ignore the opinion of those Orientalists
who maintain, that "Nirvana" is essentially
nothingness; and moreover, that the idea
involved in it has a peculiar charm for the
Hindoo mind.

"Pray," sighed he, "that this breath of
    men shall cease;
Our hell is earth, our heaven eternal
    night;
Our only godhead vague Nonentity!"

XVI.

CHRIST.

THE soul's physician thus the soul would
    kill,
    The soul's high priest its heaven-
        bound pinions stay,
    Bring from fresh beauty chaos, night
        from day,
Despair from trust, from all good prom-
    ise ill;
The outworn heart and sickened senses
    still
    Must shroud heaven's life in fogs of
        foul decay,
    Veil the swift angel, love, and hide the
        ray
Born of God's smile with masks of mor-
    bid will: —

But Truth, and Truth's great Master
    cannot die;
    While Love, the seraph, free of wings
        and eyes,
Upsweeps the realm of calm immensity.
    A thousand times our buried Christ
        shall rise
    In prayerful souls to hush their
        anguished sighs,
And dawn, not darkness, rule o'er earth
    and sky.

XVII.

A WINTER HYMN.

O WEARY winds! O winds that wail!
    O'er desert fields and ice-locked rills!
O heavens that brood so cold and pale
    Above the frozen Norland hills!

Nature is like some sorrowing soul,
    Robed in a garb of dreariest woe; —
She cannot see her vernal goal
    Through ghostly veils of mist and
        snow: —

Her pulse beats low; through all her
    veins
    Scarce can the sluggish life-blood
        start;
What feeble, faltering heat sustains
    The half-numbed forces of her heart!

Above, despondent eyes she lifts,
    To view the sun-ray's dubious birth;
Beneath she marks the storm-piled drifts
    About a waste bewildering earth!

Ah, stricken Mother! hast thou lost
    All memory of the germs that rest
Untouched by tempest, rain, or frost,
    Shrined in thine own immortal breast?

Bend, bend thine ear; yea, bend and
    hear, —
    Despite the winds' and woodlands'
        strife, —
Deep in Earth's bosom, faint and clear,
    The far-off murmurous hints of life: —

The sound of waves in whispering flow;
    Of seeds that stir in dreams of light,
Whose sweetness mocks the shrouded
    snow,
    Whose radiance smiles at death and
        night;

So, Christian spirit! wrapt in grief, —
    Beneath *thy* misery's frozen sod,
Love works, to burst in flower and leaf,
    On some fair spring-dawn fresh from
        God!

XVIII.

THE THREE URNS.

LIST to an Arab parable, wherein
The beauty of the Orient fancy shrines
A star-like truth, the iconoclastic West
Is blind to see, its shrewd material vision
Bent over on the foulest soils of earth,
If only gold may gild them! Hear and
    learn!

Nimroud, the king to whom his four-
    score years
Had brought a wisdom pure as his white
    locks,

"O weary winds! O winds that wail,
O'er desert fields and ice-locked rills."

(And spotless they as snow on Caucasus!)
One morn commanded his three sons to
    grace
His presence chamber; there in front of
    each
A mighty urn, sealed with a mystic seal,
Was duly set — the one of burnished
    gold,
Blazed like an August noon — of amber
    fair
The other — but the third (dull as a
    cloud
Seen 'gainst the bright flash of a distant
    wave.
Or 'twixt the glittering tree-tops),
    seemed, in form,
A rugged mould wrought from the com-
    mon earth.

" Choose thou, my eldest," said the
    king, deep-breathed,
" Choose thou amongst these urns, the
    urn which seems
To thee most precious," — whereupon he
    chose
The Vase of Gold, which bore in jewelled
    flame,
Clear leaping, the word " EMPIRE," —
    opened it,
And found beneath a deadly, vaporous
    fume,
(Which on the instant sickened heart
    and sense), —
Nought but a bubbling tide of vital
    blood,
Hot, as appeared, that moment from the
    veins
Of murdered manhood. The fair amber
    vase,
With " GLORY " written on it — " this
    for me!"
Exclaimed the second prince, with eager
    eyes,
And feverish hands clasping his treasure
    close,—
Too close, alas! for as he spake, the urn
Crashed on his breast, and bruised and
    tortured it,
And a rare dust, the ashes of great men,

Dead centuries since, rose from its shat-
    tered bulk
Pungent, and yet so light the feeblest
    puff
Of failing wind hath shorn and scattered
    them
Into vague air. One vase alone re-
    mained,
Which the third son unsealing, found
    therein,
Deep-graven, glittering like a planet
    keen,
Thro' gulfs of envious darkness the sole
    name
Of GOD, — " which name, O! princes,"
    said the king,
" Doth sanctify yon vase of common
    earth
Above all precious metals sought of
    men,
Since but one letter of that sacred
    three,
Outweighs all worlds, from the mild star
    of eve,
Shining on love, to those mysterious
    orbs,
Which gird the pathway of the Pleiades."

XIX.

ON THE DECLINE OF FAITH.

As in some half-burned forest, one by
    one,
We catch far echoes on the doleful
    breeze,
Born of the downfall of its ruined
    trees;
While even thro' those which stand,
    slow shudderings run,
As if Fate's ruthless hand were laid
    thereon;
So, in a world sore-smitten by foul dis-
    ease,
— That Pest, called Doubt — we mark by
    slow degrees.
The fall of many a faith that wooed the
    sun:
Some, with low sigh of parting bough,
    or leaf,

Strain, quivering downward to the ab-
    horrèd ground;
Some totter feebly, groaning toward their
    doom;
While some broad-centuried growths of
    old Belief,
Sapped as by fire, defeatured, charred,
    discrowned,
Fall with a loud crash, and long reverber-
    ant boom!

Thus, fated hour by hour, more gaunt
    and bare,
Gloom the wan spaces, whence, a power
    to bless,
Up burgeoned once, in grace or stateli-
    ness,
Some creed divine, offspring of light and
    air;
What then? and must we yield to blank
    despair,
Beholding God Himself wax less and
    less,
Paled in the skeptical storm-cloud's
    whirl and stress,
'Till all is lost — love, reverence, hope,
    and prayer.
O man! when faith succumbs, and
    reason reels,
Before some impious, bold iconoclast,
Turn to thy heart that *reasons* not, but
    feels;
Creeds change! shrines perish! *still (her*
    instinct saith),
*Still the soul lives, the soul must conquer
    Death.*
*Hold fast to God, and God will hold thee
    fast!*

XX.

THE ULTIMATE TRUST.

THOUGH in the wine-press of thy wrath
    divine,
My crushed hopes droop, like crude
    and worthless must,
That love and mercy, Father! still are
    thine,
    With reverent soul, I trust!

Though all my life be shattered by thine
    ire,
The mystic whirlwind of thy will
    august,
Still, from the din, the darkness and the
    fire,
    I lift my song of trust!

Tho' foes assail me! yea, within, with-
    out!
Harrow my heart, and hurl its joys in
    dust,
No forceful fear, nor fraud of treacherous
    doubt,
    Disarms my bucklered trust!

Though my lost years be wrapped in
    Arctic cloud,
And Grief on me hath wreaked her
    ruthless lust,
Still, like an angel's face above a shroud
    Smiles my celestial trust!

Tho', Lord! thou wear'st a mask of hate
    ('twould seem),
And for a time, I think — as mortals
    must —
That mask shall melt, as melts a night-
    mare dream,
    Before my Orient trust!

Yea! tho' Thou slay me, and supine, I
    cower,
Heart-pierced and bleeding from the
    fiery thrust, —
I know there bides in heaven a glorious
    hour,
    To crown my sacred trust!

XXI.

"A LITTLE WHILE I FAIN WOULD LINGER YET."

A LITTLE while (my life is almost set!)
    I fain would pause along the downward
    way,
Musing an hour in this sad sunset-
    ray,
While, Sweet! our eyes with tender tears
    are wet;
A little hour I fain would linger yet.

A little while I fain would linger
 yet,
 All for love's sake, for love that cannot
  tire;
 Though fervid youth be dead, with
  youth's desire,
And hope has faded to a vague re-
 gret,
A little while I fain would linger yet.

A little while I fain would linger here:
 Behold! who knows what strange,
  mysterious bars
 'Twixt souls that love, may rise in
  other stars ?
Nor can love deem the face of death is
 fair;
A little while I still would linger here.

A little while I yearn to hold thee
 fast,
 Hand locked in hand, and loyal heart
  to heart;
 (O pitying Christ! those woeful words,
  " *We part !* ")
So ere the darkness fall, the light be
 past,
A little while I fain would hold thee
 fast.

A little while, when night and twilight
 meet;
 Behind, our broken years; before, the
  deep
 Weird wonder of the last unfathomed
  sleep.
A little while I still would clasp thee,
 Sweet;
A little while, when night and twilight
 meet.

A little while I fain would linger here;
 Behold! who knows what soul-divid-
  ing bars
 Earth's faithful loves may part in
  other stars ?
Nor can love deem the face of death is
 fair:
A little while I still would linger here.

XXII.
TWILIGHT MONOLOGUE.

CAN it be that the glory of manhood has
 passed,
 That its purpose, its passion, its
  might,
Have all paled with the fervor that fed
 them at last,
 As the twilight comes down with the
  night ?

Can it be I have lived, dreamed, and
 labored in vain —
 That above me, unconquered and
  bright,
The proud goal I had aimed at is taunt-
 ing my pain,
 As the twilight comes down with the
  night ?

Can it be that my hopes, which *seemed*
 noble and fair,
 Were predestined to mildew and
  blight ?
Ah! sad disenchantment! that bids me
 beware
 Of a twilight which heralds the night!

The glad days, the brave years that were
 lusty and long —
 How they fade on vague memory's
  sight!
And their joys are like echoes of jubi-
 lant song,
 As the twilight comes down with the
  night!

All the past is o'ershadowed, the present
 is dim,
 And could earth's fairest future re-
  quite
The worn spirit that swoons, the racked
 senses that swim,
 In this dread of the twilight and night ?

There is dew on my raiment; the sea
 winds wail low,
 As lost birds, wafted wave-ward in
  flight,

And all Nature grows cold, as my heart
　　in its woe,
　At the advent of twilight and night!

From the realm of dead sunset scarce
　　darkened as yet —
Over hills mist-enshrouded and white,
A deep sigh of ineffable, mournful regret,
Seems exhaled 'twixt the twilight and
　　night!

O! thou genius of art! I have wor-
　　shipped and blessed;
　O! thou soul of all beauty and light!
Lift me up in thine arms, give me
　　warmth from thy breast,
　Ere the twilight be merged in the
　　night!

Let me draw from thy bosom miraculous
　　breath,
　And for once, on song's uppermost
　　height,
I may chant to the nations such music
　　in death
　As shall mock at the twilight and
　　night!

XXIII.

THE SHADOW OF DEATH.

I PRAY you, when the shadow of death
　　draws nigh,
To bear me out beneath the unmeasured
　　heaven;
I fain would hear the pine-trees' slum-
　　berous sigh,
And watch the cloud flotillas drifted
　　high,
　By slow, soft breezes driven
Due south, perchance toward realms of
　　tropic balms,
And the warm fragrance of the Syrian
　　palms.

I pray you, when the shadow of death
　　comes down,
Oh! lay me close to nature's pulses deep,
Whether her breast with autumn tints
　　be brown,

Or bright with summer, or hale winter's
　　crown
　Press on her brows in sleep;
So nigh the dawn of some new, marvel-
　　lous birth,
I'd look to heaven, still clasped in arms
　　of earth!

I pray you, when the shadow of death
　　draws near,
Give, give me freedom for my last, faint
　　breath;
Beneath God's liberal heaven I could
　　not fear,
His merciful winds would dry my latest
　　tear,
　His sunshine soften death,
And some fair shreds of our dear earth's
　　delight
Cling round the spirit in her upward
　　flight.

XXIV.

FINIS.

A MOMENT'S gleam, a hint of sunnier
　　weather,
　Borne from the storm-clouds and the
　　mists of fate;
Dawned, with a tender " Peradventure"
　　hither,
　A soft " Perchance it is not yet too
　　late!"

And so a transient omen magnifying,
　My soul would fain pass brightened,
　　unto thine;
But to my half-formed thought comes
　　truth replying:
"No life mounts backward from its
　　wan decline."

Would'st thou expect, drear winter,
　　ashen, sober,
　To burn with blushes of a spring-tide
　　noon ?
Would'st thou expect the hectic-cheeked
　　October
　To catch the virginal freshness of
　　young June ?

All mortal lives like the year's seasons
ever
Pass from their May dawn and rare
summer's bloom,
Down to the day when autumn winds
dissever
Life's latest sheaves to strew them
near a tomb.

And then death looms, that pitiless grim
December.
Bringing cold tears, a winding sheet
like snow,
Last, a carved stone, which bids the
world remember
One of its countless myriads sleeps be-
low.

"My thoughts are wandering on the verge of dreams, . . .
While lower, feebler, flit the fireside gleams."

XXV.
THE SHADOWS ON THE WALL.

WHAT mournful influence chills my soul
to-night ?
I watch the expiring flames that fade
and fall,
From which outleap vague shafts of
arrowy light,
Pursued by spectral shadows on the
wall.

My thoughts are wandering on the verge
of dreams,
Mist-laden, gray, and sombre as a
pall,
While lower, feebler, flit the fireside
gleams,
And darker those quaint shadows on
the wall.

The old sad voice (fraught with the cen-
    turies' tears)
  That seems through infinite space and
    time to call,
Faint with the doubts and grief of an-
    tique years,
  Years that are dim as shadows on the
    wall;

The old sad voice is whispering to my
    heart:
  Man's life, phantasmal, vain, illusive
    all,
Beholds too soon its cloud-foundations
    part,
  Melting like midnight shadows on the
    wall.

Too soon the noblest passions, worn and
    old,
  Die, or grow dulled and languid past
    recall;
Even love may wane in memory's twi-
    light cold,
  Sad, wavering, wan, as shadows on the
    wall.

And oft the loftiest nature's loftiest aim,
  Heaven-soaring once, wide as this
    earthly ball,
Sinks, a tamed eagle o'er whose eyes of
    flame
  The death-films steal like shadows on
    the wall.

A subtler voice whispers the conscious
    soul,
  "What of high hopes which held *thy*
    youth in thrall ?
Where flash *thy* chariot wheels, where
    shines *thy* goal ? "
  The mocking shadows answer from
    the wall.

With deepening dusk and faded flame
    they grow
  Fantastic phantoms, hovering over all
The tremulous space, or flickering to
    and fro
  In wild unearthly antics on the wall.

Till as the last slow ember drops in
    gloom,
  Like vassals hurrying through some
    wizard's hall,
Whirling they pass, and darkness haunts
    the room,
  No life, not even a shadow on the
    wall!

XXVI.
CONSUMMATUM EST.

I'VE done with all the world can give,
  Whate'er its kind or measure.
(O Christ! what paltry lives we live
  If toil be lord, or pleasure!).
Alas! *I* only yearn for sleep,
  Calm rest for fevered riot —
The sacred sleep, the shadows deep,
  Of death's majestic quiet.

I've done with all our earth-life lends —
  False hopes and wild ambitions,
Brilliant beginnings, futile ends,
  And long-postponed fruitions,
Those hollow shows dissembling truth,
  Vain myths that mock the real,
The dreary wrecks of peace and youth
  Above a crushed ideal.

I've done with heavenly dreams that
    wane
  At touch of earth-born dawnings,
With fervid passion, useless pain,
  Brave aims and dim forewarnings;
I've done with alien tears or smiles,
  Past days and vague to-morrows;
I've done with earth's unhallowed
    wiles,
  Brief joys and helpless sorrows.

I've done with compacts sealed in dust,
  Dull cares that overweighed me,
With promise of the Judas-trust,
  That, while it kissed, betrayed me;
With *all* save love, whose matchless
    face
  Midmost a life's undoing
Smiles in its tender angel's grace
  To sanctify the ruin.

I've done with all beneath the stars,
  O world! so wanly fleeting!
How long against time's ruthless bars
  Have the soul's wings been beating,
Till even the soul but yearns for sleep,
  Calm rest for fevered riot —
The sacred sleep, the shadows deep,
  Of death's majestic quiet!

XXVII.

THE BROKEN CHORDS.

LIKE a worn wind-harp on a barren lea,
Unstirred by subtle breathings of the
    sea,
  Though sweet south-breezes swell the
    floodtide's flow,
The lyric power in this worn heart of
    mine
Droops in the twilight of life's wan
    decline,
  While the loosed chords of song grown
    lax and low,
  Are dumb to all the heavenly airs that
    blow!

Only, sometimes along each shattered
    string
I hear the ghost of Memory murmur-
    ing
Old strains, as half in sadness half in
    scorn,
So faint, so far, they scarcely pass the
    bound
'Twixt sullen silence and ethereal
    sound, —
Mere wraiths of murmurous tone, that
    die forlorn
Ere yet we deem those faltering notes
    are born!

So, smitten chords, sink, wane, and pass
    away!
Yet have ye made soft music in your
    day
  On many a sea-swept strand or breezy
    lawn.
Once more I hear that yearning music
    rise;

Once more I see deep tears in tender
    eyes;
  And all my soul melts in me, fondly
    drawn
Back to youth's love and youth's Arca-
    dian dawn!

XXVIII.

THE RIFT WITHIN THE LUTE.

A TINY rift within the lute
May sometimes make the music mute!
By slow degrees, the rift grows wide,
By slow degrees, the tender tide —
Harmonious once — of loving thought
Becomes with harsher measures fraught,
Until the heart's Arcadian breath
Lapses thro' discord into death!

XXIX.

IN HARBOR.

I THINK it is over, over,
  I think it is over at last,
Voices of foeman and lover,
  The sweet and the bitter have passed: —
Life, like a tempest of ocean
Hath outblown its ultimate blast:
There's but a faint sobbing sea-ward
While the calm of the tide deepens lee-
    ward,
And behold! like the welcoming quiver
Of heart-pulses throbbed thro' the river,
  Those lights in the harbor at last,
  The heavenly harbor at last!

I feel it is over! over!
  For the winds and the waters surcease;
Ah! — few were the days of the rover
  That smiled in the beauty of peace!
And distant and dim was the omen
That hinted redress or release: —
From the ravage of life, and its riot
What marvel I yearn for the quiet
  Which bides in the harbor at last?
For the lights with their welcoming
    quiver
That through the sanctified river
  Which girdles the harbor at last,
  This heavenly harbor at last?

I *know* it is over, over,
  I know it is over at last!
Down sail! the sheathed anchor uncover,
For the stress of the voyage has passed:
Life, like a tempest of ocean
  Hath outbreathed its ultimate blast:
There's but a faint sobbing sea-ward,
While the calm of the tide deepens lee-
  ward;
And behold! like the welcoming quiver
Of heart-pulses throbbed thro' the river,
  Those lights in the harbor at last,
  The heavenly harbor at last!

XXX.

FORECASTINGS.

WHEN I am gone, what alien steps shall tread
  This flowery garden-close?
What alien hands shall pluck the violets sweet,
Or gather the rich petals of the rose,
  When I — drear thought! — am dead?

When I am gone, toward doubtful dark-
    ness led,
  What voices, false or true,
Shall echo round these old, familiar
    haunts
My happiest days of tranquil manhood
    knew,
  Ah me! when I am dead?

When I am gone, what museful eyes
    instead
  Of these dimmed eyes of mine,
Beneath yon trellised porch shall mark
    thro' heaven,
On cloudless eves the summer sunsets
    shine,
  When I, alas! am dead?

When I am gone, and all is done and
    said,
  One life had wrought below —
'Mid these fair scenes what other souls
    shall! thrill,

In turn, to love and anguish, joy and
    woe —
  Dear Christ! when I am dead?

Though I be dead, perchance when
    Spring has shed
  Her gentlest influence round —
Here, where love reigned, my ghostly
    feet may tread
The old accustomed paths without a
    sound, —
  Perchance — when I am dead!

Though I be dead, earth's fragrant
    white and red
  Here in spring roses met,
May to strange spiritual senses bring the
    balms
Of tender memory and divine regret,
  Yea! even to me — though dead!

Though I be dead, with faded hands and
    head
  Laid in unbreathing rest —
Dear cottage roof! thou still mayst lure
    me back,
Among the unconscious living a wan
    guest,
  Veiled, as Fate veils the dead:

A guest of shadowy frame, ethereal
    tread,
  Amongst them, yet apart —
A sombre mystery! in whose bosom
    throb
The faint, slow pulses of its phantom
    heart,
  Ah, heaven! not wholly dead!

XXXI.

APPEAL TO NATURE OF THE SOLI-
TARY HEART.

DEAR mother, take me to thy breast!
I have no other place of rest
  In all this weary world of men:
  Ah! fold me in thy love again,
Sweet mother; clasp me to thy breast!

From out thy womb, long since, I came,
A creature wrought of dust and flame;
  I knew no mortal mother's grace,
  But only viewed *thy* mystic face,
That softly went, and softly came!

I knew thee in the sunset grand,
The waveless calm, the silvery strand;
  From out the shimmering twilight-
  bars
  I saw thee smile between the stars,
Divinely sweet, or softly grand!

I heard, beneath the sylvan arch,
Thy battling winds, led on by March,
  Sweep where the solemn pine-tops
  close
  About its ravaged, dim repose —
Hushed, awed, beneath the woodland
  arch!

I heard thee, 'mid some tender hour,
In lisping leaf and rustling flower,
  In low lute-breathings of the breeze,
  And tidal sighs o'er moonless seas
Star-charmed in midnight's mournful
  hour!

I thrilled at each far-whispered tone
That touched me from thy vast un-
  known,
  At every dew-bright hint that fell
  From out thy soul unsearchable,
Yea, each strange hint and shadowy
  tone!

I felt, through dim, awe-laden space,
The coming of thy veilèd face;
  And in the fragrant night's eclipse
  The kisses of thy deathless lips,
Like strange star-pulses, throbbed
  through space!

Now mine own pulses, beating low,
Whisper the spent life: " *Thou must go;*
  Even as a wasted rivulet, pass
Beyond the light, beneath the grass,
For strength grows faint, and hope is
  low!"

*FOUR POEMS FOR SPECIAL OCCA-
SIONS.*

I.

TO THE POET WHITTIER.

ON HIS 70th BIRTHDAY.

FROM this far realm of pines I waft thee
  now
  A brother's greeting, Poet, tried and
  true;
So thick the laurels on thy reverend
  brow,
  We scarce can see the white locks
  glimmering through!

O pure of thought! Earnest in heart
  as pen,
  The tests of time have left thee unde-
  filed;
And o'er the snows of threescore years
  and ten
  Shines the unsullied aureole of a child.

II.

TO O. W. HOLMES,

ON HIS BIRTHDAY.

DEAR Doctor, whose blandly invincible
  pen
Has honored so often your great fellow-
  men
With your genius and virtues, who
  doubts it is true
That the world owes in turn, a warm
  tribute to you?

Wheresoever rare merit has lifted its
  head
From the cool country calm or the city's
  hotbed —
You were always the first to applaud it
  by name,
And to smooth for its feet the harsh
  pathway to fame.

Wheresoever beneath the broad rule of
  the sun,
By some spirit elect, a grand deed has
  been done —

Its electrical spell like the lightning's
    would dart,
Though the globe lay between, to thrill
    first in *your* heart!

Philanthropist! poet! romancer! com-
    bined —
Ay! shrewd scientist too — who shall
    fathom your mind,
Shall plumb that strange sea to the ut-
    termost deep,
With its vast under-tides, and its rhyth-
    mical sweep?

You have toiled in life's noon, till the
    hot blasting light
Blinds the eyes that would guage your
    soul stature aright;
But when eve comes at last, 't will be
    clear to mankind,
By the length of bright shadow your
    soul leaves behind!

III.

TO EMERSON.

ON HIS 77th BIRTHDAY.

" I do esteeme him a deepe sincere soule ; one
that seemeth ever to be travailing after the
Infinite ! " — *Sir Thomas Browne.*

AH! what to him *our* trivial praise or
    blame,
    Who through long years hath raised
        half-mournful eyes
Yearning to mark some heaven-descend-
    ed flame
    Light his soul's altar rife with sacri-
        fice ?

The offering of far thoughts, profound
    as prayer,
    And starry dreams, still rhythmical of
        youth,
With travail of brain that pants for lof-
    tier air,
    To the veiled mystery of immaculate
        Truth:

No Orient seer — wild woodlands, 'round
    him furled, —
    Building his shrine 'mid virginal
        vales apart,
E'er watched and waited in the antique
    world,
    For fire divine, with more ethereal
        heart!

Can life's supreme oblations still re-
    main
    All undiscerned ? or hath some mar-
        vellous levin
Hallowed his gift, and down his rifted
    pain
    Flashed the white splendor of God's
        grace from heaven ?

IV.

TO HON. R. G. H.

UPON HIS 78th BIRTHDAY.

CLOSE to the verge of fourscore crowded
    years
    Your heart is strong, your soul serene
        and bright;
As when confronting first life's hopes
    and fears—
    The star of manhood crowned your brow
        with light.

Clear thoughts are spells to keep the life-
    blood pure,
    Brave aims are medicinal, rife with
        balm;
What wonder then, with *thee* life's joys
    endure,
    And life's majestic sunset smiles in
        calm!

For thou art one whose brotherhood
    supreme
    Hath touched all circles of benign
        desire;
Therefore, thy days like some uncloud-
    ed dream,
    Are slowly melting into heavenly fire.

HUMOROUS POEMS.

HUMOROUS POEMS.

VALERIE'S CONFESSION.

TO A FRIEND.

THEY declare that I'm gracefully pretty,
  The very best waltzer that whirls;
They say I am sparkling and witty,
  The pearl, the queen rose-bud of girls.
But, alas for the popular blindness!
  Its judgment, though folly, can hurt:
Since my heart, that runs over with
    kindness,
  It vows is the heart of a flirt!

How, *how*, can I help it, if Nature,
  Whose mysteries baffle our ken,
Hath made me the tenderest creature
  That ever had pity on men ?
When the shafts of my luminous glances
  Have tortured some sensitive breast,
Why, I soften their light till it trances
  The poor wounded bosom to rest !

Can I help it if, brought from all regions,
  As diverse in features as gait,
Rash lovers besiege me in legions,
  Each lover demanding his fate ?
To be cold to such fervors of feeling
  Would pronounce me a dullard or
    dunce;
And so, the bare thought sets me reel-
    ing,
  I'm engaged to *six* suitors at once!

The first, — we shall call him " sweet
    William,"
  He's a lad scarcely witty or wise —
The gloom of the sorrows of " Ilium "
  Would seem to outbreathe on his
    sighs.

When I strove, half in earnest, to flout
    him,
  Pale, pale at my footstool he sunk;
But mamma, quite too ready to scout
    him,
  Would hint that " sweet Willie " was
    drunk!

My second, a florid Adonis
  Of forty-and-five, to a day,
Drives me out in his phaeton with po-
    nies,
  Making love every yard of the way,
Who so pleasantly placed could resist
    him ?
  Had he popped 'neath the moonlight
    and dew
That eve, I could almost have kissed him
  (A confession alone, dear, for you).

Next, a widower, polished and youthful,
  Far famed for his learning and pelf:
Can I doubt that *his* passion is truthful,
  That he seeks me alone for myself ?
Yet I know that some slanderers mutter
  His fortune is just taking wings;
But I scorn the backbiters who utter
  Such basely censorious things !

Could they hearken his love-whisper,
    dulcet
  As April's soft tide on the strand,
Whose white curves are loath to re-
    pulse it,
  So sweet is its homage and bland;
Could they hear how his dead wife's de-
    votion
  He praises, while yearning for mine —
They would own that his ardent emotion
  Is something — yes — almost *divine !*

My fourth — would to heaven I could
    paint him
    As next the high altar he stands —
A Saint John, all the people besaint
    him?
Pale brow and immaculate hands,
Ah! his tones in their wooing seem
    holy,
    Nor dare I believe it misplaced,
When an arm of the church, stealing
    slowly.
    Is folded, at length, round my waist;

Behold this long list of my lovers
    With a soldier and sailor complete:
Both swear that their hearts were but
    rovers
    Till fettered and bound at *my* feet.
Oh dear! but these worshippers daunt
    me:
    Their claims, their vain wishes, appall;
'Tis sad how they harass and haunt
    me, —
    What, WHAT, *shall I do with them all?*

LATER.

As the foam-flakes, when steadfastly
    blowing,
    The west wind sweeps reckless and
    free,
Are borne where the deep billows, flow-
    ing,
    Pass out to a limitless sea,
So the gay spume of girlish romances,
Upcaught by true Love on his breath,
With the fretwork and foam of young
    fancies,
    Was borne through vague distance to
    death.

For he came — the true hero — one
    morning,
    And my soul with quick thrills of de-
    light
Leaped upward, renewed, and reborn in
    A world of strange beauty and might:
1 seemed fenced from all earthly disas-
    ter;

My pulses beat tuneful and fast;
So I welcomed my monarch, my master
    The *first* real love, and the *last.*

A MEETING OF THE BIRDS.

Of a thousand queer meetings, both
    great, sir, and small
The bird-party *I* sing of seemed oddest
    of all!

How they come to assemble — a multi-
    form show —
From all parts of the earth, is — well
    — more than *I* know.

I only can vow that, one fine night of
    June,
In a vast, varied garden, made bright by
    the moon,

Such bird-throngs I saw, with plumes
    brilliant or dark,
As had ne'er met, I deem, since the age
    of the ark:

There the phœnix, upborne on a tall
    jasper spar,
His fair mate by his side, shone serene
    as a star;

With a calm sort of pride glancing down
    on all others,
As scorning to claim such *canaille* for
    his brothers!

He alone of earth's creatures (more wise
    far than Adam),
When Eve tempted *him,* said "Excuse
    me, good madam!

"No juice from *that* fruit shall e'er
    moisten *my* thrapple!
Delicious! perhaps . . but who gave
    you the apple ?" *

---

* Tradition says that when Adam ate of the
forbidden fruit, at Eve's instigation, the
phœnix, *alone,* of all creatures, equally tempt-
ed, did *not* fall.

Then — his tiny red optics upturned to
    this king
Of all species that court the light air
    with a wing —

Lo, the rooster! his top-knot bright crim-
    son and blue,
With his impudent strut and his cock-
    doodle-doo,

Is resolved, one can see, the king's hau-
    teur to balk!
What's a phœnix, forsooth, to such cocks
    of the walk!

Oh! he bustles along, and he bullies his
    wife,
Till the poor humbled partlet is weary of
    life —

When, phew! like a bolt of blue light-
    ning or brown,
Outflashed from the trees, a swift bee-
    bird whirls down

Upon cocky's great top-knot upreared
    like a dome,
To cut, just for once, his big high-
    ness's comb!

From the rooster's discomfiture, laugh-
    ing, I turn
To where, 'mid the garden's cool
    avenues, burn

The fair cinnamon tufts of those
    hipooes that sold
To King Solomon, once, their true
    crownlets of gold;*

And beyond where the shadow waves
    dim by the sheen,
The gay humming-bird darts — a live
    rainbow — between:

---

* The Hipooes originally had *real* crowns of
gold on their heads; but so persecuted were
they because of this possession that they
appealed to Solomon, who (the legend says)
exchanged their gold crowns for crowns of
feathers, retaining the *former* as a trifling
"compliment" for his magic skill and *kind-
ness!*

While the parrakeets glitter, the orioles
    float
Through the moonlighted mist and fine
    vapors remote;

And by sides of small streams and clear
    lakelets outspread
Stalks the long-legged flamingo, all scar-
    let and red:

In sooth, birds of all climes, whether
    wild birds or tame,
Whether dove-hued and sad, or high-
    colored like flame,

Walked, wobbled and sauntered, paused,
    fluttered and flew,
With vast blending of plumes, and, ah!
    endless ado.

The eagle's loud anger, set deaf'ningly
    loose,
Shrilled fierce o'er the arrogant hiss of
    the goose,

And a peacock, who screeched till his
    gills were half black,
Could not drown, after all, a profes-
    sional "quack;"

The nightingale pitted his voice and his
    lore
'Gainst the skylark, that never had
    trilled *thus* before;

And the cock now recovered, and fresh,
    sir, as dew,
Strove to bear them *both* down with his
    cock-doodle-doo:

Till — one volume of strange, contra-
    dictory sound,
The air, like a millwheel, whizzed round
    us and round.

And while still the white moonshine, on
    vapors of fleece,
Rained down its ineffable splendors in
    peace,

That bird congregation broke up in a
row,
Whose noises, half dreaming, I catch
even now.

But the last glimpse of all that flashed
quick on my eyes,
Ere the whole meeting faded 'twixt
garden and skies,

Was the cuckoo's unwearied, nefarious
leg
Scratching fast to discover a phœnix's
egg,

Which, if found, I've no doubt, was
close-hidden and pressed
By the vile little wretch, with quite
mother-like breast.

Yet I've seen other creatures than
creatures with wings
Who dared to make free with thrice
sanctified things,

From whose false incubation *what* creeds
came in vogue!
*Even truth's egg is marred if hatched
out by a rogue!*

———◆———

*A BACHELOR-BOOKWORM'S COM-
PLAINT OF THE LATE PRESIDEN-
TIAL ELECTION.*

[Written during the Hayes and Tilden
Controversy].

A MAN of peace, I never dared to marry,
Lover of tranquil hours, I dwelt apart;
Outside the realm where noisy schemes
miscarry;
My only handmaids, Science, Learn-
ing, Art;
Oh! home of pleasant thought, of calm
affection,
All blasted now by this last vile election!

One morn, absorbed in studious contem-
plation
Of what or whom, I cannot now recall,

A strident voice, "Rise! help to save the
nation!"
Roared in mine ear, half bellow and
half squall;
"Throw by your books, why, man, there's
treason brewing;
Come, come with me, we'll block the
march of ruin!"

My neighbor, Dobson—all the gods con-
found him!
Seized, shook and hauled me from my
cushioned seat;
(Just then I could have drugged the
wretch, or drowned him;)
But the next moment on bewildered
feet,
I trudged with him through dirty streets
and weather,
That we might vote at the next poll to-
gether.

Vote! vote for whom? I'd not the faint-
est notion;
Little I recked of modern joys or woes;
Wrapped in Greek wars and ancient
Rome's commotion,
What passed beneath my philosophic
nose,
Seemed dim as glimmerings of a mid-
night taper
Marked from afar through autumn clouds
and vapor!

At length we paused before a wood-work
wicket,
Shrining the grimy guardian of the
poll;
Into my hands they thrust a printed
ticket,
An ink-besmeared, suspicious-looking
scroll,
Which, ne'ertheless, held names of men
whose action
Would cow — they swore — the brazen
front of faction!

With scarce a glance, in vacant mood, I
cast it;
That ticket soiled into as soiled a box;

A box, I thought, half vaguely as I
    passed it;
  Whose guardian " Rough " looked wily
    as a fox,
Willing, no doubt, for any public hero,
To cheat *ad lib.* — a Brutus, or a Nero!

Well! from that day, my peace of life
    was shattered;
  Dobson *would* come, all lowering or
    ablaze
With joy, to shout — (as if the issue
    mattered')
  Now *"Tilden's won!"* now *"glorious*
    Ruthy Hayes!"
Vainly I argued, vainly vowed that d—n
    me,
I didn't care three straws for Ruth or—
    Sammy!

" Have I not Scipio and majestic Cato,
  With their grand deeds to ponder yet?"
    I cried;
" Why, dunder-headed Dobson, *will* you
    prate so,
  Of modern dwarfs of time and fate
    untried;"
" Untried!" quoth he, aghast at my
    iniquity;
" I'll back them *both*, by Jove! 'gainst
    all antiquity!"

And still he came, morning, and noon,
    and twilight,
  Bringing, at last, his party henchmen
    too;
O! how I yearned to blow them through
    the skylight,
  Or, at the gentlest, beat them black
    and blue;
Each cursed and threatened like some
    desperate Lara;
Meanwhile they quaffed and quaffed my
    best Madeira!

A point there is beyond the soul's de-
    fiance,
  Which gained, a mortal man must
    fight, or fly;

Fight, if he knows the wily tricks of
    " science," *
  Fly, if he knows not *when* to smite,
    and *why;*
Needless to say, in this disastrous mat-
    ter,
  Of the two ways, I wisely chose — the
    latter!

I left my home; I fled to shades subur-
    ban,
  Where an old aunt, as deaf as twenty
    posts.
(A fine antique, bedecked with lace and
    turban,)
  Lived in a house unknown to rats or
    ghosts;
There, far from party conflicts, proud or
    petty,
  I dwell at peace, with sober Madame
    Betty!

At peace! good lack, the universal
    virus
  Of party strife had captive made the
    air,
The light, the very sun-motes shifting
    nigh us,
  And thus, alas! it entered even
    there;
Up, down her stairs, how oft had I to
    stump it,
  Shrieking the news through her infernal
    trumpet.

Baffled, once more I sought the public
    pass-ways,
  But then, from morn to midnight's
    " witching noon,"
Monotonous as when some blatant ass
    brays,
  The same mixed clamors rose 'neath
    sun and moon;
Tilden and Hayes in never-ceasing wran-
    gle,
  Who the vexed " snarl " shall ever dis-
    entangle?

---

      * *Ring science*, of course.

Bank, hall, and market, counting-house
    and alley,
    Patrician parlor and low bar-room den,
Echoed, as 'twere, cries of retreat or
    rally,
    From brassy throats of many thousand
        men;
Such foolish boasts were blent with
    threats as silly,
Yet even the wise men babbled — *willy
    nilly.*

The very nurse-maids with their baby
    charges,
    Took sides, and squabbled; newsboys
        shouting loud,
Scuttled along the slippery pavement
    marges,
    And burst like young bulls through the
        motley crowd
Of parsons, black-legs, dandies, hack-
    men, bummers;
Swollen each moment by some rash new
    comers!

Around the telegraph stands they surged
    and battled,
    Till direful Hades seemed unloosed on
        earth;
Lies were exchanged, cudgels and brick-
    bats rattled;
    The veriest blackguard scorned the
        man of birth,
And tweaked his nose, or knocked his
    beaver double—
Ah me! the noise, the blows, the furious
    trouble!

I passed a gay "Bazaar," and glanced
    within it,
    Of silks and satins, what a dazzling
        maze!
Fair tongues were wagging smartly;
    every minute,
    "Of course 'tis Tilden!" "nay, not so,
        'tis Hayes!"
Rose, with the rustle of bright garments
    blending—
A strife of voices, eager and unending!

You'd scarce believe it; but maids fair
    and tender,
    Dancing from school, the merest slips
        of girls,
Shrilled *Hayes* or *Tilden*, and with fin-
    gers slender,
    Caught and dragged fiercely at each
        others' curls;
Ill words they spake—those inconsiderate
    misses —
From rosebud lips just framed for love
    and kisses!

.   .   .   .   .

Enough! the die is cast; from rage and
    riot,
    I'll cross o'er mountain walls and ocean
    streams,
To seek and find again, that gracious
    quiet,
    Whose charm hath left me, save in
    transient dreams;
In some far land and time, my spirit
    stilled then—
I may — who knows — forgive both
    Hayes and Tilden!

COQUETTE AND HER LOVER.

A "PETITE COMEDIE" IN RHYME.

LOVER.

COQUETTE! coquette! now, is it fair
To weave for me your magic hair,
Binding me thus, all unaware?
Till, wholly meshed in every part,
From dazzled eyes to captured heart,
Scarce can I, thro' your radiant snare,
Inhale one waft of free-born air;
Answer, coquette! now, is it fair?

COQUETTE.

O, foolish querist! what if I,
Beholding your enamored face
And every well-attested trace
Of verdant, young idolatry,
Should, after my own fashion, choose
To play the subtly-amorous muse,

Your inexperienced heart-strings touch,
Wooing the warm chords overmuch!
Or tempt you, 'twixt a smile and sigh,
To enter beauty's luminous net ?
Such snares must evermore be set

For blinded human flies like you!
Cease, therefore, this half-feigned ado,
You are a natural victim! I
Am by the same strange law's decree,
Your dear, predestined enemy!

"For full five seconds, it would seem
As if you really thought, coquette,
On something grave."

LOVER.

Is *such* the only comfort, then,
You give to thrice-deluded men ?
Suppose our life-plan quite upset,
Reversed in whole, or changed in part;
My sex your own, and feelings strong,
(Wiled by deep passion's syren song);
Yours the blind victim's tangled heart,
And *mine* to weave the tempter's net —
What then, O! honey-tongued coquette ?

COQUETTE.

Such questions! — ah! *mon Dieu! mon
Dieu! —*
Fancy I've places changed with you!
I cannot! 'tis too hard a task
Of any mortal *belle* to ask!

[ASIDE *with a half-humorous, half-solemn air.*]
Fancy *my* person changed to *his*
By some odd metamorphosis!

My fairy frame to that huge bulk
That might befit red Rory O'Fulke,
Our Irish groom!—six feet, at least,
Of stature—with that boundless waist,
Instead of mine, Titania might
Quite envy on a " round-dance " night,
By all the waltzing beaux adored!
My brow to that great, sabre-scored
Brown forehead; and my cheeks of
    rose
To bearded *puffs ;* my delicate nose—
Quel horreur ! 'tis a hideous dream!

LOVER.

For full five seconds, it would seem
As if you really *thought,* coquette,
On something grave! Slowly about
Your flower-like lips' delicious pout,
Came tiny puckerings, lined with doubt;
Your large eyes widened deep and
    blue,
As May-skies glimpsed thro' morning
    dew;
And shadows vague as noon-tide trance
Stole o'er your vivid countenance:
Coquette! show pity!—after all,
Have you resolved to free from thrall
Your wretched serf ? . . . Close, close
    your eyes
For one brief, merciful minute; try
To turn your perfect mouth awry;
Let those arch smiles which magnetize
My inmost blood be changed to scorn;
Do all a winsome lady born
To loveliness and witchery, can,
To flout a love-tormented man!

COQUETTE.

You know as well as I
What balms have soothed your slavery;
Besides, *I'm sure, whate'er you say,*
There never yet has dawned the day
On which, in truth ('tis vain to frown),
You longed to lay your fetters down.
Surely but airy chains they are,
And tenuous as the farthest star.
But *should* you break the binding net,
You'd come . . . (ah! graceless, thank-
    less loon!)

'Ere the next wax or wane of moon,
To sigh, or call on "sweet coquette!"

LOVER.

Too much! by heaven! you .heartless
    chit!
I'll *prove* you underrate my wit,
And self-respect, for all that's passed!
I will — will break these bonds at last.
Yes! look! you false, hard-hearted girl!
I dash to earth the dazzling curl
You gave me once! . . . your portrait
    too! . . .
(O, yes! I *stole* it, . . . what of that ?
'Twill soon be shapeless, crushed and
    flat,
Beneath my stern, avenging heel!
Would it were *flesh,* and so could *feel,*
. . . Where is it! *where ?*
[*He searches frantically, but vainly for the
    likeness in one pocket after another.*]

[COQUETTE—approaching with infinite sweet-
ness, rests one hand upon his shoulder, while
the forefinger of the other is archly shaken in
his angry face, that changes with ludicrous
quickness, from passion to bewilderment, and
from bewilderment to rapture]:
. . . Why, Hal, for shame! you prayed
    just now,
With earnest mien and solemn brow,
That I would sting you with hot scorn;
" *Do all a winsome lady born*
To loveliness and witchery, can,
To flout a love-tormented man."
And lo! because your bidding's done;
Half-way, and mildly; why, I've won
Such rude abuse! . . . I shall not stir,
Till you have begged my pardon, sir!
. . . Hal! *do* you love me ? . . .

LOVER.

. . . Angel! saint!
Can this be true! . . . my heart grows
    faint,
With happiness! . . . so then, despite—

COQUETTE (*interrupting*).

Yes, dear! of feigned contempt and
    slight,
— I have loved you always! who but *you*

Had failed thus long to read me true?
You dear, delightful, blundering boy.

LOVER.

. . . Cupid be blessed! Oh, love! Oh, joy!
. . . But where's that precious curl I
    threw
Rashly away? . . . Already flown
On some light wind?

COQUETTE.

—— Yes, yes, 'tis gone!
But then the whole bright, golden net
        (*shaking down her curls.*)
You've gained with me! . . . If still
    unfair
You deem this soft, imprisoning snare;
And self-respect, for all that's passed,
Demands you break your bonds at last,
Give me due warning — if you please —

LOVER (*embracing her*).

Ah! *thus* a loving seal is set
On rosy lips to keep them dumb;
Some other eve beneath the trees
Of golden summer, 'mid the hum
Of forest brooks and hive-bound bees,
I'll hearken, madcap, while you tease.
But now, my heart the future years
Sees through a mist of blissful tears;
My eyes with gracious dew are wet;
I'm dreaming! . . . No! . . . *here* smiles
    coquette!

———◆———

SENEX TO HIS FRIEND.

ABOUT THE PERIOD OF A NEW YEAR.

Dedicated to Sam'l Lord, Jr., Charleston, S.C.

YOUR hair is scant, my friend, and mine
    is scanter,
On heads snowed white by Time, the
    disenchanter;
In place of joyous beams and jovial
    twinkles,
Behold, old boy, our faces scored with
    wrinkles!

Sparkles your legal lore with salt that's
    Attic!
But, ah! those twinges (gout?), those
    pangs rheumatic!
With muse of mine no more the public
    quarrels,
But, Lord! how cold I feel despite the
    laurels!

If spiced your fame, not so your milk or
    sago:
Only mild diet suits a sharp lumbago.
While as for me — what critic "puff"
    avails one
Whose own short breath (asthmatic!)
    almost fails one?

The world we deemed so rife with fade-
    less prizes —
Which of us most its hollow show de-
    spises?
We'd yield our gains for just one mar-
    vellous minute
Of our lost youth, with all youth's glory
    in it!

Yet from this House of Life, now
    wrapped in twilight,
Gleams 'mid the shadowy roof Faith's
    magic skylight;
Whereby as night steals down through
    weird gradations,
We hail the glow of heavenly constella-
    tions.

So, as through darkness only dawn the
    graces
Of God's calm stars and lofty shining
    spaces,
That night called death which shrouds
    our bodies breathless
May flood the heaven of soul with peace
    made deathless.

———◆———

THE OBSERVANT "ELDEST" SPEAKS.

" PA vows that all gluttony's wicked;
    He's always for docking *my* meat,
And ne'er at dessert will he give me
    Enough of what's racy and sweet:

Yet he'll gorge and gorge on at *his* din-
 ners,
 As restless in mouth as in hand; —
Now, say, — if all gluttons are sinners,
 Where — where does *my* 'governor'
  stand!

"Oh! pa's most impressive on lying;
 ('Meanest crime in the annals of sin;')
Yet why does *he* tell folk (through
  Thomas)
 That he's *out* when he knows that he's
  in?
And ma's done the same, when she
 meant not
From house nor from chamber to stir:
I suppose what is punished in *me*, sir,
 Is all right in *him* or in *her!*

"Pa says, that good men must be
 generous,
 Self-denying, benevolent, kind;'
Then why does he give those poor beg-
  gars
 Just nothing? The lame and the
  blind,
Small orphan, and wan, pining widow,
 The gold-covered head and the gray,
Unsoothed and unhelped in their sor-
  rows,
 From *him* turn — how sadly — away!

"Pa counsels fair words of our neigh-
  bors; —
 Oh! he dotes on the pure 'golden
  rule;'
Yet he calls Aunt Selina 'back-biter,'
 And he dubs Uncle Reuben 'a fool.'"
And when *I* said, 'Young Reub's like
  his father,'
 On what text in reply did pa lean?
Why, 'Whoso thou fool shall dare utter,'
 Must taste — well, *you* know what I
  mean!

"Pa says, 'we must reverence our
  elders;' —
 How he harps and he harps upon
  that; —

Yet grandfather, who's ninety and up-
  ward,
 He treats like an imbecile 'flat.'
And once when poor grandpa, at break-
  fast,
 Mistook the slop-bowl for his cup,
Pa muttered, 'I wish the old dotard
 Were locked — *somewhere* — heedfully
  up!'

"I don't know what the 'governor's'
 made of;
 But truly, if *he were not he*,
(I mean if he were not *my* 'pater' —
 Alack! that *such* fathers should be,)
His name would begin as I spelt it,
 With a big blatant H, if you please,
And conclude with the tiniest, meanest,
 But most self-sufficient of e's!'"

———◆———

LUCIFER'S DEPUTY.

A MEDIÆVAL LEGEND.

A POET once, whose tuneful soul, per-
  chance,
Too fondly leaned toward sin, and sin's
  romance,
On a long vanished eve, so calm and
  clear
None could have deemed an evil spirit
  near,
Brooding ill deeds, was summoned by a
  writ,
In the due form of Hades, to the Pit;
A red-nosed, red-haired fiend the sum-
  moner,
About whose horrent head his locks did
  stir
Like half-waked serpents! "Well," in
  wrath and woe,
The poet cried, "whom the De'il drives
  must go,
Whate'er the goal! Yet much I wish
  that he
Had sent as guide some nobler fiend than
  thee,
Thou hideous varlet!"

" Come, keep cool, I say,"
Counselled the other sagely, " while *you
may !* "
Whereon, as half in scorn and half in
ire,
He haled the poet to the realm of fire.

Arrived in bounds Hadéan, a vast rout
Of fiends they met, who rushed tumultu-
ous out,
To roam the earth and those doomed
spirits snare
Who unsuspecting lived and acted
there;
Till in a few brief seconds the whole
crew
Of crowding demons — black, brown,
green and blue —
All but their haughty chief, his form up-
reared
Through the red mist, had wildly dis-
appeared.

Then said the dark archangel to the
bard :
" Thine eye is bright, thou hast a shrewd
regard;
And, therefore, ere I likewise o'er the
marge
Of Hades wing my way for some brief
hours,
To thee I choose to delegate my powers
As chief and sovereign of this kingdom
dread,
To which, if well thou guardest, by my
head
Thy recompense, when I come back,
shall be
A luscious tid bit, garnished daintily —
No meaner *entrée* than a roasted monk,
(Before he's cooked we'll make the
rascal drunk,
To spice his juices!) ; or, if thou'dst
prefer
Yon leaner and less succulent usurer,
Why, of our toil and time with trifling
loss,
We'll serve *him* up, larded with golden
sauce !"

But while the absent fiends their cunning
tasked
To trap unwary souls, thick cloaked and
masked,
One entered Hades who did soon
entice
The heedless bard to play a game at
dice,
Staking the souls he held in charge
thereon.
The stranger played superbly — played,
and won.
So, gathering round him the freed souls,
with care
And kind despatch, safe to the outward
air
He led them triumphing; and all who
now
Looked on his unmasked face and
glorious brow
Knew that St. Peter stood amongst them
there.
But when the devils, trooping homeward,
found
Their kingdom void — its conflagrations
drowned
As 'twere by showers from Heaven —
such curses rose —
Like thunder bellowing through the
strange repose
Which late had reigned — the poet's
head whirled round,
Stunned by the tumult. But ere long,
with whirr
And furious whizz, his right hand
Lucifer
Brought in such stinging contact with
one cheek
And then the other, that our minstrel,
weak
From pain and fear, sank trembling on
the floor.
But sternly Satan pointed to the door,
Where through his faithless guard, with
many a kick
And echoing thump, and one swift mer-
ciless prick
Of a keen pitchfork, was thrust forth in
shame

From out the empire of fierce grief and
    flame,
In even more woeful plight than when
    he came!
Then Lucifer upraised his arms and
    swore
A mighty oath that Hades' lurid door
No poet's form should ever enter more!

So, brother bards, whate'er ye write or
    do,
Be fearless.   Hades holds no place for
    you:
Since if on earth men deem your worth
    but small,
Why there, 'tis plain, ye have no worth
    at all!

POEMS FOR CHILDREN.

POEMS FOR CHILDREN.

LITTLE NELLIE IN THE PRISON.

The eyes of a child are sweeter than any hymn
    we have sung,
And wiser than any sermon is the lisp of a
    childish tongue!

HUGH FALCON learned this happy truth
    one day;
('Twas a fair noontide in the month of
    May)—
When, as the chaplain of the convicts'
    jail,
He passed its glowering archway, sad
    and pale,
Bearing his tender daughter on his arm.
A five years' darling she! The dewy
    charm
Of Eden star-dawns glistened in her
    eyes;
Her dimpled cheeks were rich with sun-
    ny dyes.

"Papa!" the child that morn while
    still abed,
Drawing him close toward her, shyly
    said:
"Papa! oh, won't you let your Nellie go
To see those naughty men that plague
    you so,
Down in the ugly prison by the wood?
Papa, I'll beg and pray them to be
    good."
"What, you, my child?" he said, with
    half a sigh.
"Why not, papa? I'll beg them so to
    try."

The chaplain, with a father's gentlest
    grace,
Kissed the small ruffled brow, the plead-
    ing face:

"Out of the mouths of babes and suck-
    lings still,
Praise is perfected," thought he; thus,
    his will
Blended with hers, and through those
    gates of sin,
Black, even at noontide, sire and child
    passed in.

Fancy the foulness of a sulphurous lake,
Wherefrom a lily's snow-white leaves
    should break,
Flushed by the shadow of an unseen
    rose!
So, at the iron gate's loud clang and
    close,
Shone the drear twilight of that place
    defiled,
Touched by the flower-like sweetness of
    the child!
O'er many a dismal vault, and stony
    floor,
The chaplain walked from ponderous
    door to door,
Till now beneath a stairway's dizzy flight
He stood and looked up the far-circling
    height;
But risen of late from fever's torture-
    bed,
How could he trust his faltering limbs
    and head?

Just then, he saw, next to the mildewed
    wall,
A man in prisoner's raiment, gaunt and
    tall,
Of sullen aspect, and wan, downcast
    face,
Gloomed in the midnight of some deep
    disgrace;

He shrank as one who yearned to fade
    away,
Like a vague shadow on the stone-work
    gray,
Or die beyond it, like a viewless wind;
He seemed a spirit faithless, passionless,
    blind
To all fair hopes which light the hearts
    of men, —
A dull, dead soul, never to wake again!

The chaplain paused, half doubting
    what to do,
When little Nellie raised her eyes of blue,
And, no wise daunted by the downward
    stir
Of shaggy brows that glowered askance
    at her,
Said, — putting by her wealth of sunny
    hair, —
" Sir, will you kindly take me up the
    stair ?
Papa is tired, and I'm too small to
    climb."
Frankly her eyes in his gazed all the
    time;
And something to her childhood's
    instinct known
So worked within her, that her arms
    were thrown
About his neck. She left her sire's em-
    brace
Near that sad convict-heart to take her
    place,
Sparkling and trustful! — more she did
    not speak;
But her quick fingers patted his swart
    cheek
Caressingly, — in time to some old tune
Hummed by her nurse, in summer's
    drowsy noon!

Perforce he turned his wild, uncertain
    gaze
Down on the child! Then stole a trem-
    ulous haze
Across his eyes, but rounded not to tears;
Wherethrough he saw faint glimmerings
    of lost years

And perished loves! A cabin by a rill
Rose through the twilight on a happy
    hill;
And there were lithe child-figures at
    their play
That flashed and faded in the dusky
    ray;
And near the porch a gracious wife who
    smiled,
Pure as young Eve in Eden, unbeguiled!

Subdued, yet thrilled, 'twas beautiful to
    see
With what deep reverence, and how ten-
    derly,
He clasped the infant frame so slight
    and fair,
And safely bore her up the darkening
    stair!
The landing reached, in her arch, child-
    ish ease,
Our Nelly clasped his neck and whis-
    pered:
                        " Please,
Won't you be good, sir ? For I like you
    so,
And you are such a big, strong man,
    you know — "
With pleading eyes, her sweet face side-
    wise set.
Then suddenly his furrowed cheeks
    grew wet
With sacred tears — in whose divine
    eclipse
Upon her nestling head he pressed his
    lips
As softly as a dreamy west wind's sigh,
What time a something, undefined but
    high,
As 'twere a new soul, struggled to the
    dawn
Through his raised eyelids. Thence,
    the gloom withdrawn
Of brooding vengeance and unholy pain,
He felt no more the captive's galling
    chain;
But only knew a little child had come
To smite despair, his taunting demon,
    dumb;

"Our Nelly clasped his neck and whispered:
'Please
Won't you be good, sir? For I like you so.'"

A child whose marvellous innocence en-
    ticed
All white thoughts back, that from the
    heart of Christ
Fly dove-like earthward, past our cloud-
    ed ken,
Child-life to bless, or lives of child-like
    men!

                Thus he went his way,
An altered man from that thrice blessèd
    day;
His soul tuned ever to the soft refrain
Of words once uttered in a sacred fane:
" The little children, let them come to
    me,
Of such as these my realm of heaven
    must be;"
But most he loved of one dear child to
    tell,
The child whose trust had saved him,
    tender Nell!

THE CHILDREN.

THE children! ah, the children!
  Your innocent, joyous ones;
Your daughters, with souls of sunshine;
  Your buoyant and laughing sons.

Look long in their happy faces,
  Drink love from their sparkling eyes,
For the wonderful charm of childhood,
  How soon it withers and dies!

A few fast-vanishing summers,
  A season or twain of frost,
And you suddenly ask, bewildered
  " What is it my heart hath lost ? "

Perhaps you see by the hearth-stone
  Some Juno, stately and proud,
Or a Hebe whose softly ambushed eyes
  Flash out from the golden cloud

Of lavish and beautiful tresses
  That wantonly floating, stray
O'er the white of a throat and bosom
  More fair than blossoms in May.

And perhaps you mark their brothers—
  Young heroes who spurn the sod
With the fervor of antique knighthood,
  And the air of a Grecian god!

But where, ah, where are the children,
  Your household fairies of yore ?
Alack! they are dead, and their grace
    has fled
For ever and ever more!

WILL AND I.

I.

WE roam the hills together,
In the golden summer weather,
    Will and I:
And the glowing sunbeams bless us,
And the winds of heaven caress us,
  As we wander hand in hand
  Through the blissful summer land
    Will and I.

II.

Where the tinkling brooklet passes
Through the heart of dewy grasses,
    Will and I
Have heard the mock-bird singing,
And the field-lark seen upspringing
  In his happy flight afar,
  Like a tiny wingèd star,
    Will and I.

III.

Amid cool forest closes
We have plucked the wild wood roses,
    Will and I;
And have twined, with tender duty,
Sweet wreaths to crown the beauty
  Of the purest brows that shine
  With a mother-love divine
    Will and I.

IV.

Ah! thus we roam together,
Through the golden summer weather,
    Will and I;

While the glowing sunbeams bless us,
And the winds of heaven caress us —
As we wander hand in hand
O'er the blissful summer land
Will and I.

———◆———

JAMIE AND HIS MOTHER — IN THE TROPICS.

JAMIE.

O MOTHER, what country is that I see
Far over the stream and the boulders
gray,
Where the wind-song pipes, and the cur-
lews flee,
And the little brown squirrels dance
and play
Through the boughs all day?

MOTHER.

Why, only a forest dark and wild,
A savage waste you must shun, my child!

JAMIE.

O mother, what shapes are those that sit
In the deep dun heart of the woodland
gloom?
And what those creatures that dip and
flit,
Each crowned with a golden and scar-
let plume,
O'er the tamarind bloom?

MOTHER.

Why, only the monkeys crouched from
sight,
And paroquets flashing in gay-hued
flight!

JAMIE.

O mother, what children are those that
run
So swift and light 'mid the tree-stems
bare?
They seem to twinkle from shade to sun,
And beckon me over their sport to
share
In the noontide fair!

"Go not," she cried, with a quivering
breath:
"They are Pixies, child, and their sport
is death!"

But there came a morn when the moth-
er's words
No longer dwelt in her Jamie's mind;
When he followed the flight of the whir-
ring birds
That circled and soared on the wood-
land wind,
And mother and home were far behind.

Like one in a golden dream was he,
Far over the stream and the boulders
gray;
And the wind-song pipes, and the cur-
lews flee,
And the little brown squirrels dance
and play
Through the boughs all day.

But the day grew dim, and the night-
shades fell,
And there in the dark, drear, hungry
wild,
In the loneliest nook of a mountain dell,
Where never a tender moonbeam
smiled,
Lay the weary child!

Like one in an awful trance was he,
In the deep dun heart of the woodland
gloom;
But a trance whose shadows can never
flee,
Till the mystic trump of the day of
doom
Breaks vault and tomb.

And they found him there with his
bleeding hands
So humbly crossed o'er the ragged vest,
His spirit had gone to the angel lands,
But his out-worn body they laid to
rest
In the last sad smile of the gentle west:
God guard his rest!

THE THREE COPECKS.

CROUCHED low in a sordid chamber,
  With a cupboard of empty shelves,
Half starved, and, alas, unable
  To comfort or help themselves,

Two children were left forsaken,
  All orphaned of mortal care;
But with spirits too close to heaven
  To be tainted by earth's despair,

Alone in that crowded city,
  Which shines like an arctic star,
By the banks of the frozen Neva,
  In the realm of the mighty Czar.

Now, Max was an urchin of seven;
  But his delicate sister, Leeze,
With the crown of her rippling ringlets,
  Could scarcely have reached your
    knees.

As he looked on his sister weeping,
  And tortured by hunger's smart,
A thought like an angel entered
  At the door of his opened heart.

He wrote on a fragment of paper,
  With quivering hand and soul,
"*Please send to me, Christ, three co-
    pecks,
  To purchase for Leeze a roll!*"

Then, rushed to a church, his missive
  To drop, — ere the vesper psalms, —
As the surest mail bound Christward,
  In the unlocked box for alms!

While he stepped upon tiptoe to reach it,
  One passed from the priestly band,
And with smile like a benediction,
  Took the note from his eager hand.

Having read it, the good man's bosom
  Grew warm with a holy joy;
"Ah! Christ may have heard you
    already,
  Will you come to *my* house, my boy?"

"But not without Leeze?"   "No,
    surely,
  We'll have a rare party of three;
Go, tell her that somebody's waiting
  To welcome her home to tea."

That night in the cosiest cottage,
  The orphans were safe at rest,
Each sang as a callow birdling,
  In the depths of its downy nest.

And the next Lord's Day, in his pulpit,
  The preacher so spake of these,
Stray lambs from the fold, which Jesus
  Had blessed by the sacred seas:

So recounted their guileless story,
  As he held each child by the hand,
That the hardest there could feel it,
  And the dullest could understand.

O'er the eyes of the listening fathers
  There floated a gracious mist;
And oh, how the tender mothers
  Those desolate darlings kissed!

"You have given your tears," said the
    preacher,
  "Heart-alms we should none despise;
*But the open palm, my children,
  Is more than the weeping eyes!*"

Then followed a swift collection,
  From the altar steps to the door,
Till the sum of two thousand rubles
  The vergers had counted o'er.

So you see that the unmailed letter
  Had somehow gone to its goal,
And more than three copecks gathered
  To purchase for Leeze a roll!

THE REASON WHY.

I'D like, indeed I'd like to know
Why sister Bell, who loved me so,
And used to pet me day and night,
And could not bear me out of sight,

Now always looks so cross and glum,
If to her side I chance to come,
When that great, gawky man is nigh;
I'd like to know the reason why?

That man! I *hate* him! yes, I do,
And, in *my* place, you'd hate him too.
At first, (his common name is John!)
He brought me boxes of *bon bons*,
With books, and dolls, and tiny rings,
And lots on lots of precious things,
And said, of all Miss Pontoon's girls,
Not one could match my flowing curls,
My rosy cheeks and rounded chin,
With one sly dimple nestling in.
But now, he seems so stern and high,
I scarce may catch his scornful eye,
While as for *toys!* — he has ceased to
　　buy!
Tell me, who can, the reason why?

It's mean! dear me! I'm sure it's mean!
Did I not run a " go-between "
From him to sister Bell so long,
(Although I *feared* it might be wrong),
With sweetmeats, flowers, and scented
　　notes,
Sealed by two doves with curving throats?
Of course I thought him kind and nice.
But now, he's cold as arctic ice!
And more than once I've heard him
　　say,
" That chit's forever in the way!"
While Bell — she *snaps!* till I could
　　cry.
Will no one tell the reason why?

LATER.

Think — Mr. John's my friend again.
('Twas yesternight he made it plain),
For most of our big household gone
To Friday's lecture, — left alone,
But Bell and I; *he* came to tea,
(As now he's coming constantly,)
And spoke to me quite warmly — quite :
" Lizzie, you are not looking bright;
And since both Bell and I are here,
Take Nurse, and see the circus, dear;
I'll pay, my love! accept of this."

(A wee gold dollar, and — a kiss!)
" Why don't you come with Bell?"
　　asked I;
He smiled, but would not answer why.

LATER STILL.

Good news! good news! I'm almost mad,
I feel so pleased, so proud and glad.'
To-morrow is the wedding-day;
Papa will give our Bell away,
And I'm a bridesmaid!—oh, my dress!
" Soft waves of white silk loveliness,"
Bell says, " with grace in every tuck!"
And isn't Brother John a duck?
(I call him *Brother* now, you see,)
He gave this dainty dress to me,
And said, his " little friend must look
Fair as a picture in a book."
I answered gayly, " I shall try!"
What need to ask the reason why?

THE SILKEN SHOE.

" Hie on the holly-tree !"— *Old Ballad.*

THE firelight danced and wavered
　　In elvish, twinkling glee
On the leaves and crimson berries
　　Of the great green Christmas Tree;

And the children who gathered round it
　　Beheld, with marvelling eyes,
Pendant from trunk and branches
　　How many a precious prize,

From the shimmer of gold and silver
　　Through a purse's cunning net,
To the coils of a rippling necklace,
　　That quivered with beads of jet.

But chiefly they gazed in wonder
　　Where flickered strangely through
The topmost leaves of the holly
　　The sheen of a silken shoe!

And the eldest spake to her father:
　　" I have seen — yes, year by year,
On the crown of our Christmas hollies,
　　That small shoe glittering clear;

"But you never have told who owned it,
 Nor why so loftily set,
It shines through the fadeless verdure,
 You never have told us yet!"

'Twas then that the museful father
 In slow sad accents said,
While the firelight hovered eerily
 About his downcast head:

"My children — you had a sister;
 (It was long, long, long ago),
She came like an Eden rosebud
 'Mid the dreariest winter snow,

"And for four sweet seasons blossomed
 To cheer our hearts and hearth,
When the song of the Bethlehem angels
 Lured her away from earth —

"My shoe, papa, please hang it
Once more on the holly bough."

"For again 'twas the time of Christmas,
 As she lay with laboring breath;
But — our minds were blinded strangely,
 And we did not dream of death.

"A little before she left us,
 We had deftly raised to view,
On the topmost branch of the holly
 Yon glimmering, tiny shoe;

"We knew that no toy would please her
 Like a shoe so fair and neat,
To fold, with its soft caressing
 Her delicate, sylph-like feet!

"Truly, a smile like a sunbeam
 Brightened her eyes of blue,
And once — twice — thrice — she tested
 The charm of her fairy shoe!

"Ah! then the bright smile flickered,
 Faded, and drooped away,
As faintly, in tones that faltered,
 I heard our darling say:

"'My shoe, papa, please hang it
 Once more on the holly bough,
Just where I am sure to see it,
 When I wake — an hour from now.

"But alas! she never wakened!
 Close shut were the eyes of blue;
Whose last faint gleam had fondled
 The curves of that dainty shoe.

"Ah, children, you understand me;
 Your eyes are brimmed with dew,
As they watch on the Christmas holly
 The sheen of a silken shoe."

THE BLACK DESTRIER.

A BALLAD OF THE THIRD CRUSADE.

First 'mid the lion Richard's host,
 Sir Aymer fought in Holy Land;
And they loved him well for his honest
    heart,
 And they feared, for his stalwart hand.

Once on a glorious battle eve,
 The Paynim legions wildly flying,
Sir Aymer paused from his work of
    blood,
 Where an eastern knight lay dying.

He was the latest guard of one,
 The Soldan's fair and favorite bride,
And there on the trampled and crimson
    sod
 She moaned by the warrior's side.

No strength had he to shield his charge;
 But mild the Christian victor's face;
And the lady knew, as she gazed thereon,
 That his mercy would grant her grace.

The Paynim died: "I am thy guide,"
 The brave Sir Aymer softly said;
"By my father's faith thou art safe from
    scaith,
 Wheresoever thou would'st be led."

True to his word, through friend, through
    foe,
 He bore the lady fast and far,
Till the hostile sheen of the Moslem
    spears
 Flashed under the evening star.

The Soldan's self with speechless joy,
 With glistening eyes and bated breath,
The queen of his house and heart em-
    braced,
 As if claiming his Love from death!

"Now, Christian knight, by this pure
    light,
 No vain nor empty thanks are mine;
So, name thee the guerdon a king may
    grant,
 And believe me, it shall be thine."

"No guerdon, prince, for simple ruth
 The Christian warrior deigns to take;
He has vowed to rescue the lorn and
    weak,
 For his own sweet lady's sake.'

"All proofs of zeal the grateful feel,
 Surely, fair knight, thou would'st not
    shun?
An honored guest, thou wilt tarry and
    rest,
 At least till the morrow's sun?"

Thus, in the Soldan's tent he stayed —
 What time the queen with passionate
    eyes,
Struck blind to the harem's splendor,
    dreamed
 Of his beauty with love-sick sighs:

And ere that morrow's sun had set,
 With scarce a blush her love she told;
But Sir Aymer hearkened with haughty
    mien,
 And the words that he spake were cold.

Then flushed the imperious forehead
    high,
 A dark flame glittered in her eyes,
And the hate of the deadly orient quelled
 The breath of her tender sighs.

"Sir knight, enough; thou scorn'st my
    love!
 But ere thou goest, take instead
This marvellous steed of the jet-black
    breed,
 In the land of the Magi bred.

"O stern in fight! O swift in flight!
 This matchless steed will serve thee
    well,
Whether thy lure be a lady's bower,
 Or the vanward war-trump's swell."

He took the gift, he bowed him low,
 And gained the Christian camp at
    noon;
"O courser of might in strife or flight!"
 Quoth he, "I shall prove thee soon."

.   .   .   .   .   .

The conflict joins; the hosts are hot;
  That gallant Destrier "holds his
    own;"
Aghast at the rush of his whirlwind
    course,
  Whole legions are overthrown.

In twice three mortal combats more
  The same fell ruin marked his path,
Till the Saracens deemed, as their life-
    blood streamed,
  'Twas a fiend of hell in his wrath.

But once, alas! alas! the day!
  The Moslem's sudden war-cry rose,
And the knight his "Avè" forgot to
    say,
  Ere he hastened to meet his foes.

St. Paul! what wizard spell is this?
  The Destrier spurns the hands that
    guide,
And full on the front of the *Christian*
    host
  Sweeps back through the battle tide.

Gramercy! 'twas a dreadful sight
  Which met the gathering thousands
    there,
When the war-horse charged like a blaz-
    ing star,
  Through a halo of blood-red air.

With bristling mane, and hot disdain
  Against the mail-clad lines he came;
And his red orbs burned with a frenzied
    ire,
  And his nostrils darted flame.

Thus raging from the heathen van,
  Strange steed and awful rider rushed,
And the souls of the boldest shrank
    appalled,
  And the wildest voice was hushed;

Till swift towards King Richard's camp
  The fiery-fronted portent bore,
From the fetlock firm to the horrent crest
  All reeking with Christian gore.

There, on a sudden paused the barb,
  Still, as if carved in marble black,
And from silent knight and terrible steed
  The pale throng shuddered back:

But now from out the trembling crowd
  A priest with holy water passed,
He sprinkled the knight, he sprinkled
    the steed
  With the pure lymph free and fast:

When lo! the fatal charm dissolved —
  Prone, with a hollow, rattling sound
In the clasp of his unscathed armor, fell
  The knight to the bloody ground:

They loosed his hauberk and his helm,
  But dead and wan his eyeballs shone,
As if they had gazed on a nameless
    dread
  Which had frozen their life to stone!

They felt his pulseless heart, his brow
  Dim with the death-shade's mystic
    gloom,
While ruthless and stern are the looks
    they turn
  On the demon that wrought his doom.

But pallid as a waning cloud
  Athwart the summer moon-disc blown,
The shadowy form of a demon steed
  In the ghost-like eve had grown:

Only — his supernatural eyes
  One moment shot a vengeful spark,
Ere the glimmering Syrian twilight
    closed
  On the steps of the sudden dark.

THE ADVENTURES OF LITTLE BOB
BONNYFACE.

LITTLE Bob Bonnyface went out one
    day
Into his father's fields to play;
'Twas a morn undarkened by mist or
    cloud,

With the thrush and the blackbird
    piping loud;
The locust, deep in the pine-tree wood,
Shrilled, as only a locust could;
And borne on the waft of a summer
    breeze,
Swarmed by him an army of honey-bees.
Delighted he saw, delighted he heard
The morn, the bees, and the singing
    bird;
He also sang, as he roamed through the
    clover,
Feeling *so* jolly, and free all over!

But Bob — I must tell you the honest
    truth —
Was a terribly mischievous thoughtless
    youth;
Whatever he wanted to do or say,
He did and he said in the boldest way,
Not seeming to ponder, even to care
How naughty his words or his actions
    were;
For the only aim of this reckless elf
Was — everywhere, always, to please —
    himself!

'Twas to please himself, without license
    or leave
Nor a thought how his poor sick moth-
    er might grieve,
If she missed too long, on her suffering
    bed,
The golden gleam of his curly head,
That he left his home through the fields
    to stray,
On that sunny and beautiful summer's
    day,
As the air breathed over him, blithe-
    some, but calm,
All laden with fragrance and meadow-
    balm,
And the sunshine warmed his young
    blood through,
While it dazzled and danced from the
    stainless blue,
Bob felt that a jollity, wholesome and
    sweet,
Possessed him wholly, from head to feet.

He looked around, and what should his
    eye
In an open space 'mid the clover spy,
But an ant-hole, wrought in the sandy
    drouth.
Out of its busy, populous mouth,
The dwarfish tenants — an endless train,
Emerging, covered the tiny plain;
Eastward and westward, north and
    south,
They toiled, with a constant will, to
    gain
The fairy stores of their winter's grain;
Yet Bob in his recklessness deemed it
    fun
The ants and their mansion to overrun.
By millions down in the crumbling sod
The frightened creatures he swiftly
    trod;
Filled up with dust, and grasses, and
    stone,
The entrance-ways to their home, o'er-
    thrown
Not one of the innocent horde, not *one*,
Was left to toil in the laughing sun —
But still Bob shouted, and thought it —
    fun!

Next on his wandering way he came
To a furze-bush, gleaming like yellow
    flame;
A spider as ugly and fierce as sin,
Had spread the snares of his web there-
    in;
But — cunning and sly — as Bob rushed
    up,
He hid himself deep in a thistle's cup,
Leaving above, in his worship's stead,
A bee, caught fast in his poisoned
    thread!

Now, here was a chance for Bobby to
    free
From his pain and prison this harmless
    bee;
But bless you! no! 'twas a finer thing
He thought, to pierce him from wing to
    wing;
On a pin's keen point to whirl him high,

And behold the quivering insect die,
This, too, when the barbarous act was
　done,
Seemed nothing to Bob but a moment's
　— fun.

More gleeful than ever, Bob onward
　pressed;
In the wayside thickets he found a nest,
The eggs half hatched; but he took
　them out,
And with rude hand scattered them all
　about,
Laughing to see how the egg-shells
　broke.
But hey! what's this ? with a buffeting
　stroke,
The wings of the outraged mother-bird
(Who down from her neighboring perch
　had whirred,)
So smartly smote him on forehead and
　eyes,
That Bobby in *his* turn trembling —
　flies!

(Don't you think that his was a wretch-
　ed plight ?
Just picture a *boy* from a *bird* in flight!
His heart and his knee-joints weak with
　fright.)

But soon recovered, he trudged along,
Humming the words of a ballad-song,
Till reaching a place where the grasses
　bred
Tall " hoppers " in thousands, he staid
　his tread,
And cunningly crouching, as quick as
　thought,
A " grandfather hopper " was deftly
　caught.
Bob squeezed his body, and pulled his
　thighs,
And poked a straw in his winking
　eyes;
Then, with shrill laughter, and merry
　scoff,
He wrenched both legs of the creature
　off;

And next (could the rascal have had a
　heart ?)
Its head from the body was snatched
　apart,
Till, a pitiful image of death and dearth,
Its carcass lay on the verdant earth!

I haven't the leisure to stop and tell
What other pains and evils befell
The defenceless tenants of wood and
　dell;
All wrought by an urchin's uncurbed
　will,
At length as an evening fair and still,
Shone over the wood, Bob strolled be-
　yond
The wooded glades to a quiet pond,
The home of eels, mud-fishes, and
　things
Half frog, half fish, all covered with
　stings,
And scaly armor, as bright as brass;
Then and there, reader, it came to pass
That a terrapin, lazily crawling o'er
The moistened ways of its native shore,
Bob shrewdly captured — he turned his
　back
Heedfully down on the sandy track,
And — need we say it ? — at once began
To practise as ever, his teasing plan.
He pinched the flesh of the terrapin
　sore
Racked it behind, and racked it before;
And strove — tho' just with a touch of
　awe,
The reptile's head from its shell to draw.
When hark! the sound of a vicious
　snap!
And the juvenile's fingers were in a trap
As ruthless as fate, and as sharp as
　steel;
Then, followed a piteous discord!
　Squeal,
Bellow, and shriek, the echoes around,
Woke up from the startled wave and
　ground.
Bob struggled and panted, kicked and
　cried,
Yet, his enemy's hold all efforts defied;

He thought to rise, but he would not do
    it,
For fear that his mangled flesh might
    rue it;
And still more agonized, angry, and
    loud,
His yells went up to a whirling cloud,
Which in a moment from out the
    blue,
(*Or such was his fancy*), darker grew,
Whence peered a head and a face to
    fear;
But what shall I say of the monster's
    leer,
His huge mouth stretching from ear to
    ear ?

"You have tortured," (it said) "and
    torn all day
God's helpless creatures in wanton
    play;
Now, learn, oh! cruel and coward elf!
A useful lesson of pain, yourself!
Does it burn and sting to the deepest
    nerve ?
What less do your brutal deeds deserve ?
How! groaning again! for shame! be
    done!
*You only tortured, you know, — in
    fun !*"

.   .   .   .   .

When he gained from the terrapin's
    clutch release
While resting, that night, on his couch
    in peace,
There softly dawned thro' the twilight
    gloom,
A face more fair than a white-rose
    bloom;
And a voice that seemed like the under
    speech
Of the waters that swoon on a breezeless
    beach,
Whispered as low as low could be;
"Look up! I charge thee! and worship
    me;
And yet *not* me, but the Master —
    Christ!

"My name is Pity! — I am enticed
From even the Heaven of Heavens to
    bring
Soft balms for mortal suffering;
And whosoever the frailest thing
With strength within it to feel or love,
Wounds *here* — he is torturing me
    above;
And worse — for the pangs of that
    anguish dart
Through mine, to the tender Saviour's
    heart!"

Silence! — but just as sleep was won,
And over the boy's bright eyes of brown,
The delicate lashes came drooping down,
Thro' the silvery eddies of moonlight
    mist,
There stole the shadow of lips that
    kissed
The stain from the childish soul away,
That sadly sinning, had deemed it —
    play!

———◆———

KISS ME, KATIE!

KATIE, Katie, little Katie!
Mouth of rose and eyes of blue,
(Eyes that look one frankly through!)
When I'm absent don't you miss me ?
Now I'm near you, come and kiss me!
    Katie, little Katie, kiss me!
        Katie, do!

Katie, Katie, pretty Katie!
Prettier far than Jane or Lu,
Madge or Margaret, Maud or Prue;
Graceful as a spring-born fairy,
Tuneful as your pet canary—
    Katie, pretty Katie, kiss me!
        Katie, do!

Katie, sly, deceptive Katie!
If you fly me I'll pursue.
(What though *corns* or *gout* should rue!)
Then, if I can overmatch you,
Running fast can clasp and catch you,
    Captured Katie, won't you kiss me ?
        Katie, do!

"Katie, pretty Katie, kiss me."

Katie, mute, day-dreaming Katie,
If I tell your thoughts to you,
Guess your dreams and *make* them true,
Won't you cease your coy defiance,
Vanquished by such wondrous science—
  Won't you kiss me, Katie darling?
    Katie, do!

Katie, captious little Katie!
Why that quickly tapping shoe,
Ready shrug and scornful *moue?*
Can it be you mean to scout me?
Just because I'm *grayish*, flout me?
Are you muttering, " KISS HIM! NEVER!
  No, I *can't!* and no, I *won't!*"
  O, you petulant, changeful Katie!
    Katie, *don't!*

———◆———

CAGED.

YOU think he sings a gladsome song!
  Ah, well, he *sings!* but only see
How oft on glossy neck and breast
  His bright head droops despondingly;
Or note the restless, eager bird
When a *free* minstrel's voice is heard.

You think because he pecks his grain
  With vigorous mien and active bill,
This long captivity has trained
  To tame content his roving will.
But watch, as some wild pinion flies,
Flashed near his cage, from summer
    skies:

He lifts his crest, his eyes dilate
  To yearning orbs of passionate fire;
His whole small body seems to thrill,
  And vibrate to the heart's desire:
The deathless wish once more to roam
The broad blue heaven God made his
    home.

Mark, next, the weary pant, the sigh
  Of hope deferred, that follows then;
Perchance your captive's pain is deep
  As that which haunts imprisoned *men*,
Pining behind *their* cruel bars
For sunlight or the holy stars.

Come! ope the door! he owns a soul
  As tender, sensitive and fine
As yours or mine — for aught *we* know,
  And dowered with rights scarce less
    Divine;
Come! let him choose, at least, between
God's azure and yon gilded screen!

Freed! yet he flies not! — Wait! — his
    brain
  Is dazed! — he comprehends not yet
How earnest is your proffered boon, —
  How surely his the glorious debt
Of freedom and all free-born things:
Wait! — ha! he prunes his doubtful
    wings.

Hops, perch by perch, to gain the door;
  Then, as if first conviction came,
Full-faced, and whispered, *"thou art
    free!"*
  He darts without, a wingèd flame,
And soon from far, fair cloudland floats
The rapture of his grateful notes!

———◆———

LITTLE LOTTIE'S GRIEVANCE.

MAMMA'S in heaven! and so, you see
My sister Bet's mamma to me.
Oh! yes, I love her! — that's to say,
I love her well the whole bright day;
For Sis is kind as kind can be,
Until, indeed we've finished tea —
Then (why did God make ugly night?)
She never, never treats me right,
But always says, " Now, sleepy head,
'Tis getting late! come up to bed!'"

Just when the others, Fred and Fay,
Dolly and Dick, are keen for play —
Card-houses, puzzles, painted blocks,
Cat-corner, and pert Jack-in-the-box —
I must (it's that bad gas, I think,
That makes me somehow seem to wink!)
Must leave them all to seek the gloom
Of sister Bet's close-curtained room,
Put on that long stiff gown I hate,
And go to bed — oh, dear! at eight!

Now, is it fair that I who stand
Taller than Dolly by a hand,
(I'll not believe, howe'er 'tis told,
That cousin Doll is ten years old!
And just because I'm only seven,
Should be so teased, yes, almost driven,
Soon as I've supped my milk and bread,
To that old drowsy, frowsy bed?
I've lain between the dusky posts,
And shivered when I thought of ghosts:
Or else have grown so mad, you know,
To hear those laughing romps below,
While there I yawned and stretched
          (poor me!)
With one dim lamp for company.
I've longed for courage just to dare
Dress softly — then trip down the stair,
And on the parlor pop my head
With " No, I will not stay abed! "

I'll do it yet, all quick and bold,
No matter how our Bet may scold.
For, oh! I'm sure it can't be right,
To keep me here each dismal night,
Half scared by shadows grimly tall
That dance along the cheerless wall,
Or by the wind, with fingers chill,
Shaking the worn-out window-sill
One might as well be sick or dead,
As sent by eight o'clock to bed!

———◆———

A NEW VERSION OF WHY THE ROBIN'S BREAST IS RED.

KNOW you why the robin's breast
Gleameth of a dusky red,
Like the lustre mid the stars
Of the potent planet Mars?
'Tis — a monkish myth has said —
Owing to his cordial heart;
For, long since, he took the part
Of those hapless children, sent
Hadean-ward for punishment;
And, to quench the fierce desire,
Bred in them by ruthless fire,
Brought on tiny bill and wing,
Water from some earthly spring,

Which in misty droplets fell
O'er their dwelling of unrest,
While the sufferer's faces grew
Softer 'neath the healing dew!

But, too far within that hell
Venturing, some malicious fiend,
A small devil hardly weaned,
Seized bold Robin in his claw,
Striving thro' the flames to draw
His poor body, until fled
Sight of eyes and sense of head,
Scorched he lay and almost dead!

Then, a child whose tongue and brow,
Robin's help had cooled but now,
Clutched the baby-fiend in ire,
And in gulfs of his own fire
Soused the vile misshapen elf.

Fluttering upwards, scarce himself,
After all the pain and fear
Of his horrid sojourn there
In that realm of flame and smoke,
Lo! earth's happy sunlight broke
On the bird's dazed view at last;
But the ordeal he had passed
Left a flame-spot widely spread
Where the wind-blown feathers part
Just above his loyal heart.
So the robin's breast is red!

———◆———

THE LITTLE SAINT.

AT the calm matin hour
   I see her bend in prayer,
As bends a virgin flower
   Kissed by the summer air;
Oh, meek her downcast eyes!
   But the sweet lips wear a smile;
How hard our little angel tries
   To be serious all the while!

I tell her 'tis not right
   To be half-grave, half-gay,
Imploring in Heaven's sight
   A blessing on the day;

She hears and looks devout —
　Although it gives her pain;
Still, when the ritual's almost out
　She's sure — to smile again!

She shocks her maiden aunt,
　Who thinks it a disgrace
That, do her best, she can't
　Give her a solemn face;
She'll scold and rate and fume,
　And lecture hour by hour,
Until she makes the very room
　Look passionate and sour!

Alack, 't is all in vain!
　Soon as the sermon's done
My fairy blooms again,
　Like a rose-bud in the sun.
I cannot damp her mirth!
　I will not check her play;
Is guileless joy so rife on earth,
　Hers shall not have full sway?

I asked her yester night,
　Why, when her prayer was made,
Her brow of cordial light
　Scarce caught a serious shade.
"*Father*," she said, "*you love*
　Better to meet me glad;
And so I thought the Christ above
　Might grieve to see me — sad!"

A NEW PHILOSOPHY; OR, STAR
　　SHOWERS EXPLAINED.

ONE luminous night in winter,
　All crystal clear and still,
A band of wondering children
　Were grouped by the window sill.

The window looked out northward,
　Where through the tranquil hours
The stars kept falling, falling,
　In a ceaseless shine of showers.

Ah! beautiful sight! those children! —
　As they gazed on the magic skies,
With their tiny hands uplifted,
　And their large, bright, marvelling
　　eyes.

"What is it?" asked curly Alfred,
　Of his elder brother, Gus;
"Does you think it is coming nearer?
　If it comes, can it fall on us?"

"No, stupid!" (in tones determined,)
　But soon he was touched by doubt,
And wished, as the flames waxed
　　brighter,
Somebody would put them out!

For, indeed, the radiant sparkles
　Now poured from a grander height:
And filled like a conflagration,
　The hollows and gulfs of night!

Till at last they all grew frightened;
　And the small dark heads and light
Were in a closer circle,
　While still they watched the night!

All but one sturdy urchin,
　The smallest and shrewdest there,
Whose eyes like a pert cock robin's,
　Turned up on the northward glare,

As he lisped, with an air quite final,
　And with somewhat of scorn and
　　scoff:
"*It's the Fourth of July up yonder,*
　And the wockets is whizzing off!"

BABY'S FIRST WORD.

WE watched our baby day by day,
　With earnest expectation,
To hear his infant lips unclose
　In vague articulation.

But weeks, nay weary months, passed on;
　His last wee tooth had broken
From rosy gums, yet not a word,
　Not *one* had baby spoken.

"O Rol!" I cried, "it cannot be
　A child so quick and clever,
Who hears ('tis plain he hears our talk),
　Should thus stay dumb forever!"

Rol answered sharply, vexed and red,
"What wretched nonsense, Jenny!
I never could have dreamed, my dear,
You'd prate like such a ninny!"

(Yes, that's the term, I must confess,
By which, with judgment narrow,
He dared for once, just once, you know,
To call his "winsome marrow.")

But what cared I? since as I live,
True as my name is Jenny,
From out the cradle clear and loud,
Came back the bad word "Ninny!"

Thence uprose baby all aglee,
His peaceful slumbers routed,
And thrice that naughty, naughty word
He spoke, nay, almost shouted!

Rol, glancing at my startled eyes,
His mirth could scarcely smother.
But oh! to think the rogue's first word
Should thus abuse his mother!

THE CHAMELEON.

I KNOW that I'm *like*, yet I am *not*, a
snake!
'Tis true that I glisten by boll and
by brake,
That I dart out and in, can glide, quiver
and coil
As swift as the lightning, but softer than
oil,
Yet a creature more innocent never was
drawn
From the gray of cool shadows to bask
in the dawn!

If I pause by a brook the rock-currents
divide,
I grow silvery-white as the foam of its
tide;
If 'mid dew-freshened meadows at sun-
rise I pass,
There's a shaft of pure emerald shot
through the grass.

When to gay garden-closes I joyfully turn,
'Tis mine with all hues, of their roses to
burn;
I reflect each bright blush that the
petals have won
Of their young virgin-flowers from the
kiss of the sun.
My skin's a clear mirror, a glass of the
elves,
In which all lovely tints can smile back
on themselves!
Stranger still! for on ugliness mirrored
therein,
Though it tarnish a moment, this magi-
cal skin,
On the dark and uncouth some slight
beauty's bestowed;
Why, even that dull little hunchback,
the toad,
I endow with faint outlines of sweetness
and grace,
While the newt, glancing down on his
lop-sided face,
Reflected, — in pity, — by softened de-
grees,
Almost dreams he was formed by kind
Nature to please!

Ah, therefore, sweet maiden, shrink not
when you see
My lithe body reposing by streamlet or
tree;
But kneel down where I rest, and all
mellowed behold
Your eyes of deep blue, and your ring-
lets of gold,
In my miniature mirror, my glass of the
elves,
Wherein all lovely things can smile back
on themselves!

FLYING FURZE.

AIRILY, fairily, over the meadows,
Over the broom-grasses waving and gay,
O! see how it shimmers,
How wavers and glimmers,
Flying, and flying away.

Hastefully, wastefully, over the copses,
Over the hedge-rows in scattered array,
See, see how 'tis curling
And twinkling and whirling,
Ever and ever away!

Merrily, cheerily, down the far verges,
Verges of fields growing misty and gray,
Still, still how it shimmers,
Grows fainter and glimmers,
Shimmers, and glimmers away!

———◆———

THE NEW SISTER.

Phil. SAY, Pete, do you like her?
Pete. Like! love her you mean!
Phil. Ain't she jolly and red?
Pete. And hurrah for her! just think of
her head!
Phil. As big as a pippin, and round as
a bullet!
Pete. And bald! oh! as bald as a newly-
plucked pullet!
Phil. Did you look at her eyes too?
Pete. Of course; they are blue.
Phil. Not a bit of it — black!
Pete. Blue, I tell you — ask Jack!
Phil. Jack! I've eyes of my own that
see better than his!
Pete. Brag on! but for once they have
led you amiss.
Baby's eyes are blue — very!
Phil. As black as a berry!
Pete. Blue, you ninny! but s'pose we
come down to her nose!
It's as funny and fat with an end
like —
Phil. Like a rose?
Pete. No! a small dab of putty just tint-
ed with pink!
Phil. Now, stoo-pid! how can you! I'm
sure that I think
Nothing nicer than roses so
dumpy and smug —
Pete. Pshaw! you mean it's a boo-ti-ful,
boo-ti-ful pug!
Phil. Well, you naughty old Pete! you
can't laugh at her chin!

Pete. Oh, no, it's the nattiest, sauciest,
sweetest —
Phil. The nicest, completest,
Of arch little chins, with a dimple
put in,
That winks up like a sunbeam,
Pete. And then her wee throat!
Phil. Her throat like egg-foam, or a
syllabub boat
On a lake of clear cream!
Pete. And her arms; they are nice now;
there's nothing can beat them!
Phil. So plump, round, and soft! I'm
most ready to eat them!
Pete. Of course, Phil, you kissed her?
Phil. Oh, didn't I!
Pete. Well!
Phil. Well, I put my mouth down; I had
something to tell;
Ah! close whispered close in the
shy little ear,
That seemed to turn up, Pete, half
coyly to hear,
And again, as I kissed her —
Pete. You blessed the good Lord for so
jolly a sister!
Phil. Yes, I did!
Pete. So did I!
Phil. And now, Pete, 'tis but right
We should go in once more and
bid " Baby " good night!

———◆———

HOP, SKIP, AND JUMP: A QUEER TRIO PERSONIFIED.

O! Hop is a sailor used up in the war,
With a single good leg to stand on;
And a face as dingy almost as the tar
He was wont to rest his hand on:
And he grumbles strange oaths in his
hairy throat
Whenever he sees a fair vessel afloat,
Especially one with those staring round
eyes
(Port-holes, you know)
Whence the hot shot flies
At a quaking foe;
For then his anger, it fizzles up

(Like the sputtering foam in a lager-beer
        cup),
    And he hoarsely cries,
" May witches fly off with that fellow by
        whom
I'm reduced to the cruel, contemptible
        doom
        Of tottering all day,
        In an imbecile way,
        'Twixt a single good leg
        And this base wooden peg,
        Far, far from the spume
Of the gay ocean-spray!
So, seize him, and scorch him, and fry
        him, I say!"

But Skip is a mincing lady fine;
She never was seen to breakfast or
        dine;
    And how she lives, none knoweth;
Her waist is so very slender and thin,
You fear it must snap, and topple in,
    At the first slight wind that bloweth.
Her favorite motion's an airy jerk,
With her eyeballs raised, and her chin
        a-perk,
And her little red ringlets bobbing,
    Bobbing and hobnobbing,
In a friendly fashion, each to each;
And her cheek is the hue of a delicate
        peach
(That never a shade can vary);
" *Perpetual motion* " she's sometimes
        called,
And really, truly one feels appalled
To view her galvanized skipping,
Her dancing, wriggling, whipping
Of one skirt in and one skirt out,
Her general manner of going about,
        Which lies, I ween,
        Half pitched between
The twittering, fussy, old-maidish way
        Of the restless jay,
And the airs of a sprightly canary!

Jump is a long-limbed sturdy boy,
    With such strong muscles to back
        him,

That I hardly could wish the creature
        joy
    Who should ever dare to attack him;
A four-foot fence he clears in a minute;
And if you bet from the cottage eave
(And a very tall cottage it is in sooth),
With your leave, or without your leave,
        That he cannot jump
        With a dauntless thump,
        And a thundering bump, —
Be sure that he'll quickly win it!
And, to whisper the truth, — the fearful
        truth,
I believe if whale or dragon,
The one on sea, and t'other on land,
(The biggest that either could brag on),
    Came floating, or crawling nigh,
        That this marvellous boy,
        With a ringing cry
        Of fierce, exuberant, reckless joy,
        Would, just for the fun of it,
        Make a swift run of it
Right down the jaws of whichever
        dread vermin
The turn of chance or a thought should
        determine!

So here my song ends,
And ye, charming young friends!
    Don't endeavor to pump
    My dry fancy again;
    'Tis enough I've made plain
    As Tommy's big nose
    Looming red o'er the snows,
Those impalpable ideas of Hop, Skip,
        and Jump!

DANCING.

DANCING! I love it, night or day:
    There's nought on earth so jolly,
Whether you straightly glide with May,
    Or madly whirl with Molly,
The country dance is smooth and sleek;
    But waltzes (some call vicious!)
Bring one so near a rosy cheek,
    That, Jack, they're just delicious!

At every chance, I'm bound to go,
 And join our " West End " classes,
With all about me *comme il faut,*
 To captivate the lasses.

I think they rather like me, Jack, —
 (Oh, dear! the pretty creatures!*)* —
One shyly praised — behind my back —
 She *did* — my *Roman* features!

" Dancing! I love it, night or day :
There's nought on earth so jolly."

Yet somehow, Jack, the loveliest she
 (I mean sweet Mary Whimple)
Has never, never turned on me
 A single charming dimple :
But when I try the least advance,
 Her smile is changed to sneering;
Three times she has snubbed me in the
  dance
 To please that odious Speering!

Ah! Jack, it makes my bosom swell,
 And all my life forlorner,
To think (while others like me well)
 She, *she* should be a scorner!
I cannot be revenged on *her,*
 Nor *would,* if able even;
But, oh! that long-legged **Speering**
  cur
 I wish he was — in heaven!

He has given my hopes a blighting touch
  Though lank as any mummy;
And as for *mind*, — I've seen as much
  In some poor pasteboard dummy:
But then the best of girls are queer —
  Titania loved a donkey;
So Mary airs her charms to snare
  This awkward ball-room flunkey!

Ha! now my steam is all blown off,
  Once more I'm pleased and placid;
If Mary Whimple still *will* scoff,
  Why should I too grow acid ?
With jovial smile and heart in tune
  (Ill humor's best disarmers,)
See, Jack, if I don't figure soon —
  Adonis 'mid the charmers!

———————

MOTES.

Up and down, up and down,
In the air the sunshine mellows —
Green or yellow, gold or brown,
See those gay capricious fellows!
Sparkling, glittering, frisking, dancing,
Now retreating, now advancing,
Livelier than the jolliest clown,
Tinier than the tiniest fairy
That e'er robbed a farmer's dairy
Of the luscious cream which floats
Round his frothed and brimming bowls
Buoyant, tireless little souls!
    Who can fold them,
    Catch or hold them ?
Evanescent,
  Omnipresent,
    Shy eluders,
      Bold obtruders,
Past all joking, most provoking,
  Tricksy, whisky, frisky
    Motes.

Up and down, up and down,
Light in sunshine, lost in shadow —
Green or yellow, gold or brown,
Over hill and over meadow,
    Swiftly over
Rock-ribbed height and billowy clover,

Still advancing,
  Still retreating,
    Glittering, fleeting,
Never dozing, nor reposing,
But forever dancing, dancing;
And in numberless quaint fusions,
And eye-dazzling convolutions,
    Deftly sped
      Overhead —
See (where happy sunshine mellows
All the air) those jovial fellows!
Ah! ye tricksome waifs and tiny,
Who may circumvent and bind ye ?
Can it be such creatures antic,
Unrestrained, grotesquely frantic,
Are but small nymphs out of school,
Laughing at all graver rule ?
Or loose sylphides, bent on sowing,
      Sowing,
        Sowing,
In their thoughtless mirth o'erflowing,
Naughty crops of wildish oats ?
How they jostle, whirl and hustle,
Up and down, up and down,
Through the air the sunshine mellows!
Green or yellow, gold or brown,
All those gay, capricious fellows,
    Evanescent,
      Omnipresent,
        Shy eluders,
          Bold obtruders,
Past all joking, most provoking,
  Tricksy, whisky, frisky,
    Motes!

———————

THE GROUND SQUIRREL.

Bless us, and save us! What's here?
      Pop!
        At a bound,
A tiny brown creature, grotesque in his
        grace,
Is sitting before us, and washing his face
  With his little fat paws overlapping;
Where does he hail from ? Where ?
      Why, *there*,
        Underground,

From a nook just as cosy,
And tranquil, and dozy,
As e'er wooed to Sybarite napping
(But none ever caught him a-napping).
" Don't you see his soft burrow so quaint,
      lad! and queer ?"

Gone! like the flash of a gun!
This oddest of chaps,
      Mercurial,
      Disappears
      Head and ears!
Then, sly as a fox,
Swift as Jack in his box,
Pops up boldly again!
What does he mean by this frisking
      about,
Now up and now down, and now in and
      now out,
And all done quicker than winking?
What does it mean ? Why, 'tis plain,
      fun!
Only fun! or, perhaps,
The pert little rascal's been drink-
      ing ?
There's a cider press yonder all day on
      the run!

Capture him! no, we won't do it,
Or, be sure in due time we would rue
      it!

Such a piece of perpetual motion,
      Full of bother
      And pother,
Would make paralytic old Bridget
      A fidget.
So you see (to *my* notion),
      Better leave our downy
      Diminutive browny
Alone near his " diggings" ;
      Ever free to pursue,
      Rush round, and renew
      His loved vaulting
      Unhalting,
      His whirling,
      And curling,
      And twirling,
      And swirling,

And his ways, on the whole,
      So unsteady!
'Pon my soul,
      Having gazed
      Quite amazed,
On each wonderful antic
And summersault frantic,
      For just a bare minute,
My head, it feels whizzing;
My eyesight's grown dizzy;
And both legs, unstable
As a ghost's tipping table,
      Seem waltzing, already!

Capture him! no, we won't do it,
Or in less than *no* time, *how* we'd rue
      it!

———◇———

ARTIE'S "AMEN."

THEY were Methodists twain, of the
      ancient school,
Who always followed the wholesome
      rule
That whenever the preacher in meeting
      said
Aught that was good for the heart or
      head
His hearers should pour their feelings
      out
In a loud " Amen " or a godly shout.

Three children had they, all honest boys,
Whose youthful sorrows and youthful
      joys
They shared, as your loving parents will,
While tending them ever through good
      and ill.

One day — 'twas a bleak, cold Sabbath
      morn,
When the sky was dark and the earth
      forlorn —
These boys, with a caution not to roam.
Were left by the elder folk at home.

But scarce had they gone when the
      wooded frame
Was seen by the tall stove pipe aflame;

And out of their reach, high, high, and
    higher,
Rose the red coils of the serpent fire.

With startled sight for a while they
    gazed,
As the pipe grew hot and the wood-work
    blazed:
Then up, though his heart beat wild with
    dread,
The eldest climbed to a shelf o'erhead,
And soon, with a sputter and hiss of
    steam.
The flame died out like an angry dream.

When the father and mother came back
    that day —
They had gone to a neighboring church
    to pray —
Each looked, but with half-averted eye,
On the awful doom which had just
    passed by.

And then the father began to praise
His boys with a tender and sweet amaze.
"Why, how did you manage, Tom, to
    climb
And quench the threatening flames in
    time
To save your brothers, and save your-
    self?"
"Well, father, I mounted the strong oak
    shelf
By help of the table standing nigh."
"And what," quoth the father, suddenly,
Turning to Jemmy, the next in age,
"Did you to quiet the fiery rage?"
"I brought the pail, and the dipper too,
And so it was that the water flew
All over the flames, and quenched them
    quite."

A mist came over the father's sight,
A mist of pride and of righteous joy,
As he turned at last to his youngest boy,
A gleeful urchin scarce three years old,
With his dimpling cheeks and his hair
    of gold.
"Come, Artie, I'm sure you weren't
    afraid:

Now tell in what way you tried to aid
This fight with the fire." "Too small
    am I,"
Artie replied, with a half-drawn sigh,
"To fetch like Jemmy, and work like
    Tom;
So I stood just here for a minute dumb,
Because, papa, I was frightened some :
But I prayed, 'Our Father,' and then,
    and then
I shouted as loud as I could, 'Amen.'"

———◆———

THREE PORTRAITS OF BOYS.

STURDY little form, of true
Saxon pattern, through and through;
Face as purely Saxon, too,
With a smile demure and sly,
Dimpled cheek and twinkling eye;
Robin head, with sideway perk,
O'er some cunning ruse at work;
Welcome, lad! of wholesome ways,
And true juvenile displays;
Now progressing at full speed
On your gay velocipede,
(Yet where'er it deftly goes,
Wronging no one's dress or toes);
Now, beneath the basement hid,
On a dwarfish pyramid
Toiling, with scarred bricks and stone,
After methods, all your own;
A small Cheops! scarce less shrewd
In your purpose and your mood,
Than that king of mobs and mud,
By the old Nilotic flood!
Or with flying scarf and hat,
Coursing some half-frantic cat,
Fraught with wrath, and words that rail,
Should poor Tabby save his tail!
For the " old Adam's " sometimes seen
In your actions and your mien,
But no more than must appear
In his undegenerate heir.

Grown from what seems nature's plan,
What will Henry be as man?
One of healthful, mental range,
Honored at the doors of 'Change?

Of a quick and eager mind,
At the rise of fortune's wind;
Shrewd! perchance with scores of
    friends,
And productive dividends ?

On life's middle pathway still,
By extremes of good and ill.
Evermore unvisited,
Shall we see him safely tread ?
Not ambitious of grand things,
Or the scope of eagle's wings;
But within the limits meet
Of his unpretentious feet,
A good man, perhaps a wise,
Who — (in ledger of the skies),
May — unsmutched by blots of blame,
Find, at last, his honest name ?

MARION.

URCHIN of the Syrian face,
And half melancholy grace,
With a look in your dark eyes,
Sometimes deep and overwise;
What shall be your mortal doom ?
Desert blight, or healthful bloom ?
Shall the lily, Virtue, shine
On your life, made thus divine;
Or Corinthian roses shed
Poisoned petals on your head ?
Ah! the soul that dwells in you,
Heaven hath blent of flame and dew
Mixed by subtlest art together
In your nature's changeful weather,
Whence a lightning-glitter warm,
Now and then, portends a storm;
Such a storm of tropic strain,
Scathed by fire and big with rain;
All your being o'er and under,
Thrilled as if by spirit-thunder;
Till, exhausted at the source
Of its wild imperious course
Passion — like a blast that dies
Down the slowly brightening skies,
Thro' loud sob and weary moan
Falls to plaintive monotone!

Strange child-soul, but half unfurled,
Who shall scan its complex world ?

Glimpsed 'twixt light and shadow dim,
Dare I prophesy of him ?
Subtle, mystical, refined,
Seem the thoughts that haunt his mind,
While large forces play their part
On the boy's embattled heart,

Stubborn *will* — it irks to yield,
Always watchful — under shield;
Scorn of all who do him wrong,
Keen, implacable and strong;
Yet — toward the fair and just,
Love, that's crowned with generous
    trust;
And those graces, pure and high,
Born of tender loyalty!

With a firm and wise control,
Guide the currents of his soul!
Forceful are they, and must ride
Ever, with impetuous tide,
If to duty's strand they flow,
Fraught with all pure flowers that
    blow,
Or, the Syren's lotus-lea,
Fronting death's unfathomed sea!

HERBERT.

AH! you tricksy little elf,
How you idolize yourself!
And believe the world was made
Like a gay-hued masquerade,
Just for you to sport and dance,
Ever, in a happy trance!
How I envy you the joy
Of such bright *abandon*, boy!
All your buoyant veins are rife
With the sunniest wine of life!
And if e'er a shadow strays
O'er your glad, elysian ways,
'Tis but like the doubtful mote
In the morning's eye afloat;
At the slightest breeze of fun,
Cloudless is your spirit's sun!

Still, my tricksy little elf,
Idolize your blissful self;
Dream you'll always be a boy,
And that life's a painted toy,

Just for you to hasten after,
Full of thoughtless mirth and laughter;
Soon, alack! how grim and grum,
Disenchantment's sure to come!
Life, with which you loved to play,
Slowly turns from gold to gray;
All its splendid tints are lost,
For, experience, cold as frost,
Dims the hues which undefiled,
Blessed the outlook of the child;
And we learn in mournful wise,
Earth's no longer — Paradise!

—◆—

BIRDS.

THAT's the dove, my darling!
  Murmurous, soft and tender;
  There! she's mooning, crooning,
    On a pine-branch slender.
And ah! it's the dove, the dove, dove,
  dove,
That never can coo, but she pleads of
  love,
    Of love, love, love,
  In the shadows fair and tender.

That's the wren, my fairy!
  With her wee love-pledges;
  See her playing, straying
    Underneath the hedges.
And oh! it's the wren, the wren, wren,
  wren,
That is never contented too far from
  men,
    But lives, lives, lives
  Secure in the field-side hedges.

That's the thrush, my beauty!
  Hark! and let us hear her,
  Yonder swinging, singing,
    Higher, bolder, clearer,
And oh! it's the thrush, the thrush,
  thrush, thrush,
Whose loud song wakens the noon-tide
  hush,
    The deep, deep hush
    Of the meadows and wolds, to hear
      her!

That's the mockbird, sweetheart!
  To all tones beholden,
  Which are thrilling, filling
    Glades of woodland golden,
And ah! it's a bird, a bird, bird, bird,
The sweetest that ever a mortal heard.
    Ah! sweet, sweet, sweet,
  In the sunshine, fresh and golden!

—◆—

THE DEAD CHILD AND THE MOCK-ING-BIRD.

ONCE in a land of balm and flowers,
  Of rich fruit-laden trees,
Where the wild wreaths from jasmine
    bowers
  Trail o'er Floridian seas;

We marked our Jeannie's footsteps run
  Athwart the twinkling glade;
She seemed a Hebe in the sun,
  A Dryad in the shade!

And all day long her winsome song,
  Her trebles and soft trills,
Would wave-like flow or silvery low
  Die down the tinkling rills.

One morn, midmost the foliage dim,
  A dark-gray pinion stirs;
And hark! along the vine-clad limb,
  What strange voice blends with hers?

It blends with hers which soon is stilled!
  Braver the mock-bird's note
Than all the strains that ever filled
  The queenliest human throat:

As Jeannie heard, she loved the bird,
  And sought thenceforth to share
With her new favorite dawn by dawn,
  Her daintiest morning cheer!

But ah! a blight beyond our ken,
  From some far feverous wild,
Brought that dark shadow feared of
    men,
  Across the fated child!

It chilled her drooping curls of brown,
  It dimmed her violet eyes,
And like an awful cloud stole down
  From vague mysterious skies!

At last, one day our Jeannie lay,
  All pulseless, pale, forlorn;
The sole sweet breath on lips of death.
  The mocking breath of morn!

When just beyond the o'ercurtained
    room,
  (How tender yet how strong!)
Rose through the misty morning gloom,
  The mock-bird's sudden song!

Dear Christ! those notes of golden peal,
  Seem caught from heavenly spheres;
Yet through their marvellous cadence,
    steal
  Tones soft as chastened tears!

Is it an angel's voice that throbs
  Within the brown bird's breast?
Whose rhythmic magic soars, or sobs,
  Above our darling's rest?

The fancy passed, but came once more,
  When stolen, from Jeannie's bed,
That eve along the porchway floor,
  I found our minstrel . . . dead!

The fervor of the angelic strain
  His life-chords burned apart,
And blent with sorrow's earthlier pain,
  Broke the o'erburdened heart!

Maiden and bird! the self-same grave
  Their wedded dust shall keep,
While the long low Floridian wave
  Moans round their place of sleep!

———◆———

THE LITTLE GRAND DUCHESS.

WHAT a pure and chastened splendor,
What a grace of joyance tender,
Like to starlight or to moonlight,
Melting into fairy Junelight,
Sleeps my little lady sweetly, —

In the air that answers meetly
With each soul-illumined feature,
Which the lovely, winsome creature
Lifts toward us so demurely,
That despite their candor, surely
Something of an elfish slyness
Sparkles 'round their shadowed shyness,
Though a *pose* that's sometimes stately,
(Baby brows thrown back sedately,)
Charms us by a look that such is,
She might be a wee Grand Duchess!

But anon that aspect changes,
Through all moods her spirit ranges.
Free and far as Ariel pinions
O'er a warlock's weird dominions;
Happy fields of dim romances:
Woods wherein an elve-troop dances
'Neath a noon of splendid trances,
Culling flowers, or chanting lowly
Songs of golden melancholy;
Or in stretch of wildest dreamings,
(Holding true their gracious seemings,)
Wafted into blissful vision
Of some rarer realm Elysian.

Well I know that mark the yearning
Through her snowy eyelids burning,
Shadowed by those midnight lashes,
(Quickly closed when aught abashes,
And as quickly flashed asunder,
When swift anger lightens under,)
How supreme the hidden forces
Blindly struggling at their sources
In her depths of nascent being:
Insight, but half-born to seeing,
Faint perceptions, intuitions,
And soft-murmuring admonitions,
Toned and mellowed down so finely
That their voices breathe divinely.

Ha! but see, our dainty fairy
Freed from thought, or dreamings airy,
All an embryo flirt's beguiling,
Wooes us in her roguish smiling,
Rippled into silvery laughter,
With arch glances levelled after,
Coy, coquettish, gay, capricious
Sprite! thy every mood's delicious;

Yet amid these spirit-phases
Whereupon thy poet gazes,
There is one that steals above thee;
Dewy pure from heavens that love thee.
'Tis not when thy heart is lightest,
'Tis not when thy glance is brightest,
But when sober Contemplation
Near thee takes her pensive station,
While a strange ecstatic quiet
Follows on thy childish riot.

Lo! her trifling fancies vanished, —
Lo! her baby bearing banished,
She has grown so sweetly earnest
That I'm sure the harshest, sternest
Cynic who should chance to meet her,
Must with fond caresses greet her!
Introspective, deep surmising,
Glow her eyes like moonbeams rising,
And across her face, where wonder
Seems with tremulous awe to ponder,
Smiles a glory, as if angels
Whispered her their soft evangels!

So that for the moment losing
Time and place while on her musing,
One might say, this eerie creature
Hardly owns our earth-born nature,
For she's changeling, fay and fairy,
In a word, all things that vary
Most in wizard transformations,
And the round of weird creations!

ROLY POLY.

ROLY POLY's just awakened,
    Wakened in his cosy bed;
All his dainty ringlets tumbled
    O'er his shoulders, and his head:
Roly Poly's cheeks are rounder
    Than a dumpling duly done,
While they look as rich and ruddy,
    As a freshly-dawning sun.

Roly Poly's keen for breakfast;
    Ah! he stays, he tarries not,
But as soon as mother's breeched him,
    Rushes for his "hot and hot";

Such huge sups of oatmeal porridge
    Swallows he at lordly ease,
That I'm sure in stout digestion,
    He's an infant — Hercules!

Roly Poly rises briskly
    (When repletion bids him stop),
Shall he take his kite for flying,
    Or, go out with cord and top?
Not the faintest breeze is blowing,
    So, of course, the top's preferred;
Eagerly he hastes to spin it,
    Almost flying — like a bird!

But unlucky Roly Poly
    Chooses — since the ground is hard —
As the fittest place for spinning,
    Mother's well-stocked poultry-yard;
So, what time his mammoth "hummer"
    Circles on its nimble pegs,
Roly feels a rearward *something*
    Dabbing, stabbing at his legs!

Round he turns in vast amazement,
    Round, to find erect and free,
Ruffled, ireful, a great gander,
    Quite as tall ('twould seem), as he;
But brave Roly Poly battles,
    Knight-like, on his sturdy thighs,
Battles, till the treacherous monster
    Leaves his legs, to smite his eyes!

Then, must Roly fly affrighted,
    Fly, the sudden wrath beyond,
Of that ruthless, base aggressor, —
    But to tumble in — *a pond!*
Over head and ears to tumble
    In a dark, unsavory flood,
Bubbling, doubling, kicking fiercely,
    Plucking weeds, and grasping mud!

While — as pitiless fate *would* have it —
    Ponto, panting on the run,
Thinks that Master Roly Poly's
    Only sought the pond in fun;
So, he dashes in, exultant,
    Paws the boy, with bark and bound,
And instead of gallant rescue,
    Madly rolls him round and round: —

"Roly Poly's just awakened,
Wakened in his cosy bed."

When a gasping groan and sputter
  Prove to Ponto, shrewd and true,
What is now the sacred duty
  That a faithful dog should do;
See, he tugs at Roly's trowsers,
  Tugs with steadfast might and main,
Till he brings our dripping urchin
  Safely to the shore again.

Ponto's teeth are sharp and potent,
  And impelled by need to speed,
They have made poor Roly Poly
  In no stinted measure bleed!
Therefore, with his gory garments,
  And his mud-bespattered knees,
He is like a dwarfish Sindbad,
  Sorrow-laden, by the seas!

Oh! to mark our roguish Roly
  Throw his fright and trouble off !
How he laughs at dangers vanished,
  With his merriest boyish scoff.
Decked once more in spotless trowsers
  How he makes the household ring:
Scours and scampers, shouts and dances,
  Domineering like a king.

Doubt not that at lunch and dinner,
  Fervid is the fork he plies;
Presto, how the mutton dwindles!
  Gone are sweetmeats; melted pies!
Not one drop of bygone trouble
  Bitter makes his cup, or can;
Roly! let us change our places —
  I, the boy; and you, the man!

THE IMPRISONED INNOCENTS.

[Or the Complaint of a Philosopher of Family !]

ONE morning I said to my wife,
  Near the time when the heavens are
    rife
  With the Equinoctial strife,
" Arabella, the weather looks ugly as sin!
Observe, how those mists from the ocean
    begin
To creep eastward and blend

With the sickly street vapors fantastic
    and thin;
So, (*won't* you attend ?) keep the chil-
    dren within,
Safe-housed from these damps of Sep-
    tember!
For myself — as I'm studying ' *Barret
  On Drainage*' just now — I'll go up to
    the garret,
And thus will be barred from all noises,
And tumults of infantile voices!
(Please listen, my dear! I am speaking,
    I *think*,
And put down your baby! he'll drink,
    and he'll drink
Warm tea till he pops!) so again let me
    say,
Keep the juveniles housed on this treach-
    erous day,
May I trust you, for *once*, to remem-
    ber ?"

Then, with pain (for my limbs are
    rheumatic),
  I slowly climbed up to the attic;
  And all the 'mid-stories o'er passed,
  Reached the dismal old garret at last!
" Now," thought I, " no echoes of riot
  Can break my philosopher's quiet;
  Thank heaven! all luxuries scorning
  Of stuffed couch or sofa, — I'll settle
    just here —
(Though perhaps I would like a less im-
    becile chair)
And be deep in research the whole morn-
    ing!"

Alack! for all bright expectation!
  While safe, as I fancied, from worry,
  For below me I heard,
  Ere my choler was stirred
First, a faint indefinable flurry,
Then, a deep roll, and thunder-like
    rumble,
With the shock of some terrible tumble,
  Which shook the whole house to its
    basis!
In a trice from my foolish elation
  I emerged with the blankest of faces,

And, well, I confess as a Christian I erred
  But who, my good sir, or good madam!
 Could have throttled, (just then), the
    "old Adam"?
I'm afraid that I muttered a some-
    thing
That ought to have rested a dumb
    thing!
  Yet before your stern censure you
    urge on,
  Bethink you! the same term 's been
    uttered
  Quite roundly, not stammered or stut-
    tered,
    By good men from Edwards to Spur-
      geon!
    So, pray don't confuse me,
    But kindly excuse me,
    If once in a justified passion,
    I followed their clerical fashion,
    (Albeit much modified too!)
And whispered, not shouted, a d——n!

Of course, to the doorway I scurried,
  And down the old stairs from the
    attic
    (In spite of my twinges rheumatic),
    Incontent hurried!
Having reached the back parlor, I
    trembled,
Alack! now, with fear undissembled,
For Jacky all spattered with gore,
Lay flabby and flat on the floor!
    A pestilent urchin,
Who stood much in need of promis-
    cuous ' birchin '
With his tricks and his manners un-
    stable,
He had taken to tipping the table,
(A rickety table, though heavy as lead),
And succeeded, the mischievous elf!
In tremendously tipping himself!
And then the big board like an un
    loosened rafter,
Came sundering, blundering, thunder-
    ing after,
Gave his pert shanks a majestical rap,
    And one fat little thumb,
    Round as a plum,

    Caught — as in spite,
    And held on to it tight,
    As a new patent trap!
But worst of all, he had thumped his
    head,
  Thumped his head and maltreated his
    nose,
  (Hence, the sanguine stains that dis-
    figured his clothes!)
And yet after all the ado,
We managed to rescue, and bring him
    to,
    On his pipe-like pegs
    Of ridiculous legs,
To set him up in the general view,
No longer flecked by a crimson hue,
But, a trifle black and a trifle blue!

Behold me, once more in the garret!
  This time with the door barred fast,
And locked by a rusty key,
  (As if one could banish trouble,
  By making one's fastenings double!
  "Here's peace," quoth I, " at last!
One row, and a row of such degree,
  Is surely enough 'till twilight!"
And so, 'neath the garret sky-light,
  Again I pored o'er my " Barret"
  ("Barret on Drainage," I've said),
  With calmer nerves and a cooler head;
Determined to compass the topic,
  In a mode most philosophic,
  And launching a sudden shot,
  Lightning-swift, and fiery hot,
Through an article terse and satirical,
  Those foolish savants to bring down,
Who with theories basely empirical,
  Had so startled and shocked the
    town!

  Ah! soon in order beautiful,
  To a masterly logic dutiful,
My thoughts were ranged for fight;
  I was making here and there,
  A note on the fly-leaves bare,
  When horribly higher and higher,
  Uprose the shout of " Fire!"
In a monstrous dumb affright,
  I hardly walked, but fell,

(As it seemed), from the garret's
    height,
  (Though how, I could never tell!)
I alighted beneath to find
In the parlor a spark half out,
Which the feeblest puff of wind
  From the chimney had blown about
  But the children still would shout,
    And dance, and prance, and bellow,
  In a deafening, demonish rout,
While as for their mother, low and limp,
  She lay, in a faint, by the opened
    door,
With her eighteenth-monther, a restless
    imp,
  Drawing and pawing o'er and o'er
  The folds of her rumpled dress!
Somebody in years gone by,
Had pronounced her fainting *pose*
The *ne plus ultra* of loveliness,
As she lay like a sweet white rose;
But now! perchance, perchance,
I have lost my young romance,
For, unadmiring quite,
I gazed on the touching sight,
And (I'm a brute no doubt!)
But I let the syren lie.

    Ah me, the vexations,
      Exasperations,
      And tribulations,
        Confusions,
        Obtrusions,
    And endless affrays,
Which marked with dark tracing that
  blackest of days!
Don't tell me that children are angels,
All fraught with pure heaven's evan-
  gels,
And trailing — what is it! — from
  some mystic star
Bright cloudlets of glory. I know
  what mine are,
Not a whit worse I'm sure than the rest
  of young "fry,"
Whose natures are thoughtless and
  spirits are high;
But as for your "angels!" all that's
  "in my eye!"

To enter again
On that morning of pain:
I should wretchedly blunder
In counting the number
Of times I was harried
(My thoughts all miscarried!)
By yells of shrill laughter
Or dread cries thereafter,
By accidents seen or invisible,
And mishaps high tragic, or risi-
  ble;
Young Tommy three window-panes
  shattered,
And, of course, cut his head in the proc-
  ess,
  And an old silver heir-loom
  That oft held the rare bloom
Of vintages mellow and lusciously
  fine
From the banks of Moselle or the banks
  of the Rhine,
A tankard four centuries old and no
  less,
  By wee Janet was battered,
    Disgraced,
    And defaced,
Till the Bacchus Cellini had graven there-
  on,
Was broken and wan,
And the sweep of the vine, and the curve
  of the grape,
Were twisted hopelessly out of shape.

Then Harry fell down in the cistern!
  With yells to be heard for a mile,
And in striving to fish him out,
(For the boy is portly, puffy, and stout)
  Back would he slip, and slip, and
    slip,
  E'en from the cistern's utmost lip,
Until with a wrench swift-handed,
The human gudgeon was landed,
Who made with a ghastly smile
  The half-inarticulate pledge,
That never more would he tempt the
  edge
Of well or cistern, fount or river,
Although upon earth he should dwell
  forever!

And lastly, Cornelia, aged five,
(I marvel the child is still alive!
Contrived in the subtlest, deftest way,
   From the surgery shelf, to steal, in
      play,
   A box of my pills cathartic;
   Enough (if swallowed at once) to slay
   A bear of the regions Arctic!
How many she took I cannot say,
But thereafter for many and many a day,
Supine the suffering maiden lay,
And I scarce believe that her blood has
      set
To the shore of health that is perfect, yet!

What is the moral of this, my masters?
   (To you that are fathers, I mean,
      Fathers, and students as well?)
   Tis easy enough to tell),
Would you 'scape all household disas-
      ters?
   And be cosy, sweet-tempered, serene?
Then *never, never, never,*
Make the absurd endeavor,
Because the sky's not bluish
And the wind seems somewhat shrew-
      ish,
      To pen a young regiment in,
      Of heirs to Adam's sin!